PRIVATIZATION SOUTH AMERICAN STYLE

Privatization
South American Style

LUIGI MANZETTI

OXFORD
UNIVERSITY PRESS

OXFORD
UNIVERSITY PRESS

Great Clarendon Street, Oxford OX2 6DP
Oxford University Press is a department of the University of Oxford.
It furthers the University's objective of excellence in research, scholarship,
and education by publishing worldwide in

Oxford New York

Athens Auckland Bangkok Bogotá Buenos Aires Calcutta
Cape Town Chennai Dar es Salaam Delhi Florence Hong Kong Istanbul
Karachi Kuala Lumpur Madrid Melbourne Mexico City Mumbai
Nairobi Paris São Paulo Singapore Taipei Tokyo Toronto Warsaw

and associated companies in Berlin Ibadan

Oxford is a registered trade mark of Oxford University Press
in the UK and certain other countries

Published in the United States
by Oxford University Press Inc., New York

British Library Cataloguing in Publication Data

Data available

Library of Congress Cataloging in Publication Data
Manzetti, Luigi.
Privatization South American style / Luigi Manzetti.
(Oxford studies in democratization)
Includes bibliographical references.
1. Privatization—South America. I. Title. II. Series.
HD4079.M36 1999 338.98—dc21 99–28124
ISBN 0–19–829466–2

1 3 5 7 9 10 8 6 4 2

Typeset by Graphicraft Limited, Hong Kong
Printed in Great Britain
on acid-free paper by
Bookcraft Ltd
Midsomer Norton, Somerset

To Camilla and Gabriele

Contents

List of Figures

List of Tables

List of Abbreviations

ADEBA	Asociación de Bancos de Republica Argentina
AP	Acción Popular
APRA	Acción Popular Revolucionaria del Peru
BNDES	Banco de Desenvolvimento Economico e Social
CADE	Conselho Administrativo de Defesa Economica
CEDAL	Centro de Asesoría Laboral
CEPAL	Comisión Económica para América Latina
CGT	Central General dos Trabalhadores/Cofederación General de Trabajo
CISEA	Centro de Estudios Sobre el Estado y la Administación
CLADE	Centro Latinoamericano de Analisis de la Democracia
CND	Conselho Nacional de Desestatização
CNT	Comisión Nacional de Telecommunicaciones
CONFIEP	Confederación Nacional de Instituciones Empresariales Privadas
COPRI	Comisión de Promoción de la Inversión Privada
CORFO	Coproración de Fomento
CSN	Compañhia Siderurgica Nacional
CST	Compañhia Siderurgica de Turbarao
CUT	Central Unica de Trabalhadores
CVRD	Compañhia Vale de Rio Doce
DGFM	Dirección Nacional de Fabricaciones Militares
DNPDC	Departamento Nacional de Proteçao e Defesa Economica
ECLA	[UN] Economic Commission for Latin America
FIEL	Fundación de Investigaciones Económicas Latinoamericanas
FONCODES	Fondo Nacional de Compensacion y Desarrollo Social
FUNDAP	Fundação do Desenvolvimento Administrativo
GDP	Gross Domestic Product
IDB	Interamerican Development Bank
IESP	Instituto de Economía do Setor Publico
IFC	International Financial Corporation
IMF	International Monetary Fund
INFES	Instituto Nacional de Infraestructuras Educativa y de Salud
ISI	Import-Substitution Industrialization
LASA	Latin American Studies Association
MEF	Ministry of Economics and Finance (Peru)
MYDFA	Multi-Year Deposit Facility Agreement

PDS   Partido Democratico Social
PE   Public Enterprise
PJ   Partido Justicialista
PMDB   Partido do Movimiento Democratico Brasileiro
PND   Programa Nacional de Desestatização
PRN   Partido de Reconstrução Nacional
PSDB   Partido Social Democrata Brasileiro
PT   Partido de Trabalhadores
SELA   Sistema Económico Latinoamericano
SFT   Supreme Federal Tribunal
SIGEP   Sindicatura General de Impresas Publicas
YPF   Yacimientos Petroliferos Fiscales

1

The Political Economy of Privatization

Introduction

Privatization is defined as the transfer of assets and service functions from the public to the private sector.[1] In the early 1990s, a prominent magazine described privatization as the 'sale of the Century . . . a policy that in 1980 seemed adventurous to some and unworkable to everybody else . . . is [now] economic orthodoxy worldwide' (*The Economist* 1993: 13). It has been the most controversial policy issue dominating the political agenda of many countries around the globe for over a decade, and by the mid-1990s it was progressively gaining momentum (Edwards 1995; Holden and Rajapatirana 1995; Sader 1995). Between 1990 and 1996, Latin America and the Caribbean became the developing world's leader in privatization, accounting for 53 per cent of total proceeds ($82.4 billion see Table 1.1). During such a period annual revenues averaged, in terms of Gross Domestic Product (GDP), for the region as a whole, 1 per cent (Interamerican Development Bank (IDB), 1996: 170).

The academic debate regarding privatization has traditionally focused on economic arguments. However, no matter how sophisticated economic analyses may be, they have been unable to explain why for most of the 1970s and 1980s privatization, while making perfect economic sense in many countries, failed to occur. Obviously, the problem lies else where. According to the investment report of one of the world's most respected financial institutions, the real issue is that the decision to privatize is a political one. In discussing the Latin American experience, the report states: 'In all cases, the world of politics and, more importantly, the ability to deal with it, has played a crucial role.'[2] This explanation is not an isolated case. Practitioners argue much of the same. Carlos Montoya, the architect of the Peruvian state divestiture program, admitted that privatization was essentially a political issue, which requires a clear political plan and a strong presidential leadership.[3] A Brazilian economist, who worked on the programs under the Sarney and Collor administrations, echoed such a statement by admitting that the decision to privatize rests ultimately upon political calculations as politicians are the ultimate arbiter of the decision-making process.[4] The World Bank itself, in a recent cross-national study surveying the success and failure of privatization in Eastern Europe, Asia, Africa, and Latin America, acknowledged that, 'clearly factors

TABLE 1.1. *Proceeds from Privatization by Region (US million)*

Region	1990	1991	1992	1993	1994	1995	1996	1990–6
Latin America and the Caribbean	10,915	18,723	15,560	10,487	8,198	4,615	13,919	82,417
East Asia and Pacific	376	835	5,161	7,155	5,507	5,411	2,678	27,123
Europe and Central Asia	1,262	2,551	3,626	3,988	3,956	9,641	5,467	30,491
Middle East and North Africa	2	17	70	417	782	746	1477	3,510
South Asia	29	996	1,558	974	2,666	917	889	8,029
Sub-Sharan Africa	74	1,121	205	630	595	472	745	3,843
All developing countries	12,658	24,243	26,180	23,651	21,704	21,802	25,175	155,413

Source: Lieberman and Kirkness (1998: 12–13).

other than economic efficiency determine the nature, pace, and extent of [state-owned enterprises] reform. The most important of these factors is politics' (World Bank 1995: 175).

The political science literature has attempted to identify which factors have been critical in inducing Latin American leaders to adopt privatization policies in recent years. A few scholars stress the importance of international processes in creating conditions for external pressure (Przeworski 1991; Khaler 1992). Some emphasize the tendency of many countries to adopt policies successfully implemented elsewhere, or policy emulation (Ikenberry 1990). Others underscore the power of neoconservative ideas, within which privatization is used as a means to reconfigure political coalitions and to reduce the role of politics in shaping economic decisions (Schamis 1992). However, some contend that ideological motivations are neither sufficient nor necessary conditions for policy-makers to privatize, whereas pragmatic political incentives to keep or attract the support of domestic and foreign coalitions and, to a lesser extent, pragmatic concerns over general economic governance are the most important factors leading to the decision to privatize (Armijo 1992: 24–27). Finally, others hypothesize that privatization can be used as a strategy to privilege the goals of some socioeconomic groups at the expense of others (Feigenbaum and Henig 1994).

It is quite clear, from this brief overview of the literature, that political scientists (like their colleagues in economics) are not in agreement on what factors lead to privatization. This is due first to the fact that privatization is a complex policy, encompassing various types of asset and function transfers from the public to the private sector. Second, privatization's goals have often shifted over time. While in the beginning many countries conceived state divestiture as having limited objectives (i.e. supporting stabilization programs, improving government credibility, financing budget deficits), as time went on, particularly in successful cases, goals became more ambitious (i.e. enhancing competition, improving management operations, developing capital markets, fostering corporate efficiency) and the methods more sophisticated (from direct sales to international public offers).[5] Third, it is a policy that has occurred under widely different political regimes around the world. In general, recent economic and political analyses list a variety of factors instrumental in triggering privatization policies, which will be discussed later. They fail, however, to explore the 'dynamic interrelationship' binding all those factors together (Suleiman and Waterbury 1990*b*: 2).

Thus, the focus of this book is on the politics of privatization by scrutinizing both micro and macro factors under which such a policy is likely to take place. The book will also describe the economics of achieving privatization and the most important measures introduced in the countries here examined. To accomplish this goal, the book puts forth an analytical model that will help to organize conceptually the many and sometimes conflicting factors commonly cited in the literature, which are regarded as either to encourage or deter policies of privatization in the context of Latin American politics. It will also examine those factors affecting the implementation of a policy of divestiture. The evidence, in fact, suggests that most privatization policies are rarely implemented as originally planned (World Bank 1995). From a technical standpoint, privatization is a learning process that evolves through trial and error. Politically, power coalitions that are negatively affected by state divestiture are likely to organize for the purpose of preventing policy reform. Thus, special attention will be paid to the formation of coalitions favoring privatization. Additionally, the book will examine the bureaucratic and technical predicaments affecting privatization, and possibly dooming it to failure, once launched.

In brief, the framework of analysis presented here should enable us to respond to key questions about the socioeconomic determinants of privatization policies. I took these questions coming from earlier works on policy reforms by Nelson (1990*b*: 5), Grindle and Thomas (1991: 11), and Williamson (1994: 25–6) as they fit my concerns quite well.

1. How does privatization get on the government agenda? Why do some governments respond to signs of economic crisis via privatization while others muddle indecisively for years?
2. What decision criteria—be them political, technical, ideological, bureaucratic—were important in promoting or inhibiting privatization.
3. What factors enter the choice (explicit or by default) to treat privatization as a short-term remedy only, or to adopt privatization as part of a long-term strategy of adjustment?
4. Why have some countries experimented with privatization in tandem with heterodox approaches, while others have pursued privatization through orthodox stabilization plans?
5. Why have privatization policies failed to get off the ground in some countries and forged ahead in others?
6. Why, when confronted with heated political protest, have some governments persisted, while others have modified or abandoned their courses?
7. Finally, what were the consequences (intended and unintended) that followed privatization? What can be learned from them?

Before introducing the analytical model, I will briefly sketch the historical conditions that first led first to the creation and later to the dismantling of large government-run industrial and service sectors.

The Crisis of the State, Public Sector Reforms, and Privatization
in Less Developed Countries (LDCs)

State interventionism in the economy, or *dirigismo*, began to develop in many Latin American countries as a response to the crisis created by the Great

Depression. In Argentina, Brazil, Chile, Mexico, and Uruguay for instance, conservative elites supported laissez-faire economic policies until 1930. Thereafter, they switched to *ad hoc* measures allowing state intervention in the market place in order to alleviate the effects of the economic crisis. This took the form of counter-cyclical policies aimed at protecting domestic producers, fostering some import-substitution industrialization (ISI), maintaining steady employment levels, and regulating key economic activities. The 1950s saw the advent of Keynesian-minded policies in many Western European countries. Their emphasis was on state-led development and income redistribution through the establishment of a welfare state. This coincided with the creation of the United Nation's Economic Commission for Latin America (ECLA). ECLA's economists gave intellectual consistency and broadened the scope of the piecemeal ISI policies being pursued in Latin America at the time. In many ways the ECLA's recipe for ISI shared several ideas with Keynesianism, helping the former to gain acceptance among Latin American political elites. The Europeans were expanding the responsibilities of the state by increasing welfare benefits, creating state monopolies in both manufacturing and service sectors, nationalizing private companies, regulating key markets, and sheltering their economies from foreign competition through regional integration. The Latin American countries decided to follow the European model in a typical case of policy emulation.

Thus, as state intervention became dominant in Western Europe, many Latin American countries that were already practising it found additional ammunition to further it. This occurred whether the political regime was conservative, populist, or reformist. Most governments embraced the creed of *dirigismo* and economic nationalism in one form or another well into the 1980s. The appeal of state intervention was its ability to incorporate the otherwise incompatible demands of traditional and new socioeconomic interests. Public enterprises (PEs), were one of the most tangible symbols of state interventionism. They were set up as direct instruments through which investment flows could be channeled, adequate social and economic services could be guaranteed, regional development programs could be assured, full employment policies could be pursued, fairer income redistribution could be accomplished across social classes, and sentiments toward economic nationalism could be satisfied. Equally important, however, PEs became the means for politicians to create new patronage networks. Politically, they were used to reward supporters through the arbitrary manipulation of jobs, contracts, and investments.

Steady economic growth characterized the world economy until the early 1970s. *Dirigismo*, as a result, was widely accepted and economically viable in both developed and developing countries. However, the 1973 and 1979 oil crises, and the recessions that they produced, began to undermine the economic feasibility of the model. Faced with lower or even negative growth rates, many Latin American governments saw their tax base shrinking. They were forced to fund their costly and over-extended state sectors through ever-increasing fiscal deficits and new taxes. The resulting burden imposed by financing state capitalism overwhelmed the benefits involved. Even Rosemary Thorp, a long advocate of ISI, did recognize that, 'structuralist economists like me had too much faith in the state. Today, without any ambiguity, we must recognize that the State was not sufficient, and this is the reason why we have to leave greater room for the dynamics of the market forces'.[6]

A growing number of conservative political, economic, and social groups who had supported ISI and welfare policies back in the 1950s now saw them as the root of all evil. The heterogeneous political consensus that had brought together contending groups in support of state interventionism progressively began to evaporate. This occurred most noticeably after 1982 when the debt crisis swept Latin America (Frieden 1991). The 'policy debate reopened and new conservative coalitions carried a package that proposed a return to a more market-based economy. This aimed at both removing the state from managing the overall direction of economic activity and, at later stages, moving toward the privatization of public enterprises' (Schamis 1992: 57). The political pendulum swung inexorably back to a market-driven vision of development and capital accumulation that was abandoned in the 1930s. Inevitably, PEs became a prime target of the 'rolling back the state' rationale. Conservatives charged that PEs had not solved the problems they were supposed to resolve; rather they had become a problem themselves due to their economic inefficiency, mismanagement, deficits, corruption, and political manipulations.

Thus, if nationalization of private companies was at the core of *dirigismo*, then privatization was an essential component of the market reform packages put forth by the political and economic right throughout Latin America in the 1980s (Acuña and Smith 1994; Bresser Pereira 1993). The increasingly trendy conclusion was that a policy of privatization would unquestionably improve economic performance.[7] Economic theorists contended that the private initiative was superior to *dirigismo* in pursuing goals of economic growth. Some argued that the private sector is better suited to cut costs, improve quality of service, increase output, and is more responsive to consumers' demands than are PEs. Others saw in privatization a means to slash the government fiscal deficit by ending costly subsidies to PEs. Many scholars and pundits favored privatization on the grounds that it would depoliticize business decisions, end corruption, reduce the power of unions, and bring to an end the mismanagement of conglomerates controlled by the military, which reached an apex during authoritarian periods (Yarrow 1986; Vickers and Yarrow 1988; Henke 1986; Henke 1987; Savas 1987; Hemming and Mansoor 1988; Cook and Kirpatrick 1988; Vernon 1988; Donahue 1989; Cowan 1990; Jones, Tandon, and Vogelsang 1990, Ott 1991, Bös and Peters 1991, Ramamurti and Vernon 1991; Kikeri, Nellis, and Shirley 1992). Empirical studies by the IMF, the World Bank, and the IDB, as well as a variety of think-tanks, supported many of these conclusions thus playing a pivotal role in influencing the views of many Latin American policy-makers (Haggard and Webb 1994; Edwards 1995). Perhaps, one of the biggest blows yet to ISI and *dirigismo* came from the ECLA itself. Some of the ECLA economists, after comparing the economic performance of the so-called East Asian Tigers with those of Latin American countries, concluded that combining market-oriented structural reforms with policies alleviating poverty was the only way to promote growth with social equity (Bianchi and Nohara 1988). Thus, either by conviction or disillusion, privatization became to be perceived as part of the solution toward reforming the socioeconomic role of the state and address-ing its failures (Krueger 1974; Pirie 1985; Austin, Wortzel, and Coburn 1986; Kay and Thompson 1988; Schneider 1988–89; Maciel 1989; Yotopoulos 1989; Bienen and Waterbury 1989; Glade 1989; Suleiman and Waterbury 1990*b*; Gerchunoff and Visintini 1991; CEPAL 1992; Waterbury 1993).[8]

As in the 1930s and the 1950s, two crucial elements came into play to swing the pendulum back to market-oriented policymaking: the severity of the economic crisis and policy emulation. In the mid-1980s, it became increasingly evident that heterodox economic policies (mixing elements of monetarism and Keyenesianism) although initially successful, actually ended up in greater inflation and fiscal deficits. No other alternative solu-tions seemed readily available except for neo-orthodox economic adjustments cum privatization. The neo-orthodox approach to stabilization, advocated by prominent economists since the 1960s, postulates that '. . . trade and fiscal imbalances often reflect causes deeper than excess demand. [Stabilization] therefore, called not only for corrective macroeconomic policies but also for medium-term structural reforms, including shifts towards outward-oriented trade policies, reductions in the role of the state, and public sector reforms' (Nelson 1990*b*: 11). More importantly, the neo-orthodox economic recipe, already endorsed by private banks and multilateral agencies, was embraced by Margaret Thatcher and Ronald Reagan, who made it the cornerstone of their conservative political agenda. By 1990, Williamson began to speak about the so-called 'Washington consensus', which consisted of the main policy initiatives agreed upon by US policy-makers, think-tank analysts, and multi-lateral lending agencies, which were urged on Latin America. The 'Washington consensus' thus sanctioned the 'direction in which it is desirable to trans-form the economic policy regime and made deregulation, trade liberalization, fiscal discipline and, of course privatization the economic dogma of the western world (Williamson 1994*b*: 13).[9]

The neo-orthodox approach was eventually followed, in varying degrees, by Socialist administrations in France, Spain, and Portugal, and more conservative parties with an old *dirigiste* tradition. These included the Christian Democrats in Germany and the Liberals in Japan; 'it was in part the international spread of the "culture of privatization" that made it an acceptable idea even in countries with strong *dirigiste* traditions' (Suleiman and Waterbury 1990*b*: 13). The success experienced by many industrialized countries in stabilizing their economies through the adoption of market reforms thus created a strong model for Latin American countries to emulate (Ikenberry 1990: 101). Moreover, Chile constituted an example close to home of successful implementation of these reforms. By the same token, under the influence of the United States and other industrialized countries, international lending organizations to which Latin American countries came to finance their external debts (the International Monetary Fund (IMF), the World Bank, the IDB) made credit dependent upon the adoption of market reforms (Babai 1988; Ikenberry 1990; Kahler 1992). Thus, the combination of policy emulation and external inducements was instrumental in tipping the balance toward the adoption of deregulation and privatization policies.

The Analytical Model

Privatization as a policy phenomenon has been justified, designed, and carried out in many different ways. Students of privatization have attempted to come to grips with its complexity, developing a number of theoretical explanations based upon cross national comparisons and case studies. Some scholars have tried to develop general explanations that hold true across time and space by identifying the conditions deemed necessary and sufficient for privatization to occur. These attempts have tended to focus at the 'middle level', by looking at why some countries do decide to privatize, while others dealt with the costs and benefits of privatization policies. Another group of scholars have focused on the micro-level, by concentrating on the privatization of specific economic sectors taken in isolation. However, the results have only been partial and often inconclusive. The scholarly evidence provided so far has produced several 'islands of theory' that seem to explain only a few aspects of privatization. This is because by focusing exclusively on factors either at the macro or micro level, scholars have precluded themselves from understanding how such factors are logically related to one another.

Zahariadis (1995) noted that the rationale behind privatization often shifts from country to country, and even within the same country across a prolonged period of time, and consequently tried to model these different patterns by focusing on the effects of timing on those factors that can induce or deter privatization. Moreover, the weight that different factors have in spurring privatization varies across countries depending on domestic circumstances (Armijo 1998).

The most comprehensive work to date was published by the World Bank in 1995. It encompassed nine developing market economies and three transition economies.[10] According to the World Bank study, three conditions are deemed necessary for the successful reform of PEs: political desirability, political feasibility, and government credibility. In other words:

- Reform must be politically *desirable* to the leadership and its constituencies. Reform becomes desirable to the leadership and its supporters when the political benefits outweigh the political costs. This usually happens with a change in regime or coalition shift in which those favoring the status quo lose power. It may also happen when an economic crisis makes [PE] subsidies so costly that reform becomes preferable to the status quo.
- Reform must be politically *feasible*. Leaders must have the means to implement change and to withstand opposition to reform.
- Promises central to state-owned reform must be *credible*. Investors must believe that the government will not re-nationalize privatized forms; [PE] employees and others who fear that they may lose out in reform must believe that the government will deliver on any promises of future compensation. (World Bank 1995: 10)

To integrate the findings of previous research, this work proposes a model that tries to link some of the 'islands of theory' so far developed by adopting a micro-level analysis focusing on the decision-making processes and expected utility calculations involved in privatization. It should be clear that a model is intended here as, 'a simplification of, and approximation to, some aspects of the world' (King, Keohane, and Verba 1994: 49). Models can be broadly classified as restrictive and unrestrictive (King 1989). 'Restrictive models are clearer, more parsimonious, and more abstract, but they are also less realistic. . . . Models which are unrestrictive are detailed, contextual, and more realistic, but they are also less clear and harder to estimate with precision (King, Keohane, and Verba 1994: 49). A model is successful if it provides us with the theoretical tools to comprehend complex phenomena in a simple, stylized fashion, that can be readily applied to the concrete world without losing oneself in a myriad of factors, many of which are not crucial to the development of causal explanations. Given the complexity of privatization as a policy phenomenon, the model here presented falls into the latter category, as we shall discuss in more details later.

The model starts with two basic assumptions. First, the policy-makers' ultimate goal is to keep their jobs and/or influence. In fact, it has been well documented in Latin America that the primary preoccupation of policy-makers is political survival (Ames 1987). Policy-makers are constantly engaged in the manipulation of government expenditures to create 'survival coalitions'. The object is to dispense benefits to supporters while excluding opponents, so as to retain power. This strategy becomes particularly acute in times of crisis. The unfortunate results are short-term, often disorganized and erratic policy responses rather than well thought out, long-term planning (Bates 1991).

Second, as a direct consequence of this 'survival' approach, policy-makers tend to take action in response to unfolding crises rather than working to anticipate problems. This is particularly true in LDCs. These cases include the complication that politicians often face unstable political conditions and more acute socioeconomic problems than would be prevalent in industrial societies.[11] Policy-makers' responses to crisis vary, depending upon their magnitude. For example, 'low intensity crisis', is a situation in which crisis builds up slowly. In this case, policy-makers may come to the conclusion that, although quick action might be preferable, the consequences of a reform attempt would jeopardize the government's political support base. In this situation, the forces preserving the status quo outweigh the forces for reform (Frieden 1991). Thus, as long as the crisis is not threatening the government's stability, or postponing reform, 'politics as usual', will ensue (Grindle and Thomas 1991: 14). However, a 'high intensity crisis' occurs when the seriousness of a problem picks up momentum, passing the threshold beyond which inaction becomes intolerable in the eyes of powerful socioeconomic groups key to government support (Waterbury 1993). Reform is likely to take place under these circumstances. During crisis-ridden reforms the policy-maker's agenda is dominated by concerns such as political stability, national welfare, and coalition building. Here, the greater the crisis at hand, the more likely policy-makers will adopt bold reforms. To reiterate, the model places emphasis on expected utility calculations to explain the decision-making processes involved in privatization.

Policy Substitution

In addressing the puzzle presented by the different 'islands of theory' in the field of international relations Most and Starr argued:

If international behaviors can be alternative means that different states utilize in pursuit of their . . . national goals and *under at least certain conditions* states may *substitute* one means for another, then all of the behaviors that tend to be substituted in fragmented fashion need to be conceived and studied from the outset—*not* as separate and distinct phenomena, the understanding of which will eventually be integrated—but rather as commensurable behaviors of component of parts of abstract conceptual puzzles.   (Most and Starr 1989: 99)

Such a contention suggests two things. First, given the complexity of policy-making and the different goals pursued by policy-makers, a way of solving conceptual puzzles rests not in the search for 'always true', encompassing explanations but, rather, on the design of theories and models which hold true only under explicitly prescribed conditions. Second, across time and space, 'similar factors could plausibly be expected to trigger' different policies (Most and Starr 1989: 98). The latter is the core of the *policy substitutabil-*

ity concept. In other words, if we assume that public policies are alternative means used by policy-makers to achieve their goals, then it may be plausible to expect that, when confronted with a given policy dilemma, the same decision-makers, can 'under at least certain conditions, substitute one such means for another' (Most and Starr 1989: 102). For instance, let us suppose that a president faces the task of keeping the government budget under control in an election year. He may find the continuation of a policy of high taxes pursued up to that moment no longer feasible and decide to substitute high taxes with a policy emphasizing drastic government cuts to trim the deficit. The result is taxation policy *substituted* by budgetary cuts.

Let us now turn to the case of privatization as a policy alternative. Many of the issues discussed below have been highlighted in the previous pages but are recast according to the policy-substitutability rationale. The contention is that privatization policies, in the Latin American context, can indeed be thought of as substitutes for previous public policies which were no longer considered viable by policy-makers. The substitutability concept can be useful in understanding the adoption of drastic policy departures in Latin America. Privatization, for example, as contrasted with previous policies like ISI and economic protectionism.

ISI began, in most of the region, as a response to the devastating consequences of the Great Depression on international trade. Latin American decision-makers were faced with the collapse of their export markets in North America and Europe, high inflation, and increasing foreign debts. They turned to ISI as a means to promote self-sufficiency and steady employment levels that were the necessary conditions for political stability. Accordingly, the old export-oriented development model was abandoned. This forced policy reversal creating the seeds for state interventionism and the development of PEs. This phenomenon would later become associated with the rise of populist politics in some of the most advanced Latin American countries (Dornbusch and Edwards 1989). To reiterate, the unprecedented crisis brought about the conditions for the substitution of free-market economic policies with interventionist ones. By comparison, there are several similarities between the Great Depression of 1929 and the 1982 debt crisis. Like the 1930s the 1980s saw many Latin American nations experiencing large foreign debts and fiscal deficits, high unemployment and inflation rates, sluggish growth, and unstable terms of trade with the industrialized nations. Latin American policy-makers responded first by resorting once again to neo-Keynesian economic approaches. The objective was to mitigate the harsh consequences of neo-orthodox reforms advocated by the IMF, the World Bank, the IDB, the United States and Western European governments, and creditor banks. Argentina, Brazil, and Peru tried this path through a series of heterodox stabilization policies in the mid-1980s, but ultimately failed (Bruno, Di Tella, and Dornbusch 1988; Edwards 1989; Brock, Connolly, and González-Vega

1989; Devlin 1989; Nelson 1990*b*). The heterodox debacle had the effect of convincing many Latin American political leaders that market reforms were the only option left to the multiple socioeconomic problems they were confronting. The director of the IDB described this change of heart as a 'trend toward convergence', which rested upon four policies: (*a*) macroeconomic stability; (*b*) trade openness; (*c*) poverty alleviation; and (*d*) privatization and deregulation (Iglesias 1992). Thus, the late 1980s set the stage for yet another policy reversal. The politicians' objective, however, remained essentially the same, strengthening their political power and maintaining socioeconomic stability. The difference was that state interventionism was now *substituted* with market economics and the divestiture of PEs.

Willingness and Opportunity

So far I have argued that *under at least certain conditions*, policy-makers may substitute one policy for another. What are the conditions that determine the likelihood that a decision-maker will engage in the substitution of state interventionism with privatization policies? Such conditions are shaped by two related concepts which link environmental and systemic factors: 'willingness' and 'opportunity' (Sprout and Sprout 1969; Russett and Starr 1985; Most and Starr 1989). Once again, the level of analysis here is at the micro-level as our attention is focused on the decision of the country's top policy-makers, the president and his staff.

The decision-maker's willingness is influenced by the perceived margin of advantage, that is, the degree to which the expected results of privatization are preferred to available alternatives. Willingness to privatize comes from a mixed bag of motives, which are ideological and pragmatic in nature (Fig. 1.1). A typical example of how ideology can be instrumental in shaping a leader's willingness to privatize occurred in Chile in the mid-1970s and again in the mid-1980s. In that case, General Augusto Pinochet embraced the teachings of neo-conservative economists in order to implement reforms which went beyond the economic sphere and aimed at transforming the Chilean society as a whole in a conservative direction. Privatization was at the core of his political project. It was used to weaken the labor movement and to undo many of the Christian Democratic and Socialist welfare reforms enacted between 1964 and 1973. This enabled Pinochet to emasculate unions (through the deregulation of the labor market) which constituted the support basis of his main political foes (left-wing and centrist parties). Although hardly an economist, Pinochet saw in the logic of privatization an affinity with his goals and ideological underpinnings.

A leader may adopt privatization not only because it complements a neo-conservative political project. He may also be convinced that private ownership is a superior means of promoting economic well-being. The reasoning behind this belief rests on two assumptions:

Stage I: DECISION TO PRIVATIZE	
Ideology	1. affinity with leader's goals and ideological standing
	2. free-market economics regarded as superior to state intervention
	3. emasculation of labor power
	4. popular capitalism
WILLINGNESS	
Pragmatism	1. improvement of economic efficiency
	2. modernize domestic economy
	3. strengthening capital markets
	4. improvement of business climate
	5. reduction of fiscal deficit and balance of payments deficit
	6. rationalization of state operations
	7. reward supporters
	8. lack of alternatives
OPPORTUNITY	1. availability of tenders
	2. favorable public mood
	3. foreign pressure and financial support

▲
Leadership
▼

Stage II: IMPLEMENTATION	
	GOVERNMENT CAPABILITIES
	1. cohesive economic team
	2. technical and administrative capacity
	3. bureaucratic cooperation
	4. concentrated executive authority (technopols)
	5. speed
	POLITICAL RESPONSES (opposition)
PRIVATIZATION REFORM IMPLEMENTATION	1. civil servants and PEs' employees
	2. labor unions
	3. PEs' suppliers
	4. military
	5. pro-privatization political base
	TECHNICAL DIFFICULTIES
	1. market failure
	2. inadequate financial markets
	3. difficulty in valuation of assets
	4. lack of deregulation mechanisms

FIG. 1.1. Analytical Framework

First, all transfer of ownership from the state to the private sector is understood to result automatically in greater space allocation by markets, as contrasted to allocation by command. No inquiry into the existing or expected degree of oligopolization of the sector to be privatized is thought necessary. Second, such persons believe that economic growth, and 'development,' always is furthered by any expansion of free markets, regardless of the larger political space within which the markets operates. That is, there is no room within this framework for proposing 'second best' solutions to deal with cases of market failure beyond the control of domestic policymakers, as, for example, in the empirically not uncommon case of developing countries freeing entry for foreigners into domestic markets without necessarily receiving reciprocal access in foreign markets for the products the developing country is most likely to export. Overall, this argument for privatization depends upon making the *general case for markets, rather than the specific one* that a given privatization policy empirically will increase competition, efficiency, and so on.   (Armijo 1992: 8–9)

This seems to have been the case of Margaret Thatcher in the United Kingdom in the 1980s. Repeatedly, she stressed that the transferring of public corporations to private hands would create more incentives for investments, thus strengthening the bases of a free market-dominated economy. Thatcher also contended that through the entrepreneurial spirit of the middle class the UK became the world's power in the nineteenth century.

Thatcher's proselytism added another element to the ideological justification of privatization: 'popular capitalism'. This meant that working- and middle-class people were encouraged to buy shares of companies to be privatized. Starting from the old conservative tenet that the right to property is a fundamental prerequisite in a democratic society, Thatcher argued that privatization democratized ownership of private assets because every citizen was given the incentive to become a potential shareholder. Thus, in her rhetoric, privatization served the purpose of cementing the linkage between capitalism and democracy. Again, popular capitalism was expected to ignite the spirit that had been buried by the welfare programs of the Labour and Conservative governments after World War II. In turn, Thatcher argued, the liquidation of state holdings would make the state leaner and more capable of handling its tasks.

Popular capitalism was also used in Chile during the second round of privatizations in the 1980s. The inviolability of the right to property had always been a mainstay of conservative elites in Chile. Thus, it was easily incorporated into the political rhetoric of the Pinochet authoritarian regime without, of course, any reference to those democratic values of privatization cited by Thatcher. The government offered the public shares of some of the companies and banks being privatized to the public at prices below market value. Shares were sold by granting long-term credit at zero interest and tax breaks (Meller 1992; Hachette and Lüders 1993: 59).[12] Politically, the intended outcome was to make a conservative inroad within the working-class electorate (Schamis 1992).

Although the power of ideology has been crucial in the British and Chilean experiences, usually the most common factors inducing a decision in favor of privatization rest on pragmatic grounds. In the eyes of a leader considering the adoption of privatization, the pragmatic factors that are most likely to assume particular relevance are those that led to tangible achievements in other countries. Figure 1.2 shows what some of these factors are,

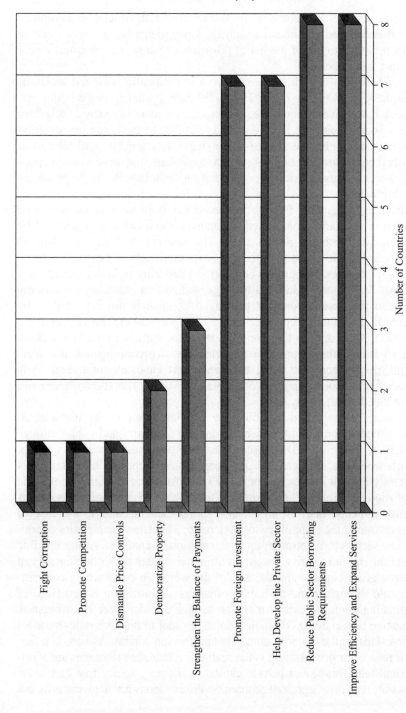

FIG. 1.2. Latin America: Major Achievements of Privatization

Source: Economic and Social Progress in Latin America. Washington, DC, 1996, p. 168.

based upon a survey of policymakers and resident IDB officials in seventeen Latin American and Caribbean countries. Coincidentally, the most cited of these factors tend to top of the list of priorities of many state divestiture programs in Latin America.

Thus, ideological arguments are decisive in politically polarized societies, such as the UK and Chile in the 1970s. When pragmatism is the major element behind the privatization drive, ideological considerations play a secondary role, as a sort of cosmetic to give more credibility to the entire privatization package. In this light, the sale of some shares to company workers and/or the general public are functions of popular capitalism that serve to soften popular opposition, thus diffusing worries that the only beneficiary of privatization is big capital.

Addressing pragmatic factors, the expected improvement in economic efficiency is constantly mentioned by many economists and is adopted by politicians who embrace privatization. The rationale behind the enhanced efficiency argument is that privatizing a state monopoly and breaking it into smaller private ones encourages competition resulting in better service at a lower cost for society. Additionally, improvements in efficiency supposedly come from the assumption that privatized companies are expected to be run according to purely economic rather than political criteria (Leyden and Link 1993). According to the empirical evidence gathered by a World Bank (1995: 6) study, 'the greater the participation of private agents in ownership and management, the better enterprise performance'. As a result, it is assumed that the corruption that often plagues state corporations should end or be reduced significantly.

One factor closely tied to efficiency considerations is the understanding that privatization should modernize domestic industry and public utilities (World Bank 1995: 25–53). These businesses, while under state ownership, have often become obsolete and undercapitalized. Repeated budgetary cuts consistently make it impossible for many Latin American countries to provide new infusions of capital. The assumption here is that private capital has powerful reinforcements; first, the financial resources and, second, in the case of foreign investors, the technology to modernize. This allows companies operating in key sectors to be brought up to international standards. Along this line of reasoning, failure to privatize would ultimately widen the technological gap between a given country and the rest of the world. In cases where companies are sold through domestic public offerings, privatization is perceived as strengthening domestic capital markets through a wider share of ownership. Privatization is also a flag commonly flown in order to improve state–business relations. This applies to both domestic and foreign capital. As noted earlier, a major reason for privatization is the realization that state resources are virtually exhausted. This leaves private capital as the only source that can invest and possibly revitalize depressed economies. Privatization aims at giving business

a clear signal that the government is serious about retreating to more fundamental tasks, thus leaving the role of promoting growth to private capital (World
Bank 1995: 12–13). However, given that private domestic capital is often too
small and lacks the technological sophistication to pick up the slack, foreign
investments then become crucial. Privatization is a primary, powerful incentive, for the arrival of foreign investors *en masse* (Boeker 1993; Sader 1995).
This is particularly true if it is accompanied by the dismantling of regulations restricting foreign ownership and repatriation of capital.

The need to reduce large fiscal deficits, under which many Latin American
governments operate, can convince even nationalist leaders of the need for privatization. Indeed, although many governments present privatization as a means
to improve economic efficiency in the long-term, several studies show that
state divestiture programs, particularly in their early stages, are often adopted
to finance fiscal deficits (Vernon 1988; Suleiman and Waterbury 1990*b*; Castelar
Pinheiro and Schneider 1994; SELA 1995). Transferring state operations
to private companies can make an important contribution toward balancing
the budget. This is because sales bring money into the government's depleted
coffers. By the same token, companies will no longer create additional deficits
for the state (Devlin 1993). This can be done by selling assets in return for
cash, government securities (issued to finance the domestic debt) and foreign
debt-equity conversion bonds. Privatization via debt-equity swap arrangements
and purchases in hard currencies can also make an important contribution to
a country's foreign debt (Ramamurti 1992). Moreover, privatization may have
long-term effects on the balance of payments. This becomes especially true
if the new private owners reorient production from domestic to export markets.

By privatizing, the state's tasks are reduced and the complexity of its
operations simplified. This streamlining process should allow the state to
redefine its priority areas and become more selective in its intervention.
Consequently, at least in theory, this should bring an improvement in the provision of public services as more human and capital resources can be allocated more efficiently. Yet, there are also some implicit political advantages
in reducing the state to basic functions. For instance, through privatization,
policy-makers can unload to the private sector some costs of welfare provision like pensions and health coverage (Suleiman and Waterbury 1990*b*: 17).
Additionally, privatization serves the purpose of rewarding supporters or finding new ones. According to Bates (1991) and Kiewiet and McCubbins
(1991) policy reform can be highly distributive and tailored to further the
interests of specific economic groups. An administration can sell PEs to sympathetic private businesses, under very profitable conditions. Thus, privatization may turn into a form of patronage, a reward for campaign contributions
or a means to lure future support. Examples are the United Kingdom, France
in the 1980s (Feigenbaum and Henig 1994), and Mexico in the 1990s (Nelson
1994). Some have also emphasized that the sustainability of market reforms

can be enhanced if governmental policies are designed to hasten the emergence of socioeconomic groups that benefit from them and in turn will be supportive. A final crucial factor is (as noted earlier) that a decision-maker may be faced with a situation in which privatization is the only viable option left if other alternative courses of action have been tried and failed before.

However, willingness alone may not suffice If leaders do not have the opportunity to implement their policy agenda. 'Opportunity' delimits the range of possible options open to decision-makers. Often governments want to get rid of deficit-ridden enterprises but may encounter strong public opposition or are unable to find buyers due to market availability, markets' willingness to assume risk, and the supply of available investment opportunity. Therefore, the availability of tenders is a condition which circumscribes a decisionmaker's opportunity.

A favorable public mood is another crucial element in shaping privatization opportunities. Ironically, (as noted before), such an opportunity may be brought on by the severity of the economic crisis. The greater the economic crisis, the greater the likelihood that a decision-maker will adopt a policy of state divestiture. For example, hyper-inflationary spirals create a basic consensus across society about the need for economic stability, even at the cost of higher unemployment, lower salaries, and radical structural reforms, particularly after half-hearted attempts had proven ineffective (Schvarzer 1992).

A further opportunity can be offered by exogenous factors like external support in the form of foreign aid and intellectual help (Haggard and Webb 1994). International lending agencies, along with the United States, Japan, and Western European nations in the late 1980s made the adoption of privatization policies a precondition for receiving loans and discounts on the foreign debt through conditionality agreements (Edwards 1995: 57). Thus, if privatization is essential for a government's credit-worthiness in order to improve the domestic business climate and attract foreign investors, it is equally crucial for the improvement of a country's international standing and its accessibility to international financial markets in order to service its foreign debt. A decision-maker who favors privatization can argue before relevant constituencies that privatization is necessary to meet foreign obligations. As Sachs (1994: 504) bluntly put it in describing his experience as a consultant to the Polish and Russian governments, 'the market cannot do it all by itself, international help is critical'.

The fact that multilateral institutions like the World Bank and the IDB offer special loans and technical assistance to countries willing to privatize lowers the costs of a state divestiture policy effort and thus gives a decision-maker further incentives to privatize. Moreover, to the extent that privatization is perceived as a world-wide phenomenon sponsored by the (so-called) First World, a policy-maker may argue that if his/her own country does not follow suit it will miss the 'train of history' and remain behind forever

(Schneider 1990: 228). Therefore, policy emulation issues, based upon the positive results of previous privatization experiences in other countries, provide additional incentives for privatization.

In short, 'it is through willingness that decision-makers recognize opportunities and then translate those opportunities into alternatives that are weighed in some fashion' (Siverson and Starr 1990: 49).

Opportunity and willingness are linked in a number of ways. They do not create mutually exclusive categories. Anything that affects the structural possibilities of the environment or environments within which decision-makers must act also affects the incentive structures for those decision-makers. Opportunity and willingness thus become more than organizing concepts. They take on theoretical characteristics when we understand that they describe the conditions that are necessary for the occurrence of events. (Siverson and Starr 1990: 49)

Consequently, it is hypothesized here that policy-makers decide to embark on a privatization scheme if their willingness coincides with an opportunity to do so. In other words, 'opportunity represents macro level (environmental and structural) factors, willingness represents the choice processes that occur on the micro level, that is, the selection of some behavioral option from a range of alternatives' (Siverson and Starr 1990: 48). It is precisely by combining both macro and micro factors that the model tries to improve upon previous research. Indeed, as long as our data is consistent with and adds more implications to the theory, whether they come from different levels of analysis is irrelevant (King, Keohane, and Verba 1994: 48). Thus, following the model, 'opportunity' and 'willingness' are jointly necessary conditions for privatization to take place. In other words, 'opportunity' and 'willingness' must be considered as clearly interactive concepts (Starr 1978: 363–87). Such concepts enable us to discern a decision-maker's policy priorities and how such priorities are circumscribed by environmental factors. By the same token, while most scholars have concentrated on 'the' factors that are conducive to privatization, the use of 'opportunity' and 'willingness' as organizing concepts help us to see how those factors are logically related to each other and to privatization in general (Most and Starr 1984: 324).

To summarize, by examining the expected utility calculations involved in the privatization decision, the model aims at both explaining under what specific circumstances we should expect privatization to take place. Likewise, the model has also predictive capabilities. In this respect, one may argue that willingness and opportunity are ex-post rationalizations of what happened. However, we should bear in mind that the logic of scientific inquiry is rooted in the observation of phenomena by following valid procedures. As noted early on, theories and models are scientific simplifications of reality. They also serve as a guidance to collect the evidence necessary for theory building. None the less:

theory and data interact. As with the chicken and the egg, some theory is always necessary before data collection and some data are required before any theorizing. Textbooks on research tell us that we use our data to test our theories. But learning from the data may be as important a goal as evaluating prior theories and hypotheses. (King, Keohane, and Verba 1994: 46)

Thus, as applied in our case, if willingness and opportunity may seem at first glance ex-post rationalizations, it is precisely because they are organizing concepts based upon empirical observations. Their strength, in theoretical terms, is precisely to organize the facts pertaining to privatization in terms of observable implications for our model.

Political Leadership

While willingness and opportunity are essential in identifying the conditions leading to policy substitution, they may not suffice to successfully implement a privatization scheme. According to Sachs (1994: 509), 'the key reform input that is missing in most economic analyses is political leadership'. One recent study based on the privatization of the telecommunication sector in Argentina, Brazil, Chile, and Uruguay, confirms this point by concluding that successful implementation rests on the ability of the political leadership to control the bargaining process among the parties involved during the divestiture process while preventing opposition groups from expanding the scope of the policy debate (Molano 1997). Indeed, there is widespread consensus among scholars, as well as practitioners, that the decision to go ahead with a privatization program is not the most problematic issue to success. As Williamson aptly stated it (1994*b*: 20), 'the most difficult part of a reform program is not introducing the reforms but sustaining them until they have a chance to bear fruit and thus generate political support from potential beneficiaries', and sustaining reforms requires strong and skillful leadership. In fact, past experiences indicate that the probability of privatization programs being abandoned or seriously diluted in mid-course can be traced back to lackluster executive leadership.

Executive leadership in the Latin American context usually means presidential leadership. Leadership here entails two basic features. First, it takes 'a visionary leader with a sense of history; an individual prepared to take a long-term view of what is at stake regardless of the short-term political costs' (Williamson and Haggard 1994: 577). An example that is often cited is that of Pinochet who, as I discussed before, saw in market reforms the policy tool to drastically transform Chilean society. However, Pinochet was a dictator, who could decide rather freely. Today's Latin American leaders are instead elected and rule within the context of a competitive political system, which requires a second essential feature to overcome political and technical difficulties, political skill. In fact, theoretically a president could have willingness and opportunity but not have the skills to get privatization past his opponents. For instance, shortly after being elected, President Bill Clinton was determined to push through the US Congress a sweeping bill on health care, and public opinion polls showed strong support for such an initiative. However, according to many observers, Clinton and his wife, Hilary, eventually failed due to their naivety. Unaccustomed to the complexities of Washington politics and relying upon a bright but often inexperienced staff, the Clintons were caught unprepared in dealing effectively with powerful opposition from Congress and interested lobbies. Privatization is no less a controversial policy as it affects negatively many vested interests. Overcoming their resistance require skilled political leaders.

What is skill then? Presidential scholars have usually emphasized psychological traits by pointing out how dynamic, positive-thinking presidents are the most likely to succeed in their tasks because such traits allow them to be resilient, learn from past experiences, tackle multiple tasks, and take criticism with confidence (Barber 1992). Others have argued that an efficient management style to problem solving is crucial to a successful presidency. This can take the form of a competitive style where the president solicits different points of view from his staff, or even provoke them. Opposite to it is the collegial style, where the president encourages cooperation from a small group of trusted advisers. Some presidents opt for a hierarchical, formalistic style in which part of the authority is delegated to a strong chief of staff. Yet no matter what style is adopted, a president constantly faces an overwhelming amount of information, must decide how much authority he can delegate to his subordinates, and has to strike a nice balance with regard to the amount of dissent desirable within his inner circle to avoid disruptive factionalism (George 1980).

Providing strong leadership is not easy even in Latin America where traditionally the executive is all powerful (Mainwaring and Shugart 1997). In fact, presidents are often elected through broad political alliances supported by several parties. As a result, a cabinet usually represents the various political forces that have contributed to a candidate's election. There are cases in which a party is able to win an election alone. However, often there exists factions and conflicting interests within the party that must be reconciled through the appointment of some of their prominent leaders. Often disagreement occurs among coalition partners or party factions regarding privatization. Attempts are then made to stop it at the cabinet level and, if this fails, threats are made in Congress on other key legislation by withdrawing support for the president. A president facing opposition from within becomes extremely vulnerable. Anti-privatization forces outside the government are likely to exploit the situation, torpedoing the policy or at least slowing it down (Molano 1997).

Thus, political leadership must be present both at the decision-making as well as at the implementation stage. Figuratively speaking, it is the glue that holds the whole process together from start to finish and thus must be present every step of the way to give coherence to the policy process. This is particularly so at the implementation stage.

Policy Implementation

The current literature on privatization has heavily scrutinized the motives behind this policy but has paid much less attention to the problems involved with its implementation. Such problems, as noted earlier, are none the less crucial because sustaining privatization at the implementation stage invariably poses the toughest challenges even to the most determined leaders. By the same token:

The characteristics of particular reforms determine the type of conflict and opposition that surround their implementation. In fact, characteristics of a policy have a powerful influence on whether it will be implemented as intended or whether the outcome will be significantly different. . . . Implementation becomes a filter that often alters the intended policy. Thus, anticipating where reaction to new policy initiatives is likely to occur—in a public or political arena, or in a bureaucratic arena—and who the principal figures in such a reaction are likely to be, is critical to successful implementation. Such analytic capacity has the value of enabling the analyst to determine whether a policy reform is actually feasible.   (Grindle and Thomas 1991: 6)

What factors best explain variations of the degree in which successful implementation is achieved? Figure 1.3 displays what policymakers commonly regard as the factors posing the greatest challenge to privatization, based on the crossnational IDB survey mentioned earlier. In this book, I have tried to be more systematic and bring such factors into broader, but more cohesive categories. I have grouped them into three sets. Of course, each group may be closely interrelated to the others but together they shed light on explaining the extent to which the implementation of a given scheme is carried out as planned. They are: 'governmental capabilities', 'political responses', and 'economic difficulties' (Nelson 1984) (Fig. 1.1). Political skill is thus required to confront all of them, often simultaneously.

The first set, 'government capabilities', includes a cohesive economic team, technical and administrative capacity, state institutions, bureaucratic cooperation, and speed. In explaining the success of Chile's market reforms under the Pinochet regime, Piñeira (1994) ascribed a substantial amount of the credit to the cohesiveness (in terms of shared views) of the economists at the helm. This view was confirmed by Nelson who, in summarizing the results of policy reforms in seventeen developing countries in the 1980s concluded that, 'the cases of clear failure all traced collapse in large part to deeply divided economic teams' (1990*b*: 347).

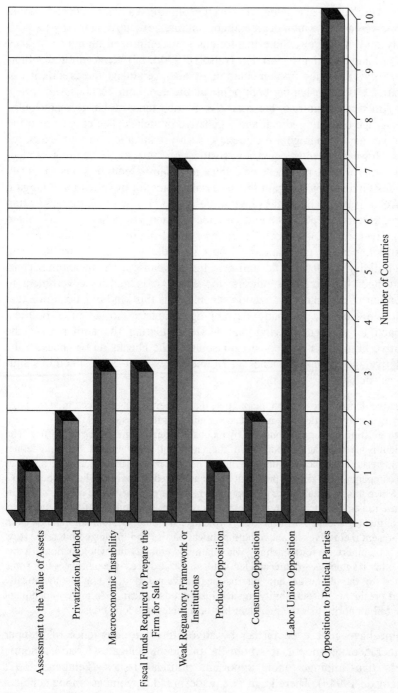

FIG. 1.3. Latin America: Major Difficulties in Privatization

Source: Economic and Social Progress in Latin America. Washington, DC, 1996, p. 168.

However, Nelson also added that even economic teams, to succeed, should be empowered with a high degree of concentrated executive authority to move quickly and effectively. State institutions and centralized authority are key (Haggard and Kaufman 1995). For Nelson (1990*b*: 25), 'concentrated authority directly facilitates implementation; it also heightens the credibility of programs, crucially shaping both political and economic responses'. In most Latin American countries, the executive branch tends to have greater political leverage over the judicial and legislative branches. The case of a strong executive may encourage a president to rush privatization through executive orders. However, in most countries privatization legislation often requires legislative approval. A president who does not enjoy a congressional majority must design a strategy to gain the necessary votes for privatization (Haggard and Webb 1994). This could prove to be costly politically as the opposition may request unacceptable changes or side payments on other issues (Molano 1997). Even in the instance of a congressional majority, opposition parties can still appeal to the Supreme Court in order to forestall privatization, while building support for the anti-privatization cause in the meantime. Thus, the stronger the executive powers, the easier it is for the government to implement its original privatization scheme. It is this kind of calculation that has led presidents, in many developing countries, to adopt a political approach to problem solving that while insulating the authority of the executive branch simultaneously emasculates the checks an balances of the legislative and judicial branches. O'Donnell (1994: 59–58) defined this situation as 'delegative democracy'.

Delegative democracies rest on the premise that whoever wins an election to the presidency is thereby entitled to govern as he or she sees fit, constrained only by the hard facts of existing power relations and by a constitutionally limited term of office. The president is taken as the embodiment of the nation and the main custodian and definer of its interests. The policies of his government need bear no resemblance to the promises of his campaign—has not the president been authorized to govern as he (or she) thinks best? Since this paternal figure is supposed to take care of the whole nation, his political base must be a movement, the supposedly vibrant overcoming of the factionalism and conflicts associated with parties. Typically, winning presidential candidates in DDs present themselves as above both political parties and organized interests. How could it be otherwise for somebody who claims to embody the whole nation? In this view, other institutions—courts and legislatures, for instance—are nuisances that come attached to the domestic and international advantages of being democratically elected president. Accountability to such institutions appears as a mere impediment to the full authority that the president has been delegated to exercise.

Some have gone even further by advocating the emergence of a super technocrat, or technopol, to whom the president delegates broad economic powers that impinge upon important political issues (Feinberg 1992; Williamson 1994*b*). There is, in fact, widespread agreement among scholars and practitioners that, 'good economic policymaking requires that economic decisions be made by technocrats' (Bates 1994: 30). According to this view, technopols are likely to have a high degree of independence that allow them to overcome the roadblocks posed by multiple ministerial jurisdictions, constitutional bans, and legal interpretations invoked by Congress or local government (state legislatures and municipalities).

Coherence and concentrated decision-making authority in the hands of technocrats, however, are not enough if they are not matched by technical and administrative capacity. The design of a privatization policy entails a high level of expertise by government planners. There exists a lack of well-trained economists and lawyers capable of designing such policies, particularly in the poorer countries of Latin America. However, highly qualified professionals, even when available, may not be sufficient. Ministers in charge of privatization and their staff may find themselves in a complete policy vacuum if the public bureaucracy does not have an adequate institutional capacity for implementation. To this end, countries that already have special development agencies with a strong expertise in dealing with PEs may have a greater chance of success. None the less, special agencies put in charge of privatization may achieve little if they are unable to depend upon the cooperation of other bureaucratic institutions.[13]

Speed is another major factor. Addressing the case of Eastern Europe, Sachs (1991) emphasized the importance of speed in carrying out a privatization policy, 'the need to accelerate privatization . . . is the paramount economic policy issue. . . . If there is no breakthrough in the privatization of large enterprises in the near future, the entire process could be stalled for years to come.' The sooner an administration can devise and implement a privatization policy, the quicker a government can sell its PEs. Expediting policy allows an administration to prevent anti-privatization lobbies from organizing and mounting effective campaign to slow down the process. Conversely, a long period of gestation increases the risk that the policy may be diluted or abandoned altogether. 'Fire sales' do have their own drawbacks, however. Hastily designed privatization policies can run into a multitude of economic and political problems, at times giving the opposition further ammunition against state divestiture. Thus, decision-makers often find themselves in a 'catch-22' situation caught between 'doing the right thing' and doing it 'quickly' (Przeworski 1995). Privatization tends to occur after a presidential inauguration. The president is likely to enjoy a brief 'honeymoon' period with the public at this juncture that enables him to overcome his political foes who have been eclipsed by the electoral defeat (Haggard and Webb 1994). By contrast, privatization rarely occurs prior to mid-term elections because short-term employment effects are likely to be negative.

'Political responses' by key socioeconomic groups are a second set of variables that constrain leaders' capacity to implement privatization. It is indeed true that responses do affect decision-makers' opportunities but here they are treated separately for the sake of simplicity. How and in what sequence opportunities and responses occur are questions that can be answered only by examining the real world of policy-making. In this arena it is just as likely to find unscheduled decision-making behaviors as behaviors that conform to a rational model. However, the systematic comparison of public policy is difficult to achieve without some conceptualization of the stages of the decision-making process. Political responses are shaped by private and public interest groups alike. It has already been made evident that opposition for privatization can come from a president's own party or from the coalition parties that helped him win office. This can spring from nationalist motives. A more potent reason, however, is that PEs have traditionally been used by politicians to sustain their own patronage networks. Privatization can thus spell political disaster at the next elections. Likewise, civil servants and officials of public corporations have accrued power and benefits by overseeing PEs' operations. PEs provide ministries with powerful policy tools with which to implement their policy agendas. Labor unions fear a drop in employment levels. Private suppliers of state corporations are concerned with the loss of rent-seeking advantages established over time through lucrative contracts (Frieden 1991). The armed forces, in some developing countries, may also have strong interests in thwarting privatization. First, because they often directly manage companies producing military equipment. Second, because they see privatization as a threat to national security. In the end, they all constitute potentially hostile interest groups, because of their organization, awareness, and control over important assets.

The final factor regarding 'political responses' is the popular support (or lack of it) ensuing from the privatization reform. The stronger the social consensus and the support base, the more secure a leader tends to feel in carrying out a privatization effort. A 'support base' refers to those groups bound to the government by durable ties of ideological commitment, party loyalties, and political clienteles. Reactions to privatization are muted or heightened by the security or precariousness of the government and by the nature and strength of opposition parties. When they were first announced in the 1980s, privatization programs did not elicit much popular support in Europe and Latin America. The right-of-center parliamentary coalition in France was voted out of office in 1988 partly because of strong popular opposition to the privatization program launched in 1986. Aside from the groups mentioned above, if the remainder of the society perceives no benefit or is indifferent to privatization (i.e. if there is no constituency for it), then governments can expose themselves to accusations of selling the 'family silver' at advantageous prices to private domestic and foreign interests. This may be especially damaging in countries where substantial investment was made in previous decades to justify the creation of PEs as the only means of correcting inequities in income distribution and achieving social justice and economic independence.

It was noted above that a president facing congressional opposition to privatization must come up with a coalition strategy to turn out the votes, which requires a substantial leadership effort from the president himself. However, the coalition building effort does not end there. An equal or stronger effort is necessary to 'sell' the privatization policy to the general public and to the interest groups affected by it (Piñeira 1994). An administration should engage in media campaigns to convince the public that private ownership, particularly in the service sector, will result in superior performance. The sooner newly privatized companies can show improvements, the better. Failure to provide improved service in a relatively short time may eventually jeopardize the privatization of other PEs at a later stage. In situations where a favorable public mood already exists, it is important to mobilize the 'silent majority' to counter those groups opposed to privatization that are likely to organize quickly and be very vocal about it.

If the mobilization of public opinion pro privatization constitutes the ground floor upon which a coalition building effort is based, drafting the support and cooperation of key interest groups is also essential. Privatization invariably encounters strong opposition from private groups that have made profitable business through the provision of goods and services to PEs, often at inflated prices with little or no competition. To thwart their opposition, compensation schemes for potential losers are powerful means to turn potential enemies into decisive allies (Haggard and Webb 1994). An administration can forge counter alliances with domestic and foreign private groups that favor privatization. This can be achieved by allowing private groups to bid for PEs under very favorable conditions, thus allowing them to acquire monopolistic or oligopolistic status in their respective markets. Union opposition may be softened by intimidation (e.g. using the threat of closing down a PE if it is not sold), cooperation (by involving union leaders in the design of procedures for the privatization process), or compensation (e.g. early retirement and severance pay packages for displaced workers).

'Economic difficulties' play an equally important role. Unless accompanied by liberalization measures, it is unlikely that privatization of PEs will result in significant gains in economic efficiency. The proper scheduling of privatization and liberalization thus becomes a critical issue for policymakers. Also important is the extent to which one may be substituted for the other. Generally speaking, greater economic and social benefits may be achieved by a privatization *qua* liberalization of the economy and a reduction in domestic barriers protecting economic rents. Market failures must be addressed in addition to liberalization (i.e. lack of competition or adequate providers of goods and services). Indeed market failures were often behind the creation of the PE sector from the 1930s through the 1970s. Where market failure exists, any practical privatization scheme must solve them. The absence of adequate financial markets, particularly in the poorer Latin American countries, also complicates privatization. Where stock exchange markets are very small, it is very difficult for the state to make large public offerings of shares. Since widespread share holding is not feasible, ownership is likely to benefit a small group of private companies. Even then, often there does not exist a mechanism for risk sharing, thus buyers must be willing to assume substantial risk. This is particularly troublesome for domestic companies that often are short in liquidity. Domestic groups that are interested in purchasing a firm are still responsible for arranging financing. However, because of the large size of many PEs, financing their purchase may become problematic due to the limited domestic sources for these kinds of operations. Within this context, foreign corporations have the advantage in gaining control of the enterprises as they are better capitalized.

A final compelling problem is the valuation of assets. Evaluating the assets of a PE and making accurate estimates of the future flow of profits are complex tasks requiring levels of expertise not commonly found in less developed economies. The task becomes more difficult where no capital markets are present to provide share values for comparison purposes. Future profit expectations, not book value, are the key to a company's worth. Nevertheless, profit expectations depend upon the condition of the fixed assets as well as upon future economic and political conditions.

Of course, the model just described has limitations. On the one hand, the elements making up 'willingness' and 'opportunity' at the decision-making stage, and those spelled out in the implementation part, are often closely related. On the other hand, their inclusion in one part of the model rather than another may look arbitrary at times. Indeed, regarding the first concern, it is undisputable that if the model could be quantified and tested through a regression equation, it would suffer of inextricable multicollinearity problems. This is why I opted for an unrestrictive, qualitative-type of model that allows for a contextual, detailed explanation more suitable for a complex policy like privatization. This is also why the different elements of the model are referred as factors, rather than variables, since often they cannot be measured with great accuracy. None the less, what we lose in precision we gain in the number of observable implications to evaluate the model. Organizing 'willingness,' 'opportunity,' 'government capabilities,' 'political responses,' and 'technical difficulties' into a list of 'specific observable implications' of a model, after all, 'helps reveal the essential scientific purpose of much qualitative research' (King, Keohane, and Verba 1994: 47).

Regarding the second problem, the assumption that one factor makes up one dimension of the model rather than another is dictated by the need to systematize the data in the most coherent fashion possible. Thus, if for instance 'popular capitalism' is listed under 'willingness-ideology' instead of being considered as one of the incentives used to gain workers' support in the 'polit-ical responses' dimension, it is because in the former case popular capital-ism brings more information to bear on the model.

Another potential problem comes from the absence of an explicit time dimension. The model simply distinguishes between the decision-making stage followed by policy implementation. Admittedly, the assessment of policy management is somewhat problematic. One is tempted to judge policy-makers according to the fit between intentions and outcomes of their policies based upon clear sequential actions. As straightforward as this seems, it can be terribly misleading. Policy implementation, for instance, is an ongoing process, a voyage of discovery. The experiences of the country here examined point out, in two cases out of three, that stop-go patterns were more common than linear ones. The road to privatization is a bumpy and often unpre-dictable one. Thus, rather than being constrained in a rigid time-dimension straight jacket, the model accommodates the analysis of policy sequences in the qualitative description of each country study.

Methodology

The test of the analytical framework presented above will be based upon the experience of Argentina, Brazil, and Peru. However, the focus will remain on privatization as a policy phenomenon. Hopefully, the findings discussed here may be applied to other countries facing similar challenges in Latin America.

Case selection was based upon the 'Most-Similar-System-Design' approach (Przeworski and Teune 1970). The basic premise of this method is that 'systems as similar as possible with respect to as many features as possible constitute the optimal samples for comparative inquiry' (Przeworski and Teune 1970: 32). In the event that some important differences are found among three essentially similar countries, as in our case, 'then the number of factors attributable to these differences will be sufficiently small to warrant explanation in terms of those differences alone' (Przeworski and Teune 1970: 117–26). Put in other words, the initial assumption is that the units of observation are similar. The goal is to identify the differences that exist among such similar systems.

Argentina, Peru, and Brazil seem to fit the prerequisites of the 'Most-Similar-System-Design' quite closely. All three are located in the same geographical area, South America. They also have similar cultural and political histories, political institutions, and development patterns.[14]

Additional criteria induced the case selection. First, I chose administrations that were contemporaries of one another to avoid time lag problems.[15] Second, consistent with the Most-Similar-System-Design approach, I wanted to focus on countries that used similar approaches to privatization within the context of market-oriented reforms.[16] Third, analysts regarded Argentina, Brazil, and Peru, more than any other countries in South America, as the main test cases for the feasibility of privatization in that region.[17] Fourth, they were similar in terms of political regime, characterized by democratic-ally elected governments.[18]

As noted earlier, the study will be qualitative. While this approach is not as precise as if we were employing quantitative methods, it is more reliable in terms of the accuracy of the observed phenomenon. Following this ration-ale, in the country-by-country analysis the method used will be that of struc-tured, focused comparison. The strength of this method is that it allows the researcher an in-depth definition and standardization of the data requirements of the case studies by 'formulating theoretically relevant general questions to guide the examination of each case'. Accordingly, data were collected on the same factors across unit of analysis in order to strengthen the causal infer-ence ensuing from each country analysis.

Although each country is here examined individually, comparisons among cases are made throughout the chapters, particularly the ones on Brazil and Peru, which chronologically followed Argentina in their privatization effort. The periods analyzed in the country chapters (3, 4, and 5) will be the admin-istrations of Presidents Carlos Menem of Argentina (1989–99) and Alberto Fujimori of Peru (1990–99). In the case of Brazil, the analysis will center on the Collor–Franco administrations (1990–4) and, to a lesser extent, the Fernando Enrique Cardoso first administration (1995–8).

Besides the collection of statistical data not available in the United States, the field research involved extensive open-ended, structured interviews carried out between 1990 and 1998 in all three countries with 310 people. These interviews included cabinet ministers, high-ranking government bureaucrats, representatives of multilateral lending organizations and foreign governments, congressmen, journalists, pollsters, and businessmen. All information used in the text was thoroughly double-checked through documentary sources (government documents, congressional inquiries), secondary sources (press reports), and the corroborations of structured interviews.

Endnotes

1. For a thorough discussion of the theoretical definition of privatization and its methods, see Adam, Cavendish, and Mistry (1992).
2. Swiss Bank Corporation Warburg (1997: 8).
3. COPRI (1993*a*: 12).
4. Interview with David Moreira, São Paulo, August 1993. See also Suleiman and Waterbury (1990*b*: 3).
5. Swiss Bank Corporation Warburg (1997: 2).

6. *El Peruano*, 30 July 1992, p. A4.
7. Privatization can take many forms. Here again it is mainly understood as a transfer of assets and services from the state to the private sector. A typology of privatization policies can be found in Glade (1986: 2–23).
8. These works questioned the feasibility and even the utility of privatization by pointing to a number of economic and political difficulties that could thwart attempts at state divestiture. Obstacles to privatization will be discussed later in the chapter.
9. Williamson's (1990) list of reform policies consisted of: fiscal discipline, public expenditure priorities, tax reform, financial liberalization, exchange rates, trade liberalization, foreign direct investment, privatization, deregulation, and property rights.
10. In the former group we find Chile, Egypt, Ghana, India, Mexico, the Philippines, the Republic of Korea, Senegal, and Turkey. In the latter were included China, the Czech Republic, and Poland.
11. This assumption has been questioned with the argument that decision-makers 'are not simply forced by events, pressure by interest groups, or external agencies to make particular choices: generally, they have a significant range of options in the management of public problems' (Grindle and Thomas 1991: 2).
12. Practically, the government subsidized the sale of shares. The scheme was so lucrative that a limit was imposed on the number of shares that an individual could purchase.
13. Haggard and Webb (1994: 13) argue that ministers and bureaucrats within the government are the 'most vociferous opposition' of all to any change in the status quo. This is why, in many LDC countries, executives ascribed the authority to design and implement market reforms to small, insulated groups of technocrats often coming from outside the public administration.
14. The selection of South America led, automatically, to the exclusion of Mexico and Central America.
15. This led to the exclusion of Chile, which privatized most of its PEs between the mid-1970s through the late 1980s.
16. This led to the exclusion of Ecuador, Venezuela, and Uruguay where market reforms proceeded at an ad hoc manner due to strong political opposition.
17. Accordingly, Bolivia and Paraguay were excluded. Colombia had one of the smallest PE sectors in South America to begin with and began to privatize some companies only in the mid-1990s.
18. This last criterion led to the exclusion of Mexico, one of the most important cases in Latin America, thus reducing the focus to South America. There is strong consensus among specialists that the Partido Revolucionario Institucional's monopolistic power makes Mexico a semi-authoritarian political regime.

2

Privatization in the 1980s: Politics as Usual

The debt crisis that affected most of Latin America since the early 1980s came at a time of regime change in many countries as the military governments that took power in the 1960s and 1970s returned to the barracks having proven unable to tackle mounting socioeconomic problems. Civilian administrations were therefore elected in Peru (1980), Argentina (1983), and Brazil (1985).

All these countries, with the exception of Argentina, experienced a rapid growth of the public sector in the 1970s. Between 1970 and 1982, the outlays of PEs in GDP terms doubled in Brazil and grew eigthfold in Peru (Table 2.1). According to Kuczynski (1988: 55), 'The rapid growth in the role of state enterprises in the 1970s was . . . accompanied by rising nationalism and a growing tendency to regulate investment flows and prices. The same set of circumstances favored the larger established private enterprises as well . . . [while] foreign investment was in effect discouraged through restrictions on ownership and profit remittance as well as by red tape.' Thus PEs became major players in domestic economies. By 1983 Argentine PEs accounted for 42 per cent of the public sectors investments. In 1984, Brazilian and Peruvian PEs' investments were respectively 3.8 per cent and 4.8 per cent of total public investments (Table 2.2). Yet, during the 1970–82 period, the public sector deficit of all four countries (as a percentage of GDP) also skyrocketed (Table 2.1). In Argentina and Brazil, PEs contributed heavily to their countries' external debt as they obtained foreign loans to finance their investments and current expenditures (Table 2.2).

TABLE 2.1. *Growth of Public Sector in Argentina, Brazil, and Peru, 1970–82*

Country	Public Sector Outlays				Estimated Share of PEs in GDP (%)	Public Sector Deficit as % of GDP	
	as % of GDP		of which PEs (%)				
	1970	1982	1970	1982	1978–80	1970	1982
Argentina	33	35	11	12	20	1	14
Brazil	28	32	6	11	39	2	17
Peru	25	57	4	32	15	1	9

Source: Kuczynski (1988: 54).

TABLE 2.2. *Amount of Public and Private Investments (as % of GDP) and External Debt by Country, 1980–4*

	Argentina		Brazil		Peru	
	Average 1980–81	1983	Average 1980–81	1984	Average 1980–81	1984
Public sector investments (% of GDP)	12.7	11.9	6.7	6.1	6.6	7.8
of which PEs (% of GDP)	4.9	5.0	4.3	3.8	3.5	4.8
Private sector investments (% of GDP)	7.7	4.2	15.6	10.2	9.0	6.8
Public sector deficit (% of GDP)	5.7	15.7	8.1	10.5	7.4	7.1

	Argentina			Brazil			Peru		
	1980	1982	1984	1980	1982	1984	1980	1982	1984
Oustanding external debt by PEs (US$ billions)	14.4	28.6	37.6	32.0	46.7	53.3	3.08	5.4	6.08
Total external debt (US$ billions)	27.2	43.6	48.8	70.9	92.8	105	9.98	12.23	13.16

Source: Kuczynski (1988: 62); Total external debt from World Bank Tables, 'External Debt of developing Countries', ii, 1990–1; CEDAL 1992; Saulniers (1988).

The outbreak of the 'debt crisis' in 1982 called into question the role of PEs. By the mid-1980s, a rapidly deterioating economic situation forced these countries to take action. This was easier said than done. At times policy-makers acknowledged that some kind of reform was necessary. However, they also realized that such reforms would negatively affect the economic rents and political privileges of powerful economic, bureaucratic, and political groups (Frieden 1991). These sectors in turn were likely to torpedo any initiative aimed at the alteration of the status quo. The dilemma was summarized as follows:

In the name of efficiency and development, many changes of the 1980s implied a significant decentralization of decision-making, a shrinking of the size of the public sector, and an important shift in the strong role of the state in the economy. For decision makers schooled in the importance of state building, practiced in the methods of centralizing power in order to survive politically, familiar with the use of the public sector for patronage and regulation, and imbued with development doctrines emphasizing planning and control, the logic of many proposed reforms was not always politically or philosophically obvious.   (Grindle and Thomas 1991: 3)

The policy response to the debt crisis of the 1980s was usually tentative and tried invariably to avoid an economic adjustment program that encountered the opposition of powerful lobbies (like those sectors of the business community that benefitted from high import barriers and generous state contracts and subsidies, labor, the military, and the government bureaucracy.) Moreover, at least until the mid-1980s, many presidents failed to grasp the severity of the crisis. They believed that through the manipulation of macroeconomic variables, time could be gained to weather the storm. Although decision-makers saw the need for a fiscal adjustment through government reform, market deregulation, and privatization, they also believed that the political cost of these reforms was too high. A 'politics as usual' approach thus ensued, based upon incremental changes whose palliative nature did not address the distribution of political power and economic resources, which was at the core of the crisis.

Despite being under the extreme pressure of the IMF, the United States, and the international banking community, Argentina and Peru, in 1985, and Brazil in 1986, opted instead for a heterodox approach. However, by 1987 all three attempts had miserably failed resulting in a deeper economic recession. Little was accomplished considering that the stabilization efforts, at least in Argentina and Brazil, called for some privatization policies to be enforced.

The lack of privatization efforts in the 1980s should come as no surprise since most of the elements making up the 'willingness' and 'opportunity' model presented in Chapter 1 were absent. Accordingly, I now turn to a close examination of those factors hindering a coherent privatization policy in each country.

Argentina (1983–1989)

Privatization never materialized although it was on the Argentine government's agenda since the Frondizi administration (1958–62). During the military rule of the 1976–83 period, grand announcements were made regarding market deregulation and privatization by the then Minister of the Economy, José Alfredo Martínez de Hoz (1976–81). Despite all hype, little was accomplished. Some nationalist factions within the military actually coalesced with PEs' managers, private suppliers of PEs, and union leaders to thwart Martínez de Hoz's 'irresponsible dismantling' of the state (Fontana 1986: 69). Between 1976 and 1981 only 120 privatizations were completed, most of which were of negligible importance (Schvarzer 1981: 30). Sales affected mostly service companies and a few industrial companies that had gone bankrupt and were thus acquired by government-owned creditor banks. None of the largest PEs were privatized. In fact, not only did the military regime fail to privatize but it actually kept expanding the number of PEs. This was done, as in the past, through the acquisition of troubled companies like Austral Líneas Aereas and Compañía Italo Argentina de Electricidad or by creating new ones like Nuclear Mendoza, Astilleros Domeq García, and Empresa Nuclear Argentina de Centrales Eléctricas.

Raúl Alfonsín, the leader of the Radical Civic Union (Unión Cívica Radical, UCR), won the presidential election of October 1983 with 52 per cent of the popular vote. This was quite a remarkable achievement considering that the last Radical victory had been in 1928. Since the 1950s the Radicals' presidential candidates averaged only 28 per cent. In 1973, Alfonsín was the leader of the Movement Renovation and Change, a minority, left-wing faction of the UCR with strong nationalist overtones. The Radicals, despite their name, were predominantly moderate and scarcely ideological. It was not until 1981, when the old party leader Ricardo Balbín died, that Alfonsín emerged as the UCR's spokesman. By the time he was elected, Alfonsín had abandoned many of his former left-wing stands (usually targeting foreign multinationals and the US 'imperialist' foreign policy) and began to portray himself as a social democrat with a Latin American twist, placing heavy reliance on personal charisma and populist rhetoric.

The Alfonsín administration was characterized at first by strong *dirigiste* rhetoric. Upon taking office, Alfonsín and his cabinet neither understood the severity of the economic crisis they inherited nor they were prepared to solve it (Torre 1993). The President promised to reform the state bureaucracy and make PEs more efficient but also reasserted the primacy of the state in economic development over the private sector. In view of the economic recession of the 1981–83 period, Alfonsín made economic growth the number one priority of his administration. Given the unwillingness of the private sector to invest, Alfonsín's Minister of the Economy, Bernardo Grinspun reasoned that substantial government spending was necessary to jump-start the economy. While the means that Grinspun used were highly criticized, his basic object-ive encountered little opposition. During the military regime Argentina went through a series of half-hearted horthodox stabilization efforts only to ex-perience a threefold increase in its foreign debt, and a severe contraction in investments, employment, and the purchasing power of wage earners, in addition to increased inflation. During his campaign Alfonsín promised a more equitable distribution of income in order to improve the living standards of the middle class and the working class who had suffered the most under the erratic economic policies of the military regime. He later came under pres-sure to deliver on his promises. At the same time, many business associa-tions lobbied the government to spur demand to avoid bankruptcy.

Alfonsín also took a tough stand toward the renegotiation of the country's foreign debt (the third largest in the world after Brazil). Commercial banks and the IMF, warned that Argentina could eventually call for a unilateral mora-torium. In the President's view, the demands imposed on the young demo-cracy by the international financial community were unfair for two basic reasons. First, the bulk of the debt resulted from the speculative operations allowed during Martínez de Hoz's tenure. Second, in 1982 then Chairman of the Central Bank Domingo Cavallo decided that the government would take over the debt contracted abroad by domestic private companies (often to fund speculative operations) in order to avoid a financial collapse. During the first year of his term, Alfonsín unsuccesfully explored the possibility of forming a cartel of debtor countries with other Latin American governments in order to win concessions from the IMF and the commercial banks.

Alfonsín tried, also unsuccessfully, to break union power immediately after his election. The President wanted to undermine labor because the major-ity of Argentine unions supported the major opposition party in Congress, the Justicialist (Peronist) Party (Partido Justicialista, PJ). The unions had tradi-tionally regarded themselves as the 'backbone' of the Peronist movement, which was created by Juan Perón in 1945. Although he had defeated the PJ at the polls, Alfonsín recognized the power of the Peronist unions. These unions had such a large following and organizational skills that they could easily torpedo any presidential initiative (McGuire 1997). However, privatization was not used to emasculate union power. Instead, the administration relied on more conventional means. In early 1984, Minister of Labor Antonio Mucci sent a bill to Congress that passed the House of Deputies but was narrowly defeated in the Senate.

Thus, if we look at those ideological factors influencing the willingness to privatize it becomes apparent that none of them seemed to apply to Alfonsín. Privatization did not fit the President's ideology and ultimate goals, nor did Alfonsín believe in popular capitalism or in the superiority of market eco-nomics vis-à-vis *dirigismo*. Alfonsín did pursue the emasculation of union power but his reasoning was based on practical rather than ideological grounds. Peronist unionism was not a threat (to Alfonsín) because of incompatible ideological beliefs but (rather) because of labor's affiliation with the PJ. In fact, in the mid-1980s both the Radicals and the Peronists still supported state-led economic development. The most important political cleavages rested up on disagreements about the policy to be adopted with regard to human rights violations during the military regime and bread-and-butter issues.

Pragmatism was the motivation behind the privatization effort that occurred under Alfonsín, yet the emphasis changed over time. In 1984, Minister of Public Works and Services Roque Carranza clearly stated that privatization was to be interpreted as an additional means to foster economic growth. In his view, 'if private capital is willing to invest in existing productive activities in areas where security does not demand the present degree of state participation, the revenues realized can be directed toward new investments with higher priority'.[1] However, by early 1985 things quickly deteriorated. Grinspun's attempt to simultaneously pursue economic growth and income distribution goals proved fatal. It came at a time when the tax base was shrinking and interest on the foreign debt was climbing. Yearly inflation rose from 343 per cent in 1983 to 626 per cent in 1984.

Grinspun's economic team was replaced by a new one headed by Planning Secretary Juan Sourrouille in February 1985. Unlike Grinspun, Sourrouille and his economists were primarily technocrats with little or no formal ties to the Radicals. This fact, later on, created problems in garnering support within the UCR for controversial economic measures.

As the crisis began to unravel quickly in the Spring of 1985, so did the view of the new economic team toward privatization. The overall emphasis changed appreciably. The sale of PEs was no longer considered as contributing to growth but rather as a means of alleviating the fiscal crisis (Gónzalez Fraga 1991: 79; Domíngues 1988: 59). Sorrouille and his team argued that as long as the state retained ownership of money-losing enterprises, the fiscal deficit woud continue. In addition, some of these PEs had a de facto autonomous status that allowed them to spend and borrow, thus making the ministry of the economy's task to control the fiscal deficit all the more complicated (Machinea 1993). Sourrouille's argument to privatize was thus based on both the need to bring under control governmental expenditures to fight inflation and his inability to invest in PEs. As the government was expected to have less money to invest in PEs, their privatization was deemed as the most practicle solution to avoid a deterioration of their performance. In June 1985, with the financial support of the IMF and the backing of some of Argentina's largest conglomerates, Sourrouille launched a bold stabilization attempt, called the Austral Plan.

The Austral Plan took an 'heterodox' approach toward combating inflation. It combined some of the main tenets of monetary and fiscal policy advocated by the IMF and neoorthodox economists with a 'heterodox' shock treatment of inflation based upon monetary reform (a new currency was created, the austral, and pegged to the US dollar), and wage and price controls. Juan Carlos Torre (1993: 78–9), who at the time served as an advisor at the Ministry of Labor, explained the rationale behind this economic approach in these terms:

The search for a heterodox alternative was prompted not only by technical considerations but by a non-monetarist interpretation of the causes of inflation. Political considerations were also influential—for example how to minimise the social and political costs of the anti-inflationary drive so as not to endanger the process of democratic reconstitution nor damage the future electoral ambitions of the governing party. The energies of officials at the Ministry of Economy were concentrated both on meeting these requirements and on responding urgently to a rapidly deteriorating situation. All other considerations were of secondary importance.

Once inflation was under control, Sourrouille planned to enact a several reforms eliminating a number of 'bottlenecks' causing economic stagnation. The Austral Plan's unexpected success fueled unwarranted optimism. It increased pressure upon Alfonsín to concentrate on economic growth rather than on structural reforms, which negatively affected many powerful vested interests. One of Alfonsín's aides commented that the economic stability that ensued under the Austral Plan, 'lulled the willingness to reform'.[2] Unfortunately, this proved to be a costly mistake. The half-hearted measures of the new program were only able to provide the Argentine economy with a brief respite. The postponement of structural reforms doomed the plan to failure.

The resurgence of high inflation by February 1987 forced Alfonsín's team to adopt yet another set of restrictive monetary and fiscal policies supported by a tenuous accord with some Peronist trade unions. The new plan, Australito, marked a further development in the administration's economic stance. Unveiling the content of his new plan, Sourrouille acknowledged that the old state-led development model had created too many monopolistic interests. Such groups prevented serious reforms exclusively through monetary and fiscal policies. Hence, it was necessary to eliminate market inefficiencies by implementing a reform of the state that then allowed the private sector to play a greater role. Streamlining the state, opening up the economy to foreign imports, and reforming the domestic capital markets were the prominent measures of the Australito, and privatization was again included as one of the components of the state reform package. None the less:

privatizations did not result from an overall government belief in the expediency of transferring productive assets to the private sector, nor did they spring from convictions about the advantages of deregulation that privatization implies. The sales responded to practical case-by-case advantages and to isolated pressure. The absence of an intense ideological argument had one positive and one negative aspect. On the positive side, if ideological discussion had started, it would still be going on and nothing would have been sold. The negative aspect is that, lacking an ideological base, each privatization effort fell under attack by interest groups opposing privatization. (Gónzalez Fraga 1991: 85)

The Alfonsín administration's ad hoc approach toward privatization stemmed from the necessity to respond to the unfolding economic crisis depending upon the circumstances of the moment. Despite repeated pledges for structural reforms, privatization always occupied a secondary role on the government's agenda. It was not perceived as a long-term policy (Domíngues 1988). The main pragmatic motive behind privatization was the reduction of the fiscal deficit with attempts to sell money-losing enterprises. Other arguments were secondary in the government's calculations, like the improvement of economic efficiency, the modernization of the economy through the infusion of private capital in areas where the government could no longer invest, the rationalization of state operations by keeping PEs in strategic sectors while unloading those acquired through bankruptcy procedures. Additional factors like strengthening capital markets and rewarding supporters played no tangible role.

Only in mid-1988 did the government try to implement some policies toward market deregulation. This is the year that the Spring Plan was launched as the last anti-inflationary attempt. However, even then, capital markets were slightly affected. The handful of privatized PEs also did not seem to respond to a clear strategy aimed at rewarding supporters in the business community. Part of the reason for the lack of privatization was the general perception within the Alfonsín administration, at least up until 1987, that more politically appealing alternatives existed to the neo-orthodox formula. This is evident not only in official statements but also in the design of stabilization policies. Starting from Grinspun's gradualist, neo-Keynesian approach, Alfonsín's policies progressively turned to neo-orthodox measures as the crisis deepened in intensity. However, when in 1989 the administration came to grips with the necessity of bold market reforms in order to stop stagflation, Alfonsín had become a lame duck President, lacking the legitimacy to enforce meaningful changes (Torre 1993).

Turning now to opportunity, we note that the conditions conducive to privatization were not ripe in Argentina. First, the availability of tenders was limited. From the beginning, domestic entrepreneurs showed scant interest in privatization. Many domestic conglomerates that had flourished under fat government contracts as suppliers or sub-contractors, saw greater incentives in keeping the government in business rather than buying out its PEs. The few PEs which were eventually sold went to bidders from different economic sectors who saw privatization as a chance to diversify their business (Gónzalez Fraga 1991: 85). Second, given that the government subsidized the prices charged by PEs in public services, prospective buyers initially requested that such charges be raised in order to make operations profitable (Gerchunoff and Visintini 1991: 187). In some cases, private entrepreneurs tried to convince the Alfonsín administration to sell them unprofitable PEs in return for future state contracts or government-subsidized loans. To meet business' demands, the government offered instead to finance up to 80 per cent of a purchase over a six-year period. The total price paid, in the end, was considerably less than the amount originally agreed upon by the two parties, taking into account the high inflation of the late 1980s and the fact that government financing was much cheaper than it could have been otherwise obtained from commercial banks. Third, unless the government was willing to make generous concessions, many private groups saw few incentives for acquiring PEs that were invariably deficit-ridden and whose reorganization was likely to cost additional funds. Fourth, indecision and ineffectiveness on the part of the government in confronting the crisis created an inhospitable environment for privatization. Sharp fluctuations in the exchange rate and high inflation shortened the time span for decisions and made investments extremely risky. Fifth, Alfonsín's intention to create joint ventures with private capital by allowing the state to retain control of 51 per cent of the shares in the most important privatizations attempted, drove away many prospective buyers. Sixth, privatization often became a controversy over national sovereignty issues when the government sought foreign buyers to compensate for the lack of credible domestic bidders. Domestic entrepreneurs, who resented the intrusion of foreign groups, joined the opposition in Congress by charging Alfonsín with the 'selling out' of the country.

The public mood remained set against privatization. Beginning in the mid-1940s with Juan Perón's ascendance to power, Argentines grew accustomed to a state that not only intervened heavily in the economy through business regulations, but also provided cheap social services through PEs and a host of welfare benefits (like medicare, social security, and unemployment compensations). The thrust of these policies remained basically unaltered until 1983. In describing public attitudes toward the state in the 1980s, Edgardo Catterberg, Alfonsín's pollster, noted:

Argentine political culture . . . shows strong signs of statism, reflected in the population's support for protectionist policies on the part of the state, and in the decided backing of state action in areas perceived as close to daily life, such as controlling prices, freezing rents, and providing jobs. That is to say, the positive view of state intervention is maintained by its image as an agency whose function and responsibility is to contribute to the well-being of the population.   (Catterberg 1991: 15–16)

Fifty-eight per cent of the people surveyed in 1986 agreed that, 'the state should provide public services without worrying about losses' (Catterberg 1991: 17). Opinions like this were skillfully exploited by the Peronist opposition and affected the way Alfonsín and his cabinet weighed the feasibility of a privatization program.[3] However, toward the end of the Radical administration, the provision of public services continued to deteriorate. The public mood began to change. It is not by chance that Alfonsín's most ambitious plans for privatization were attempted in 1988, when opinion surveys registered an approval rating of 75 per cent for that policy (Mora y Araujo 1993: 313). Still, the Radicals had no working majority in Congress after an embarrassing electoral defeat in the mid-term congressional elections of September 1987, thus, Alfonsín was unable to capitalize on the swing in public mood.

Foreign pressure on Alfonsín to push market reforms came primarily from the IMF and commercial banks. Initially, the President took a tough stand in the negotiations with both the IMF and its private lenders, to increase his popular support at home and to gain more concessions from lending institutions. However, the severity of the crisis in early 1985 left the President with little room for maneuvering, as foreign creditors were no longer willing to give additional loans to Argentina unless an agreement with the IMF was reached. Yet, Alfonsín made the best of a poor situation. With Brazil and Peru threatening a debt moratorium at the time, the IMF needed a large South American country to point to as a 'role model' for the region. Moreover, the Alfonsín administration pleaded to the Reagan administration to help the young Argentine democracy by interceding on its behalf with the IMF. In fact, both the Reagan administration and the US Federal Reserve Bank strongly lobbied the IMF about the desirability of adopting a conciliatory behavior toward Argentina. As a result, the IMF grudgingly accepted the price and wage control features of the Austral Plan. Hence, Alfonsín's team was allowed greater control over its own destiny than the IMF had permitted to previous Argentine administrations or to contemporary Latin American governments, save Mexico (Stiles 1987). This also became evident with with the Australito too. Although by July 1987 Argentina was out of compliance with many of the requirements spelled out in the letter of intent agreed upon with the IMF in 1985, Alfonsín secured additional financing and some changes in macroeconomic targets from the Washington-based lending institution. In 1988, when the IMF refused to support the Spring Plan, Alfonsín turned to the World Bank and obtained the necessary funds. It is worth noting that on each agreement signed with both the IMF and the World Bank, Argentina was required to promote specific market reforms, including privatization, and on each occasion it fell short. The Alfonsín administration's ability to bargain hard with its creditors until 1988 allowed it to gain enough financial assistance to buy time. Ironically, this was also instrumental in postponing a tough economic adjustment program as desired by international lenders.

The implementation of Alfonsín's privatization policy was equally plagued by problems that impaired its execution. In terms of government capabilities, it was clear from the beginning that there was little government cohesiveness over the privatization issue. Grinspun and the old guard of the Radicals opposed state divestiture. Sourrouille and his economic team favored it but their intentions often found the veto of cabinet ministers more preoccupied with keeping electoral clienteles within entrepreneurial and labor lobbies (Torre 1993). A typical example of this internecine conflict was the 1987 squabbles between Sourrouille and Minister of Labor Carlos Alderete (a union leader) over the general thrust of economic policy. Although Sourrouille eventually prevailed, he had to water down many of his policies, including privatization in order to appease his critics within the cabinet. To complicate matters, Alfonsín's reluctance over market reforms intensified the struggle among rival factions within the administration. Such struggles mirrored the lack of cooperation among different ministries.

In December 1983, the executive created a special commission comprised of representatives from several ministries and state banks in charge of laying out plans for the transfer of formerly privately-owned enterprises. The lack of tangible results led to the creation of the Ministry of Growth Promotion in July 1984. Consistent with the privatization philosophy dominant at the time (which was examined above) its mandate was to look for private investments in areas that had traditionally been the exclusive monopoly of the state. However, by January 1986, the ministry lacked strong support from the executive and quickly fell prey to its critics. It was therefore unable to carry out any privatization. At the end of that year, this situation led to the creation of yet another agency in charge of government reform, the Directorio de Empresas Públicas (DEP) which was dependent upon the Ministry of Public Works and Services. The DEP's official mandate was to suggest improvements in the economic efficiency of PEs and whether or not they should eventually be sold. The administration strategy at that time was still to promote growth through the inclusion of private capital in the provision of public services, preferably via joint ventures. The Ministry of Growth Promotion was disbanded by 1987, but multiple jurisdictions continued to be a source of squabbles between the DEP, the Ministry of the Economy, and the Ministry of Public Works and Services. In 1988, the power struggle finally ended with the latter assuming leadership (Terragno 1992). It is not by chance that the greatest effort toward privatization was made during this year. The privatizations that Minister of Public Works and Services Adolfo Terragno attempted in 1988 took place with little coordination with the Ministry of the Economy nonetheless (Domíngues 1988: 57).

Despite the few privatizations carried out during the military regime, government agencies had little experience in selling PEs. The Banco Nacional de Desarrollo, the state development bank, which had acquired many bankrupt companies in the 1960s and 1970s, was the only agency with some expertise on the issue. Many were the technical flaws that emerged during Alfonsín's term, spanning from the methods used to the legal frameworks in the organization of the sale. These problems were generally ascribed to the lack of experience. In order to solve them, the government hired domestic and foreign consulting firms. In the case of major sales, like the airline Austral, the International Bank for Reconstruction and Development supervised the transfer.

State institutions played a key role in preventing privatization from taking off under Alfonsín. Although the Argentine executive had historically been more powerful than either Congress or the Supreme Court, the sale of PEs required congressional approval.[4] Alfonsín was in trouble from the start with the opposition controlling the Senate since 1983 and, after 1987, the Chamber of Deputies as well. When the President finally decided to go ahead with the sale of Aerolíneas Argentinas and ENTel in 1988 (respectively the country's flag carrier and telephone monopoly) he faced a hostile Congress. The Peronist congressmen decided to deal another political blow to the President by blocking both privatizations, despite that in the administration's proposal the state was going to retain majority ownership of both companies.

Alfonsín's indecisiveness, poor cohesiveness within his cabinet, an appreciable opposition against privatization within the UCR, the lack of mechanisms to assure bureaucratic cooperation among departments and government agencies, made it virtually impossible to mount a coherent, well-planned privatization program during the Radical administration (Torre 1993). Valuable time was wasted in the process. Enough government consensus to privatize did not come until 1988, at the end of Alfonsín's term, when the President was too weak politically to push major legislation through Congress.

Some of the political responses have already been mentioned in the previous paragraphs. Unions displayed the strongest opposition to privatization. The locals of those companies slated for privatization, with the support of the national umbrella organization, the Peronist-dominated General Confederation of Labor (Confederación General de Trabajo, CGT), mounted an effective campaign to sabotage the policy arguing that the transfer of PEs to private owners went against the 'national interest'. Even in those few cases in which privatization materialized, like the case of the Siam conglomerate, unions won important concessions in terms of employment guarantees, production, and workers' benefits (Gónzalez Fraga 1991: 84). The managerial staffs of PEs, unwilling to let the private sector enter markets traditionally dominated by the public sector and afraid of the losing their jobs, joined forces with labor to attack the government's initiative (Machinea 1993). Fearing the end of lucrative contracts, private suppliers of PEs lobbied strongly to forestall privatization. Describing this behavior, the economist Guido di Tella, a Peronist deputy in 1987 and later head of the Ministry of Foreign Affairs under the Menem administration, stated in 1988, 'the most lucrative companies in the Argentine economy are those that sell to the state. For them it is fundamental that the state remains in "business"' (CLADE 1988: 31). The military had a particularly rocky relationship with the Alfonsín administration, which tried to prosecute human rights violations perpetrated by the armed forces during the 1970s. Privatization just added a further strain in government-military relations. Since the 1920s the military had developed several industries in areas considered vital to national security and beyond. In 1941 the various companies run by the three armed services were grouped into the General Directorate of Military Factories (Dirección Nacional de Fabricaciones Militares, DGFM), a vast industrial conglomerate. Growing in breadth and scope after World War II, DGFM companies became notorious for their inefficiency, making them potentially prime targets for privatization.

To appease his critics, early on Alfonsín's privatizations were limited only to companies that had been acquired through bankruptcy procedures and did not impinge on the state role in economic development of 'strategic' economic sectors. Even when, in 1988, the administration tried to sell its airline and telephone companies, which were traditional symbols of the country's economic independence, it did so in a manner that would not rouse nationalist sentiments. For instance, in the case of Aerolíneas Argentinas the government offered its potential partner, Scandinavian Airlines System, to manage the company and 40 per cent of its shares. The state would retain control of the company, keeping 51 per cent of the voting shares, while the employees would be given the remaining 9 per cent. Moreover, a provision was included that required a 70 per cent majority of the company's board of directors in order to approve the most important decisions. In the case of ENTel, the private partner, Telefónica de España, agreed in principle to similar terms.

These limits to private ownership notwithstanding, the opposition in Congress thought they did not go far enough. The party whip of the Peronists in the Senate, Eduardo Menem, led the charge against privatization arguing that, 'the administration is making a deal which goes against the national interest and, worst of all, is compromising the country's sovereignty and national security'.[5] To make things worse, an Argentine-led consortium made an alternative offer for the privatization of Aerolíneas Argentinas in July 1988, which was used by the government opposition to postpone a final decision.[6] As a result, the employees of the PEs and domestic entrepreneurs joined forces with the anti-privatization lobby in Congress and succeeded in frustrating the effort.

The Alfonsín administration was rather ineffective in creating a pro-privatization coalition, despite the fact that by 1988 consensus on privatization was growing. The most outspoken supporters of market reforms were the conservative think-tank Fundación de Investigaciones Económicas Latinoamericanas (FIEL 1987) and right-wing political parties like the Union for the Democratic Center (Unión del Centro Democrático, UCEDE; Gibson 1996). However, the profound political divisions separating the Radicals from the conservative economic and political groups in Argentine society made it difficult for Alfonsín to forge a new alliance with the latter. Concerned with preserving his administration's independence, the President thought that such an allaince could alienate many of his center-left supporters (Torre 1993). Alfonsín was also unsuccessful in mounting an effective pro-privatization media campaign. Such a policy remained a secondary issue on the administration's priority list and Public Works Minister Terragno often behaved as if he were acting in a political vacuum.

Technical difficulties were also instrumental in undermining the whole policy. Alfonsín's team tried to sell PEs operating in monopolistic markets without first deregulating the economy, which is a precondition for effective gains in economic efficiency to ensue from privatization. This fact exposed the government to a lot of criticisms.[7] The lack of a comprehensive legal framework to carry out the policy was also detrimental. The executive sent a legislative proposal to Congress in early 1987 but it soon died there. The methods adopted to privatize also turned into a political issue. The inadequacy of the Argentine capital markets posed several problems, preventing the sale of PEs through the Buenos Aires stock exchange and thus narrowing Alfonsín's options. The Radical administration ultimately opted to sell PEs either through a public auction, as in the case of Austral, or through direct negotiations with prospective buyers, as in the case of Aerolíneas Argentinas and ENTel. The latter means became a source of controversy. The Peronists in Congress believed that a public auction was the best way to proceed whereas selling to a pre-established private partner raised the issue of possible collusion between government officials and potential buyers (Blanco 1993: 19). The valuation of assets added to tensions. Private business argued that the price demanded by the government for its PEs, based on the company's book value, was grossly inflated. To soften business opposition, the treasury offered generous financing conditions and, in the case of Aerolíneas Argentinas and ENTel, the elimination of most of those companies' financial liabilities prior to the transfer of assets. This, once again raised the opposition of the anti-privatization lobby, which accused the government of subsidizing the sale.

All things considered, privatization under the Radical administration had negligible results. When Alfonsín assumed power in December 1983, the state owned 305 PEs.[8] When he left office five-and-a-half years later, only four companies had been privatized (Table 2.3) for a total of less than $32 million (Gónzalez Fraga 1991: 80). The PEs that were sold were all formerly private companies. Thus, it seems more appropriate to speak of reprivatization rather than privatization. Moreover, such companies had been slated for sale under the military regime. The Radical administration's new initiatives, like the partial sale of Aerolíneas Argentinas and ENTel were to symbolize the beginning of the state-shrinking process, instead they failed miserably.

TABLE 2.3. *Argentine PEs Privatized During 1983–8*

Company	Date	Buyer	Price US$ Thousands
Siam Servicios Asistensiales	Dec. 1985	Sedimed	275
Division Siat	Feb. 1986	Comatter	12,360
Electromecanica	Aug. 1986	Sade	2,866
Electrodomestica	Dec. 1986	Aurora	1,642
Lagos del Sur (Sol Jet)	Apr. 1986	Centrex	715
Opalinas Hurlingham	Jun. 1986	Industria del Vid. Plano	1,077
Austral Lineas Aereas S.A.	Dec. 1987	Cielos del Sur	12,800
TOTAL			31,735

Source: Gonzalez Fraga (1991: 80).

Brazil (1985–1989)

Similar to Argentina, the role of the Brazilian state in the economy increased substantially after the Great Depression through business regulations and public sector investments in manufacturing and services. The idea that the state should ascribe itself to the role of guiding the country's socioeconomic development and deciding upon the allocation of economic resources gained progressively acceptance among Brazilian political, business, and military elites (Wirth 1970; Sikkink 1990). Government-sponsored ISI gained momentum in the 1950s and continued under the military regime (1964–85) with the promotion of inward-looking development policies aimed at self-sufficiency. Most PEs were created at this time (Schneider 1990: 322). Between 1967 and 1978 the military administrations made large investments to create new domestic industries (i.e. computer) while spending heavily on infrastructure, heavy industry, and consumer goods (*The Economist* 1987). Some data illustrates the point; between 1965 and 1979 government investments (out of total investments) rose from 38.1 per cent to 43.7 per cent of GDP (Reichstul and Coutinho 1983). PEs' production, in GDP terms, increased from 16.2 per cent in 1970 to 18.3 per cent in 1980 (Longo 1982). Within the same period PEs' investments, in terms of gross fixed capital formation, climbed from 20.3 per cent to 22.7 per cent (Reichstul and Coutinho 1983: 45). However, it had become clear that only a small number of PEs were responsible for the state sector's economic performance. In the 1980s, the six largest PEs accounted for 81 per cent of all government sales, 69 per cent of outlays, 80 per cent of investments, and the bulk of PEs' debt (Schneider 1988–9: 96).

The consensus over the primacy of the state sector in promoting economic development began slowly to break apart as a result of the oil crisis of 1973. After averaging a spectacular yearly growth of 10 per cent (GDP) during the

1969–73 period, the Brazilian economy, heavily dependent on oil imports, slowed down. The growth of GDP from 1974–9 averaged only 4 per cent a year. This coincided with an increase of PEs' losses as the fiscal resources of the government for new investments became progressively scarce. Several business sectors began to ascribe the roots of the country's poorer perform-ance in the second part of the 1970s to the inefficiency of the entrepreneurial state and more specifically to PEs. The last military President, General João Figueiredo (1979–85), addressed some of these concerns in July 1979, when he announced the establishment of a National Program for Public Sector Rationalization (Decree 83740). A new decree (86215) that same month estab-lished the rules for the sale of some PEs to the private sector. To manage the sale of assets the government set up a commission comprised of re-presentatives from the ministries of finance, planning, and public sector. Interestingly, one of the rules imposed by the military, which would continue to characterize the Brazilian privatization process later on, banned foreign investors from acquiring PEs. However, the debate over privatization, or *destat-ização* as it came to be known in Brazil, was overshadowed in the early 1980s by the intense political events that led to the demise of the military regime. The number of PEs had declined from 530 to 420 by 1985, but the change was superficial. Only seventeen PEs were actually sold, the rest were either dissolved, absorbed by government agencies, reclassified, or transferred to states and municipalities (Schneider 1988–89: 97). Revenues from these sales amounted to approximately $190 million, a figure that constituted only 0.6 per cent of the total assets of PEs (Mendes 1987). In conclusion, privat-ization under Figueiredo was a token policy and consequently produced very modest results.

The Brazilian military withdrew to the barracks in 1985, allowing an ad hoc electoral college to elect the first civilian President since 1964. Tancredo Neves, the leader of the largest opposition party in Congress, the Partido do Movimiento Democrático Brasileiro (PMDB), emerged as the winner. His running-mate was José Sarney, a former senator of the pro-military Partido Democrático Social (PDS), who had defected from his party only a few months prior to the elections. However, Neves died suddenly before taking office thus leaving to an ill-prepared Sarney the task of leading Brazil through the difficult political transition.[9]

The exceptional circumstances that led him to the presidency plagued Sarney throughout his term in office. Brazilians expected Neves, who had enjoyed large popular and congressional support, to be the President. When Sarney took office, many questioned the legitimacy of his mandate as well as his democratic credentials.[10] How could a long-time ally of the military build the foundations of the new Brazilian democracy? Sarney inherited a cabinet that had been largely selected by Neves and whose policy priorities did not exactly match his own. Moreover, Sarney lacked a majority in

Congress and the length of his term in office remained unclear. Neves had promised to be in office for four years but Sarney wanted to stay in power for five, like his military predecessors. Sarney was also caught in a situation in which he was expected to live up to the popular expectations raised by Neves's campaign promises targeting social and economic reforms for the reduction of income inequalities. The transition from authoritarian to democratic rule, as in the case of Argentina, set into motion a series of previously repressed redistributive claims on the government from parties, business organizations, labor unions, and grass roots movements. Similar to the case of Alfonsín's, for Sarney, 'it became difficult to separate the objectives of redemocratization from substantive policies aimed at a rapid improvement of depressed living standards' (Kaufman 1990: 74). Such demands, however, were hard to reconcile with the need to address economic problems like triple digit inflation, high unemployment, and the world's largest external debt. Given his lack of legitimacy, Sarney struggled for political survival throughout his term (Haggard and Kaufman 1995). His efforts concentrated on the manipulation of macroeconomic policy to appease as many constituencies as possible in return for political support. The easiest way to do so, while honoring Neves' pledges, was to promote economic growth. According to Roett:

The [Sarney] administration, desperate to build support for a five-year term office for the President, and highly susceptible to appeals for public funds from state and local officials in the North and Northeast (President Sarney's home state, Maranhão, greatly benefitted from his presidency), would hear nothing of fiscal restraint. Contracts were awarded for unneeded construction projects; new public sector positions were authorized when there was a surplus of workers in government; and little interest was manifested for privatization. (1992: 124)

Negotiations with the IMF to reschedule part of Brazil's external debt, had been initiated under the Figueiredo administration. Their collapse in 1985 allowed Sarney to postpone a politically unpopular fiscal adjustment policy as the economic austerity of the last years of the military regime had borne no tangible results. Challenging the IMF and foreign creditor banks was a calculated maneuver to garner support for a weak President by striking the cord of nationalism. Sarney repeatedly stated that Brazil would not give in to foreign pressure and would not pay the debt with the 'hunger of the people' (*The Economist* 1987). Initially, the administration was split between those who supported austerity policies and an agreement with the IMF (Finance Minister Francisco Dornelles, a Neves appointee) and those who argued in favor of a growth-oriented approach (Planning Minister João Sayad). Finally, in August 1985, Sarney broke the impasse by appointing a new economic team headed by Finance Minister Dilson Funaro, a development-minded economist and an outspoken critic of the IMF. This unequivocally signaled the administration's intent to favor growth over austerity concerns.

Taking this scenario into account, it is not surprising that ideological factors played no meaningful role in Sarney's willingness to privatize. The President from the beginning supported *dirigismo*. Sarney was an influential politician from the state of Maranhão in economically depressed northern Brazil. Like many others from this region, he had built his power base through clientelistic networks based upon pork-barrel politics. These schemes were often financed by development projects to boost the economically depressed North during the military regime. A clear example of this activity was Sarney's effort, with the support of the military, to build a new railway line linking the south to the north eventually ending in his home state of Maranhão. The project, a multi-billion dollar investment, was widely regarded as a waste of public money at a time of financial restraints. Marred by irregularities in the bidding process, the railway was pure pork that the President used to reward his supporters. Additionally, the railway was meant to boost Sarney's reputation as a 'developmentalist', in the tradition of Juscelino Kubitscheck, the popular Brazilian President who embodied the ideals of *dirigismo* in the 1950s. A further example that the administration still favored the central role of the state in economic development became apparent in the Plano de Meta, an ambitious plan unveiled in 1986 that set the government investment priorities (Kaufman 1990: 76). Thus, state-shrinking and neo-orthodox economic principles were alien to Sarney and the interests he represented, as was popular capitalism. Sarney, despite his often rocky relations with labor, did not seem to perceive privatization as a tool to emasculate it. Rather, he used carrot-and-stick tactics to overcome union opposition. Sarney did not believe in privatization as a vehicle for the promotion of economic reform and on rave occasions when he did pledge to act upon it as such, he did so reluctantly.[11]

Much as in Argentina, pragmatic factors were the main reasons behind the few privatizations that occurred during Sarney's term. 'Sarney had no ideological commitment to privatization, but appeared willing to endorse it when officials could convince him that the financial crisis of the state was more pressing than his political agenda' (Schneider 1990: 327). Actually, Sarney's political agenda was usually paramount in his calculations and privatization was endorsed in an ad hoc manner, whenever such a policy fit the circumstances of the moment. In fact, despite the President's repeated commitment to state divestiture, very little was accomplished until 1988 (Baer 1993).

Sarney's economic teams first headed by Dilson Funaro (August 1985 –March 1987) and later by Luis Carlos Bresser Pereira (March–December 1987) held a center-left political orientation and perceived privatization, at best, as a policy with limited scope. Their belief was that it should not jeopardize the role of the state in economic development. Privatization until 1987 was perceived in both the executive and legislative branches, as a means to alleviate the government's fiscal crisis without abandoning growth and development goals. This perspective was consistent to that of Argentina's. The main proponent of this thesis was Ignácio Rangel, a well-respected leftist, nationalist economist and a former executive of Brazil's development bank, the Banco Nacional de Desenvolvimiento Econômico e Social (BNDES). The fiscal crisis prevented the government to further invest in enterprises like public utilities. Investments in public utilities were badly needed, and only the private sector had the necessary liquidity. Rangel, in turn, welcomed the transfer of PEs in that sector to private owners. The government by doing so could accomplish a double objective: (1) it would free itself from unprofit-able enterprises while allowing those sectors renewed growth through the infu-sion of private capital; and (2) it would divert scarce resources to strategic economic areas thus remaining under state monopoly, i.e. oil (Rangel 1987). These statements were echoed by Paulo Galleta, the executive secretary of the Interministerial Privatization Council, who stated, 'privatization is one of the only instruments of promoting growth' (Schneider 1988: 100).

The Cruzado Plan was a heterodox stabilization plan launched by Funaro's team in February 1986 for the purpose to stemming an inflationary spiral that was quickly getting out of control. The new economic policy reasserted the concept of 'stabilization with growth'. Similar to the Austral Plan in Argentina, the Cruzado's main features included price freeze (but not on government spending), the ending of price and contract indexation, and the creation of the a new currency unit, the cruzado. However, the Austral Plan at least in theory, aimed to pave the way for some structural reforms to follow. The Cruzado did not. In fact, the Cruzado Plan placed high priority on short-term distributive and expansionist goals. The inclusion of real wage increases and the maintenance of prices at relatively low levels had the purpose of enhancing the purchasing power of salaried workers. All of these measures were designed with an eye on the November congressional elec-tions.[12] These elections were crucial to Sarney as they would elect the Congress that would draft the new constitution and decide on whether the President would be in charge for four or five years. Although the Cruzado's success was short-lived, (compared to the Austral) it was crucial in boosting Sarney's popularity from a negative approval rating (36 per cent in January 1986) to a positive 68 per cent approval in March (The Economist 1987: 9).

Pro-government candidates won by a landslide as was anticipated by the administration.[13] Unfortunately for the President, it proved to be a Pyrrhic victory. Inflationary pressures regained momentum by November. This im-petus forced the administration to hurry a new emergency package, the Cruzado II. Its failure led to internal conflicts within the economic team and, ultimately, to Funaro's resignation in March 1987. Privatization fared no better under his replacement, Bresser Pereira. The new Finance Minister's top priority remained inflation. Privatization was once again placed on the back burner. Sarney, facing plummeting approval rating, became progressively ineffectual and politically weak. Much of the President's effort was concentrated in 'buying' congressional support in order to earn a one-year extension on his mandate. His strategy was the allocation of new discretionary funds targeting sympathetic legislators. Unable to control the budget deficit, Bresser Pereira quit in December of 1987.

Maílson Pereira de Nobréga was Bresser Pereira's successor. He was a more conservative economist and thus it comes as no suprise that privatization gained some momentum. His appointment marked a move away from the traditional growth-centric developmentalist strategy (Kaufman 1990: 87). The failure of the growth model prompted Sarney to rely on a more conventional approach against inflation based upon tighter monetary policy. The change in philosophy of the economic team also altered, to some degree, some of the motives behind privatization. Consistent with the case of Argentina, the fiscal crisis turned from bad to worse. Privatization became less of an alternative means to promote growth and more of a source for restructuring the public sector and slashing its debt.[14] Additional factors were ofted cited, including, gains from economic efficiency, the contribution of private investments to the modernization of obsolete PEs, and streamlining the state, but these arguments usually played a secondary role. Other factors like the improvement of capital markets and the business climate were noticeably absent. The small amount of privatization that took place did not seem to reward political allies of the President. Sarney publicly promised to sell a company a month in June 1988. Given the President's track record on the issue, nobody seemed to take him seriously.[15] The Brazilian privatization program, like that of Argentina, remained in limbo until the end of the administration's term. The reason being that for most of his term Sarney and his advisors believed that market reforms were politically unwise and economically detrimental to the role of the state. It took over three years of trial and error for Sarney to realize that the economic crisis could not be solved even with unconventional heterodox measures. By that time it was too late. As was the case in Alfonsín's Argentina, the Sarney administration had no government experience and failed to realize the magnitude and severity of the crisis at hand.

Starting on an expansionary swing in 1985, Sarney's economic policies turned progressively to mild economic orthodoxy by end of his term. By 1989, his last year in office, Sarney's prestige and legitimacy reached an all-time low, making it impossible for him to make any sweeping reform.

Conditions to privatize in the second-half of the 1980s in Brazil were feeble in terms of opportunity. First, the Interministerial Privatization Council created in November 1985 enforced the restrictions barring foreign tenders from participating in the privatization process engineered under the military regime. The only difference was that of allowing foreign groups to acquire former PEs at a later date (Decree 91991). Although such restrictions were justified on the grounds of 'economic nationalism', they substantially reduced the number of prospective buyers as foreign groups could count on greater financial resources than their Brazilian competitors. This flaw became apparent when the government was forced to disqualify bidders from public auctions because they did not meet the minimum requirements established by the Intraministerial Privatization Council. The government, as a result, was often left with few competitive bids and, frequently, with bids far short the minimum floor, which forced the cancellation of several auctions. Second, most of the PEs slated for privatization belonged to the BNDES, which had taken them over through bankruptcy procedures.[16] BNDES restructured several of these PEs by the time they were privatized in order to facilitate the sale. However, others continued to lose money and attracted little or no interest from the private sector. This occured despite the fact that BNDES, as was the case in Argentina, provided very generous financing to private investors.[17] The most successful transfers involved highly profitable companies like Aracruz Celulose. Third, Sarney's lack of commitment to privatization and to economic austerity in general strained the administration's relations with sectors of the business community, thus creating an extremely unstable investment climate. Fourth, the fact that the state often retained voting shares or some management functions discouraged some potential buyers interested in taking total control of a PE.[18]

The public mood was generally indifferent or anti-privatization. The general public, from the outset seemed to be rather ill informed or not informed at all regarding the likely impact of privatization. As was the case in Argentina, Brazilians had consistently benefitted from cheap public services since the establishment of the first welfare policies in the 1940s. Most of the PEs slated for privatization were in the manufacturing sector. However, the anti-privatization lobby made up of unions, left-wing and populist parties, and some entrepreneurial groups, effectively mounted a campaign depicting privatization as an attack upon the national interest and on 'social justice'. The tremendous popularity of the price freeze under the Cruzado Plan was used as a example that the people wanted more rather than less government control in the provision of public goods.

Foreign pressure, which played a considerable role in forcing Alfonsín to push for greater monetary and fiscal austerity, was much less a factor in the Brazilian case. Unlike Argentina, whose reserve by early 1985 had fallen dangerously low, Brazil was able to generate, between 1985 and 1986, trade surpluses of $12 billion and $9.5 billion respectively. This was more than enough to serve the interest on the country's foreign debt. Thus, Sarney was also able to avoid going to the IMF for financial assistance, which would have implied economic austerity measures unacceptable for Funaro and his team.

Relations between Brazil and its foreign creditors reached their lowest point in February 1987 when Funaro decided to declare a moratorium on Brazil's medium- and long-term commercial debt payments. Talks with the IMF and Brazil's creditor banks did not resume until 1988. The administration began to lift some protectionist trade barriers and to ease business regulations in May, a move which led to new loans from foreign banks and the IMF at mid-year. None the less, Brazil retained a considerable bargaining power with foreign creditors. The country's advantage was its ability to generate substantial trade surpluses that could sustain a debt moratorium for a short term (in the event that negotiations would collapse again). Fearing that Brazil's position could trigger a similar response by other debtor nations, international bankers were less adamant in their request for market reforms as long as the Sarney administration resumed debt payments and made some strides toward economic liberalization.

The lack of willingness and opportunity to privatize negatively affected the policy implementation process. There was little government cohesiveness about the need to privatize, as was mentioned before. Funaro and Bresser Pereira failed to include privatization as an integral part of their stabilization plans and, on ideological grounds, were opposed to a full scale state divestiture policy. Privatization was thus treated as an ad hoc policy, entrusted to special committees with limited decision-making powers. The Interministerial Privatization Council was created in 1985. It comprised representatives of several ministries and was reorganized in 1986 and again in 1988. This was done to solve the problems caused by multiple jurisdictions that were claimed by different ministries slowing down the privatization process in the first three years of the Sarney administration. Although on each occasion the council's executive powers were strengthened, its decisions remained heavily dependent upon the executive branch, the finance ministry, and Congress. The real force behind privatization was BNDES, which owned the majority of the PEs up for sale. BNDES, under the council's supervision, hired auditing and consulting firms to assess the financial and legal issues at stake and coordinated the role of the different ministries involved in the transfer of public assets in order to assure transparency. Unlike the Banco Nacional de Desarrollo in Argentina, BNDES had already acquired considerable expertise in privatization during the military regime, which allowed it to expedite activities once the decision to privatize had been reached. This, in turn, served as partial of compensation for the slow action on the part of the politicians and bureaucrats.

In the case of Brazil, state institutions became an obstacle to any substantial reform effort, including privatization. The executive branch retained many of the strong prerogatives over policy-making of the military regime (the authoritarian constitution of 1967 remained in place until 1988). Even so, Sarney lacked a clear mandate. As a minority President, he faced a Congress comprised of many parties, which required a constant effort at coalition-building. Adding to the challenge, party allegiances remained volatile as congressmen's voting patterns were often dictated by pork-barrel considerations rather than the pursuit of the public good. Many ministers and congressmen had customarily regarded PEs as a source of jobs and capital for rewarding their clienteles. It comes as little surprise, then, that even cabinet members and pro-administration legislators openly opposed privatization as it tended to undermine their political fiefs.

Following the collapse of the Cruzado II at the end of 1986, the situation further deteriorated as the President no longer had the capacity to control the political agenda. He thus became progressively weak vis-à-vis Congress, which forced him to rely on the military and on political patronage. Through these channels, Sarney enlisted the support of individual legislators and governors for the sole purpose of political survival. Sarney, under these circumstances, increased his use of executive orders to enact his legislative proposals (Power 1994). Privatization gained momentum after Congress finally agreed to extend Sarney's term for one year in mid-1988. Yet, this success was short-lived. The Constituent Assembly passed a new constitution in November that not only strengthened the autonomy of Congress and the states, but also explicitly prevented the privatization of some state monopolies in the petroleum and telecommunication sectors. Sarney entered his last year in office in 1989. By this time, he had become a lame-duck President incapable of pushing any meaningful reform policy (Rosenn 1990).

The most effective political responses to privatization were usually negative. Predictably, the labor movement tried to derail the policy. The two major labor umbrella organizations, the Central Unica de Trabalhadores (CUT) and the Central General dos Trabalhadores (CGT), opposed privatization fearing the loss of jobs and benefits. This fear became particularly acute in 1988 as triple digit inflation, coupled with economic recession, worsened wages' purchasing power and increased unemployment. The left-wing CUT, the most militant of the two, also added ideological motives to these bread-and-butter issues. The government tried to win the workers' compliance on occasion by offering them 5 per cent of a company's shares as was the case with the SIBRA and Aracruz companies. Generally speaking, such a strategy elicited little enthusiasm. Unions were often joined in their opposition by the managerial staffs of the companies to be transferred as was the case in Argentina. Many PE managers had been previously appointed according to 'political' criteria with reason to fear that their jobs would be terminated under private ownership. Despite government statements to the contrary, individuals and financial institutions that owned public bonds were also skeptical about privatization. They feared that, 'the inducement to convert public debt into equity in public enterprises might eventually provide the legal basis for a compulsory swap' (Werneck 1991: 70).

The private sector's response, despite much rhetoric favoring market economics was quite ambivalent in practice (Payne 1994). PE suppliers were fearful of loosing business and, as to be expected, opposed privatization. This was also the case of other countries. A larger numbers of firms followed suit on different grounds. Over the years, both military and civilian governments had kept PEs's prices below cost as they related to the provision of goods and services. The reasoning behind this approach spanned from promoting better income distribution and keeping inflation under control, to favoring specific political clienteles within the business sector. Regardless, the net result was that in so doing PEs heavily subsidized the private sector, thus creating powerful vested interests with much to loose from privatization (World Bank 1989). Private groups were, on several occasions, successful in stopping the privatization of PEs that provided such subsidies (Schneider 1988–9: 111). State governors also turned out to be a stumbling block with considerable importance. For instance, the governor of Bahia, along with the congressional delegation from that state, convinced the executive to cancel the privatization of the Caraíba copper mines located in his state despite the disastrous financial performance of that company (Werneck 1991: 71).

The Sarney administration, for the most part, made no tangible effort to create a pro-privatization support group in defiance of its critics. The responsibility for sustaining the privatization effort was left to the bureaucrats of the Interministerial Privatization Council and the management of BNDES. The latter wanted to unload many unprofitable enterprises acquired in previous decades. These industries had no association with the development of strategic economic sectors, which was BNDES's original task. BNDES's policies over the years had lost focus as a result of forced acquisitions. Its resources for investments had shrunk considerably as a result of the required financing of too many unprofitable companies. The PEs' deficit, which had averaged 5.4 per cent of GDP during the 1980–1985 period, soared to an all-time high of 23.1 per cent by 1988.[19] For many BNDES managers, privatization was an instrument for shedding unnecessary firms and free capital for strategically important investments (Schneider 1990: 327). Despite their commitment, however, neither the federal bureaucrats of the Interministerial Privatization Council nor the BNDES management could count on Sarney's support. This was a serious drawback that led to the resignation to several key officials.[20]

Many technical difficulties that were discussed in the Argentine case also became apparent in Brazil. Though the Brazilian capital markets were larger and more sophisticated than those of Argentina, high inflation and strong barriers to financial services considerably reduced the size and cost-efficiency of capital markets (Welch 1993: 8). Additional factors including multiple jurisdictions, difficulties in the valuation of assets, the absence of a legal framework for privatization, and no market deregulation prior to the transfer of public assets to private ownership, created substantial technical problems. Last but not least, the Interministerial Privatization Council had a small staff relative to the quantity of work it was responsible for accomplishing.

The Sarney administration sold twenty-one PEs of the original sixty-seven slated for privatization for approximately $550 million (Castelar Pinheiro and Oliveira 1991; Mello 1992; Prado 1993). The majority of these companies were transferred between 1988 and 1989. Contrary to official statements, sales apparently did not follow criteria aimed at enhancing competition and economic efficiency. For instance, Eletrosiderúrgica Brasileira merged with its private competitor, which increased the latter's control over the manganese alloys market to 85 per cent (Werneck 1991: 67). The real objective was cutting BNDES's financial losses. Yet, the impact of these sales on the budget deficit was meaningless because while, on the one hand, BNDES tried to sell PEs, on the other, the government was still investing in existing ones or even creating others (Schneider 1990: 328). Worth noting is the fact that, consistent with the Argentine case, such transfers were actually reprivatizations of firms that BNDES had acquired from previous private owners and many of them had appeared in the privatization plan of the Figueiredo administration. Moreover, the PEs actually sold were medium- or small-size enterprises. When Sarney disclosed his emergency economic bill that included the privatization of seventeen PEs in August 1989, Congress blocked the sale as several slated for privatization included those symbolized the heyday of dirigismo, like USIMINAS (steel).[21]

Peru (1980–1990)

Peru was the last of the three countries examined to embark on full scale ISI. This came about during the first administration of Fernando Belaunde Terry (1963–8), the leader of the centrist, reform-minded party Acción Popular (AP). The conservative elites that dominated Peruvian politics until the early 1960s had assigned the state few fundamental tasks and kept its intervention in the economy to a minimum. Economic policies followed a fairly orthodox laissez faire model which ascribed to the private sector, centered around the exploitation of natural resources, the task of promoting growth and employment (FitzGerald 1979). Within this context, foreign companies occupied a dominant position in the two most important sectors, mining and petroleum. However, starting in 1962 private investments began to decline (Burneo 1993). To offset this trend the Belaunde administration decided to finance new industrial sectors and public infrastructures through lax monetary and fiscal policy. In so doing, Belaunde hoped to address popular demands for a more equitable income distribution and better social services (Belaunde Terry 1994). Unfortunately, the Peruvian ISI strategy was plagued by faulty planning and a limited tax base. Public spending quickly outstripped the administration's economic means forcing Peru to seek foreign credit in order to fill the financial breach, causing a steady increase in government indebtness. This debt had become among the highest in South America by the late 1960s (Devlin 1985). Moreover, many of the initial reform projects were either abandoned or substantially weakened as a result of the stiff opposition from conservative parties that controlled Congress. The end result was increased political polarization, widespread disillusion in the face of unfulfilled promises, and macroeconomic inefficiency, giving the military a perfect excuse to stage a coup in 1968 (Kuczynsky 1977; Cotler 1978).

The military regime that followed, unlike its Argentine and Brazilian counterparts, took a decisively left-wing, populist approach. General Juan Velasco Alvarado, its first President, reasoned that Belaunde had failed because his reforms stopped short. Having muted all political opposition, Velasco implemented a radical land reform, accelerated and expanded existing ISI projects, and further pushed the redistribution of income through new social programs (Thorp 1977). Velasco made an explicit, though contradictory, effort to alter the pattern of capital accumulation by assigning to the state the shaping of economic development while relegating private capital to a secondary role.[22] This trend can be seen in few economic data. Private investments 1960 were seven times greater than public investments. By 1974, public investments for the first time surpassed private ones, although only momentarily (Burneo 1993).

Velasco's goal was to destroy the political and economic power of Peru's conservative elites (Sheahan 1987). Accordingly, the military regime tightly regulated private investments and financial transactions, resorted to the widespread nationalization of domestic and foreign companies in the mining, petroleum, electricity, and manufacturing sectors, and encouraged worker ownership of the means of production (Portocarrero 1983).[23] It is estimated that the state owned between eighteen to forty PEs (Alvarez Rodrich 1992: 20). Velasco, to foster his project of state-led capitalism, gave even greater precedence to PEs than did Belaunde, particularly during the 1970 period. Newly nationalized firms (either bankrupt or strategically important to the government) became part of the public sector while new enterprises were created, reaching a total of 177 PEs by 1977. The increase is evident in that PEs' share of GDP rose from 1 per cent in 1968 to 20 per cent in 1975 (Wise 1994: 90). Despite strong growth rates and low inflation between 1968 and 1971, military-sponsored populism ran into trouble by 1975. During that year the deficit of the non-financial PEs rose to a record level of 4.4 per cent of GDP (Table 2.4). This is because the great expansion of PEs took place in a chaotic fashion. Lacking any clear legal and administrative framework they fell prey of the typical syndrome associated with PEs in other countries. The symptoms included inefficiency, mismanagement, redtape, and corruption. Many PEs remained heavily dependent upon the purchasing of foreign technology and raw materials while the lack of an economy of scale kept production prices very high. Moreover, the government's deliberate manipulation

TABLE 2.4. *Brazilian PEs Privatized During 1986–7*

Enterprise	Ministry of Public Enterprise Group	Industry	Date	Type of Sale	Price US$ thousands
Cia. Melhoramentos de Blumenau (hotel)	Finance Ministry	Hotel	Jun. 9, 1986	Competitive bid	420.2
Cia. Nacional de Tecidos Nova America S. A.	BNDES	Textile	Jun. 9, 1987	Auction	15,855.70
Maquinas Piratininga do Nordeste S. A.	BNDES	Capital goods	Jul. 23, 1987	Competitive bid	1,363.0
Maquina Piratininga S. A.	BNDES	Capital goods	Sep. 15, 1987	Competitive bid	106.6
Ferritas Magneticas S. A.	CVRD	Magnetic alloys	Nov. 26, 1987	Competitive bid	not available
TOTAL					17,745.70

Source: Werneck (1991: 66).

of the exchange rate and its decision to have PEs supplying public services and other products ended in subsidizing important sectors in private hands (Burneo 1993).

Velasco's ability to finance its multiple projects relied primarily upon foreign loans, which further jeopardized Peru's external debt position. Unprecedented government spending led to an escalation of the fiscal deficit which approached 10 per cent of GDP by 1975 (Sheahan 1987: 261). The lack of a coherent economic plan to optimize resource allocations and improve efficiency resulted in a lot of waste as was the case under Belaunde. The economic impasse at this point provoked an internal coup within the military that replaced Velasco with the more moderate General Francisco Morales Bermúdez in 1975. The military took a neoorthodox approach to combat mounting inflation and fiscal imbalances under Morales Bermúdez, but with no appreciable success. In 1978 the military government, through decree 22402, put on the auction bloc several PEs, but none of them were actually sold for lack of offers (Alvarez Rodrich 1992).

The armed forces' reformist attempt had turned into a failure by the end of the 1970s and the initial popular support enjoyed by the military in 1968 degenerated into widespread opposition from all levels of Peruvian society (McClintock and Lowenthal 1983). By 1978, Peru, first among Latin American nations, found itself unable to honor its foreign debt obligations (Palmer 1990). That year, facing popular unrest and widespread strikes, the generals conceded defeat allowing the election of a constitutent assembly for the drafting of a new constitution. Two years later, the country returned to the polls and voted for a new President and Congress. Belaunde, the very man that the military had deposed twelve years earlier, won again.

During his second term in office (1980–5), Belaunde was besieged by contending needs. On the one hand, he had to revive the economy in order to keep popular support. On the other, he had to enforce strict monetary and fiscal policies in order to bring inflation and the fiscal deficit under control. Initially, the President could count on an ideal situation. He had a comfortable majority in both houses of Congress and a new constitution gave him ample freedom to legislate through executive orders. Moreover, Belaunde's first economic team, headed by Manuel Ulloa, had the strong financial and technical backing of the IMF and the World Bank. Ulloa's power was formidable as he simultaneously occupied the position of prime minister. Between 1980 and 1982, Ulloa tried to enact a neoorthodox package of economic measures. His purpose was to contain government spending while at the same time promoting several reforms whith the goal of undoing many interventionist, loose-money programs instituted under Velasco. However, while Ulloa preached fiscal responsibility, Belaunde's concern for mid-term local and congressional elections postponed and diluted the austerity package. Furthermore, the President often failed to prevent, and on occasion actually

TABLE 2.5. *Peru: Economic Results and Non-Financial Public Sector Investments, 1970–81 (% of GDP)*

	1970	1971	1972	1973	1974	1975	1976	1977	1978	1979	1980	1981
Economic Results of the												
Non-Financial Public Sector	0.6	1.2	2.4	4.0	5.9	8.1	8.8	8.6	5.3	0.?	3.9	6.7
Central Government	1.1	2.6	3.1	3.4	2.7	4.6	5.6	6.6	4.4	0.?	2.4	3.8
PEs non-financial	0.4	0.9	0.1	0.8	3.9	4.4	3.6	2.4	1.2	0.?	1.8	2.8
Other PEs	0.9	0.5	0.6	0.2	0.7	0.9	0.4	0.4	0.3	0.?	0.3	0.1
Financing	0.6	1.2	2.4	4.0	5.9	8.1	8.8	8.6	5.3	0.?	3.9	6.7
External	1.0	0.2	1.4	2.7	3.9	4.1	3.0	4.2	1.9	2.3	0.8	1.7
Internal	0.4	1.0	1.0	1.3	2.0	4.0	5.8	4.4	3.4	1.4	3.1	5.0
Public Investment	3.9	3.9	4.2	4.7	7.0	7.4	7.1	5.6	4.8	4.8	6.0	7.3
Central Government	2.0	2.4	2.5	2.0	2.5	2.4	2.3	2.3	2.2	2.6	3.0	3.3
PEs non-financial	1.3	1.0	1.3	2.4	4.2	4.8	4.5	3.1	2.5	1.9	2.6	3.3
Other PEs	0.6	0.5	0.4	0.3	0.3	0.2	0.3	0.2	0.1	0.3	0.4	0.7
Economic Results of PEs/Results of Non-Financial PEs	66.7	75	4.2	20	66.1	54.3	40.9	27.9	22.6	55.6	46.2	41.8
Investment of PEs/Total Public Investment	33.3	25.6	31	51.1	60	64.9	63.4	55.4	52.1	35.6	43.3	45.2

Source: Statistical Summary of the Non-Financial Public Sector, 1970–87. ('Compendio Estadistico del Sector Publico no Financiero, 1970–87') and Burneo (1993).

encouraged, the excessive spending in infrastructure and social programs that his ministers and Congress wanted.

The reforms advocated by Ulloa included privatization of several PEs. Unfortunatelly, he was unable to carry these out. In the early 1980s the government owned between 150 and 200 PEs (depending on the definition of PEs used to calculate them) with an 11 per cent share GDP (Saulniers 1988: 71, 106). Belaunde returned radios, television stations, and newspapers that Velasco had expropriated in the mid-1970s, to their original owners, but he went no further. Actually, his administration 'featured the worst portfolio performance because the President failed to take key decisions and lacked the administrative clout to follow through on enunciated polcies' (Saulniers 1988: 180). In defense of his record Belaunde cited the fact that the economic situation of the country in the early 1980s was so shaky that neither domestic nor private groups were willing to take any risk with PEs.[24] Although there may be some truth here, others have argued to the contrary. Ulloa's measures, including privatization, 'challenged popular ideas and political taboos, yet were announced with no prior search for a political mandate nor any effort to convince either key political players, even within Belaunde's party, or the public at large' (Webb 1994: 365). This became problematic as privatization required congressional approval and strong presidential backing, which soon appeared to be missing elements. To begin with, opposition to privatization came from within Belaunde's party (Alvarez Rodrich 1992). In addition, labor unions, opposition parties, business organizations, opinion leaders, the media, and academic circles saw Ulloa's reforms as flawed and radical. All these vested interests effectively mobilized public opinion, in one way or another, against change.[25]

The military veto against reversing key nationalizations was also a key factor in aborting Ulloa's privatization initiative. Anticipating situations similar to those that occurred in Argentina and Brazil a few years later, the Peruvian public after enduring years of mismanagement from its military leaders was tired of hearing about additional sacrifices. The transition to democratic government was identified with a return to redistributive policies while maintaining those social programs (subsidized services supplied by PEs) and reforms (like land distribution) that had experienced popular approval. In the meantime, the fiscal position of PEs continued to deteriorate. 'State enterprise spending was being driven by presidential prodding, by exaggerated forecasts, of projected deficits in energy, water, and other services, and by the political cowardice of state enterprises, which often ducked the need to make unpopular price increases' (Webb 1994: 361).

State divestiture was against Belaunde's ideological beliefs, deeply rooted in *dirigiste* tradition. Richard Webb, who served as chairman of Peru's Central Bank under Belaunde, described the President's attitude as follows:

Belaunde had an almost physical aversion to economics. He heavily discounted the preaching, and warnings of his economic advisers, and during his entire political career he took every opportunity to push for vast schemes of public works. During his first two and a half years in office, he continually sought to postpone the adjustment measures and to dilute reforms that he had originally approved.   (Webb 1994: 371)

Belaunde's contradictions and indecision proved fatal. A sharp fall in commodity prices for Peruvian exports by 1982, came at a time of stagnating non-traditional exports, and diminishing foreign credit as a result of the onset of the debt crisis. This squeezed the financial support upon which the government's macroeconomic policies were based. Ulloa came into open conflict with Belaunde at the end of that same year. Demanding greater powers to fight escalating terrorism, the Minister clashed with the President who increasingly felt upstaged by his second in command. The squabble ended with Ulloa's resignation. He was later succeeded by three more economy ministers. Peru went into a deep recession in 1983 and in November (of that year) Belaunde's Acción Popular suffered an embarrassing defeat in municipal elections, including those in Lima, at the hand of center-left opposition parties. In 1983, making the events more dramatic, Peru underwent the devastating consequences of *El Niño*, a weather phenomenon associated with floods in the northern Peru and droughts in the south. *El Niño* wiped out vital agricultural and fishing production. It also depleted the scarce financial reserve of the Belaunde administration forcing it to spend valuable resources on disaster relief programs.

Under pressure from the IMF and the World Bank, Belaunde, in spite of policy inconsistencies, authorized an even stronger dose of neo-orthodox measures that only two years earlier he had refused to endorse.[26] Amidst the strong opposition of his party, the President allowed the elimination of many subsidies, steep increases in taxes and interest rates, and budget cuts between 1984 and 1985. All of these sacrifices generated a small current account surplus in 1985, reducing the fiscal deficit to 3 per cent of GDP as opposed to 12 per cent in 1980 (Stallings 1990: 136). Nonetheless, unemployment rose significantly, wages' purchasing power deteriorated, and inflation continued to climb. Belaunde was besieged by the opposition of both labor and entrepreneurial organizations as his term came to a close. At the same time, a violent left-wing terrorist movement spearheaded by the Maoist Sendero Luminoso (Shining Path) and the Movimiento Revolucionario Tupac Amaru (MRTA) drove the country into a state of virtual civil war.

Declining standards of living, political violence, and ineffective macroeconomic policies played into the hands of Belaunde and AP's political opposition. The 1985 elections sanctioned, for the first time in the country's history, the victory of the candidate of the Acción Popular Revolucionaria del Peru (APRA). The new President would be Alan García. APRA was a populist political party that, similar to the Peronists in Argentina, had been ostracized by the military who had annulled its victory in the 1962 elections. García represented the left-wing faction of the party. A man of strong personal charisma, he quickly centralized political authority in the hands of himself and a selected group of trusted advisers, leaving much of the party machine outside the decision-making process. García contacted a team of left-wing researchers who had been tied to the Velasco regime for the purpose of drafting his administration's economic plan. García and his economists rejected the IMF-sponsored neo-orthodox measures of the second half of the Belaunde administration. For García's economists these measure only depressed business activity while failing to tackle inflation.

Peru's problems, it was reasoned, did not stem from excess demand, but rather from supply side bottlenecking, fluctuating prices for exports, and capital flight. In promoting a growth-oriented model, García hoped to revive the economy ultimately creating new jobs and allowing higher wages. The President feared that if high growth rates could not be sustained in the years to come, then Shining Path was likely to take over the country by exploiting the profound alienation of poor Peruvians who had suffered most severely from the prolonged recession.

Attempting to tackle the crisis, García's first economic team adopted a heterodox approach to economic stabilization, like those tried in Argentina and Brazil. The administration froze prices in the short term and, as time went on, adjusted them periodically, decreased interest rates and several taxes, established a fixed exchange rate, and implemented controls on imports and capital outflows (Carbonetto *et al.* 1987). The long-term growth strategy was assigned to the state and its PEs. Renewed empahsis was given to import-substitution and export-promotion schemes. However, the government asked the private sector to play its part too. Evidently, García's political behavior was two-faced. In public he constantly used his left-wing, populist rhetoric, punctuated by attacks on international capitalism and domestic power elites. Meanwhile, the President cultivated a close relationship with Peru's twelve largest conglomerates well before his election. His intent was to convince big entrepreneurs to contribute to his administration's policies with substantial investments. García offered in return an array of incentives including tax breaks, subsidized exports, preferential exchange rates, exceptions on price controls, and heavy protection from foreign competition. Such a strategy was not unsual, as Alfonsín did much of the same in Argentina to garner support for the Austral Plan. Thus, García enjoyed a honeymoon with the country's largest conglomerates in the first two years of his term, at the expense of the peak organizations which represented the most important economic sectors. Among them there was the prominent Confederación Nacional de Institutciones Empresariales Privadas (CONFIEP). This cooperation relationship led to the creation of the National Investment Council and the Fund for Investment and Employment in early 1987, two institutions set up to facilitate government-business relations. None the less, the unwillingness of big business to invest, coupled with García's fear of losing political initiative at a time of declining economic conditions and escalating terrorist attacks, led him to reverse his conciliatory approach (Durand 1987: 53–56). In July 1987, the President announced the nationalization of the domestic banking sector, which was partly owned by some of Peru's largest conglomerates. This move created a backlash from the opposition in Congress and big business, eventually forcing García into an embarassing withdrawal of his original proposal.

The economic situation took a turn for the worse by the end of 1987, after an initial success in 1986. The President constantly came under attack both from opposition parties and from the business community. Strained relations abroad magnified the unraveling domestic crisis. García, upon coming to office, severed Peru's ties with the IMF, which rejected his administration's heterodox plan. The President challenged the IMF and foreign creditors by announcing a unilateral decision to use only 10 per cent of export earnings to service Peru's foreign debt. This initiative was far from a debt moratorium, and Peru's debt disbursement in 1986 and 1987 continued well above the 10 per cent self-imposed ceiling. Peru's political position remained isolated among Latin American nations. This isolation proved counterproductive because with foreign reserves nearly depleted García was not able to locate any appreciable foreign financing for the purpose of alleviating the fiscal crisis beginning in 1988. It was at this time that all payments were stopped and arrears began to pile up quickly reaching $6.5 billion out of a total external debt of $23 billion. These facts were enough to establish Peru as an international pariah. By late 1989 capital flight was endemic and, 'the secondary market prices for Peru's debt were the lowest of all Latin American countries at 6 cents to the US dollar (compared with 68 cents for Colombia, 43 cents for Mexico and 17 cents for Argentina)' (Palmer 1990: 6).

With the country experiencing a hyperinflation spiral, opinion polls in September 1988 showed that the President approval rating had plummeted to 16 per cent from 96 per cent in August of 1985 (Stallings 1990: 148). Confronted with political collapse, the APRA conservatives forced García to replace his 'heterodox' economic team. They favored one that would turn back the clock to a more orthodox management style hoping to re-open negotiations with the IMF and the World Bank. Unfortunately, 'the result of two poorly planned and poorly implemented packages of orthodox measures, on top of the previous heterodoxy, created even greater economic chaos' (Stallings 1990: 148). In 1988 alone the economy shrank by 8.3 per cent of GDP and a further 11.6 per cent in 1989. Inflation rose by 1,772 per cent and 2,775 respectively.[27] Adding to the economic paralysis were a number of 'general strikes' imposed by Shining Path. Betweeb 1988 and 1989 terrorist activities marked a bloody crescendo claiming the lives of 275 public officials and police officers (Palmer 1990: 5). The combination of economic depression and guerrilla insurgency left Peru broke and on its knees. By 1989, the 'informal' or underground economy (which escapes taxation) was regarded to be as much as 40 per cent of the formal sector (De Soto 1989). This mirrored the deterioration of real wages that by then were only 52 per cent of what they used to be in 1970 while well over half of the population was either unemployed or under-employed (Palmer 1990: 5).

As portrayed above, it is evident that under Belaunde, and even more so under García, willingness (both ideological and pragmatic motives) to privatize was virtually non-existent (Burneo 1993). The few sales that took place under García were merely cosmetic actions. According to Alvarez Rodrich (1992: 28):

In 1986 the State sold its shares in Prolansa (14.4 per cent) and Adesur (5.8 per cent) for US$650,418 and US$69,346, respectively; in 1987 [the State] sold the assets of Daasa for US$807,628 and 40 per cent of the shares of Festa belonging to the State; in 1988 the assets of Modasa were transferred; and in 1989 workers acquired 71 per cent of Compasa, all the shares in Emcohol, and the minority shares in Prolacsur through a direct sale . . . Likewise, in 1989 the government placed at the Stock Exchange 29 per cent of the shares of Cementos Lima, but without any major success.

In December 1988, the executive had Congress pass the Law of Entre-prenurial Activities of the State (24948), which established the norms for the sale of PEs. However, other measures point to García's unwillingness to abandon *dirigismo*. In 1986, the government nationalized Belco Petroleum leading to the creation of a new PE, Petromar. Nine more PEs were created thereafter.[28] Under García the government forced many PEs to set prices below their market costs in order to control inflation. This attempt not only failed but further deteriorated the already precarious financial position of many PEs.[29] A World Bank (1988) study estimated that below-cost-charges cost PEs like Petroperú, Electroperú, Ecasa, and Enci financial losses equal to 6.7 per cent of GDP in 1987 alone. According to Burneo (1993: 18), PEs losses rose from $83 million in 1985 to $503 million in 1989. These amounts were not small if one considers that in 1988 the total assets of non-financial PEs amounted to $5.5 billion (World Bank 1988).

Alan García's ambiguous ideology, rooted in state-led development and left-wing populism, was averse to the theoretical tenets behind state divest-iture. Privatization was not an option, even on pragmatic grounds. García had rejected the IMF orthodox measures that had failed under Belaunde. He believed that the true alternative was in economic heterodoxy. Heterodoxy promised growth and new employment opportunities, which appealed to García's core constituency made up of traditional unionism, middle classes, and urban poor. Peru's ability to attract foreign investments vanished rapidly as a result of García's severed relations with the international financial community and increased terrorism. This had negative effects with regards to opportunity.

The general public mood, at least early in García's term, seemed also to point to a rejection of the orthodox model. This included any privatization, as was the case under Belaunde. The general political and economic context that García inherited in 1985 was not conducive to privatization. There was no support for it, at the time, not even among the country's largest domestic conglomerates, which instead lobbied for tariff protection and the preservation of oligopolistic market conditions.

Conclusions

The discussion of the three countries examined above establishes that for most of the 1980s privatization was a token policy issue as the conditions shaping willingness and opportunity were missing. Primarily, ideological motivations deterred privatization. Alfonsín, Sarney, Belaunde, and García, were presidents who believed that the state, rather than the market, should be in charge of promoting economic development. When Alfonsín and Sarney finally decided to include privatization in their respective administrations' stabilization policy, they did so when they ran out of options. Their advisors convinced these two presidents that the sale of several PEs was necessary for raising needed capital for the state while, at the same time, unloading profitless companies. Even at times in which some major privatization was attempted, as in the case of Aerolíneas Argentinas, the Alfonsín administration aimed at retaining 51 per cent of the company's shares while allowing the potential private owners to manage the air carrier.

Pragmatic motives spurred the few privatizations that did materialize. In Argentina and Brazil (we have already seen that in Peru state divestiture under Belaunde and García was ephemeral) privatization was intended to: improve the business climate; induce private investments; reduce the fiscal deificit; and to rationalize state operations by selling PEs in economic sectors regarded as being of little or no 'strategic' importance. Although definitions varied slightly among countries, a basic consensus existed in regarding steel, telecommunications, aviation, mining, mail services, electricity, oil, petrochemicals, banking, nuclear energy, rail transportation, and military-related production, as areas of the economy with strategic importance. Politicians and government bureaucrats were usually willing to sacrifice companies that were acquired by government banks and agencies from defaulting private businesses. These for the most part remained unprofitable and thus added to the government deficit. Such PEs encompassed sectors ranging from textile to home appliances, all of which had no strategic importance.

Opportunity was another missing element in the 1980s. Chile was the only country that had privatized extensively in Latin America. The financial collapse in 1982, which involved many economic groups that acquired former PEs, forced the authoritarian regime of General Augusto Pinochet to re-acquire many of those companies. This event, as well as the tainted reputation of the Pinochet regime, caused privatization in Latin America to be identified with 'faulty' policies and the remnants of authoritarianism in the region. Thus the Chilean experiment was considered a non-viable one in the eyes of policy-makers. When a government showed an intent to privatize, it generally aimed at selling unprofitable PEs. Salvaged for its own purposes were those that generated profits and monopolies, as in the petroleum and telecommunication sectors, which although temporarily unprofitable could be streamlined to retain profitability. Concurrently, private investors, both domestic and foreign, remained unconvinced about the government's commitment to market reforms. Thus, they were reluctant to embark upon deals with strings attached as in the Alfonsín's privatization scheme. Moreover, the small size of capital markets in these countries, and widespread inside-trading practices, made privatization through public offers extremely difficult. This, in turn, made the promotion of a Thatcher-styled 'popular capitalism' unfeasible.

Another missing element of opportunity is that, in general, most people viewed any state shrinking policy with suspiciousness and hostility. Critics of privatization argued that such a policy would unravel many of the social welfare rights that the poorer classes had gained since World War II. Decades of state-led development had created a societal consensus over the state's responsibility for maintaining minimum standards of living for all citizens via welfare programs, cheap public services, and minimum wage policies. Thus, arguments against privatization came not just from opposition parties but also from influential members of the government.

In Argentina, the powerful union movement and the Peronist party, the largest opposition bloc in Congress, effectively made it impossible for Alfonsín to privatize Aerolíneas Argentinas (González Fraga 1991: 89–91).[30] Compounding matters, many Radical congressmen were ideologically opposed to privatization. Some also feared that their party would loose popular support as this policy would inevitably provoke substantial layoffs. In Brazil unions, left-wing parties, and even the Catholic Church were equally opposed to privatization with the difference that the Sarney administration had a narrower support base than Alfonsín's. Sarney, in fact, held together a heterogeneous coalition of parties whose mutual vetoes on key economic issues prevented any coherent policy reform. Sarney and his allies had grown accustomed to use PEs as a means for consolidation and expansion of their political patronage. They had little interest in dismantling the vast economic empire constructed by the state since Vargas' times. Unsurprisingly, the new constitution approved in 1988 barred the state from selling PEs in 'strategic' sectors. In Peru, not only did Belaunde and García face opposition from labor, business interests, and the military but also from the congressional ranks of their own parties.

Generally, in all three countries, the greatest supporters for privatization were some government technocrats who had reached the conclusion that privatization was necessary to alleviate unecessary state responsibility while, at the same time, enabling the executive to cut the budget deficit thus devoting funds to more urgent needs. International pressure was present but not strong enough to swing the balance in favor of privatization. This can partly be attributed to the fact that the economic crisis had not reached yet its zenith. Policy-makers continued to believe that they could continue to manage the situation with mild policy reforms appeasing powerful domestic lobbies crucial to their electoral support. It must also be emphasized that business support for privatization was lukewarm in many quarters. This was partially a function of private companies' uncertainty about the government's commitment to market reforms. Equally important, however, is the fact that powerful economic groups initially thriving under generous government contracts (both as suppliers or contractors) had much to lose from state divestitutre.

When privatization took place in Argentina, Brazil, and Peru it was carried out incoherently. Little or negligible attention was given to efficiency concerns in terms of possible consequences of market changes. The few PEs privatized on occasion, ended up in the hands of their private competitors, thus increasing monopolistic or oligopolistic conditions. Invariably, the overall concern for policy-makers was to raise cash and cut losses in order to trim the deficit and make better use of government resources. This took precedence over redesigning the state's role according to conservative political and economic principles. Ultimately, in all three cases the fiscal impact of privatization was negligible.

Endnotes

1. Cited in González Fraga (1991: 79).
2. Statement released by former Secretary for Economic Coordination Adolfo Canitrot (*Noticias*, 18 September 1989, p. 16).
3. Interview with Edgardo Catterberg, Buenos Aires, May 1993.
4. Law 20.705 prevented the privatization of PEs originally created by the state, as opposed to companies acquired through bankruptcy procedures.
5. *Diarios de Sesiones del Senado de la Nación*, 27 April 1988.
6. Argentine businessmen Menotti Pescarmona and Gilberto Montagna led the consortium supported by Alitalia and Swissair. Their proposal was actually less favorable to the government as it offered to buy out 55 per cent of Aerolíneas (Blanco 1993: 20).
7. This was the case also in areas where the government wanted to sell its shares to its private partners in private mixed companies. 'If a sector's survival depends on state regulation of prices and quotas, the private sector will not welcome a

break in its alliance with the state unless it believes the rules of the game will not change' (Gónzalez Fraga 1991: 93).

8. PEs where the state had complete or majority ownership numbered 305 (of these, 117 were national or binational companies, 182 belonged to the provinces, and 6 belonged to municipalities.) If we add to this number 222 companies where the state had a minority share, the total amount reached 527 (Fundación de Investigaciones Económicas Latinoamericanas. *El Gasto Público en la Argentina 1960–1985*. Buenos Aires: FIEL 1987).

9. Sarney was the President of the PDS until 1985 when he left it because of personal disagreement with PDS' candidate, Paulo Maluf. However, after becoming President, Sarney never gained an appreciable support within the PMDB.

10. According to some commentators, 'Mr Sarney lacked Neves's democratic credentials. He had long supported the departing generals, and was put on the ticket as part of a backroom deal to ensure a Neves victory, and because no one more important wanted to be vice-President. Even he conceded he was ill-prepared to be President' (*The Economist*, March 1988, p. 46).

11. Interview with former Executive Secretary of the Interministerial Council on Privatiazation David Moreira. São Paulo, August 1993. See also 'David Moreira critica demora na privatização,' *O Globo*, 13 January 1988.

12. On the poor implementation of the Cruzado Plan and its populist features see Bresser Pereira (1996).

13. The PMDB won 259 of the 559 seats in the new Constituent Assembly (46.3 per cent), whereas Sarney's newly formed party, the *Partido da Frente Liberal* (PFL) secured 115 seats, thus making the President heavily dependent on the PMDB support.

14. *Journal do Brasil*, 10 April 1988.

15. Between April 1986 and December 1987 the government sold less than a dozen PEs worth about $30 million. Conselho Interministerial de Privatização, Secretaría de Planejamento da Presidência da República, 'Relatório de atividades desenvolvidas pelo Conselho Interministerial de Privatização, Exercício de 1987' (Brasilia, mimeo, 1988).

16. The government's criteria for the privatization of PEs were as follows: (1) former private companies that the government had acquired to save them from bankruptcy; (2) PEs in economic areas where private competitors were able to replace the state in the provision of goods and services; and (3) subsidiaries of public enterprises that were unfairly competing with private companies (Werneck 1991).

17. In the most important privatizations the government financed up to 80 per cent of the sale spreading across an eight-year period (Mello 1992).

18. *Gazeta Mercantil*, 27 January 1988.

19. The First National Bank of Boston, 'Newsletter Brazil,' no. 5, 17 April 1989, p. 2.

20. David Moreira, who headed the Interministerial Privatization Council, resigned in 1988 citing Sarney's lack of support.

21. *O Estado de S. Paulo*, 17 August 1989, p. 1b.

22. Still, Velasco gave private businesses generous tax breaks, financial incentives for investment, and high tariff protection.

23. Firms were forced to distribute some of their profits to workers in the form of company shares until the latter would own 50 per cent of their company.
24. Interview with the author, Lima, 12 August 1994.
25. Interview with former Peruvian government officials, Lima, August 1994.
26. The IMF also recommended to draw plans for the privatization of PEs but things did not go beyond the discussion stage (Burneo 1993: 24)
27. Data provided by the Central Bank of Peru.
28. These were Flopesca, Conaa, Whisky, Electronor-Oeste, Mesa, Larcarbon, Sedajunin, Sedapuno, and Prolacsur (Burneo 1993: 24).
29. According to Alvarez Rodrich (1992) the prices charged by PEs for electricity and gasoline in 1990 were 7.4 per cent and 7.8 per cent of what they used to be in 1985, respectively.
30. González Fraga (1991: 89–91).

3

Argentina

Argentines turned out at the polls in May 1989 to choose a successor to President Raúl Alfonsín of the Radical Civic Union. The winner was Carlos Menem, the candidate from the largest opposition group, the Justicialist (Peronist) party. While on the campaign trail Menem pledged that if elected he would faithfully adhere to Peronist doctrine as originally postulated by Juan Perón. The party creed emphasized economic nationalism, strong state regulation of the economy, economic growth through direct government investments and financing of the private sector, and social justice favoring workers through income redistribution (Borón 1991; Wynia 1992; Peralta Ramos 1992). Menem, with this rhetoric, harnessed the support not only from the traditional labor-dominated Peronist constituency, but also from the middle classes who voted for Alfonsín in 1982, only to be frustrated by five and a half years of broken promises and economic disasters. Menem skill-fully avoided specific details about policy plans, but few questioned his real intentions. After all, his Peronist credentials were impeccable. Menem was a three-time governor of La Rioja, one of Argentina's poorest provinces. He had successfully put half of that province's work force on the state payroll by dispensing thousands of jobs. When the Radical government curtailed the disbursement of federal funds to La Rioja, he went so far as to print cur-rency himself. However, in 1989, with the Argentine treasury depleted, the country was experiencing the worst economic crisis of the century. Menem realized shortly before taking office that there was no room for the redistributive measures he had promised so vehemently. The consolidation of democracy had been all-important for the Alfonsín administration. Menem's top prior-ity would be to resolve the economic crisis.

In the most stunning policy reversal in Argentina's modern history, Menem reached the conclusion that turning the economy around no longer rested in the traditional populist, nationalistic, redistributive approach. The key to success was instead the establishment of a free market economy through the implementation of a sweeping market-oriented reform program worthy of Thatcher and Reagan's applause. Oddly, it took a Peronist President to undo most of Perón's welfare and ISI policies of the 1940s (Landi and Cavarozzi 1991: 18). Economy Minister Domingo Cavallo later admitted that, 'Menem is changing all that Perón did after World War II.'[1] However, Menem's adop-tion of a neoconservative economic approach was not an isolated case in Latin

America but actually part of a regional trend. Traditional proponents of state intervention and economic nationalism like Presidents Víctor Paz Estenssoro in Bolivia, Carlos Andrés Pérez in Venezuela, Patricio Aylwin in Chile, and later populist Alberto Fujimori in Peru, once elected, converted themselves into enforcers of free market economics.

Initially, Menem left the solution of the economic crisis in the hands of a team from Bunge & Born, the country's largest agribusiness conglomerate, which had opposed Perón's policies during the 1950s. The Bunge & Born plan's primary objective was to stop hyperinflation. It also mandated structural reforms including deregulation of the economy, slashing the fiscal deficit, reforming the tax system, and downsizing government bureaucracy.

However, the cornerstone of Menem's market approach to resolving the country's problems was a radical privatization effort. Only 46 days after his inauguration Menem demanded approval from the Peronist-controlled Congress of the State Reform Law (23.696) authorizing the executive branch to place trustees in charge of all state companies for 180 days, renewable for an additional 180. The law gave the executive full authority to immediately privatize 32 of the 400 state enterprises. Most importantly, according to the new law, Congress delegated to the executive the power to privatize through decrees (the equivalent of an executive order in the United States), and unlimited discretion on the means and criteria to be implemented. Equally as important, Law 23.696 also eliminated many legal impediments and appeal procedures that might be used to derail privatization.[2] The Law of Economic Emergency (Law 26.697) was a second bill that Congress passed shortly thereafter. It gave the President the right to suspend the costly industrial promotion subsidies and tax breaks while sheltering the state from pending lawsuits and contractual obligations with government contractors. As we will see later, decree powers, either delegated by Congress or used in an indiscriminate, arbitrary fashion, will have profound consequences on the divestiture process.

Menem, citing the country's state of hyperinflation threatened Congress that if legislators failed to approve the two bills quickly, he then would implement them simply through decree. The government warned Radical congressmen that, if they tried to stop the passage of the two bills, the executive was going to uncover alleged corruption scandals that had taken place during the Alfonsín administration. None the less, at the time of the vote, some disgruntled congressmen from both the opposition and the Peronist ranks failed to attend, thus undercutting the necessary voting quorum. Attempting to solve the problem, government backers ushered congressional employees claiming to be legislators into the voting session of the House of Deputies. The impostors cast the decisive ballots (Cerruti and Ciancaglini 1992: 98). Given the intimidating scenario, neither Peronist nor Radical legislators objected to the validity of the vote. Conclusively, in less than two months Menem had established the legal instruments for expediting privatization without any independent oversight. To appease criticisms about the government's bold-ness in achieving its ends, Menem asked Congress to form an ad hoc bicameral commission with the goal of monitoring the privatization process.[3] Menem accepted that a privatization advocate, Liberal Alberto Natale, be its chairman. This appointment maintained a façade of impartiality, while ensuring that the policy would not be jeopardized.[4]

Unveiling the first stabilization package, Menem accentuated the drastic approach, describing it as 'surgery without anaesthetic'. However, despite some initial progress, the government's weak measures to curb expenses, com-pounded by decreasing tax revenues, failed to achieve long-lasting fiscal equilibrium. Thus, a new inflationary spiral ensued by the end of 1989. This event forced the resignation of the Bunge & Born team, which was replaced by another economist outside the Peronist movement, Christian Democrat Erman González. The neo-conservative content of the administration's policies became more orthodox. Under González's tenure (December 1989–February 1991), the administration refused to concede to the lobbying of the faltering labor and business interests. Yet 1990 marked the third consecutive year of negative economic growth. Although González made drastic cuts to balance the budget, the improvement was marginal. A rapid expansion of money supply in February 1991 ended in a new burst of hyperinflation.

Menem, at this point, asked his Foreign Minister Domingo Cavallo, a well-known economist and a PJ outsider, to replace González. He accepted immediately, designing a comprehensive reform program that merged the necessity of fiscal discipline with market deregulation and privatization. Unlike his predecessors, who usually resorted to decrees to usher in economic packages, Cavallo had the new measures approved by Congress in the Spring of 1991 through the Covertibility Law, giving them enhanced credibility. The main tenets of the Convertibility Law were: (1) the Central Bank could no longer finance the government fiscal deficit; (2) the Central Bank was forced to back 100 per cent of the monetary base with foreign exchange and gold reserves, creating a de facto 'gold standard' system; (3) the establishment of a new foreign exchange system fixing the parity of the US dollar at $1 per Argentine peso; (4) the requirement that any new devaluation was to receive congressional approval; and (5) the elimination of all indexation mechanisms from contracts as they created the so-called 'inertial inflation' effect.

The Convertibility Law coerced the government to strict compliance with budget guidelines. Congress approved the federal budget from 1991 on. This event was remarkable since for decades this practice had been abandoned. It also imposed a major overhaul of the federal administration, and the elimina-tion of tens of thousands of jobs. Privatization was no longer an ad hoc policy but was incorporated as an integral part of the administration's economic plan. The quasi-fiscal deficit of the Central Bank was eliminated. Likewise changes were made to the pension and social security system. The government

Argentina

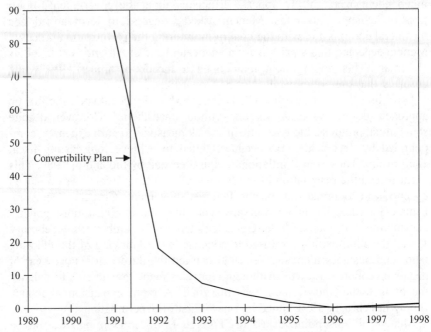

FIG. 3.1. Argentina: Inflation Rate 1989–98
Source: World Bank, 1998.

also restructured the domestic and foreign debt of the public sector. More-over, the federal government transferred the responsibility for the provision of health, education, and social welfare to the provinces.

The fiscal and monetary discipline resulting from the Covertibility Law provided the base for a stable currency. Privatization receipts, in the mean-time, generated the foreign reserves necessary to maintain a fixed parity with the US dollar until a fiscal balance was attainable. The Covertibility Law, much to the surprise of many critics, succeeded in a relatively short time in bring-ing price stability and fiscal balance. Inflation, which had increased to 4,923 per cent in 1989, dropped to 3.7 per cent in 1994 (Fig. 3.1). In 1992, for the first time in decades, the Argentine government recorded a fiscal surplus (Fig. 3.2). Along with economic stability the GDP grew by 8.9 per cent in 1991, 8.7 per cent in 1992, 6.0 per cent in 1993, and 7.1 per cent in 1994 (Fig. 3.2). Foreign reserves grew faster than the country's external debt (Fig. 3.3). A new climate of economic stability followed the Convertibility Law. Additionally, the greater coherence of Cavallo's reform policies gave new momentum to privatization, which had stumbled upon several problems between 1989 and 1990, as we shall see below.

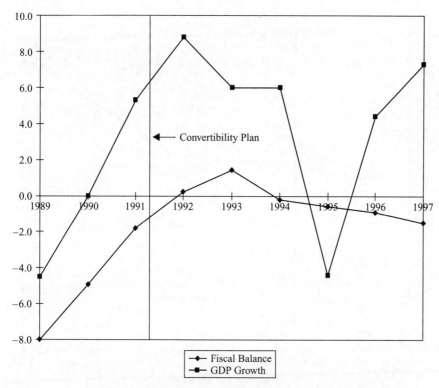

FIG. 3.2. Argentina: Fiscal Balance (% of GDP) and GDP Growth (%) 1989–97
Source: World Bank, 1998.

As a result of new political alliances and legislative measures, Menem had virtually completed, by the end of his first term in 1995, one of the world's most radical privatization programs. What induced Menem to privatize? What turned a long-time populist into a free-marketeer? It was argued in Chapter 1 that leaders, when faced with a policy dilemma, at least under certain conditions, can substitute one policy for another. Perón, in the mid-1940s, under favorable economic and political conditions, consolidated his power by emphasizing ISI policies, nationalizing foreign companies, and expanding government intervention and regulation. By 1989, however, the old Keynesian model based upon state-led ISI, economic protectionism, and strong regulation of the private sector had exhausted its capacity to promote sustainable growth. It had created, on the contrary, a large and inefficient government bureaucracy, money-losing PEs, and a huge fiscal deficit. Resources were channeled into an unproductive public sector, while at the same time import barriers protected inefficient PEs and private industries. Thus, the state had

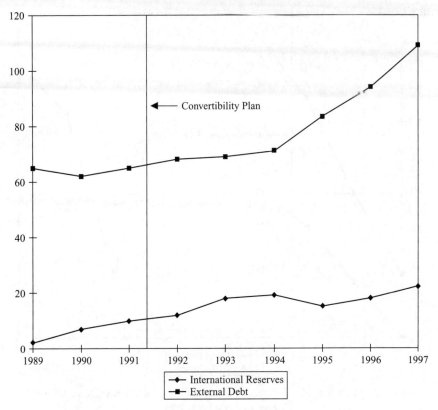

Fig. 3.3. Argentina: External Debt and International Reserves (US$ billion) 1989–97
Source: World Bank, 1998.

grown increasingly incapable of infusing the economy with fresh money while
the private sector proved unable and/or unwilling to pick up the slack due to
lack of incentives. Alfonsín recognized all this, but strong opposition by the
Peronists (as well as many Radicals) to market-oriented reforms, in addition
to his personal bias toward maintaining a strong government role, doomed
his short-lived reform attempts. However, by 1989 the situation reached its
climax. Confronted with an unprecedented economic crisis and civil unrest,
Menem concluded that, if he wanted to achieve political stability and economic recovery, the substitution of state interventionism with privatization
and deregulation policies was essential (Palermo and Novaro 1996). Given
this background, it now seems appropriate to examine the conditions leading
to such a policy substitution.

Willingness

In Chapter 1, I argued that a political leader's decision to engage in policy substitution can take place under certain conditions. I then used the concepts of willingness and opportunity to refer to these conditions. In turn, a leader's willingness is shaped by both pragmatic and ideological factors. How do these concepts fit the case of Argentina under Menem?

Ideologically, there is no doubt that Menem was the typical conservative politician of the Argentine north-west (Borón 1991; Cerruti 1993). In fact, if urban Peronism found its strongest support in the working class, in rural areas like La Rioja it was a considerably more conservative phenomenon based upon traditional political, religious, and social values.[5]

During his Presidential campaign Menem had promised 'to change history' and, once in office, it became clear that he wanted to reshape Peronism according to his own political agenda. Thus, the old populist movement would become loyal to him rather than to Perón (Di Tella 1990; Moreno 1991). By 1991, Menemism was increasingly replacing Peronism in the political discourse of both the administration and the Peronist party. The President himself put it, 'Current Peronism is a totally updated Peronism. . . . If the world changes, the political parties must change. I would be a fool or a slow-witted person if I wanted to practice in 1991 the Peronism practiced in the 1940s.'[6] Menem, in another public speech paraphrasing Lenin's famous statement about Marxism, reiterated, 'Menemism is the highest stage of Peronism' (Cerruti and Ciancaglini 1992: 124). Thus, Menem's strategy aimed at forging a new conservative alliance with big domestic capital and conservative parties from Buenos Aires and other provinces of the country at the expense of unionism, the strongest and best organized group within the Peronist movement (Landi and Cavarozzi 1991: 18).

The emasculation of Peronist unionism, through privatization, became a crucial element in Menem's plans to consolidate his own power within the Peronist movement (Palermo and Novaro 1996: 20). Historically, unionism had been the backbone of Perón's movement. Both during Perón's exile (1955–73) and after his death (1974), Peronist union bosses attempted to exercise their hegemony over the movement at the expense of party politicians (governors and legislators). Not surprisingly, union bosses like Lorenzo Miguel, Luis Barrionuevo, and Jorge Triaca were instrumental in running and financing the Presidential campaigns of 1983 and 1989, respectively (McGuire 1997). Yet although Menem was elected with labor support, he had no intention of allowing powerful union bosses to become part of the decision-making process, as many of them had anticipated (namely, Miguel of the Metalworkers' Union and Saúl Ubaldini, leader of the CGT, the equivalent of the AFL-CIO in the United States). Indeed, a policy of privatization could weaken the bargaining power of unions both economically and politically, as was the case in Chile and Great Britain. Thus, it is plausible to argue that, like Pinochet in Chile, Menem found in privatization a policy with an affinity to his own goals.

Ultimately, Menem substituted state intervention with state divestiture to achieve essentially the same goal as Perón, the consolidation of his own power. However, according to Iazzetta (1996), while the initial decision may have been dictated more by default than by conviction, the determination with which Menem pursued privatization throughout his first term (1989–95) suggests that, as time went on, he embraced the new economic philosophy. He explained, '[I] have adopted privatization because [I] am in favor of a modern and efficacious State, that will no longer be the shelter of paralyzing bureaucracies.'[7] On another occasion, he was even more explicit when he said:

Some politicians, political scientists, and union leaders who pretend to keep the old state of affairs have not understood what is going on in the world. And those who do not take into account what is going on in the world will not understand Argentina ... There are many political costs but this president, and friend of yours, takes absolute and sole responsibility for the costs and risks that this change imposes, because the president is not thinking about next year's elections but rather about the next generation ... make no mistake because there is no possibility to go back.[8]

Statements of this kind, which Menem reiterated particularly early in his first administration when reforms were slow in producing results, led a respected economist like Canitrot (1993: 91) to conclude that Menem's privatization was, 'driven by an ideological credo bent on the destruction of the core of the corporatist system that was built in Argentina since the end of the First World War'. As the quote above may suggest, it is also likely that Menem saw neo-conservative economic thinking as a means to redefine and infuse his plans with new ideas for reshaping society and politics in a way that would consolidate his power for many years to come (Palermo and Novaro 1996). In August 1994, with the consent of Raúl Alfonsín, Peronists and Radicals agreed to amend the Constitution to allow Menem to run for re-election in 1995; although the term in office was reduced from six to four years.[9] In sum, it is likely that Menem perceived free market policies and privatization as closely attuned to his pragmatic goals and conservative ideas, but it is much more doubtful that he was a conservative ideologue à la Thatcher.

The government attempted popular capitalism when it sold its shares in the largest companies that sprung from the privatization of ENTel and the oil company Yacimientos Petroliferos Fiscales (YPF). On both occasions the floating of the shares in the Buenos Aires stock market was oversubscribed and the government earned much more than the initial forecasts had anticipated.[10] However, this was an option available only to these two large privatizations. It also seemed to be dictated not by ideological considerations (spreading ownership) but, rather, by many foreign investment funds' interest in lucrative markets like telecommunications, petroleum, and gas.

However, pragmatic factors were clearly more relevant in Menem's willingness to privatize. As governor, Menem had built his personal power by creating an extensive patronage network based upon political clienteles to which he gave state jobs and contracts in return for electoral support (Cerruti 1993). In a poor province like La Rioja, with scarce economic resources and a weak diversification of business activities, government is at the same time the largest employer and investor. This enables a governor to manipulate it to his or her own benefit. Menem's 'statism' and anti-privatization positions in the mid-1980s were exemplified by the following statements:

Now it is fashionable to say that 'it is necessary to shrink the State in order to make the Nation great again'. This was Martínez de Hoz's point of view. [However,] in the end what they did was to downgrade the Nation like never before and leave our economy in the hands of the multinationals. In countries like ours, the State must direct the national economy. This is the justicialist philosophy, which makes the man the brother of his fellow man; unlike [conservative] liberalism that only makes a man the enemy of his fellow man.[11]

Some solve everything very easily: they want to privatize companies and shed 100,000 public employees. They do not think about the social cost of this kind of action, about the unemployment that this action would create . . . Today some pretend that we privatize the basic elements of our economy; that we must eliminate deficit-ridden companies and those that are engaged in activities superfluous for the Nation. I agree. However, before saying that our large enterprises are deficit-ridden, let us try to administer them well and with an Argentine sense of purpose. (Béliz 1986)

Menem's social conservatism, characteristically populist, relied heavily on personal charisma. He adopted an almost messianic style during the 1989 Presidential campaign. He toured the country with a mobile home renamed 'Menemovil' and successfully portrayed himself as 'a man of the people', the defender of the poor and underprivileged, running against the corrupt party system.[12] One of his favorite slogans during the campaign was, 'Follow me, I am not going to betray you!' Menem's electoral platform called for a 'productive revolution', a nebulous concept mixing issues like economic independence from foreign countries and multinationals, industrialization, workers' rights, human rights, and the creation of a social democracy (Menem and Duhalde 1989). However, the May 1989 presidential victory quickly appeared to have been an easy task compared to the problems confronting the incoming Peronist administration. The Alfonsín transition team quickly informed Menem that he was going to inherit a bankrupt country. Hyperinflation broke out in the following months of June and July, with retail prices soaring to 100 per cent and 200 per cent respectively. The situation was aggravated by a fiscal deficit amounting to 15 per cent of the GDP, a high internal debt subsidized through extremely costly interest rates at a short maturity, a foreign debt of $60 billion whose interest payments had been stopped in 1988, and a severe capital flight. Moreover, Argentina's international reputation had been tarnished due to the inability of the Alfonsín administration to fulfill its obligations with foreign banks and international lending institutions. This happened at a time when foreign capital was sorely needed and the country's investment-risk rating had become one of the worst in the world.[13]

In the weeks preceding his inauguration (Menem assumed power six months beforehand) the new President-elect realized that four decades of socioeconomic instability had made Perón's socially minded conservatism obsolete. In other words, traditional Peronism could no longer work for Menem as the Argentine state was simply insolvent. In addition, it became evident that the President-elect, despite his campaign promises had never developed a serious economic plan, nor had he assembled a team of qualified economists to do so. Menem was caught in dire straits. He desperately needed foreign aid and investments to revitalize an economy that had grown at about one per cent annually since 1975. He and his closest advisers clearly understood that, in order to receive a substantial reduction of the country's debt under the auspices of the Brady Plan, Argentina had to first regain the support of the United States, the IMF, the World Bank, and the European Economic Community.[14] Testifying before the Bicameral Commission on Privatization in 1990, Minister of Public Works and Services Roberto Dromi described Argentina's state of prostration in dealing with foreign governments and bankers as follows:

[Ours is] a country that is internationally disqualified, *on its knees*, *shamefully so* . . . our debt . . . forces us to go looking for forgiveness, almost like a beggar . . . I warn you that to find investors here . . . cost the Radical government a lot but is costing us much more, and without investments dear congressmen, without investments we are not going to come out [of the crisis] an [inch].[15]

A policy of privatization, particularly if it was complemented with a stringent stabilization plan was aimed at accomplishing the following goals:

1. The recovery of internal and external public credit worthiness that had deteriorated since the inception of the debt crisis in 1982.
2. Complete re-establishment of relations with multilateral lending institutions.
3. An Extended Fund Facility agreement with the IMF.
4. Sustained improvement on the conditions for the new placements of debt.
5. The restructuring and reduction of the external public debt through the Brady Plan.
6. The use of debt-equity swaps at nominal value to diminish the country's foreign debt.
7. The recovery of short, medium, and long-term solvency of the state.[16]

Menem understood that there was no longer time nor margin either for experiments or easy talks and synthesized in his mind those that would be the fundamental decisions of his government: give the green light to the alliance with Bunge & Born and with the liberal conservatives who seemed to have the economic answers that he lacked and knew how to open the doors to bring the support of the United States; severe the alliance with the recalcitrant CGT headed by Saúl Ubaldini and return to a policy of government manipulation of unionism.   (Cerruti and Ciancaglini 1992: 97)

Indeed, not only could a policy of privatization be supported by multilateral lending agencies, foreign governments, and creditors, but also served the purpose of improving the business climate. It could convince both domestic and foreign entrepreneurs that it was once again safe to invest in Argentina, and new investments in turn could alleviate high unemployment caused by the recession and thus turn the economy around (Landi and Cavarozzi 1991: 23). In the weeks prior to his inauguration, Menem and his advisers met with representatives from the largest domestic conglomerates in order to convince them that Peronism was the only political force capable of privatizing and downsizing the state, controlling salaries, and ending union unrest. Menem, aware of how the domestic conglomerates had sabotaged the economic policies of the last two years of the Alfonsín administration, decided to avoid his predecessor's mistakes. He stated plainly, 'Alfonsín in the end quarrelled with everyone and I am not going to do the same' (Cerruti and Ciancaglini 1992: 67). Thus, in what constituted a watershed in Argentine history, Menem turned the traditional confrontation between Peronism and big domestic capital into an alliance for profit. He had the votes and the political power, while big capital had the money and the international connections to revive economic activity; together they could strike a deal (Majul 1993 and 1994).

Privatization, in addition to stimulating investments, was expected to help reduce the external debt and the fiscal deficit. In the mid-1960s, the prices charged by PEs in the public utility sector began to fall behind operating costs considerably.[17] The military regime (1976–83) attempted to bypass the problem by encouraging PEs to contract large loans abroad. This strategy proved disastrous. According to Pirker (1991: 82), between 1980 and 1989 the total external debt of PEs in current US dollars rose from $7.8 billion to $16.4 billion, a cumulative increase of 106 per cent, at a rate of 8.4 per cent annually. Other studies reached the conclusion that PEs increased Argentina's foreign debt by $29 billion in 1991 current dollars (Bour 1993: 226). The oil giant YPF was the largest debtor of these companies (see Table 3.1). The selling of unprofitable state companies, whose estimated deficit in 1989 alone was $5.5 billion, would stop the government financing of money-losing firms, thus relieving such a burden from the state budget.[18] Its proceeds would go to refurbishing the empty coffers of the treasury by bridging the fiscal gap and reducing the principal of the external debt through debt-equity swap operations (Keifman 1991: 211).

TABLE 3.1. *Argentina: Foreign Debt by Company in 1980, 1985, and 1989*

Company	1980		1985		1989	
	US$ million	% share	US$ million	% share	US$ million	% share
YPF	2,906.0	36.93	4,684.0	35.30	5,604.0	34.49
Gas	452.3	5.75	1,849.6	13.94	2,405.7	14.81
YCF	118.0	1.50	179.0	1.37	222.6	1.37
Water & Electricity	1,496.6	19.02	2,180.0	16.43	2,613.0	16.08
SEGBA	661.2	8.40	724.8	5.46	783.6	4.82
Hidronor	281.6	3.58	652.0	4.91	1,120.6	6.90
FFAA	439.5	5.58	1,101.4	8.30	966.1	5.95
Airlines	515.5	6.55	826.6	6.23	773.0	4.76
AGP	33.0	0.42	9.4	0.07	4.1	0.03
Elma	663.5	8.43	446.2	3.36	957.7	5.89
ENTel	293.0	3.72	608.0	4.58	790.2	4.86
Encotel	9.3	0.12	7.0	0.05	8.6	0.04
TOTAL	7,869.5	100.00	13,268.0	100.00	16,249.2	100.00

Source: Sindicatura General de la Nación.

Privatization was an essential tool in the administration's efforts to rationalize state operations, as the government could assign to the private sector the provision of public services that it was no longer able to afford. To address the problem posed by the large debts that PEs contracted in the late 1970s, subsequent administrations imposed drastic cutbacks across the board. These reductions negatively affected new investments, which during the 1984–9 period alone declined by 17.8 per cent (Pirker 1991: 80). This decrease, in turn, led to a sharp deterioration of public service provision (Menem and Dromi 1990). Generally speaking, well before Menem took office, forceful arguments were made from some quarters of Argentine society that a policy of divestiture would increase economic efficiency after decades of devastating government interference in the marketplace. It would end political manipulation by government officials, remove bureaucratic red tape and administrative chaos, lower production costs, and eliminate the endemic corruption that characterized PEs (FIEL 1987; Bour 1993: 226–7).

There is little doubt that Menem used privatization to reward his supporters. Earlier we saw that he tried to draft business support for his policies. For their part, the largest domestic conglomerates (that is, economic groups involved in various business activities), once it was clear that Menem was going to win the presidency, generously funded his campaign in return for future economic payoffs. It is not mere coincidence that such conglomerates later played an important role in the first round of privatizations, when they acquired PEs in the most lucrative markets under monopolistic or oligopolistic conditions (Schvarzer 1992). Equally important is the fact that the regulatory agencies that theoretically were supposed to control these newly created monopolies or oligopolies actually were not set up before, as most experts suggest, but after the privatization of PEs (Azpiazu and Vispo 1994). In so doing, these regulatory agencies found themselves in a de facto situation where the new private owners had already drawn up the rules of the game (including new prices) to their advantage with the tacit consent of the executive (Gerchunoff and Cánovas 1995). According to Majul, the amount of business seized through privatization by the largest Argentine conglomerates was directly correlated to their 'donations' to Menem's campaign fund in 1989.

In the privatization [process] there were concessions so [overt] that no one cared to analyze them. The tariffs charged by the Pérez Companc group in Edesur, Metrogás, and in Gas Ban Natural, and those charged by the Soldati group in Aguas Argentina are all very high and guarantee [these groups] millions [of US dollars] in profits. It is a brutal transfer of resources, a government gift.[19]

Allegedly, in the months preceding Menem's successful re-election bid in 1995, the largest conglomerates generously contributed to his campaign.[20] When in March of that year the Central Bank suffered heavy currency losses, as people began to buy dollars for fear of an imminent devaluation, the country's largest business groups bought $1 billion worth of pesos in a show of support for the administration's policies.

The positive results evidenced by privatization policies in a number of European countries, Mexico, and neighboring Chile may also have had some impact on Menem's pragmatic considerations. Finally, the failure of neo-Keynesian stabilization efforts under Alfonsín, together with the collapse of the socialist economies in Eastern Europe and Cuba, left neo-conservative economic policies as the only credible alternative.

Opportunity

As proposed in Chapter 1, although willingness is necessary to initiate a privatization process, it must be accompanied by an opportunity to do so. Three factors were emphasized as crucial in creating the opportunity to privatize: (1) the availability of investors who are interested in taking over PEs; (2) a favorable public mood; and (3) international pressure and financial support.

In terms of availability of investors, we have seen that under the Alfonsín administration the Scandinavian airline SAS and Telefónica of Spain had expressed interest in acquiring management control and minority shares in Aerolíneas Argentina and ENTel respectively. It is true that the Menem administration initially found itself considerably in a much weaker bargaining position with potential buyers than did Alfonsín as a result of the hyperinflations of 1989 and 1990. However, it is also true that many foreign and domestic companies expressed their interest in the privatization of potentially lucrative state monopolies, like telephones, airlines, oil, and electricity (Bozas and Kaifman 1991).

Privatization became a hot subject during the 1989 presidential campaign. It was proposed by the conservative UCD of Alvaro Alsogaray as well as by the Radical party candidate, Eduardo Angeloz (the constitution barred Alfonsín from running for a second consecutive term at the time). Yet it was not only conservative politicians and some business circles that supported privatization, but also many common citizens tired of the poor performance of state-run monopolies in public services. According to Gerchunoff and Coloma (1993: 253), 'Following the hyperinflation in 1989 and a drop in GDP for three consecutive years, [privatization] became as popular as nationalization had been in the 1940s. The prevailing view was that the public enterprises' problems would disappear if they were transferred to the private sector.' These conclusions were confirmed by studies based upon survey research. Mora y Araujo's (1993) public opinion data, for instance, showed that by the late 1980s a large number of Argentines had switched from supporting *dirigismo* and

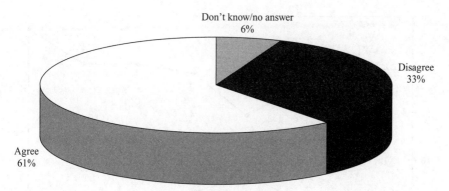

FIG. 3.4. Argentina: Opinion Poll about Privatization in 1994
Source: SOCMERC, poll taken in metropolitan Buenos Aires.

government ownership of key economic sectors to pro-market ideas. According to Mora y Araujo, in the eyes of many frustrated citizens, state intervention, instead of creating a fairer society, had led to a host of new privileges
whose costs were dumped on everyone else. People 'wanted an economy
capable of producing more, not distributing better' (Mora y Araujo 1991).
They wanted less state intervention and union power and hoped that market-
oriented economic policies, including privatization, could address the problems of economic stagnation and inefficiency. 'The privatization plan was
perceived by the population as the milestone of the economic reform program. Since its inception . . . the privatization philosophy did count . . . with
a large popular support' (Mora y Araujo 1993: 316). Support for privatization gained momentum beginning with the unraveling of the Austral Plan in
1987 and peaked in December of 1991. The approval rate of privatization
was very strong from 1989 through 1991, and remained fairly steady well into
1994 (Fig. 3.4).[21] In 1993, more detailed surveys in metropolitan Buenos Aires
showed growing consensus over the privatization of public services (Fig. 3.5;
Table 3.2). Thus, there seemed to be widespread consensus, at least in the
Buenos Aires area, that the private sector could provide services better than
the state. As noted in Chapter 2, Alfonsín in 1983 had gained the presidency
by portraying himself as the defender of democracy and human rights. These
were the dominant issues at a time when Argentina was coming out of a
bloody military dictatorship. However, by the mid-1980s people's main concern had shifted to fighting inflation. Meanwhile, Alfonsín kept emphasizing
democracy and human rights, which by then had become of secondary importance.[22] In a country where the President's approval rating is 'inflation-
dependent', Alfonsín's inability or unwillingness to change policies according
to the new public mood meant political suicide for him and his party.

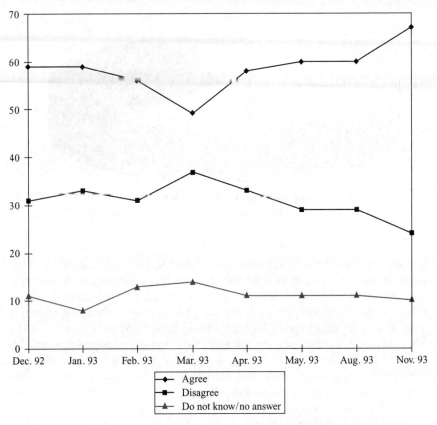

FIG. 3.5. Argentina: Public Opinion on the Country's Convenience to Privatize (%)
Source: SOCMERC, poll taken in metropolitan Buenos Aires.

Menem, unlike Alfonsín, apparently was very sensitive to public opinion trends, understood the changed public mood and was determined not to repeat the same mistake (Natale 1993: 30). He perceived that the hyperinflation outbursts of 1989 and 1990 had increased popular demand for bold, if not autocratic leadership, even at the cost of measures that a few years earlier would have been unthinkable. By the same token, years of polarized conflict pitting against one another labor unions and business organizations had seemingly created deep internal divisions and discredited them before public opinion, thus weakening their bargaining power vis-à-vis the executive. As Palermo and Novaro (1996: 236) noted, the 'virtue of hyperinflation—in contrast with the previous attempts at economic stabilization—was its persuasive role as it created a fertile ground for a political initiative aimed at creating a collective identity' behind a strong charismatic leadership.

TABLE 3.2. *Argentina: Public Opinion over the Privatization by Sector in 1993*

Company	It was good that privatization occurred						Privatization was well carried out					
	Mar. 93	Apr. 93	May 93	Jul. 93	Aug. 93	Nov. 93	Mar. 93	Apr. 93	May 93	Jul. 93	Aug. 93	Nov. 93
TV stations	61	71	66	72	65	79	28	41	40	43	38	47
ENTel	51	64	63	63	60	78	19	26	29	29	28	32
Electricity	47	56	57	57	55	72	15	23	26	26	24	31
Railways	47	53	56	56	52	68	13	13	18	20	17	24
Highways	43	48	45	54	48	59	12	14	18	19	18	23
Water	43	50	52	57	56	67	15	17	24	23	25	29
Somisa	40	48	49	56	48	63	9	15	16	19	18	22
Aerolineas A.	41	54	52	54	48	67	7	11	14	15	11	20
Gas del Estado	47	53	54	57	53	71	15	23	25	27	24	30
YPF	37	n.a.	n.a.	51	48	65	15	n.a.	n.a.	23	22	29

Source: SOCMERC, polls taken in Buneos Aires and its metropolitan area.

Quite intelligently, Menem linked hyperinflation to ISI and protectionism while depicting privatization and deregulation as the indispensable antidotes to bring about economic stability. From the start of his first mandate the President portrayed himself as the sole interpreter of the popular will for change as opposed to the narrow interests of labor and business lobbies that, according to the President, had driven the country to the brink of collapse.

Menem reasoned that, if successful, the cost of his market reform agenda would be outweighed by the benefits of economic stability. He capitalized on this widespread sense of despair (Canitrot 1993). He knew that structural reforms were the only solution and that, if his gamble paid off, he could emerge from the crisis in a remarkably stronger political position.

International pressure was intense, as was previously noted. Foreign governments, as well as multilateral lending agencies and creditor banks, had made clear to the Menem administration that further financial aid was contingent upon the adoption of a strict stabilization plan with structural reforms. The Bush administration's policy for debt reduction, framed within the Brady Plan, was the clearest example of the industrialized nations' approach to resolving the Third World debt. Some macroeconomic results were required in order to start negotiations for debt restructuring. However, multilateral lending agencies also provided incentives for structural reforms through loans aimed at: (1) hiring foreign and domestic consultants to assist in the management of privatization; and (2) providing financial support for the downsizing and reorganization of PEs in preparation for their sale. Such loans proved crucial to sweeten the bitter pill of the economic adjustment process. Between 1991 and 1995, the World Bank granted Argentina loans for a total of $1.5 billion.[23] The first of this loans issued in 1991, the Public Enterprise Reform Adjustment Loan (Peral I) of $300 million, helped the restructuring of PEs in the telecommunication, railway, and mining sectors. Half of this money was used for early retirement programs in PEs slated for privatization. By 1995, 114,538 employees of PEs had taken advantage of early retirement incentives.[24] The World Bank also provided a 'technical assistance and support' loan of $23 million in August 1991, so that the Argentine government could engage the services of international consulting firms that specialized in privatization.[25] Subsequently, in 1992, the World Bank approved $300 million for the Peral II, which helped restructuring PEs in the defense sector. In 1993, an additional loan of $400 million went to the reform of the government owned banking system.

These loans were made in collaboration with the IDB, which disbursed an additional $325 million to support the reform of the public administration and $200 million for the adjustment programs carried out by local government. To complement this effort, in 1989 the International Financial Corporation (IFC), a multilateral institution that since 1956 has promoted private investments in Third World countries, created two corporations (Argentine

Private Development Trust Co. Limited and Corporación de Inversiones y Privatización S. A.) with the Midland Bank, the Bank of Tokyo, and the Banco Río de la Plata to finance private companies, both domestic and foreign, which were willing to participate in the privatization process. Following the approval of the Convertibility Law, the IMF granted Argentina a stand-by loan of $1.4 billion, in July 1991. The agreement obliged the Menem administration to generate a fiscal surplus of $4.9 billion between July 1991 and July 1992 (including $1.7 billion in privatization receipts) and to disburse $6.3 billion in debt payments.[26] Although not all these targets were met during these periods, and in subsequent agreements, the multilateral agencies financial and political support continued unabated well into 1998, when the IMF approved a three-year $2.8 billion extended facility for Argentina. In fact, under Menem, for the multilateral lending agencies Argentina had become a model used to convince reluctant governments around the world to act likewise.[27] Thus, the three factors crucial in creating the opportunity to privatize were either present by the time the Menem administration embarked on the divestiture process or materialized later resulting from the government's structural reform program.

Implementation

Government Capabilities

The Argentine privatization program can be divided into three broad phases. The first one, between 1989 and 1991, used proceeds to reduce the foreign debt. During this time, the tariffs of PEs up for privatization in public utilities increased sharply in some cases, and regulatory frameworks were poorly designed. In the second phase, from March 1991 to 1994, financial goals were of secondary importance, as fiscal problems came under control. As a result, the administration paid greater attention to allocative efficiency concerns, by creating a more competitive environment prior to privatization (i.e. electricity) and designing some sound regulatory frameworks. It is during this period that Argentina was able to sign an agreement with its creditors according to the Brady Plan clauses. The third stage begins in early 1995 and would continue throughout 1998. As Argentina was hit hard by the consequences of the Mexican crisis of December 1995, financial concerns became paramount again. Accordingly, the sale of the remaining PEs and government shares in privatized companies became an important means to bridge the government deficit. Coincidentally, this last phase marked a step back to the old problems of the first one, that is, political manipulations, poorly designed regulatory frameworks, and the executive's strong propensity to bypass congressional and legal roadblocks by pushing privatization through decrees.

Keeping this sequence in mind, I will now examine the implementation of the Argentine privatization effort. The framework of analysis discussed in Chapter 1 proposed three sets of factors affecting the policy implementation process: government capabilities, political responses, and technical difficulties.

Regarding government capabilities, government cohesiveness plagued the privatization effort for most of its first phase (August 1989–February 1991), although the administration made a concerted effort to shelter the policy from public scrutiny by removing those public officials who voiced their concerns.[28] Interestingly, despite the fact that the administration took charge of the legislative agenda, the cabinet experienced considerable infighting over policy control and procedures. Initially, the policy followed a fairly decentralized scheme, with government-appointed trustees in charge of individual privatizations under the supervision of José Roberto Dromi, Minister of Public Works and Services, who designed its legal framework as mandated by the State Reform Law and the Law of Economic Emergency. Dromi was a well-known corporate lawyer and university professor, and a former aid of Senator Eduardo Menem, the President's brother. He prepared the speeches against the privatization plan of the Alfonsín administration that the senator from La Rioja pronounced in Congress in the late 1980s. In 1988, Dromi openly attacked the partial privatization of Aerolíneas Argentinas (Blanco 1993: 29). Once he became minister, Dromi not only did not make any excuses for his past stands but wanted to privatize everything, at any cost, as quickly as possible (Natale 1993: 45).

Sharp disagreements soon emerged between Dromi, on the one hand, and Economy Minister Erman González and ENTel's trustee María Julia Alsogaray, on the other (González and Alsogaray would later have differences of their own). González, for example, strived to make the privatization effort compatible with the stabilization programs he carried out between December 1989 and February 1991. This implied greater financial control over Dromi's ministry and over the use of privatization revenues. It also meant that the Public Works and Services Ministry had to be subordinated to the Economy Ministry, but Dromi was able to maintain his autonomy for most of his tenure. Meanwhile, Alsogaray had a big feud with Dromi over which foreign investor was best suited for the privatization of ENTel. Whereas Alsogaray favored Bell Atlantic, Dromi and the Foreign Ministry supported the bid of a French–Italian consortium.[29] Bell Atlantic's withdrawal from the competition eased tensions later on, but the feud itself testified to deep cleavages within the administration.[30]

Dromi eventually came under fire for alleged cases of corruption in the privatization of the two largest enterprises (ENTel and Aerolíneas Argentinas). In February 1991, and again in 1992, he was officially charged by federal prosecutors with fraud and abuse of authority while in public office in two separate incidents. Dromi was forced to resign as a result and his ministry was merged into the Economy Ministry in February 1991.[31] This allowed the Economy Ministry, by then under Cavallo's leadership, to gain direct control over the design and implementation of the second round of privatizations scheduled to begin in late 1991. The verticalization process that ensued affected the internal organization of the divestiture program. The micromanagement of individual privatizations was put under the control sector-specific bureaucratic units within the Ministry of the Economy. Their activities were coordinated by the undersecretariat for privatization, which responded directly to the Minister of the Economy.

Cavallo's managerial style, coupled with a series of measures aimed at further deregulation and opening the economy to foreign competition, gave the overall impression of greater unity of purpose and technical expertise of his team in carrying out its structural reforms. To accomplish this goal, Cavallo brought along about 200 trusted economists and technocrats and placed them in the most sensitive posts of his ministry and other agencies (Palermo and Novaro 1996).[32] Moreover, both the Minister and his closest aids had excellent contacts with domestic entrepreneurs, international bankers, and officers of multilateral lending agencies, which facilitated the administration's relations with the parties just mentioned. None the less, even Cavallo would have failed like many of his predecessors had Menem withered in the face of mounting opposition, the most dangerous of which came from Peronist legislators and cabinet members who resented being left out from the most important decisions affecting their political clienteles. The President's strong leadership style should be credited for keeping the privatization policy on track, despite many scandals and reversals that plagued his administration.

Technical and administrative capacity, along with bureaucratic cooperation, seemed to be missing in the first two years of the privatization effort. The need to act quickly, coupled with inexperience in dealing with the complexity of privatizing large monopolies, partially explain the many errors made during the preparation of several transfers. The squabbles among Dromi, González, and María Julia Alsogaray mentioned above also point to a lack of cooperation among ministries. Realizing these problems Cavallo not only centralized the decision-making process affecting technical matters but, by December 1992, he also gained complete control over government expenditures, including those of PEs. As noted, the ministry of the economy under Cavallo experienced a substantial overhaul. More qualified people were hired from the private sector to improve the policy design and give more credibility to the reform effort. Moreover, the World Bank's advising role increased substantially, after Cavallo took office, primarily through the hiring of foreign consulting firms.[33]

O'Donnell's (1994) 'delegative democracy', discussed in Chapter 1, seems to fit Menem's approach to problem solving quite closely. In fact, the emasculation of state institutions was a crucial step in allowing quick implementation of the privatization program. Consistently from the onset, the Menem administration made an explicit effort to prevent Congress, the judiciary, and the government bureaucracy from derailing state divestiture as was the case with Alfonsín. Claiming the need to act quickly in the face of an unprecedented economic crisis, Menem forced Congress to delegate to him the authority to privatize via decree. The Bicameral Commission on Privatization had no veto powers as it could only demand information from the executive about forthcoming privatizations and express non-binding opinions (Natale 1993: 33). For instance, in October 1990 the Bicameral Commission requested that the sale of Aerolíneas Argentinas be annulled as it was marred by irregularities. The commission's position was supported by the agency monitoring the fiscal accounts of state enterprises, the Sindicatura General de Impresas Públicas (SIGEP). Yet, the executive ignored both and proceeded with the sale that ultimately resulted in disastrous problems that the commission and the SIGEP had feared. In other cases, like the privatization of the highways and the railways, the commission's criticisms had some effects, but this was more the exception than the rule.

In the first phase of privatization, during the Dromi-González era, the government carried out divestitures through executive decrees as contemplated by laws 23.696 and 26.967. When Cavallo took office he promised to make the process more transparent and involve Congress in the final decision. The sales of YPF, Gas del Estado, and SEGBA were executed through special laws approved by Congress.[34] Yet, even in these cases where Congress did vote, it did so quickly without any real debate. There was no discussion over the goals and means of these privatizations because the Peronists in Congress wanted to rubber-stamp whatever Menem recommended (Natale 1993: 31). In many cases, even under Cavallo, privatizations were implemented via the so-called 'decrees of necessity and urgency'. Through such decrees the executive assumes legislative powers without congressional approval. From 1853 to 1989 they were adopted in twenty-five instances. Menem, between 1990 and 1994, used them over 300 times, and they continued to be used in highly controversial privatizations like those of the postal service (1997) and the airports (1998). Equally important is the fact that although the Argentine constitution restricts the use of such decrees to constitutional and national security matters, Menem invoked them primarily for administrative purposes, thus running afoul with the spirit of the constitution (Goretti and Ferreira Rubio 1994). In addition, to prevent Congress from changing important legislation affecting the privatization program, Menem also made an unprecedented use of total and partial presidential vetoes (Mustapich and Ferretti 1994).

Some of Cavallo's aids justified the frequent use of necessity and urgency decrees in the following terms, '[The] use of these decrees obviated the need to go to Congress where special interests could kill or slow down deregulatory actions' (Rojo and Hoberman 1994: 167). Cavallo himself admitted that without the power of decrees he could have accomplished only 20 per cent of his reforms.[35] For the Minister the end justified the means, even if in the process constitutional 'formalities' were violated.[36]

Menem also undermined the independence of the judiciary to prevent enemies of privatization from appealing to federal courts to uphold the executive's decisions (Verbitsky 1993). The first target of this strategy was the Tribunal de Cuentas, responsible for monitoring the Treasury's operations. Subsequently, in an unconstitutional manner, the President removed the chief of the National Court of Administrative Investigations, leaving the court practically inoperative. Then, in April 1990, the President proceeded to 'pack' the Supreme Court with government backers, by increasing the number of justices from five to nine, with the approval of the Peronist-controlled Congress. One of the new justices, Rodolfo Barra, prior to his appointment had been a close associate of Dromi in the Ministry of Public Works and Services. Barra contributed in drafting the legal framework of the controversial highways privatization. In 1990, Deputy Moisés Fontela denounced some irregularities regarding the impending privatization of Aerolíneas Argentinas before a federal judge, Oscar Garzón Funes. Fontela asked for the suspension of the sale. Barra tried to convince the judge to reject the case, upon Dromi's insistence. Failing, Dromi asked the Supreme Court to deal directly with the case due to the 'institutional gravity' that could result from the ruling of a lower court. The Supreme Court accepted Dromi's petition and overruled the jurisdiction of the federal judge by claiming the case for itself (de Michele 1993). This extraordinary measure, called *per saltum* procedure, had never before been used in Argentine history and had no constitutional grounds for application in that specific case (Carrió and Garay 1991: 31). Unsurprisingly, in a few minutes, the Supreme Court ruled against Fontela's request and the Aerolíneas Argentina's privatization was saved. Later, the Supreme Court sanctioned the constitutionality of privatization via decree, without Congressional approval, under the State Reform Law and the Law of Economic Emergency. Explaining the legal philosophy of the Supreme Court under Menem, Barra stated that, 'The [Supreme Court] has to look after the policies of the government so that they will be juridically well [designed], without obstructing the [government's] action' (Blanco 1993: 56). Subsequently, comparing the decision of the Brazilian Supreme Court to stop some of President Collor de Mello's privatizations with the Argentine Supreme Court action, Barra commented that the latter's position in the case of Aerolíneas Argentinas rescued the whole policy from failure (Blanco 1993: 57).

Speed was also a major feature of Menem's privatization effort. The President selected privatization as the testing ground for his administration. His decision to privatize first Aerolíneas Argentinas and ENTel had a clear political content: he wanted to prove that he could succeed where Alfonsín had failed (Petrecolla *et al.* 1993). Menem's repeated pledge that there would be no PEs left by 1992 and his stubbornness in carrying out some transfers, like those of Aerolíneas Argentinas and the highways, which were clearly headed for trouble, were meant to earn credibility for his administration, both at home and abroad. Moreover, Menem's privatization was a clear break with the past as it aimed at dismantling the entrepreneurial state and weakening the socioeconomic groups that had benefitted from it; to do so effectively it was indispensable to act immediately before an anti-privatization lobby could mobilize both in and outside Congress (Rojo and Hoberman 1994: 168). Indeed, Menem's insistence to have all transfers completed by 1992, regardless, was the reason for the hurried decisions and numerous mistakes made by the government officials during the process (Natale 1993: 256). Retrospectively, such worries were well justified, as by the end of Menem's second term in 1999 political opposition to the remaining privatizations, as well as his economic reforms in general, had intensified in Congress, across opposition parties (as well as his own), and within the labor movement.

Political Responses

Menem's greatest accomplishment was his ability to succeed where all his predecessors had failed, that is, making the implementation of market reforms politically feasible over a decade. To do so, his strategy was twofold. On the one hand, he had to lure into his new coalition political and economic groups that had traditionally been bitter enemies of Peronism. On the other hand, he had to keep opposition to his reform agenda within his own party at a minimum to retain a majority in Congress which, although emasculated in many of its prerogatives, could still present a major stumble block had Peronist defectors and Radicals joined forces.

To achieve the first goal, he successfully diffused traditional cleavages that had plagued Argentina since the 1940s, pitting labor against business, the military against civil society, and Peronists against anti-Peronists. He convincingly argued that he had the solutions to solve Argentina's crisis but he also needed the collaboration of all sectors of society. Those who wanted to help were welcome to do so without necessarily becoming Peronists. Thus, people were asked to back a concrete government program, not a party ideology. Of course, the mediation between the conflicting interests that were about to join in rested upon the charismatic leadership of the President, not government institutions, as noted earlier, since such institutions could slow down or impede the implementation of the program itself.[37]

The policy U-turn came with a change in the coalition supporting presidential policies. Electoral allies like minor center-left and left-wing parties (the Movement for Integration and Development, the Christian Democratic Party, and the Intransigent Party) and some unions, which opposed the new course, were replaced by the conservative political and economic right.

Menem formed a center-right coalition with a long-time enemy of Peronism, Alvaro Alsogaray. Alsogaray, was a former army officer and Minister of the Economy, and leader of the small but influential UCD conservative party. He had vigorously campaigned on a platform calling for orthodox, free-market economic policies during the 1989 presidential race. Once in office, Menem asked Alsogaray to join his administration as presidential adviser for the negotiation of the foreign debt. As noted earlier, Alsogaray's daughter, María Julia, was later appointed trustee of the ENTel state telephone company with the explicit objective to privatize it. Menem, in adopting their agenda, by 1994 had completely co-opted many UCD leaders who abandoned their party to join the Peronists. Adelina D'Alessio de Viola, an influential councilwoman from the Federal District, was one of the many.

The conservative parties of the interior were also brought into Menem's camp. Heavily dependent on federal funds for their provinces' survival, several of these parties agreed to support the executive's policies in Congress in exchange for continued pork-barrel programs. Between 1990 and 1993, this came in the form of a series of 'federal pacts', which bolstered the impoverished finances of local government at a time when the federal bureaucracy was undergoing severe budgetary cuts. Moreover, in 1992 Cavallo, in order to win the support of oil-producing provinces for the privatization of YPF, transferred the ownership of the oil and gas reserves located within each province to local government upon expiration of the exploration permits and exploitation concessions to private companies.[38] To appease the general public, the administration made promises (often not kept) to earmark some of the proceeds of privatization for funding social policies previously neglected, like education, health, public housing, and social security (Petrecolla *et al.* 1993).

The bond between Menem and Argentina's largest conglomerates intensified over time. While initially skeptical, big domestic groups (which are family-controlled) eventually established close relationships with Menem. Their strong support for his administration was unmatched even by that which they gave to the military regime (1976–83). This is because privatization provided local conglomerates like Pérez Companc, Techint-Rocca, Bunge & Born, Bridas-Bulgheroni, SOCMA-Macri, Soldati, Loma Negra, Benito Roggio, and Astra-Grüneisen with golden business opportunities (Palermo and Novaro 1996: 169).[39]

Political opposition to privatization came from many quarters of Argentine society; yet, it was largely ineffective. This was due partially to the inability of the heterogenous opposition groups to coalesce into a united front and to the President's ability to divide and rule. Menem, proceeded quickly to mute internal dissent within his own party by threatening to cut off pork-barrel programs that governors and legislators needed to maintain their respective political clienteles. Peronist politicians were left with only two options;

either supporting the President in the hope of reaping some benefits or moving on to the opposition with little chance to alter the course of events. Most of them chose the first one because, as one local boss put it, 'if Menem calls us tomorrow one by one and tells us "shut up and take this" everyone rushes to grab what he can because no one has strong enough individual resources to resist him.'[40] Only eight Peronist legislators broke off with the President and became a focal point of congressional opposition, but theirs remained an isolated case.

Menem, however, was not only careful in putting down internal opposition. He also made an explicit effort to retain the support of the Peronist voters, particularly those coming from the poorer sectors of society in both urban and rural areas. As public opinion polls showed in the late 1980s, these people demanded a sense or direction and an end to the inflationary spiral (Palermo and Novaro 1996). Menem's strong leadership and his ability to put an end to inflation delivered on both fronts, and such popular sectors remained loyal to the President by voting overwhelmingly in his favor in 1995, as demonstrated by electoral returns in poor suburban and rural districts.

Thus, within the Peronist movement, the main potential obstacle to successful privatization was represented by the opposition of the unions whose companies were up for sale. Yet, the union response to privatization was rather divided, which played into Menem's hand. According to Palermo and Novaro (1996), unions followed three different patterns of behavior: tough opposition, collaboration, and negotiation.

Ubaldini, the CGT leader, headed the group of the intransigent unions that from the outset completely repudiated the administration's policy. The 'collaborators' comprised unions whose leaders had been prone to cooperation under the Alfonsín administration, like Jorge Triaca (plastic workers), Roberto García (taxi drivers), and Adolfo Cavalieri (commerce). The 'negotiators' responded primarily to Miguel and his metal workers, one of the most powerful Peronist unions. Their aim was to stay as independent as possible from Menem while striking compromises with the government depending on the situation of the moment.

Menem, proceeded immediately to undermine Ubaldini's authority by giving open support to his rival in the other two groups. By 1990, the CGT had split into two rival organizations, the CGT-Azopardo made up by Ubaldini's loyalists, and the pro-Menem CGT-San Martín. Interestingly, the unions that joined Ubaldini were primarily concentrated in the state sector which was the main target of Menem's restructuring program. Membership in the CGT-San Martín, however, came primarily from unions in the private sector, which were largely unaffected by the privatization policy. Menem kept using a carrot-and-stick approach throughout 1989–98. The carrot came in a variety of forms. Several cooperating union leaders were appointed to government positions, like the leader of the telephone workers Julio Gullian who was appointed secretary of communications. Menem treated unions supporting him favorably when it came to wage negotiations and the transfer of welfare funds from the social security agency to individual union funds (Blake 1994). The government also invited cooperative union leaders from the largest PEs to be part of the committees in charge of the privatization of their companies. Moreover, the government provided some incentives like early retirement programs, re-training programs, and workers' ownership of stock (10 per cent of total) in privatizations affecting large PEs like ENTel, YPF, Gas del Estado, and SEGBA.[41] In some cases, privatization opened up for unions new lucrative business opportunities as they were allowed to set up companies managing the shares transferred to workers.[42]

The stick was used to break strikes of defiant unions by invoking the new legislation, enforced by decree in 1990, regulating the right to strike. The administration adopted massive layoffs affecting employees who had participated in strikes regarded as illegal in the telephone, railway, and oil companies between 1990 and 1991. In some cases, the government even went as far as jailing and starting legal proceedings against some strikers. Menem was also quick in isolating recalcitrant unions from public opinion by using a media campaign in which he accused them of defending only their vested interests as opposed to those of the country.

The administration's tough stance softened labor opposition and dissuaded many unions from striking, as many workers were afraid of losing their jobs in the midst of the deep recession between 1989–90 (Acuña 1994). By 1992, many union leaders who had initially opposed Menem's state-shrinking policies understood that the process was irreversible and it was politically wise to jump on the President's bandwagon before it was too late. A typical example of this 'change of heart' came from José Pedraza, the leader of militant Unión Ferroviaria, which lost thousands of jobs due to privatization, who said, 'The project [of the railway privatization] must be profitable to work out. If it is necessary to close tracks, they must be closed; if it is necessary to lay off half of the personnel before all would lose their job, so be it' (Natale 1993: 260).

Up until 1997, Opposition parties were equally divided and bewildered. With the President using decrees at will, they found themselves powerless as it was impossible to use Congress as a means for checking on the executive's initiatives. The Radicals, the largest minority party, splintered into rival factions which weakened its bargaining position. Angeloz attempted to compromise with Menem, supporting privatization but criticizing the methods used to implement it. Alfonsín instead remained dead set against the President's policies, but Menem easily dismissed his criticisms by simply pointing out that he was trying to rescue the country from the economic disaster that took place under his predecessor. The left was also plagued by internal squabbles, which undermined its credibility.

Private companies that had long enjoyed generous fat government contracts for supplying the bureaucratic apparatus and PEs also rose up in arms. The administration's new policy meant the end of profitable business for many of them. The Menem administration, among other things, repealed old legislation passed in the 1960s by the Radical President Arturo Illia through which domestic companies enjoyed preferential status when bidding for government contracts. This legislation had allowed private companies to sell to the state without competition. According to a 1988 estimate of the Public Works Ministry, this system resulted in a waste of $2 billion a year.[43] None the less, domestic suppliers were ineffective in mounting a persuasive lobbying effort. They were also unable to form an alliance of convenience with the CGT-Azopardo (Landi and Cavarozzi 1991: 24).

The military was considered by many to be a potent deterring factor against Menem's policies, but it remained relatively quiet. Since the early 1920s the military in Argentina had developed companies in key sectors like steel, chemicals, aviation, petroleum, and later nuclear power. Attempts were made to privatize some of these unprofitable companies, mostly controlled by the holding company DGFM during the 1976–83 military regime. These attempts were generally thwarted by nationalistic officers who believed that privatization jeopardized Argentina's national security. None the less, when the Menem administration disclosed its plans to privatize many military properties and companies belonging to the DGFM by 1992, the armed forces' establishment voiced only minor complaints.[44] One reason is that military officers acknowledged that they had badly mismanaged those industries under their direct control.[45] Moreover, the administration promised to allocate part of the revenues from privatization to improving officers' salaries and purchasing badly needed equipment and spare parts (Barham 1991). Equally important was that since withdrawing from power in 1983 the military had fallen into such disrepute that its political leverage had vanished.

Finally, the new conservative coalition forged by Menem gave the President important support at critical times that enabled him to thwart his opposition. An attempt by Ubaldini's CGT-Azopardo to stage a 24-hour general strike against the administration's policies, at the end of March 1990, failed miserably. The anti-government demonstration held in front of Congress by the rebellious unions drew only 60,000 people. Two weeks later Bernardo Neustadt, the host of a popular talk show, and pro-Menem union leader Barrionuevo masterminded a counter-demonstration, which gathered twice as many people as Ubaldini's rally. The difference in support for the two rallies represented both a boost of confidence for the administration and an embarrassment for Ubaldini and his followers. In the years that followed, Neustadt and other television and opinion leaders actively endorsed privatization, thus providing an important means to garner consent within the general public.

Last but not least, as earlier noted, the consistent international support from the United States government, the European Economic Community, the IMF, the IDB, and the World Bank was also instrumental in boosting the credibility of the administration's divestiture program at home. For instance, in July 1997 the IMF decided to enhance Argentina's credit line because of that country's 'good governance' record.[46]

Technical Difficulties

It is here that the Argentine privatization process encountered the greatest setbacks. The program was marred by all kinds of problems, especially under Dromi's leadership. Argentina lacked an expert management agency in privatization like Chile's CORFO (Corporación de Fomento) or Brazil's BNDES (Banco de Desenvolvimento Economico e Social).[47] CORFO and BNDES over the years acquired experience in running state corporations. This experience enabled them to design plans to restructure firms prior to their privatization. Once this was accomplished, they were able to deal with potential private buyers from a position of relative strength. In Argentina, on the other hand, privatization took place almost in an institutional vacuum, granting Dromi extensive discretionary powers. Thus, he was able to cover up many ministerial irregularities by rushing several sales.[48] Many theorists argue that in order to maximize profits PEs should first be reorganized and made profitable to lure potential investors. Contrary to this belief, Dromi decided to sell deficit-ridden companies for less under weak bargaining conditions. He claimed that restructuring would have required too much time and money, neither of which the administration could afford (Galiani and Petrecolla 1999). The overall concern, again, was to act quickly in order to gain credibility with foreign investors, raise cash to finance the fiscal deficit, and preventing the organization of anti-privatization lobbies. Thus, the argument followed that any gradual approach was inoperable given the conditions facing the Menem administration in 1989 (Bour 1993).

In general terms, the Argentine experience differed from those of Mexico and Peru, as Menem preferred to privatize before achieving economic stability, which was attained only after 1991. Another problem arose from the initiation of privatization before, rather than after, the deregulation of the economy, which caused market distortions as bad as the ones the divestiture effort meant to remove (the long-waited deregulation decree came only in October 1991). To overcome the lack of attractiveness of many privatizations, Dromi's strategy provided a number of incentives, in the forms of quasi-rents, that went against criteria of economic efficiency and competition (Petrecolla *et al.* 1993; Azpiazu and Vispo 1994). In fact, the government: (1) allowed the private sector to acquire PEs under monopolistic (commercial air cargo services), or oligopolistic conditions (telecommunications, secondary oil fields, gas, and steel); (2) sharply increased the prices charged by PEs in public utilities prior to the transfer in order to assure the new private owners a substantial profit in the first few years of operation; (3) allowed the new private owners to fix prices and business operations prior to the establishment of regulatory agencies (see above); (4) cut a number of taxes or gave special tax exemptions to the new private owners; and (5) took upon itself most of the debts (save for some labor debts and commercial liabilities) and other financial liabilities incurred by PEs prior to their privatization (Petrecolla *et al.* 1993: 71–2). In light of the government's weak bargaining position and lax regulatory framework, during the first stage of privatization several companies engaged in collusion practices, which resulted in non-competitive bids. In the privatizations of the petrochemicals, television and radio stations, railways, and the highways, for instance, it seemed highly suspicious that only one bidder offered an amount just above the minimum set by the government. This turned the bidding process into a de facto direct sale.[49]

Dromi made an effort to diffuse widespread criticisms triggered by this situation. In the case of public utilities under concession, he attached both quantitative and qualitative requirements to the contracts of transfer. These requirements fixed amounts of investments and quality standards for the provision of services (telecommunications, highways, gas, and electricity). Yet, it soon became clear that the weak status of the regulatory agencies made the enforcement of such requirements difficult if not impossible (in the case of air passenger cargo Dromi did not create a regulatory agency).

Other problems were typical of privatization policies abroad. One of them involved market failures. On several occasions the government was stuck with a single bidder (Aerolíneas Argentinas, railways, highways) or found no bidders at all (railways). In several cases, some domestic groups failed to meet the financial and technical prerequisites imposed by the terms of transfer. This left the government in the difficult situation of either postponing the sale for lack of alternatives or risking the fate of unreliable prospective buyers. In other cases, like that of the shipping company ELMA and the national insurance and savings bank Caja Nacional de Ahorro y Seguros, the government failed to draw any serious offers.

Another factor adding to the problem was the inadequacy of the domestic financial market through which the state could sell the shares of its companies to the public. The Buenos Aires stock exchange is notoriously very small, highly speculative, and dominated by a few large players who engage in collusive practices. The high inflation marking the first phase of privatization added to the volatility of the domestic stock exchange. Operating under such limitations, Argentine policy-makers opted to auction shares of big state companies through a bidding mechanism, which inevitably ended with the concentration of property in the hands of large foreign investors and their domestic partners. Only after the Convertibility Law had produced both economic stability and small investors' confidence was the government able to sell its remaining shares in the new private telephone companies and YPF through the stock market, with noticeable success. The auctioning of the state's shares (30 per cent of total) in Telefónica and Telecom produced $827 million and $1.2 billion respectively. The auction of YPF's share (45 per cent of total) earned the state an additional $3.0 billion.[50] A final round of sales for minority shares took place in 1996 and 1997 (Table 3.3). Yet, even in this case, the experience was limited to only a handful of large companies, like YPF, Metrogas, and EDENOR and was cut short by the mid-1998 world financial crisis.

Several other problems arose from privatization methods. The Alfonsín administration had attempted to privatize by negotiating directly with prospective buyers while the Menem administration chose a public bidding system. Direct negotiations did occur, however, when only one bidder came through. This led to a host of problems to be discussed later. The actual transfers were made in the form of: (1) sale of shares; (2) sale of assets; and (3) exclusive concessions for the exploitation of natural monopolies for a fixed period of time. Usually, the government sold PEs to the highest bidder, but on several occasions other criteria were used based upon investments and technical qualifications.

Initially, for the largest privatizations, the government accepted either cash or a combination of cash and debt equity papers. The structure of the sale involved the establishment of a three-party consortium composed of: (1) foreign investors who had the necessary technological expertise and who eventually would manage the company; (2) a minority domestic partner(s); and (3) foreign banks that would finance purchases by securing the amount of debt spelled out in the terms of transfer. This complex organization soon proved to be cumbersome and often unreliable because of feuds among the members of the consortia as each of them tried to maximize their interests at the expense of their partners. Under this scheme, banks garnered tremendous bargaining power because they were the only ones to hold a large share of the foreign debt bonds required by the government as part of the agreed-upon financing. The faltering of some consortia prior to or following a transfer often originated from disagreements between the banks and their business partners. Moreover, the use of debt-equity swaps ultimately undervalued the assets purchased (in 1989 the Argentine bonds were traded at 13 cents as opposed to the nominal value of one US dollar). These two factors eventually led Cavallo, in July 1992, to replace this system with one using cash and integrating debt titles into the privatizations. According to Cavallo's scheme:

Firms participating in the bidding process [would] now make their offers according to the effective value of the debt titles, rather than their nominal values. At the moment they hand[ed] in the titles, the firms [would] be able to make a deposit in dollars . . . in an escrow account. After this, the Central Bank [would] have a period of one

TABLE 3.3. *Argentina: Privatization Transactions 1990–8*

Company	Sector	Type of Transfer	Date	Cash (US$ million)
LS84 Canal 11	Telecommunic.	15 year concession	Jan. 90	8.2
LS85 Canal 13	Telecommunic.	15 year concession	Jan. 90	5.7
10,000 Km. of highways	Transport		Sep. 90	00.0
Monomeros Vinilicos	Petrochemicals	Sale (30%)*	Oct. 90	9.3
Inductor	Petrochemicals	Sale (30%)*	Oct. 90	17.8
Petropol	Petrochemicals	Sale (30%)*	Oct. 90	4.5
Polisur	Petrochemicals	Sale (30%)*	Oct. 90	14.1
28 marginal areas[a]	Petrochemicals	Concession	Oct. 90	241.1
9 marginal areas CPI/90[b]	Petrochemicals	Concession	Nov. 90	15.8
ENTel	Telecommunic.	Sale of 60%	Nov. 90	214.0
Aerolineas Argentinas	Transport	Sale of 85%	Nov. 90	260.0
Subtotal 1990				890.5
Radio Stations	Telecommunic.		Feb. 91	
Llalo-Llao Hotel	Tourism	Sale	May. 91	3.7
YPF oil areas: Puesto Hernandez	Oil	Association contract	Jun. 91	560.1
YPF: Vizcacheras, El Huemul, etc.	Oil		Jun. 91	
22 marginal areas CPI/91	Petrochemicals	Concession	Aug. 91	140.5
YPF: Shares of oil areas[c]	Oil		Oct. 91	243.3
Rosario-Bahia Blanca railway	Transport	30-year concession	Nov. 91	59.8
Tandanor-shipyards	Defense	Sale	Dec. 91	55.0
YPF: Central Area, Santa Cruz I	Oil	Association contract	Dec. 91	830.0
ENTel	Telecommunic.	30% of Telefónica Arg.	Dec. 91	,892.4
Subtotal 1991				

YPF: Central area, Tierra del Fuego	Oil	Association cont. (70%)	Jan. 92	143.5
5 marginal areas CPI/91	Petrochemicals	Concession	Jan. 92	18.8
YPF: Central Area, Santa Cruz II[d]	Oil	Association cont. (70%)	Mar. 92	141.6
Petroquimica Rio Tercero	Petrochemicals	Sale (39%)*	Mar. 92	7.3
ENTel	Telecommunic.	Sale (30%) of Telecom	Mar. 92	1,226.9
Altos Hornos Zapla—steel	Defense	Sale	Apr. 92	3.3
SEGBA: Central Puerto SA	Electricity-Water	Sale (60%)	Apr. 92	92.3
Mitre Railway Line—cargo	Transport	30 year concession	Apr. 92	
SEGBA: Central Costa Nera SA	Electricity-Water	Sale (60%)	May 92	90.1
Mercado de la Hacienda de Liniers[e]	Commerce	10 year concession	Jun. 92	
22 marginal areas CPI	Petrochemicals	Concession	Jun. 92	48.0
Grain elevator of BA port[f]	Agro-Industry	Concession	Aug. 92	1.1
Grain elevator of Neuquen port[g]	Agro-Industry	Concession	Aug. 92	2.9
Edesur (distribution)	Electricity-Water	Sale (51%)	Aug. 92	30.0
Edenor (distribution)	Electricity-Water	Sale (51%)	Aug. 92	30.0
Central Alto Valle (95 MW)	Electricity-Water	Sale (90%)	Aug. 92	22.1
Grain Elevator of Diamante port	Agro-Industry	Sale	Sep. 92	2.0
Central Guemes (305 MW)	Electricity-Water	Sale (60%)	Sep. 92	10.0
Hipodromo Argentino[h]	Recreation	Concession	Sep. 92	61.5
Delta-Borges Railway	Transport	30 year concession	Sep. 92	
SOMISA	Defense	Sale (80%)	Oct. 92	140.0
Central Dock Sud (211 MW)	Electricity-Water	Sale (90%)	Oct. 92	25.0
Central Pedro de Mendoza (58MW)	Electricity-Water	Sale (90%)	Oct. 92	8.5
EDELAP SA (distribution)	Electricity-Water	Sale (51%)	Nov. 92	5.0
YPF: Campo Duran Refinery	Oil	Sale (70%)	Nov. 92	64.1
YPF: Central Area Palmar Lago	Oil	Association cont. (70%)	Nov. 92	36.0
YPF: Central Area Aguarague	Oil	Association cont. (55%)	Nov. 92	143.7
Distribuidora Gas del Litoral	Gas	Sale (90%)	Dec. 92	14.0
Distribuidora Gas Cuyana	Gas	Sale (60%)	Dec. 92	26.0
Distribuidora Gas Noroeste	Gas	Sale (90%)	Dec. 92	10.0
Gas del Estado: Trans Gas Sur	Gas	Sale (70%)	Dec. 92	100.0

TABLE 3.3. *(cont'd)*

Company	Sector	Type of Transfer	Date	Cash (US$ million)
Distribudora Gas del Centro	Gas	Sale (90%)	Dec. 92	18.0
Distribudora gas Buenos Aires Norte	Gas	Sale (70%)	Dec. 92	28.0
Distribudora Gas del Sur	Gas	Sale (90%)	Dec. 92	14.0
Distribudora Gas Metropolitano	Gas	Sale (70%)	Dec. 92	44.0
Distribudora Gas Pampeana	Gas	Sale (70%)	Dec. 92	18.0
Transportadora Gas del Norte	Gas	Sale (70%)	Dec. 92	28.0
Obras Sanitarias	Sewerage	30 year concession	Dec. 92	
Urquiza Railway Line—cargo	Transport	30 year concession	Dec. 92	
San Martin Line—cargo	Transport	30 year concession	Dec. 92	
General Roca line—cargo	Transport	30 year concession	Dec. 92	
Subtotal 1992				2,553.7
Central Sorrento (226 MW)	Electricity-Water	Sale (90%)	Jan. 93	5.0
YPF: Dock Sud Distillery	Oil	Sale	Jan. 93	11.7
YPF: Ebytenʲ	Oil	Sale (70%)	Jan. 93	19.0
YPF: Pipeline of Valle	Oil	Sale (70%)	Jan. 93	77.0
YPF: Distillery San Lorenzo	Oil	Sale	Jan. 93	12.2
ECAᵏ	Defense	Sale	Feb. 93	12.4
Fabrica Militar de Sintetico Tolueno	Defense	Sale	Feb. 93	0.8
Fabrica Militar de Acido Sulfurico	Defense	Sale	Mar. 93	1.6ᵣ
Centrales Termicas de Noroeste	Electricity-Water	Sale (90%)	Mar. 93	0.4
Centrales Termicas de Noroeste	Electricity-Water	Sale (90%)	Mar. 93	2.0
YPF: Twenty tankers	Oil	Sale	Mar/Dec. 93	27.0
Fabrica Militar General San Martin	Defense	Sale	Apr. 93	8.5
Central San Nicolas (770 MW)	Electricity-Water	Sale (88%)	Apr. 93	10.0
Port Unit San Pedro	Agro-Industry	Sale	May 93	4.1
YPF: Sea Transport Petroleros	Oil	Sale (70%)	Jun. 93	41.8

	Sector	Type	Date	Amount
Grain Elevator of Villa Constitucion[l]	Agro-Industry	Lease	Jul. 93	3.5
Port Unit III of Rosario Grain Elevator	Agro-Industry	Sale	Jul. 93	
Grain Elevator Port Ing. White[m]	Agro-Industry	30 year concession	Jul. 93	30.0
Transener	Electricity-Water	Sale (65%)	Jul. 93	
YPF Oil Co.	Oil	45.3% in sale of shares	Jul. 93	3,040.0
Hidroelectrica Alicura	Electricity-Water	Sale (59%)	Aug. 93	48.0
Hidroelectrica Cerros Colorados	Electricity-Water	Sale (59%)	Aug. 93	27.0
Hidroelectrica El Cochon	Electricity-Water	Sale	Aug. 93	87.0
YPF: Aerosol Plant Dock Sud	Oil	Sale (42%)*	Sep. 93	0.9
Cerboquimica Argentina	Petrochemicals	Sale (49%)	Sep. 93	0.3
YPF: Interpatrol	Oil	Sale (49%)	Sep. 93	8.7
YPF: Sea Terminal Patagonicas	Oil	Sale (70%)	Oct. 93	10.0
Grain Elevator Mar Del Plata Port[n]	Agro-Industry	Concession	Nov. 93	2.6
Central Termicas Patagonicas[o]	Electricity-Water	Sale (51%)	Nov. 93	2.0
SEGBA: Central Puerto	Electricity-Water	30% in public offer	Nov. 93	133.6
FEMESA: General Urquiza L. & Sub.	Transport	20 year concession	Nov. 93	
SEGBA: Central Costanera	Electricity-Water	30% in public offer	Dec. 93	97.0
Hidroelectrica Piedra del Aguila	Electricity-Water	Sale (59%)	Dec. 93	100.0
Subtotal 1993				3,822.5
Transnoa	Electricity-Water	Sale (90%)	Jan. 94	2.0
Belgrano Railway North Line—pass.	Transport	10 year concession	Jan. 94	
San Martin Line—passengers	Transport	10 year concession	Mar. 94	
Caja Nacional de Ahorros y Seguros	Finance	Sale (60%)	Apr. 94	86.3[s]
CAP Cuatreros	Agro-Industry	Sale	May 94	1.9
Transportadora Gas del Sur	Gas	Public Offer (27%)	May 94	505.6
Belgrano Railway South Line—pass.	Transport	10 year concession	May 94	
Transpa	Electricity-Water	Sale (51%)	Jun. 94	1.0
Terminal 4 of Puerto Nuevo (BA)	Transport	Concession	Jun. 94	
Fabrica Militar Pilar	Defense	Sale	Jul. 94	2.8
Centrales Termicas del Litoral	Electricity-Water	Sale (90%)	Jul. 94	0.5
Centrales Termicas del Litoral	Electricity-Water	Sale (90%)	Jul. 94	0.5
Yacimientos Carboniferos Fiscales	Mining	10 year concession	Jul. 94	

TABLE 3.3. *(cont'd)*

Company	Sector	Type of Transfer	Date	Cash (US$ million)
Terminales 3–6 Puerto Nuevo (BA)	Transport	Concession	Jul. 94	14.6
Acceso Ricchieri	Transport	22 year concession	Jul. 94	102.5
Acceso Oeste	Transport	22 year concession	Jul. 94	4.0
Acceso Norte	Transport	22 year concession	Jul. 94	
Lineas Maritimas Argentinas-8 ships	Transport	Sale	Jul./Sep. 94	
State Properties	Real Estate	Sale of 986 properties	Aug. 94	2.0
Hidroelectrica del Diamante	Electricity-Water	Sale (59%)	Sep. 94	4.1
Terminal 1–2 of Puerto Nuevo	Transport	Concession	Sep. 94	1.5
Lineas Maritimas Argentinas-1 ship	Transport	Sale	Sep. 94	2.0
Hidroelectrica Rio Hondo	Electricity-Water	Sale (98%)	Dec. 94	1.0
Hidroelectrica Ameghino	Electricity-Water	Sale (59%)	Oct. 94	746.0
Centrales Termicas Mendoza	Electricity-Water	Sale (51%)	Oct. 94	
Transnea	Electricity-Water	Sale (60%)	Oct. 94	
Subtotal 1994				
Hidroelectrica Futaleufu[p]	Electricity-Water	Sale (59%)	Jun. 95	225.6
Transportadora Gas del Norte	Gas	Int. Public Offer (25%)	Jul. 95	141.6
Hidroelectrica Rio Juramento[q]	Electricity-Water	Sale (98%)	Nov. 95	41.1
Edesur	Electricity-Water	Int. Public Offer (39%)	Dec. 95	390.0
Edenor	Electricity-Water	Int. Public Offer (19.5%)	Dec. 95	156.1
Subtotal 1995				954.4
Hidroelectrica San Juan	Electricity-Water	Sale (98%)	Mar. 96	12.3
Edelap	Electricity-Water	Int. Public Offer (39%)	Apr. 96	55.3
Transportadora Gas del Sur	Gas	Stock Auction (1.98%)	Jun. 96	36.2
Edenor	Electricity-Water	Int. Public Offer (19.5%)	Jun. 96	164.0
Hidroelectrica Tucuman	Electricity-Water	Sale (98%)	Jun. 96	4.6
Subtotal 1996				272.4

Metrogas	Gas	Stock Auction (1.76%)	Jan. 97	8.5
YPF	Oil	Stock Auction (9.57%)	Jul. 97	988.4
Encotesa	Mail	Concession	Aug. 97	2,046.0
Subtotal 1997				3,042.9
National Airports	Transport	Concession	Jan. 98	5,130.0
Subtotal 1998				5,130.0
TOTAL				19,491.1

Source: Ministery of the Economy, Public Works, and Services and Economic and Commercial Section of the Argentine Embassy in the United States (1998).

Notes:

a International public auction 1/90.

b Includes OPTAR and 55% of the capital stock of Buenos Aires Catering. The State owned 43%. From March 1994, the State has only 5%, employees 10%, and an international private consortium 85%.

c Broadening of the private share in Puesto Hdez, Vizcacheras, el Huemul, and Tordillo (Decree 1727/91).

d Cuenca Austral.

e Concession for 10 years, with payment of 12% of total income of the concessionary.

f Concession US$3/t loaded and a tax of 15 cents.

g Concession US$3.5/t loaded and a tax of 4 cents.

h Concession, 8.5% of the debts plus 30% of ticket price.

i Concession of 30 years, coefficient 0.731.

j Includes the Shell station and sea port of Puerto Rosales.

k Eca: Frabrica Militar de Vainas y Conductores Electricos.

l Tax of 38 cents per ton.

m Concession for 30 years, tax of 38 cents per ton.

n Concession, tax during the concession of US$ 2.4 million for the elevator and US$ 250,000 for office space.

o Explorer of the sea terminal Caleta Cordoba and Olivia.

p The province of Chubut acquired 39% of stock.

q The province of Salta acquired 47% of stock.

r US$ 320,000 in cash. The rest of the payment will be done in three yearly installments of US$ 420,000.

s Corresponding to 27.99% of the debt of CNAS with Banco de la Nacion Argentina, which is at US$ 303 million.

year to buy the debt titles on behalf of the firm that deposited the dollars, which [would] complete the payment, no matter which quantity of debt titles were obtained with the dollars deposited.   (Petrecolla *et al.* 1993: 74)

Dromi's weak regulatory framework designed to give the executive a free hand, and to private buyers substantial incentives, led to a host of legal problems immediately after the sale. As was the case in several of the first privatizations, there were constant modifications of the terms of sale. These amendments were due to pressure from the private groups, resulting in frequent and embarrassing renegotiations, which inevitably ended in penalizing the state at the advantage of the private buyer. Furthermore, the loopholes in the legal framework opened windows of opportunity for corrupt practices as the whole process lacked transparency (Verbitsky 1991; Moreno Ocampo 1993).[51] For instance, article 18 of the State Reform Law contemplated the direct negotiation process in order to select potential buyers. Yet the criteria upon which such a selection was to be based offered government officials ample room for discretionary decisions. Such subjective criteria were used for the privatizations of Aerolíneas Argentinas and the highways, deals where strongest was the suspicion of corruption (Natale 1993: 30). Moreover, government officials granted rights to the new private owners which were not included in the terms of auction (in sectors like air passenger cargo, railways, and highways) and compensations that had no justification. This was done in open violation of the original bid. The scandals that resulted from these arbitrary decisions induced Cavallo, in the beginning, to promote greater transparency than under Dromi in the process of transferring natural monopolies to private hands through the enforcement of a more rigorous regulatory scheme. The case of electricity services is an optimal example, but unfortunately remained more the exception than the rule. In fact, Cavallo himself, during a World Bank-sponsored seminar in September 1993 declared that he needed three years of passive behavior from the part of regulatory agencies.[52] Indeed, as we shall see in a moment, he paid lip service to sound regulatory policy and transparency when they did not fit his own agenda. The focus will now shift to the major privatizations of the 1989–98 period, leaving aside other minor privatizations. The goal will be to highlight some of the problems discussed above.

Telecommunications.   The privatization of ENTel, which was to set the tone for the whole policy process, was initiated as follows. A presidential decree was issued in September 1989 stipulating the sale of 60 per cent of the company to corporations through competitive bids, 10 per cent to employees, and 5 per cent to domestic cooperatives, with the remaining 25 per cent to be sold through a public offer. In order to make the company lucrative for potential investors, trustee María Julia Alsogaray increased telephone charges by 2,300 per cent in the first quarter of 1990. Domestic rates became more expensive than international ones (making telephones a luxury for the middle class).[53] Moreover, Alsogaray guaranteed investors a net profit margin of 16 per cent annually for the first two years following privatization. The decision created a public uproar. There appeared to be no justification for the exorbitant price hike when telephone service was steadily deteriorating. The measure created a big feud within the cabinet as well. A week later, economy minister Erman González overruled Alsogaray postponing the price increase. Other issues creating controversy included the official valuation of the company at $1.9 billion (well below the $3.6 billion estimated during the Alfonsín administration) and the provision calling for the split of ENTel into two regions (north and south), basically dividing a state monopoly into two smaller private ones. It soon became evident that the government was in a hurry to close the deal. The greatest concern was to erase ENTel's losses (which amounted to $1.46 billion in 1989 alone). In an attempt to slash part of the country's foreign debt, potential buyers were forced to pay most of the price in debt and/or equity papers purchased in the secondary market rather than in cash.

However, when the bids were disclosed at mid-year, a consortium led by Telefónica of Spain had made the best offer for both regions (only three bidders came forward).[54] This violated one of the initial rules prohibiting a single bidder from gaining control of more than one half of ENTel. Thus, Telefónica chose the more profitable southern region. It paid the Argentine government $114 million in cash, $202 million in notes, and the remaining $2.7 billion in bonds. The northern region was left to the second-best offer for that area, made by the US Bell Atlantic–Manufacturers Hannover consortium. Unfortunately, the deal fell through when Bell Atlantic was unable to obtain the necessary bonds from its partner, Manufacturers Hannover, which was responsible for financing the operation. Bell Atlantic requested additional time but Dromi refused. His decision once again caused a heated controversy since the same minister had allowed unlimited postponements for the contemporary privatization of Aerolíneas Argentinas. Moreover, as it came to be known later, neither of the other two private consortia that eventually took over ENTel possessed the necessary debt financing (Natale 1993: 134–5). Bell Atlantic accused Dromi of favoring its competitors but eventually withdrew to be replaced, through an executive order, by a consortium which included the Italian communication company STET, France Télécom, J. P. Morgan, and the Argentine conglomerate Pérez Companc. Such a consortium had offered the third-highest bid consisting of $100 million in cash, $178 million in notes, and $2.3 billion in bonds.[55] ENTel was finally transferred to its new owners on November 11, 1990, for a total price of $5.5 billion. The new companies, called Telefónica Argentina S.A. and Telecom Argentina S.A. were granted exclusive rights to provide telephone services for seven years, renewable for an additional three upon satisfactory completion of investment requirements.

Yet the disruption caused by the series of unexpected events led the government and the private consortia to revise the original contracts after the sale.[56] Initially, it was agreed that the new owners could increase rates according to inflationary levels or through a complex mechanism which took into account the depreciation of the exchange rate and inflation. In the first half of 1991, however, the government notified both Telefónica and Telecom Argentina that the index-linking clauses granted under the privatization contract would be eliminated in compliance with the stabilization policies launched in March 1991. In return, Dromi tried to compensate for the income loss by cutting the value-added tax and allowing tariff increases linked to international inflation.

In the end, even President Menem acknowledged that the ENTel privatization had been badly mismanaged. The new owners were upset by the changes in the rules imposed by the administration. Consumers were outraged because basic fees and charges for long distance calls (both domestic and international) were the highest in Latin America until 1997.[57] Moreover, several court rulings established that the new phone companies had been engaging in overbilling and unfair business practices. In 1996 and 1997, the courts also suspended government decrees allowing phone companies to increase rates. Adding to the frustration, phones continued to be inoperable during rainstorms.[58]

Many criticisms were made prior to and following the ENTel privatization. First, it seemed odd that a state enterprise like ENTel was purchased by European companies whose main stockholders were, at the time, the Spanish, French, and Italian governments. Second, the division of the country into two smaller monopolies defied the very notion upon which privatization rests, that is, increasing competition and quality of service through deregulation (Petrazzini 1995; Wellenius 1998). This was quite troublesome in view of the fact that, despite the provision of the law, the Comisión Nacional de Telecomunicaciones (CNT) failed to effectively regulate the phone duopoly. Cavallo, as much as Dromi, preferred to bypass the agency and make agreements directly with the phone companies on a number of sensitive issue (Vispo 1998), in open violation of the law.[59]

A year after the transfer of ENTel to its private owners, Argentina's financial situation became unexpectedly positive. The success of the stabilization program launched by Economy Minister Cavallo in March 1991 turned things around. By October Argentina was experiencing its lowest inflation rate in two decades, interest rates plummeted, industrial production and employment levels began to recover, and substantial amounts of foreign capital were entering the country. All of these conditions were instrumental in creating a boom in the small Buenos Aires stock exchange, which turned out to be the most profitable worldwide in 1991. When the government decided to sell its 30 per cent share of the Telefónica and Telecom companies, the stock market was ripe for substantial subscriptions. The sale was a huge success for the government. Both auctions, the largest ever in Latin America at the time were oversubscribed. The Telefónica shares yielded $847.7 million, 45 per cent higher than anticipated earnings.[60] The sale of the Telecom Argentina shares was even more successful, earning the government $1.2 billion rather than the expected $650 million.[61] The sale was also a success for the two private consortia. The value of their shares appreciated rapidly. By 1998, both Telefónica and Telecom investments in Argentina had generated net incomes nearing $2 billion.[62] By 1998, the same companies had also gained a dominant position in the very lucrative cellular phone and internet business.

Transportation. The privatization of the flag carrier Aerolíneas Argentinas turned out to be the most troublesome privatization of all. The government called for tenders to sell 85 per cent of the company, as was the case for ENTel. The state was to retain 5 per cent, while the remaining 10 per cent would go to employees. The minimum floor for the auction sale was set at $220 million in cash and $310 million in a combination of debt and equity papers (Gosman 1991: 250–1). Foreign investors could purchase up to 49 per cent of the company's ownership, and no single foreign carrier could own more than 30 per cent of Aerolíneas. Bidders were required to present a five-year investment plan. In return, the government granted a monopoly of domestic traffic rights for five years and international traffic rights for ten years. President Menem signed a decree in December 1989, which allowed the privatization of Aerolíneas to be accomplished by June 1990.

Despite numerous problems, including an aging fleet, overstaffing, and a debt of $46.3 million, Aerolíneas was an attractive prospect because it had showed profits in recent years. Most importantly, controlling it would enable the new owner to operate very profitable routes under monopolistic conditions.[63] Initially, it followed that several foreign airlines, including Varig, SAS, Alitalia, American Airlines, KLM, and Iberia, expressed interest. However, all the foreign carriers except Iberia eventually withdrew. Several reasons accounted for the massive pull-out. First, some bidders were scared off by the corruption involved in the sale. Allegations were made that government officials had requested bribes from prospective buyers to 'ensure equal treatment' (Mead 1990: 21). Second, there was no clear assurance by the Argentine government that the new owner would have the prerogative to slash employment levels in order to make Aerolíneas more efficient. Third, there were few reliable domestic partners with whom to form joint ventures, as required by the bidding terms. Fourth, most of the banks that held Aerolíneas' debt were unwilling to support privatization until the Argentine government paid them first.[64] Fifth, disagreements between banks and interested foreign airlines made the creation of alternative consortia impossible. Consequently, the Argentine government was left with only one bid from the Iberia consortium. The Spanish carrier offered $260 million in cash. Approximately $130 million was to be paid immediately, with the remaining amount to be disbursed over ten months. Additionally, Iberia pledged to buy up to $2 billion in debt equity swaps and invest $683 million over five years (primarily in the acquisition of fifteen new planes). Iberia was to hold 20 per cent of the 85 per cent purchased. The rest would be disbursed among several domestic groups completing the consortium, including Cielos del Sur, the owner of Austral, the other major (private) Argentine airline.[65]

Initially, the sale appeared to be a good deal for the government: it received more than the minimum payment required despite the lack of competition. Although Aerolíneas was officially transferred to the new owners at the end of November 1990, the deal began to unravel when Cielos del Sur was unable to pay its share. Indeed, none of Iberia's domestic partners met the financial prerequisites specified in the government auction (Natale 1993: 58–61). Cielos del Sur (as well as other Argentine partners) dropped out of the consortium, selling most of its ownership to Iberia, whose shares climbed to 85 per cent of the total. This was in clear violation of Law 19.030, which stipulated that in order to retain its flagship status, the majority of Aerolíneas Argentinas shares remain in Argentine hands and the company had to be managed by Argentines. Despite Menem's public statements that he would not allow a postponement of the first down payment (as he had done in the case of Bell Atlantic), Iberia finally received a ninety-day extension for the purchase of debt for equity paper.

Further strains between the administration and Iberia developed when the Spanish carrier disclosed plans to sell some of Aerolíneas' aircraft to meet the deadline for the payment of the first $130 million cash installment. When the administration threatened to cancel the contract, the carrier backed off and paid in full. Still other problems arose. Iberia postponed payment of the second $130 million installment, claiming that it had first to be compensated for $40 million worth of tickets that had been sold prior to divestiture (Gosman 1991: 253–54). Only in September 1992, were Iberia and the Argentine government able to agree on a final settlement according to which the former pledged to pay a revised sum in dollar-denominated government bonds, allowing the Spanish carrier to save $560 million.[66] In what constituted a re-nationalization process, the Argentine government bought back 28 per cent of the airline's capital, adding to the 15 per cent it already possessed, which raised the total to 43 per cent.

After privatization, conditions at Aerolíneas worsened as mechanical failures worsened and safety standards deteriorated alarmingly.[67] This further complicated matters. Despite laying off hundreds of employees (and cutting 23 per cent of domestic flights) the company showed large losses under the new ownership.[68] This was most surprising as Iberia had a virtual monopoly of the domestic market until the mid-1990s, having acquired both Aerolíneas

Argentinas and Austral in a market left free of regulation. By 1998, Iberia had entered talks to sell Aerolíneas to American Airlines.

The poor handling of the ENTel and Aerolíneas privatizations led to Dromi's downfall and ultimately embarrassed the government as Iberia not only failed to pay on time, but by the time the ordeal was resolved it had paid much less than previously agreed.[69] The Spanish carrier was able to achieve this by exploiting the government's weak bargaining position. In fact, revoking the privatization of Aerolíneas was perceived by the administration as jeopardizing the whole policy. Menem and his advisers had reached the conclusion that, all things considered, a bad deal was better than no deal at all.

Aside from the points raised above, Aerolíneas' privatization suffered from the same shortcomings as ENTel. First, a state monopoly operating international flights had been transferred into the hands of a privately run company. Iberia's monopolistic control of the domestic market enabled it to maintain air fares at substantially higher rates than neighboring countries. Second, as with ENTel, Aerolíneas ironically was sold to a consortium headed by a state-owned enterprise (the Spanish government is Iberia's largest stockholder).[70] Third, the haste with which the process was carried out forced the government to look for investors before clear regulations could be designed. This turned out to be exceptionally costly, as offers were accepted before contracts were signed. The end result was a series of legal battles with the new owners that invariably forced the government to retreat. Fourth, the lack of transparency in both privatizations prompted accusations of widespread corruption and discrimination against some bidders.[71] The greatest merit of the ENTel and Aerolíneas privatizations was the creation of additional revenues for the government and the large profits for the telephone companies. As far as consumers were concerned, however, some tangible improvements occurred in telephone service but not in the air passenger business.

Highway privatizations were the second most important divestiture in this sector. Argentina has one of the most extensive highway infrastructures in Latin America (28,000 km.). However, the lack of investments in road repairs, at a time of steady increases in truck transportation due to the deterioration of the railway cargo system, resulted in only 36 per cent of the national highways in 1989 being in fit condition (Natale 1993: 141). A proposal by the Alfonsín administration to find private partnerships to revamp the highway infrastructure was stopped in Congress by the Peronist opposition, as was the case of ENTel and Aerolíneas. Conversely, once in office, Menem maneuvered rapidly to auction the highways. The government auction called for a 12-year concession of 9,800 km. of some of the most important highways to be awarded to the highest bidder. The objective was twofold: generating revenues and transferring the responsibility for repairing the highway system to the private sector. The government's initial specifications required the future private owners to fulfill several strict conditions prior to charging tolls. Private companies were required to make a series of investments for road improvements and other highway related services. The new owners would also be made liable for accidents resulting from road deficiencies during the period of concession.

In September 1990, the government approved the contracts transferring the highway infrastructure for which private companies paid $890 million. Dromi failed to inform the Bicameral Commission on Privatization about the bids he received and the content of the contracts.[72] This came as no surprise as the bidding process seemed suspicious from the start. It seemed that the main competitors also had previously agreed amongst themselves also for which routes they would compete. Interestingly, most of the bidders had been former government contractors for road maintenance and construction. Foreign companies were conspicuously absent. Moreover, members of the private companies involved had helped the government design the bids. In 1991, many new owners, without starting repairs, immediately began to charge tolls in open violation of the waiting period specified in the contracts. Equally alarming was the fact that they were charging $2.50 per 100 km. as opposed to the $1.50 spelled out in the concession contracts. The highway privatization suddenly became a lucrative business for the private companies which had a rate of return on the investment estimated at 40 per cent per year (Gerchunoff and Coloma 1993: 280).

The popular outrage resulting from the toll hike forced Cavallo, who had inherited the whole mess, to renegotiate the concession contracts. In March 1991, much to people's relief, the highway companies agreed to reduce the toll rate to the original $1.50 per 100 km. in return for the elimination of the concession fee ($780 million), cuts in business taxes ($285 million), and the provision of subsidies ($690 million). The total cost to the government was $1.7 billion (Gerchunoff and Coloma 1993: 281). In September 1992, after a year-and-a-half of exhausting negotiations, government and private companies sealed new contracts (Decree 1.817). The government claimed victory, because it had averted the collapse of the privatization deals and was no longer spending money for road maintenance (roughly $150 million yearly). On the positive side, many highways showed signs of improvement as time went on, although tolls remained quite high. Unfortunately, as in other sectors, controls of government regulators in charge of monitoring the compliance of the contracts remained spotty at best and let private companies ignore several contractual obligations (Natale 1993: 153) to the detriment of consumers.[73]

Petroleum.   The privatization of the oil sector proceeded incrementally and was accompanied by some deregulation. Traditionally, YPF had enjoyed a virtual monopoly on extraction and a dominant market role in other related activities, including refining, distribution, and sale.[74] Beginning in 1990, the government obtained $400 million by auctioning off the exploitation rights for secondary oil fields. Subsequently, the government auctioned the exploitation rights (in cooperation with YPF) of high productivity areas, receiving about $600 million. Existing contracts of associations between YPF and private contractors were amended giving the latter ownership for 25–35 years of the reserves they had been exploiting. As a result, YPF shares of oil extraction dropped from 98 per cent in 1989 to 43 per cent in 1991 (Petrecolla *et al.* 1993). However, with only five companies controlling 75 per cent of the private production of crude oil after privatization, it appears that the sector as a whole retained very strong oligopolistic features (Gerchunoff and Coloma 1993: 285).

Partial privatization also occurred in the refining sector, with YPF selling three major refineries, but still retaining a 52 per cent of the total market share (Gerchunoff and Coloma 1993: 285). Taking into consideration that Exxon and Shell owned an additional 34 per cent, it becomes clear that privatization did little to break existing oligopolistic conditions even in this sector. In terms of retail distribution and marketing, the government also deregulated prices and lifted restrictions on gas station permits in 1991. However, this had little effect on gasoline prices because distributors remained dependent upon a few refineries that had little interest, given the oligopolistic nature of their market, in waging a price warfare.

In contrast to the divestitures of the 1989–1 period, the one affecting YPF was marked by several differences, which made it in many ways a benchmark for the Argentine privatization program. First, due to the size of the company and its large debt, the government initially decided to restructure it. The aim was to make YPF a profitable business that could attract more foreign investors than in the past and, hopefully, better prices. YPF's payroll was cut from 51,000 in December 1990 to 8,000 in December 1993.[75] As noted above, the government sold marginal oil fields, refining and marketing operations, some shipping vessels, and other non-strategic holdings. From a deficit of $576 million in 1990, YPF earned a profit of $400 million in 1992 (Natale 1993: 185). Second, in the case of YPF the government did not go for total privatization, as had been the case with ENTel and Aerolíneas Argentinas. The executive turned YPF into a corporation through a decree in 1990, paving the legal ground for the subsequent sale of shares. Instead of instituting a bidding process, the government chose to sell the company through an international public offering (the largest of its kind in Latin America at the time), while retaining a substantial minority share. The initial offering amounted to 45.3 per cent of total shares. The remaining shares were sold in different tranches in later years. Third, the government retained management control of YPF following its partial privatization. Fourth, the placing on YPF's shares at the international stock exchange markets assured those transparency requirements that had been absent during the 1989–90 period. Congress, despite some initial opposition, later sanctioned through a law the initial government decree.

Electricity.   Electricity sector PEs in Argentina had over the years suffered substantial losses resulting from illegal connections made by private users (primarily in the Buenos Aires metropolitan area) as well as from technical flaws and mismanagement.[76] For example, SEGBA (Servicios Eléctricos del Gran Buenos Aires), one of the largest PEs, suffered annual losses of $1 million (Natale 1993: 171). During the last two years of the Alfonsín administration lack of adequate electricity supply reached crisis proportions. This was particularly the case in Buenos Aires where economic activity was brought to a standstill on several occasions due to power shortages.

Electricity privatization began in 1991. Government planners tried to make the best of other countries' experiences and avoid past mistakes, such as those made in the ENTel privatization. Under pressure from the World Bank, which heavily financed the project, and interested investors, the government introduced competition and transparency of rules in the electricity market prior to privatization. Such a pressure aimed at avoiding the repetition of the saga that characterized the ENTel privatization.[77] In 1992, the Argentine Congress passed Law No. 24.065, which established a new regulatory framework. The law, complemented by Decree 1398/92, left the enforcement of regulation to Ente Nacional Regulador de La Electricidad (ENRE), a new agency that started operating in 1993, and was financed in a way resembling the Comisión Nacional de Telecommunicaciones (CNT).

Thus, the Menem administration initiated the sale of controlling interests in the electric power services of Buenos Aires and its metropolitan area, as well as other less lucrative markets in the interior. Following a procedure tried in England, existing monopolies were divided into power generation, transmission, and distribution companies and then auctioned separately. Under this scheme, companies operating in power generation competed among themselves to sell electricity to a power pool supervised by Cammesa, a non-profit agency jointly owned by the government, power companies, and major users. For their part, the transmission companies then charged a fixed rate to send power to distribution companies that, in turn, competed fiercely to attract customers, as their prices were subject to consumers' demand and efficiency criteria. In fact, large users were left with the option of contracting directly power generators, thus bypassing distributors.

In 1992, SEGBA was split into three different companies, one for generation, which kept the name Servicios Eléctricos del Gran Buenos Aires, and two for distribution (EDENOR and EDESUR), of which 51 per cent of each company's respective shares were auctioned to interested bidders. French and Chilean consortia won EDENOR and EDESUR, respectively. These two privatizations were generally regarded as exemplary because of the competent and transparent manner in which the government conducted them. They also attracted quite a number of very competitive bids. This gave support to the premise that a good regulatory framework in place prior to state divestiture actually increases the attractiveness of the deal rather than deterring bidders.

Initially, however, the 32 electricity generation companies that resulted from the Argentine privatization process engaged in such cut-throat competition tactics that by 1993 their tariffs were lower than before privatization.[78] Companies' profit margins turned into deficits between 1992 and 1993.[79] In 1995, tariffs eventually rebounded but were still 40 per cent below their pre-privatization levels. Competition was also enhanced by the fact that entry barriers for new entrants were lifted. As a result, investors, taking advantage of the abundance of natural gas in Argentina, built new gas-powered generators that began to compete with older hydroelectric and coal-fueled plants. Of course, consumers were the main beneficiaries of this new trend, since they received cheaper and better services than they had ever imagined.

In sum, freed from the urgency and political manipulations that characterized the ENTel privatization, the Menem administration, with the technical assistance of foreign consultants, proceeded with the electricity sector privatization in a transparent, professional manner, maximizing revenues and efficiency gains. Moreover, the electricity sector's clear regulatory framework attracted many investors. This was just the opposite trend from that seen in the case of ENTel, where unclear rules had actually discouraged foreign companies (Urbiztondo, Artana, and Navajas 1997).

Post Office. The transfer to the private sector of the post office, or Encotesa, was one of the longest and surely one of the most controversial. By 1994, when plans were drawn for its divestiture, it was the last largest PE under government control and one that produced hefty losses.[80] The financial crisis that hit Argentina the following year, made its transfer all the more urgent as once again privatization had become a primary means to bridge the fiscal deficit. From a technical standpoint, two factors characterize Encotesa from other divestitures. First of all, it went through a restructuring process. Second, it was the only case in the whole program where a regulatory agency was functioning prior to the privatization of a monopolistic PE. Politically, it was also marked by the most bitter fights within the executive. To closely control Encotesa divestiture process, Cavallo appointed as its trustee Haroldo Grizanti, his right-hand man. Together they drafted a plan, to be submitted to Congress, that required, as principal manager of the business, the participation of a company with long experience in mail service and substantial financial assets. The intention was to attract a major foreign mail carrier in partnership with smaller domestic investors. However, it became clear over time that other people within the Menem administration and the Argentine Congress had different plans. In August 1995, in a surprise move, Cavallo accused 'old-style' politicians of derailing his plan to favor 'mafia-like cartels'.[81] More specifically, Cavallo claimed that many legislators, along with prominent administration officials, were trying to change the Encotesa privatization bill in Congress so that the only possible bidder could be

Alfredo Yabram, a businessman and one of Menem's personal friends, who already controlled 70 per cent of the private couriers working in Argentina.[82] According to Cavallo, if passed in the amended form, the bill would not only allow Yabram to acquire a virtual monopoly of mail service, but would have also enabled him to ship items in and out of the country without any control from law enforcement officials. For Cavallo this was most disturbing as he claimed to have evidence that Yabram was involved in narcotics trafficking. The Economy Minister also charged that Yabram was thwarting his attempt to break the monopoly of the national customs that one of Yabram's companies and the Airforce jointly administered on behalf of the federal government. Cavallo added that Yabram had physically intimidated a former secretary in charge of deregulation and other senior officials in the national post office, including Grizanti. The Minister also lamented that senior officials in the Justice Ministry not only had ignored his previous denunciations but were actually part of the plot.[83] In fact, according to his thesis, some state prosecutors were investigating several of Cavallo's closest aids in key ministries and agencies, using false allegations to force their resignations. The ultimate goal of this strategy, according to former Public Revenues Secretary Carlos Tacchi, was to get rid of Cavallo.

Unlike previous corruption charges, Cavallo's accusations could not be easily dismissed. Although the minister did not mention names it was clear that his charges were aimed at Menem's inner circle, including the President's brother Eduardo (majority leader in the Senate), Chief-of-Staff Eduardo Bauzá, Jorge Matzkin (Speaker of the House of Deputies), Interior Minister Carlos Corach, former Economy and Defense Minister Erman González, the Argentine Ambassador to Washington Raúl Granillo Ocampo, and Justice Minister Elías Jassan, all of whom had close ties to Yabram.[84] As a response, a furious Menem announced that he was planning to reduce Cavallo's status as a super minister by diminishing his prerogatives.[85] The President openly defended Yabram and even flew back to his home state of La Rioja on Yabram's personal jet days after the scandal erupted.

The feud ended with no clear winners. In the Fall of 1996 Menem, using as an excuse the persisiting sluggish status of the economy, forced Cavallo to resign. As for Yabram, he eventually abandoned the bidding process.[86] The terms of the 30-year concession in its final draft underwent significant changes from Cavallo's original proposal. By the time the government awarded Encotesa to its new private owners, many of the prospective foreign investors had dropped out because of the political clouds surrounding the transfer and the profitability of the business venture. In fact, the only two bidders turned out to be local investors without much of a track record in the business. The winners were the consortium of Siderca (Macri group) and the Banco de Galicia, which offered $2.0 billion and additional $250 million in future investments.[87]

Airports. The privatization of the thirty-three federally-owned airports was the last large transaction that Menem carried out and one that through its sloppiness and various political manipulations, seemed to resemble the disastrous management style of the Dromi years. According to some observers, in the haste to privatize and favor some investors over others, the government crafted a bill that left much to be desired.[88] The project, announced in 1994, had first received the backing of the World Bank. However, by late 1997 the multilateral institution had withdrawn its assistance due to the lack of transparency of the whole process.[89] As Congress began to question the details of the bill for the 30-year concession contract, Menem tried on several occasions to usher the privatization process via executive order. As the procedures the government used openly violated the terms of transfer, opposition legislators filed law suits to stop the process. In January 1998, Judge Martín Silva Garretón suspended the process because there was no regulatory agency overseeing the sector as mandated by the law. The following April the same judge issued another restraining order as the executive branch had failed to name a provincial representative to the regulatory agency board. Finally, in May 1998, the government decided to comply to all requirements and transferred the airports to a consortium made up by the US Odgen company, along with Italy's Simpset and Milan Societá Esercizi Aeroportuali, that agreed to pay $171 million in annual royalties during the concession period and to invest $2.2 billion in new infrastructures. None the less, it was clear to most that the regulatory framework remained weak and the chairman of the regulatory agency, the former Supreme Court Justice and Justice Minister Rodolfo Barra, due to its close ties with the administration offered no assurances of impartiality and transparency.

By the time Menem's second mandate came to a close, only a handful of PEs were left to privatize. Some of those that could not find takers remained in government hands. The few remaining federal privatization plans under preparation in 1999 affected PEs in nuclear power generation, banking, and companies formerly controlled by the military. Indeed, the bulk of the privatization effort had shifted to the provincial governments. However, most provinces found themselves either unwilling or ill-prepared to do so despite the federal government repeated request to act quickly since 1993. In addition, the small size of provincial PEs and the uncertain legal framework provided by local courts, which were highly susceptible to political manipulations, did not offer great incentives to foreign investors.

Conclusion

Menem's privatization program was remarkable for its breadth and scope. It took place very quickly and accomplished its most immediate macroeconomic goals. From a political standpoint, the privatization gamble paid high dividends to the administration. In the 1991 and 1993 mid-term congressional and gubernatorial elections, Peronist candidates did well. Exit polls indicated that people wanted to reward the administrations's economic policies, of which privatization was an integral part. In May 1995, Menem won a second consecutive term under the new provisions of the revised Constitution passed by the Constituent Assembly in 1994. He obtained 49.5 per cent of the total vote, more than he had garnered in 1989. In the same election, the Peronists, who already had the majority in the Senate, also captured an absolute majority in the House of Deputies, leaving the President in control of Congress. Regardless of the Menem administration's many scandals, people in 1995 rewarded the President for having restored political stability and economic growth, which they had desperately wanted in 1989 (Palermo and Novaro 1996: 279).

The speed with which Menem forced the market reform policies, coupled with his uncanny ability for putting together a powerful pro-privatization coalition, proved to be the decisive combination for defeating political opposition. The more moderate elements of the main opposition party, the Radical Civic Union, applauded privatization while limiting themselves to calls for greater transparency in future initiatives and greater emphasis on social policies. Until 1997, Alfonsín and left-wing parties were completely unable to put forward any credible alternative. Finally, labor union bosses, surprised and intimidated by Menem's expedient changes, appeared increasingly resigned to conforming to the new rules, thus accepting privatizations in return for the retention of a few old privileges. By 1999, privatization and economic deregulation, had significantly weakened union power.

Despite the many, well justified objections, Menem replied to his critics that privatization, no matter how poorly carried out in many instances, had been the necessary step to breaking new ground and instilling domestic and international confidence in the government's overall economic plans. The privatization program undoubtedly had positive effects.

First, revenue wise, according to the Financial Times, Argentina under Menem was the third largest 'privatizer' in Latin America, after Brazil and Mexico, with $31 billion earned.[90] My own calculations, shown in Table 3.3, are somewhat lower because they discriminate cash from debt bonds, given that for the latter private companies paid considerably less than their book value. The Menem administration earned about $19.5 billion in cash between the 1989–98 period. Debt bonds totalled $17 billion in nominal value, but their actual market value was actually $8 billion (Table 3.4). Of all the privatizations concluded during the Menem administration through 1998, the $5.7 billion coming from oil accounted for the largest amount of revenues, followed by transportation $5.5 billion (of which $5.1 payable over 30 years), telecommunications $2.2 billion, the post office $2 billion (over 20 years),

TABLE 3.4. *Argentina: Proceeds from Debt-Equity Transactions 1990–4*

Company	Debt Market Value (US$ million)	Nominal Value (US$ million)	Transferred Debt (US$ million)
Aerolineas Argentinas	392.7	1,193.7	0.0
ENTel	1,257.0	5,028.0	380.0
YPF	2,702.5	2,970.0	51.8
SEGBA	1,012.0	2,176.0	374.0
Agua y Energia Electrica	465.0	902.7	172.6
Hidronor	632.0	1,231.5	1,128.5
Gas del Estado	1,541.0	3,314.0	1,110.0
Elma	0.0	0.0	0.0
Defense industry	7.7	46.2	0.0
Other Companies	36.0	143.8	0.0
TOTAL	8,045.9	17,005.9	3,216.9

Source: Ministery of the Economy, Public Works, and Services, 1995.

TABLE 3.5. *Argentina: Summary by Year and Sector 1990–8*

Year	Cash (US$ million)	Sector	Cash (US$ million)
1990	890.5	Oil	5,623.9
1991	1,892.4	Transportation	5,506.6
1992	2,653.7	Telecommunications	2,284.8
1993	3,822.5	Mail	2,046.0
1994	832.3	Electricity-Water	1,919.1
1995	954.4	Gas	991.9
1996	272.4	Petrochemicals	517.5
1997	3,042.9	Defense	229.2
1998	5,130.0	Real Estate	202.5
		Finance	86.3
		Recreation	61.5
		Agro-Industry	18.1
		Tourism	3.7
TOTAL	19,491.1	TOTAL	19,491.1

Source: Ministery of the Economy, Public Works, and Services, 1995.

and electricity/water with $1.9 billion (Table 3.5). Debt equity swaps played an important role both in percentage and dollar value terms in 1990, but lost importance thereafter as they were replaced by cash and cash equivalents.

Second, the fiscal impact of the privatization program was positive in the short-term (Castelar Pinheiro and Schneider 1994: 17). Such an impact can be clearly seen between the 1993–5 period when the primary surplus of the government totalled $10.7 billion. Once privatization revenues were added, the total reached $16.8 billion.[91] Overall, the government was able to: (1) save on its debt servicing as a result of the private companies' bond purchases; (2) earn cash payments; (3) accrue taxes from the newly privatized companies, which often went uncollected under state ownership; and (4) save money used to cover deficits or make investments had such companies remained under state ownership.

In 1994, for instance the telephone companies alone paid in taxes $304 million to the federal government and $120 million to provincial governments.[92] On the saving side, the annual losses averaging $1.3 billion in oil and gas, and $500 million in electricity, were terminated. In the case of the railways, the government continued to pay yearly subsidies averaging $100 million, but this figure was only a fifth of what the same sector's annual deficit was prior to privatization.[93] In addition, the new private companies absorbed PEs outsanding debts worth $3.2 billion (Table 3.4). As for the revenues earned through August 1994, about 40.2 per cent went to finance the bankrupt social security system, 34.4 per cent was allocated to eliminate the foreign debt, and the remaining 25.4 per cent was used to finance other expenditures of the treasury (early retirement, current expenditures, transfers to the provinces).

Third, Cavallo's ability to create economic stability lured foreign investors back into Argentina. The contribution of foreign investors through privatization was substantial, accounting for 59.34 per cent of total revenues (Table 3.6). European investors from Spain, Italy, and France, played a predominant role particularly in the first stage of privatization, while US, Chilean, Canadian, and British companies came on strongly in the second. The US companies were, overall, the most important investors (16.2 per cent), followed by Spanish (12.5), and Chilean companies (7.6 per cent). It must be noted, however, that whereas US companies bought in a wide range of activities, Spanish and Chilean groups concentrated their efforts in transport-telecommunications and electricity respectively (Table 3.7).

Fourth, other measures including economic deregulation, terminating discrimination against foreign investors, lifting most import restrictions, simplifying tax collection, and reforming the Buenos Aires stock exchange, contributed to the improved business climate, thus reducing Argentina's perceived country risk, and strengthening the domestic capital markets.[94] In the first two phases of privatization (1989–94) private capital flows, both domestic and foreign, after marking a $4.3 billion deficit in 1989, experienced positive record growth levels in 1992 and 1993, $7.8 billion and $5.0 billion respectively. Privatization aside, investments were in the form of stocks, bonds, and real estate as well as mergers and acquisitions of domestic companies.[95] Privatization was also expected to play a strong role in future investments. Newly privatized companies were to invest $8.3 billion during the 1993–6

TABLE 3.6. *Argentina: Shareholding in Controlling Consortia in Privatized Companies*

Rank	Nationality	Share
1	Argentina	40.66
2	United States	16.27
3	Spain	12.5
4	Chile	7.67
5	Italy	7.51
6	France	6.05
7	Canada	3.19
8	United Kingdom	2.34
9	Australia	0.57
10	Switzerland	0.52
11	Panama	0.47
12	Belgium	0.46
13	Cayman Islands	0.40
14	Saudi Arabia	0.38
15	Japan	0.37
16	Brazil	0.34
17	Uruguay	0.08
18	Korea	0.08
19	Liberia	0.06
20	Cyprus	0.04
21	Ecuador	0.02
22	Netherlands	0.02
TOTAL		100.00

Source: Investment Undersecretariat, October 1994.

period and an additional $5.4 billion in the following 1997–2000 period, making up roughly 34 per cent of all investments in Argentina during the same period, according to the forecasts based upon private companies' pledges as stated in the transfer contracts of former PEs.[96] These cash inflows were important not only because they provided new investments but also because they permitted the government to sustain the fixed exchange rate policy instituted by the Convertibility Plan, which was at the core of economic stability. However, the Argentine experience also shows the perils of relying on privatization as an alternative to serious fiscal adjustment. This appeared plainly when in 1995, partly as a result of speculative maneuvers following the Mexican crisis of December 1994, the country faced a new fiscal emergency that could no longer be financed by large privatization revenues, which scared investors and drove the economy into a recession.

Fifth, the privatization policy played a key role in Argentina's ability to enter the Brady Plan. Seeking to achieve this goal, Menem uniquely and

TABLE 3.7. *Argentina: Privatized Companies by Buyer 1990–4**

Sector	Date	Company	Type of Sale	Buyer	%	Country
Telecommunications	Dec. 91	ENTel	Sale of 30%	Citicorp	20.00	USA
				Banco Rio de la Plata	14.5	Argentina
				Telefonica de Espana	10.00	Spain
				Techint	8.31	Argentina
				Banco Central de Espana	7.04	Spain
				Soldati	5.00	Argentina
				Banco Hispanoamericano	5.00	Spain
				Manufacturers Hanover	4.0	USA
				Bank of Tokyo	4. 6	Japan
				Bank of New York	4. 6	USA
				Bank of Zurich	4_6	Switzerland
				Southel Equity Co.	4.00	USA
				Arab Banking Co.	4.31	Saudi Arabia
				Rep. of NY Financing	2.50	USA
				Centro Banco de Panama	1.40	Panama
				Venegas	0.25	Panama
				Banco Atlantico	0.75	Panama
				Bank of Nova Scotia	0.10	Panama
	Mar. 92	ENTel	Sale of 30%	Stet	32.50	Italy
				Cable et Radio	32.50	France
				JP Morgan	10.00	USA
				Perez Corpanc	25.00	Argentina
Transportation	Nov. 90	Aerolineas Argentinas	Sale of 85% (later reduced)	Banco Hispanoamericano	8.82	Spain
				Banesto	8.82	Spain
				Cofivacasa	.71	Spain
				Amadeo Riva	1.76	Spain
				Devi Construcciones	7.00	Argentina
				Medefin	.35	Argentina
				Riva SA	9.00	Argentina
				F. de Vircenzo	5.25	Argentina
				Iberia Airlines	35.30	Spain

Petrochemicals	Oct. 90	Polisur	Sale of 30%	Ipako	100.00	Argentina
	Oct. 90	Petrocol	Sale of 30%	Indupa	100.00	Argentina
	Oct. 90	Monomeros Vinicolos	Sale of 30%	Indupa	100.00	Argentina
	Mar. 92	Petroquimica Rio Terecro	Sale of 39%	Egerton Finance	100.00	Argentina
	Sep. 92	Carboquimica Argentina	Sale of 42%	Safety-Procamet	100.00	Argentina
Oil (YPF Central Areas)	Jun. 91	Tordillo	Ass. Cont. 90%	Tecpetrol	47.50	Argentina
				St. Fe Energy	20.00	USA
				Energy Development Co.	12.50	USA
				Perez Companc	20.00	Argentina
	Jun. 91	El Heumul	Ass. Cont. 70%	Total Austral	100.00	France
	Jun. 91	Puesto Hernandez	Ass. Cont. 60%	Perez Companc	57.00	Argentina
				Oxy	5.83	USA
				Oxy (Arg. Cap. Nort.)	34.67	USA
				Petrolera Patagonica	1.25	Argentina
				Inter Rio Holding	1.25	Argentina
	Jun. 91	Vizcacheras	Ass. Con. 90%	Astra	50.00	Argentina
				Repsol	50.00	Spain
	Dec. 91	Santa Cruz I	Ass. Con. 70%	Quintana Petroleum	28.57	USA
				Marc Rich	25.00	Switzerland
				Compania Gral de Comb.	46.43	Argentina
	Jan. 92	Tierra del Fuego	Ass. Con. 70%	Bridas	14.29	Argentina
				Valdana	38.08	Argentina
				Chauvco Resources Ltd.	33.34	Argentina
				Coastal Argentina	14.29	USA
	Mar. 92	Santa Cruz II	Ass. Con. 70%	Perez Companc	40.00	Argentina
				Astra	40.00	Argentina
				Inter Rio Holding	20.00	Argentina
	Nov. 92	Aguarague	Ass. Con. 55%	Tecpetrol	35.72	Argentina
				Ampolex	35.71	Australia
				Gral. de Combustibles	29.50	Argentina
				Dong Won	20.00	South Korea

TABLE 3.7. *(cont'd)*

Sector	Date	Company	Type of Sale	Buyer	%	Country
Oil (YPF Asset Sale)	Nov. 92	Campo Dura Refinery	Sale of 70%	Perez Companc	40.00	Argentina
				Pluspetrol	30.00	Argentina
				Astra	15.00	Argentina
				Isaura	15.00	Argentina
	Jan. 93	Ebytem	Sale of 70%	Isaura	100.00	Argentina
	Jan. 93	Duck Sud Distillery	Sale of 100%	Destileria Arg. de Petroleo	100.00	Argentina
	Jan. 93	Pipeline del Valle	Sale of 70%	Perez Companc	33.00	Argentina
				Bolland	20.00	Argentina
				Bridas	17.00	Argentina
				Pluspetrol	17.00	Argentina
				Astra	10.00	Argentina
				Tecpetrol	3.00	Argentina
	Jan. 93	San Lorenzo Distillery	Sale of 100%	Perez Companc	42.50	Argentina
				Gral. de Combustibles	42.50	Argentina
				Pasa	15.00	Argentina
	Jun. 93	Sea Transp. Petroleo	Sale of 70%	Antares Naviera	55.00	Argentina
				Ciamar	10.00	Argentina
				Delbene	10.00	Argentina
				Ultragas	25.00	Panama
	Sep. 93	Interpetrol	Sale of 49%	Solfina	100.00	Argentina
	Sep. 93	Aerosol Plant Dock Sud	Sale of 100%	Arpetro	100.00	Argentina
	Sep. 93	Sea Term. PatagonicaS	Sale of 70%	Perez Companc	19.70	Argentina
				Astra	8.60	Argentina
				Bridas	6.90	Argentina
				Depetrol	11.20	Argentina
				Amoco	25.00	USA
				Cadipsa	7.60	Argentina
				Asociadas Petroleras	4.50	Argentina
				Total	16.50	France

Sector	Date	Asset	Sale	Buyer	Value	Country
Tourism	Mar/Dec. 93	Twenty Tankers	Sale of 100%	Antares Naviera		Argentina
				Lunmar		Argentina
				Naviera Sur Petrolera		Argentina
				Constant Shipping Ltd.		Italy
				Global Marketing System		India
				Melton Trading		Panama
				Naviera Sur Petrolera		Argentina
	May. 91	Hotel Llao Llao	Sale of 100%	Citicorp	45.00	USA
				Choice Hotel International	10.00	USA
				Cafica y Sur Hotel	45.00	Argentina
Electricity	Apr. 92	Central Puerto	Sale of 60%	Chilgener	50.00	Chile
				Chilena de Elect. V Reg.	16.40	Chile
				Chilectra V Region	33.40	Chile
	May. 92	Central Costanera	Sale of 60%	Endesa	50.10	Chile
				Enersis	15.00	Chile
				Dist. Chilectra Metropol.	5.00	Chile
				Perez Companc	12.50	Argentina
				Inter Rio Holding	12.50	Argentina
				Costanera Power Co.	4.90	USA
	Aug. 92	Edenor	Sale of 51%	Astra Caspa	40.00	Argentina
				Electricité de France	20.00	France
				Endesa de Espana	10.00	Spain
				Emp. Nacional Hidroel.	20.00	Spain
				Societe D'Amenag. Urb.	10.00	France
	Aug. 92	Edesur	Sale of 51%	Perez Companc	32.50	Argentina
				Grupo PSA Energy	8.00	USA
				Dist. Chilectra Metropol.	20.00	Chile
				Enersis	18.50	Chile
				Endesa	11.00	Chile
				Entergy	10.00	USA
	Oct. 92	Central Pedro de Mendoza	Sale of 90%	Acindar	75.00	Argentina
				Massuh	25.00	Argentina
	Oct. 92	Central Duck Sud	Sale of 90%	Polledo	100.00	Argentina
				Techint	51.00	Argentina
	Nov. 92	Edelap	Sale of 51%	Houston Power Co.	49.00	USA

TABLE 3.7. *(cont'd)*

Sector	Date	Company	Type of Sale	Buyer	%	Country
Electricity	Nov. 92	Central Alto Valle	Sale of 90%	Alto Valle Hodling, Cooperativa Provincial, and Comunit. de Neuquen Dominion generation and MGMT/Dominion Energy	40.00	Argentina
	Sep. 92	Central Guemes	Sale of 60%	Duke Power	60.00	USA
				Soc. Comercial del Plata	25.00	USA
				Iberdrola	20.00	Argentina
				The Argentine Invest. Co.	15.00	Spain
				Tew Americas Develop.	15.00	Cayman Isl.
	Jan. 93	Central Sorrento	Sale of 90%	Malvicino	18.00	USA
				Iate	18.00	Argentina
				Eleprint	4.00	Argentina
				Argon	60.00	Argentina
	Apr. 93	Central San Nicolas	Sale of 88%	AES San Nicolas	81.00	Argentina
				Ormas Saicic	19.00	USA
	Mar. 93	Centrales T de Nore. Ar.	Sale of 90%	Iate	100.00	Argentina
	Mar. 93	Centrales T. del Noroes.	Sale of 90%	Fed. de Trab. Luz y Fuerza	40.00	Argentina
				Giacomo Fazio	15.00	Argentina
				Horizonte	15.00	Argentina
				Atahualpa	15.00	Argentina
				Camino	15.00	Argentina
	Jul. 93	Transener	Sale of 65%	Electrica del Plata	15.00	Argentina
				Sade	15.00	Argentina
				Inter Rio Holding	15.00	Argentina
				Duke Transener Inc.	15.00	USA
				Enetergy Transener Inc.	15.00	USA
				International Grid Finance	15.00	UK
				The Argentine Invest. Co.	10.00	Cayman Isl.

Date	Company	Transaction	Buyer	%	Country
Aug. 93	Central Alicura	Sale of 59%	Sei Holding Inc.	80.00	USA
			Asociados de Electricidad	14.00	Argentina
			Diecisiete de Avril SA	5.00	Argentina
			Resource Dev. Consultants	1.00	USA
Aug. 93	Central Cerros Colorado	Sale of 59%	Dominion Generating	85.00	USA
			Louis Dreyfus Argener	15.00	USA
Aug. 93	Central el Choco	Sale of 59%	Hidroelectricidad	55.00	Chile
			CMS Generation	30.00	USA
			Bea Inversora	8.00	Argentina
			Sawgrass Ltd.	7.00	Spain
Nov. 93	Centrales Patagonicas	Sale of 51%	Iate	33.33	Argentina
			Fed. de Trab. Luz y Fuerza	33.33	Argentina
			Eleprint	33.33	Argentina
Dec. 93	Central Piedra del Aguila	Sale of 59%	Duke Hidronor	33.33	USA
			Transalta Energy Arg.	33.33	Canada
			Hidroandes	27.83	Chile
			Emerging Market Gr. Fund	5.00	USA
			New World Fund	0.51	USA
Jan. 94	Transnoa	Sale of 90%	Banco Feigin	45.00	Argentina
			Fed. de Trab. Luz y Fuerza	23.00	Argentina
			Iate	23.00	Argentina
			Tecsa	7.00	Argentina
Jun. 94	Transpa	Sale of 51%	Trelpa	40.00	Argentina
			Aluar	15.00	Argentina
			Grupo CG Argentina	5.00	Argentina
			Camuzzi	25.00	Italy
			Various Cooperatives	15.00	Argentina
Jul. 94	Centrales T. del Litoral	Sale of 90%	Fed. de Trab. Luz y Fuerza	100.00	Argentina
Sep. 94	Hidroelectrica Diamante	Sale of 59%	EDF International	50.00	France
			Nucleamiento Inversor	42.50	Argentina
			Banco de Galicia	7.50	Argentina
Oct. 94	Hidroelectrica Ameghino	Sale of 59%	Hidroelectrica del Sur and	60.00	Argentina
			Camuzzi		Italy
Oct. 94	Centrales T. mendoza	Sale of 51%	Transmisiones Elect.	20.00	Argentina
			Cooperativa A.P.R.	20.00	Argentina
			CMS Generation	80.00	USA
			Ormas Saicic	20.00	Argentina

TABLE 3.7. *(cont'd)*

Sector	Date	Company	Type of Sale	Buyer	%	Country
Electricity	Oct. 94	Transnea	Sale of 60%	Iate	40.00	Argentina
				Argon	20.00	Argentina
				Fed. de Trab. Luz y Fuerza	20.00	Argentina
				Eleprint	20.00	Argentina
	Dec. 94	Hidroelectrica Rio Hondo	Sale of 98%	Apauye	33.00	Argentina
				Necon	34.00	Argentina
				Jose Chediak SAICA	33.00	Argentina
Gas	Dec. 92	Gas del Estado	Sale of 70%	Enron Pipeline	25.00	USA
				Perez Companc	25.00	Argentina
				Citicorp	25.00	USA
				Arg. Private Dev. Trust Co.	25.00	Argentina
	Dec. 92	Transp. Gas del Norte	Sale 70%	Novacorp International	25.00	Canada
				Transcogas Inv.	36.00	Canada
				Wartins	39.00	Argentina
	Dec. 92	Distrib. Gas Pampeano	Sale 70%	Camuzzi	100.00	Italy
	Dec. 92	Distrib. Gas del Litoral	Sale of 90%	Tractebel	40.00	Belgium
				Iberdrola	20.00	Spain
				Garovaglio y Zarraquin	20.00	Argentina
				Diecisiete de Abril	20.00	Argentina
	Dec. 92	Distrib. Gas del Centro	Sale of 90%	Sideco Sudamericana	75.00	Argentina
				Societa Italiana Gas	25.00	Italy
	Dec. 92	Distrib. Gas de Cuyana	Sale of 60%	Sideco Sudamericana	75.00	Argentina
				Societa Italiana Gas	25.00	Italy
	Dec. 92	Distrib. Gas del Noroeste	Sale of 90%	Cartellone Construcciones	40.00	Argentina
				Banco Frances	20.00	Argentina
				Cia de Consum. de Santiago	40.00	Chile
	Dec. 92	Distrib. Gas del Sur	Sale of 90%	Camuzzi	100.00	Italy
	Dec. 92	Distrib. Gas Metropolitano	Sale of 70%	British Gas	41.30	UK
				Perez Companc	25.30	Argentina
				Astra	20.30	Argentina
				Invertrad	14.30	Argentina
	Dec. 92	Distrib. Gas BA Norte	Sale of 70%	Gas Natural	54.30	Spain
				Discogas	25.30	Argentina
				Manra	21.30	Spain

Sector	Date	Company	Type of sale	Buyer	%	Country
Defense	Dec. 91	Trandanor	Sale of 100%	Banco Holandes	2.90	Netherland
				Sid Marine	5.00	France
	Apr. 92	Aceros Zapla	Sale of 100%	Argentina de Maritimos	92.10	Argentina
				Aubert Duval	14.00	France
				Sima	19.34	France
				Pensa	28.33	Argentina
				Penfin	5.00	Argentina
				Citicorp	33.33	USA
	Oct. 92	Aceros Parana	Sale of 80%	Propulsora Siderurgica	90.00	Argentina
				Siderca	10.00	Argentina
	Feb. 93	Fab. Militar Tolueno Sintetic	Sale of 100%	Rutilex e Hidrocarburos	100.00	Argentina
	Feb. 93	ECA	Sale of 100%	Consorcio Metacab	74.00	Argentina
				Ind. Electricas de Quilmes	26.00	Chile
	Mar. 93	Fab. Militar Acido Solfurico	Sale	Maspro	100.00	Argentina
	Apr. 93	Fab. Militar San Martin	Sale	Talleres Sudamericanos	100.00	Argentina
	Jul. 93	Fab. Militar Vta. Pilar	Sale	IAMP	100.00	Argentina
Agro-Industry	Sep. 92	Elevetor Puerto Diamante	Sale of 100%	Consortium of Cia Continental, Sacimfa, and Granero	100.00	Argentina
	May 93	Unid. Puerto San Pedro	Sale of 100%	Servicios Portuarios	100.00	Argentina
	Jul. 93	Elevetor Term. de Rosario	Sale of 100%	Servicios Portuarios	100.00	Argentina
Agriculture	May 94	Corp. Argentina Productores	Sale	Incopp	50.00	Argentina
				Frigorifico Bahia Blanca	50.00	Argentina
Finance	Apr. 94	Caja de Ahorros y Seguros	Sale of 60%	Leucadia National Co.	50.00	USA
				WSA	40.00	Argentina
				Banco Mercantil Argentino	10.00	Argentina
Transportation	Feb/Jul. 94	Empresa Lineas Maritimas	Sale of 100%	Seabound Maritime	n.a.	Liberia
				Prudent Int. Shipping	n.a.	India
				Aspen Marine	n.a.	Cyprus
				Ocenbulk	n.a.	Cyprus
				Altamira Nautical	n.a.	Panama

Source: Boletin de Subsecretaria de Inversiones, Ministry of the Economy, Public Works, and Services, 1995.
* Concessions are not included.

TABLE 3.8. *Argentina: Changes in Performance of Privatized Utilities 1993–5 (%)*

Performance Indicator	Electricity distribution	Gas distribution	Water distribution	Telecoms
Efficiency[a]	6.26	8.84	4.86	11.28
Labor productivity[b]	17.59	4.79	−27.58	21.25
Investment[c]		4.56	75.97	28.10
Quality[d]	10.00	27.80	6.12	4.56
Real average tariffs[e]	−9.50	−0.50	7.20	28.40

Source: Chisari, Estache, and Romero (1997)
[a] Intermediate input costs as % of total sales
[b] GWh for electricity, 000m3 for gas, population served for water, lines in service for phones—all relative to staff.
[c] In concession contracts for gas and actual investments for other sectors.
[d] Ratio of losses to production and gas, of water unaccounted for to production for water, of lines in repair to lines in service for phones.
[e] Ratio of total sales value to production.

aggressively pursued a foreign policy aimed closely at aligning Argentina with the United States. He was ultimately successful. Argentina's entry into the Brady Plan meant that the country received a discount of 35 per cent, or $10 billion, on its foreign debt (including $3 billion in debt equity swaps earned by the new round of privatizations) and a rescheduling of the remaining outstanding debt.[97] The IMF, World Bank, and IDB provided special loans exceeding $5 billion. Concurrently, foreign governments praised the Menem administration's bold policies as a model for the new Latin American leadership, affording the President his long-sought international prestige.

Sixth, several sectors of the federal administration were streamlined and overstaffing was curtailed. By 1995, employment in PEs had dropped to 66,731 as opposed to 347,240 in 1989.[98] At the end of that year, and for the first time in decades, some of the remaining PEs were able to post an overall profit (Castelar Pinheiro and Schneider 1994: 17).

Seventh, the main privatized companies demonstrated clear improvements. A preliminary study (Chisari, Estache, and Romero 1997) showed that during the 1993–5 period, that is, a few years after being privatized, companies in telecommunications, as well as distribution in electricity, gas, and water improved their performance in terms of efficiency, labor productivity, investment, quality, and real average tariffs (Table 3.8). Another study looking at the telecommunication sector's performance, shows that the main telephone lines in service during the five-year period preceding and following privatization grew from 5 per cent a year before privatization to 12 per cent a year after privatization. The digitalization of phone lines went from 11 per cent to 76 per cent. Productivity, measured by the number of main telephone lines in service divided by the number of full time employees, rose from 60 to 186 (Wellenius 1998). The average time to get a new telephone dropped from six years to one month. The numbers of phones per 100 inhabitants grew from 6 to 19. Moreover, the quality of goods provided improved appreciably thanks to heavy investments in upgrading technology in the oil, telecommunications, water supply, and electricity sectors. Telecom Argentina alone claimed to have invested $6 billion in its first seven years of operations.[99] The quality and management training of the staff also saw significant improvements (Galiani and Petrecolla 1999).

These were the positive achievements. However, in other respects, the economic record was quite mixed if not altogether negative. To begin with, as Hill and Abdala (1996) underscored, the divestiture program took place in a heavily rent-seeking society. It was also marked by a weak institutional setting, an unreliable and politically manipulated judicial system, and a public bureaucracy prone to corruption. Adding to these problems was the fact that the rush to privatize in 1989–92 and again in 1995–8, within the context of macroeconomic instability, led to a series of poorly made decisions and even worse implementation. Only when the macroeconomic picture improved dramatically in 1993–4, so did the design and execution of several privatizations that followed. However, in the meantime, considerable damage had been done.

First, too frequently, in lucrative markets like public services, the government's eagerness to attract buyers resulted in detrimental concessions, including the preservation of monopolistic or oligopolistic markets, under new private ownership, within the context of weak regulation (Petrazzini 1995, Vispo 1998). This phenomenon created economic rents sheltering private enterprise from competition, which ultimately penalized consumers.[100] In such markets, including air passenger cargo, telecommunications, petrochemicals, highways, trains, and steel this caused the government to surrender efficiency in exchange for funding (Gerchunoff and Coloma 1993: 258). To make things worse privatization occurred in the context of trade liberalization, resulting in the creation of a dysfunctional two-sector economy. In fact, we have now, on the one hand, a private sector facing foreign competition and being forced into making drastic economic adjustments in order to survive. This has been particularly difficult to do after the enactment of the Covertibility Law, which has caused the steady appreciation of the Argentine peso vis-à-vis the US dollar, in turn raising domestic costs of production to comparatively higher rates than those of other countries. On the other hand, a new private sector now exists, controlling former state monopolies in services and petrochemicals, which faces little or no competition, is not affected by an over-valued exchange rate and, consequently is highly profitable.

Second is the problem of regulation, which is closely related to the issues raised above. For example, 'the lack of a clear regulatory regime offset the revenues obtained by the fiscal authorities. It obliged interested buyers to under-value the acquired assets . . . the income given up by the state in the pres-ence of uncertainty regarding the regulatory regime represented [in the case of the marginal oil field areas] 32 per cent of the total income [earned]' (Petrecolla *et al.* 1993: 79). In another study, Chisari, Estache, and Romero (1997: 43) estimated about $915 million worth of losses from ineffective regulation of public utilities that, on average, resulted into a 16 per cent addi-tional tax per household for such services. Conversely, effective regulation seemed to have a positive impact on income distribution since the poorest sector of society stood to gain the most in terms of electricity, gas, and water provision, whereas the middle class was the biggest winner in telecommun-ication service.

From an organizational standpoint, of the fifteen regulatory agencies and secretariats in operation in 1998, only the one overseeing the mail service was fully operational prior to, rather than after, privatization. In general, only the electricity and to a lesser extent the gas regulatory agencies seem to work fairly well. The remaining sectors have very weak regulatory agencies lacking funds, adequate staffs, and independence from the executive. Con-siderable criticism was raised against the government as many regulatory agency members had close links to the private companies that they were supposed to monitor. This brought up issues of conflicts of interest.[101]

Back in 1993, the chairman of the Bicameral Commission on Privatization had already shown concern, explicitly stating after the major privatizations were complete, 'now the time has come to control public services, to demand the [private companies'] compliance [with] the accords [they] subscribed, to rigorously verify the fulfillment of contractual obligations, to assure that the services provided be efficacious as expected' (Natale 1993: 271–2). In 1997, the Argentine General Accounting Office report on privatized firms confirmed Natale's misgivings. It stressed that many companies in public utility services did not comply with their contract agreements and the regulat-ory agencies overseeing their activities failed to sanction wrongdoings. The situation, the report continued, was particularly alarming in the provision of telephone, gas, water, and railway service.[102] Moreover, the extension of the monopoly status to the telephone companies (up until 1999) and to the urban railway operators (for 20 more years, which included a 90 per cent tariff hike to finance infrastructures) generated widespread controversy since such decisions were made by the executive, instead of the competent regulatory agency, and increased the suspicion of collusion.[103]

By 1998, regulation had become one of the most controversial issues as newspaper reports portrayed widespread dissatisfaction with the provision of many privatized services.[104] Feeling the changed public mood, opposition parties, as well as many Peronist legislators, began to seize the initiative and call for stricter government controls, possibly through the creation of a 'super agency'.

Third, the lack of transparency involved in the administration privatization process and the independence of the judiciary were troublesome factors even for many business supporters favoring Menem's reforms. 'The abuse of decrees of *need* and *urgency* from the part of the executive bring about worrisome questions . . . Between the importance and the urgency, society (and the government) . . . must give top priority to the consensus over the importance of the changes introduced [by the economic reform program]' (Bour 1993: 263–4). Lack of transparency resulted in alleged instances of corruption that were never seriously investigated because of the heavy government influence in the judiciary. This situation made people uneasy, as testified by the fact that only a quarter of the people surveyed in 1993 thought that public services were privatized well (Table 3.2).[105] The same applies to business people who feared that, having the executive used emergency powers to privatize, it was entirely possible for a new government, under a different leadership not committed to market reforms, to invoke the same means in order to breach property rights acquired by private companies in the future (Estache and Martimort 1998). In point of fact, a precedent already exists in Argentina. Months after winning the 30-year concession of the local water company in the province of Tucuman, in the north-west region of the country, the French giant Vivendi found itself in this very situation when a new governor used decree powers to alter tariff rates, causing the company large losses.[106]

Fourth, Menem's explicit effort to reward his business supporters coming from the largest domestic conglomerates has a potentially negative effect on efficiency and competition for the near future.[107] To be sure, by 1990, they had already acquired a substantial political clout:

For the first time, since the launching of the import substitution industrialization policy in the 1930s, the national bourgeoisie plays a central role so openly in the political scenario . . . not only has there been an increase of the economic power for the dominant domestic economic interests over the last 15 years, but there has also been . . . an increase in the power and political presence of those interests, particularly where public decisions are made, which affect the different aspects of the country's economic life.   (Ostiguy 1990: 17, 35)

Yet privatization strengthened the ascendancy of the ten largest domestic conglomerates (Table 3.9), which were particularly active in the divestiture process during 1990–2 period. Often in partnership with foreign groups, the country's conglomerates acquired PEs at bargain prices. Those included Astra, Bunge & Born, Bridas, Loma Negra, Macri, Pérez Companc, Soldati, Techint, and Zorraquín. Privatization gave them the oligopolistic or monopolistic

TABLE 3.9. *Argentina: Top 25 Companies by Ranking in 1984 and 1992*

Ranking 1984	Ranking 1992
1 YPF (PE)	1 YPF*
2 Esso (foreign)	2 Siderca (Techint Group)
3 Shell	3 Perez Companc
4 Acindar	4 Acindar
5 Molinos Rio de la Plata (Bunge & Born Group)	5 Esso
6 Ford	6 Bridas Energy (Bridas Group)
7 Somisa (PE)	7 Alto Parana
8 Nobleza Picardo (foreign)	8 Celulosa Argentina (Massuh Group)
9 Renault (foreign)	9 Astra (Gruneisen Group)
10 Dalamine	10 Ladesma (Blaquier Group)
11 Massalin Particulares (foreign)	11 Shell
12 Bridas (Bridas Group)	12 Alpargatas (Roberts Group)
13 Sevel (Macri Group)	13 Sevel (Macri Group)
14 IBM (foreign)	14 Aluar (Madanes Group)
15 Mastellone (Mastellone Group)	15 Impsa (Pescarmona Group)
16 Fabricaciones Militares (PE)	16 Sancor
17 Propulsora Siderurgica (Techint Group)	17 Arcor
18 Aluar	18 Pasa Petroquimica (Perez Companc Group)
19 Alpargatas (Alpargatas Group)	19 Propulsora Siderurgica (Techint Group)
20 Aluar Molinos Concepcion	20 Ipako
21 Astra (Gruneisen Group)	21 Cargill (foreign)
22 Volkswagen (foreign)	22 Loma Negra (Fortabat Group)
23 Perez Companc	23 Ciadea
24 Ladesma (Blaquier Group)	24 Iasura
25 Ducilo	25 Ciadea Iasura Cerveceria Quilmes

Source: *Prensa Economica*, September 1985 and November 1993.
* Privatized through public and international public offer.

control of very lucrative markets within the service sector such as telephones, highways, railways, oil exploitation, gas, electricity, and media (Tables 3.10 and 3.11) (Sguiglia 1992: 102). Often, private conglomerates acquired their competitors from the state sector. Ironically, it was the same state companies that, after 1945, had helped the expansion of private conglomerates through subcontracts and the provision of goods and services at inflated prices. Astra, Bridas, and Pérez Companc strengthened their oligopolistic control over the petroleum sector with the privatization of YPF. Acindar and Techint con-solidated control over the steel sector once the government sold them its companies, especially Somisa. For all these groups, privatization proved a golden opportunity not only to expand business ventures but also to increase the vertical and horizontal integration of their subsidiaries (Azpiazu and

TABLE 3.10. *Argentina: Selected Companies Acquired by Domestic Conglomerates 1990–8*

Conglomerate	Companies Acquired
Perez Companc	Telecom (ENTel); Telefonica (ENTel); YPF central areas; highways; SEGBA (Edesur); SEGBA (Central Costanera); Destileria Campo Duran; Transportadora Gas Sur; Distribuidora Gas Metropolitano; Ferroexpreso Pampeano; Oleoducto Allen-Coronel Rosales; Destileria San Lorenzo
Techint (Rocca)	Telefonica (ENTel); highways; Somisa; SEGBA (Edelap); YPF (seconday fields); Transportadora Gas Norte; Ferroexpreso Pampeano; YPF (central fields)
Soldati	Channel 11; Telefonica (ENTel); Ferroexpreso Pampeano; YPF (central areas); YPF (secondary fields); Thermic Power Station Guemes; Railway Delta-Borges; Destileria San Lorenzo; Obras Sanitarias; Transportadora Gas Norte; Distribuidora Gas Buenos Aires Norte
Astra (Gruneisen)	YPF (central areas); YPF (marginal areas); SEGBA (Edenor); Destileria Campo Duran; Distribuidora Metropolitana Gas; Oleoducto Allen-Coronel Rosales
Richard	Iductor; Petropol; Monomeros Vinicolos
Zarraquin	Polisur
Noble-Clarin	Channel 13
Acindar-Acevedo	Central Pedro de Mendoza; Railway Roca-Cargas
Massuh	Central Pedro de Mendoza
Macri	Distribuidora Centro Gas; highways; Distribuidora Cuyana Gas; potable water; Correo Argentino (Encotesa)
Bunge & Born	Distribuidorara Pampeana de Gas; Distribuidora Gas Sur
Bemberg	Distribuidora Gas del Litoral
Fortabat	Railway Roca-Cargas
Roggio	Subway of Buenos Aires; highways; YPF marginal areas
Bridas	YPF (central areas)

Source: Ministry of the Economy, Public Works, and Services, 1995.

Vispo 1994). As a result, in 1995, the ten largest conglomerates accounted for 56 per cent of the total revenues earned by Argentina's 200 most important companies (Azpiazu 1998: 50). During the same year, the nine largest conglomerates that had actively participated in the privatization process posted a 20 per cent increase in net revenues, which was the highest rate among all firms that participated in the privatization process (Table 3.12). Such a good performance is all the more striking if one considers that 1995 was a recession year in Argentina. The explanation again rests on the fact that

TABLE 3.11. *Argentina: Main Business Interests of Argentina's Largest Conglomerates*

Conglomerate	Business Sector
Perez Compano	Oil, construction, power, banking, telecommunications
Soldati	Petrochemicals, construction, energy, telecommunications
Techint (Rocca)	Construction, steel, engineering, telecommunications, railways
Astra (Grunesien)	Oil, construction
Bridas (Bulgheroni)	Oil, gas, media, fishing
Benito Roggio	Construction, transportation
Loma Negra (Fortabat)	Cement manufacturing, ranching, finance, media
Bunge & Born	Food, textile chemicals, petrochemicals
SOCMA (Macri)	Construction, automobiles, relecommunications, software, mail service
Bemberg	Beer
Zarraquin	Petrochemicals
Roberts	Textile
Blaquier	Sugar, paper
Madanes	Aluminium
Massuh	Paper
Arcor	Food
Acindar-Acevedo	Steel
Clarin (Noble)	Media
Urquia	Oilseeds
Richard	Petrochemicals
Terrabusi-Montagna	Food
Bagley-Nunez	Food
Penaflor	Wine
Cartellone	Metallurgy, construction
Pescarmona	Metallurgy, services

Source: *Latin Finance*, February 1993, pp. 49–53; *Prensa Economica*, November 1993; Economic and Commercial Section of the Argentine Embassy in the United States.

conglomerates concentrated their privatization effort in monopolistic sectors hardly affected by competition. By contrast, firms that did not participate in the state divestiture program, and were likely to be exposed to competition, posted an average revenue growth rate of only 1.7 per cent (Table 3.12). One author described the economic clout achieved by the largest Argentine conglomerates by 1993 as follows:

Chances are that if you plan to purchase non-consumer exports from Argentina, you will buy from one of them. And if you should decide to bid on any major Argentine industrial expansion or public works project, you will end up with one of them as your local partner—or fiercest competitor. Part of every major economic lobby, they are present and active in a multitude of chambers, associations, committees, and councils. (Newland 1993: 49)

TABLE 3.12. *Argentina: Distribution of Sales and Net Income According to the Type of Participation in the Privatization Process 1994–5*

Type of Company	Number of Companies	Sales in 1995 (US$ million)	(%)	Revenues in 1995 (US$ million)	(%)	Net Income (%) 1994	1995
Companies involved in privatization	67	28,903.0	39.2	3,773.0	82.8	8.5	13.0
Mixed companies	1	4,970.1	6.7	793.1	17.4	12.8	16.0
Companies pursuing vertical integration	27	7,705.1	10.5	685.0	15.0	-2.4	8.9
Companies resulting from privatization	30	13,017.5	17.7	1,630.3	35.8	9.9	12.5
Conglomerates	9	3,210.0	4.3	664.6	14.6	18.5	20.7
Companies not involved in privatization	133	44,750.7	60.8	783.2	17.2	3.3	1.7
TOTAL	200	73,653.7	100.0	4,556.2	100.0	5.3	6.1

Source: Azpiazu (1998: 62).

It is also important to underscore that many of these privatizations at bargain prices were offered as compensation to those conglomerates suffering the termination of fat government contracts and subsidies (Azpiazu and Vispo 1994, Majul 1993 and 1994). By 1995, the symbiosis between political and economic power reached an unprecedented level as the largest conglomerates generously funded Menem's campaign re-election and their chief executive officers figured prominently on the list of special guests travelling abroad with the President to procure new business.

This cozy relationship, according to some, was worrisome because domestic conglomerates, having captured important markets and established lucrative rents through privatizations, were likely to resist any effort aimed at changing the oligopolistic privileges they have acquired (Azpiazu 1998). Indeed, the economic clout that they presently have provides them with a negotiating power that hardly any government can ignore, making the prospects for greater efficiency and less collusion in Argentina in the future as doubtful as they were in the past (Canitrot 1993: 91).

Having said that, domestic conglomerates, while being highly visible, were not the only winners. Foreign investors won big too, particularly those who operated under little or no competition, as in the telecommunication sector that generated rates of return on fixed assets between 24 and 33 per cent yearly (Petrazzini 1995: 135). Workers who kept their jobs in privatized PEs also experienced appreciable salary increases and some needed extra income through the shares reserved for them under the privatization scheme. Although popular capitalism, *strictu sensu*, did not materialize, about 100,000 employees in telecommunications, gas, electricity, and oil became shareholders of what became blue chip companies under private management.[108] Those union leaders who decided to go along with Menem managed to retain many of their privileges, acquired some new ones and, in some cases, appeased their political ambitions as they were nominated to government posts. Likewise, politicians coming from the PJ and small conservative parties, acquiescent judges, sympathetic media people, and technocrats of different creeds found in Menem a generous master, as long as their services were needed.

On the losing end, one could find the usual suspects: opposition politicians cut off from patronage networks, the 163,000 laid off workers many of whom were either too old and/or whose skills were too outmoded to land another job, and small entrepreneurs who, once they lost the PEs' contracts, were left out from major privatization deals and were unable to reconvert their business ventures.

As Menem's second term drew to a close in 1999, he could rightfully claim that he truly changed his country's history as very few of his predecessors had done. The reforms that he introduced had radically changed for the better not only the economy but also his people's attitudes in a number of ways. In many respects, Argentina is entering the twenty-first century as a much more modern and self-confident country. If one looks back at Argentina's conditions in 1989, these are achievements that only fall short of a miracle. On some dimensions, the Argentine experience became a textbook case on how to build a pro-reform political coalition and technically manage a complex divestiture program, as in the case of electricity. However, in terms of transparency and regulatory policy Argentina was equally an illustrative case on how things should not be done.

In fact, the dark side of Menem's success was not so much its high social cost, as unemployment and poverty almost tripled. That was expected. Rather what was troublesome was Menem's arbitrary style and disregard for the rule of law that did nothing to improve the country's institutions in terms of legitimacy and efficiency. Indeed, throughout his tenure Menem ruled under the state of emergency legal clauses, which allowed him much discretion. His quick and dirty approach, and the alleged cases of corruption ascribed to his administration, surely tarnished the image of his policies, including privatization. In the beginning people thought that this was a necessary evil to be tolerated for a greater good, but still in 1998, Menem was trying to push major legislation through decrees, pointing out the fact that he had not changed his attitude. However, while he showed no intention to change his ways many Argentines in the meantime did. In November 1997, capitalizing on issues like corruption, unemployment, poverty, and lack of government transparency the Radicals and the left-wing FREPASO movement (Frente Pais Solidario) joined forces and scored a stunning victory in mid-term congressional elections depriving Menem of a congressional majority for the first time since 1991. As the country moved from a situation of economic bankruptcy to one of political and economic stability, people progressively began to expect more from their politicians in terms of accountability and performance on issues other than inflation. The old slogan 'follow me, I am not going to betray you', that served Menem so well in 1989, did not seem to do the trick anymore, particularly among middle and upper-middle-class voters.[109] While Menem had well understood his country's mood in 1989, by 1997 he failed to realize that the stakes of the game had changed and demanded more honest and efficient government performance. Coincidentally, after the electoral debacle, opposition to the government's remaining privatizations in banking and power plants, both in and out of Congress, and within his own party, mounted to an unprecedented level and brought the process to a virtual standstill.

Endnotes

1. *La Nación*, 11 February 1992, p. 13.
2. The law also allowed the executive to change the internal organization of PEs, break them apart, merge them, or dissolve them at will. It gave great discretional

power to new government-appointed trustees in choosing the methods of privatization. Sales could take the form of public auctions or competitions with or without a minimum floor price. The law also preserved existing labor contracts, union rights and internal organization, and social security benefits. It spelled out a system of workers' ownership in PEs to be privatized as well.

3. The Senate and the House of Deputies both named six members. Of the twelve, six were Peronists, four Radicals, and two were conservatives from small regional parties.

4. The term 'liberal' actually means conservative in Argentina and the rest of Latin America and Southern Europe. Deputy Natale was from the Progressive Democratic party of Santa Fe.

5. Traditionally, the Peronist movement has been strongest in the urban areas (particularly within the working class) and in the less developed provinces of the country where there persists a strong conservative tradition based upon a patronage system (Snow 1979; Turner *et al.* 1988; Mora y Araujo 1991; McGuire 1997).

6. *Foreign Broadcast Information Service*, 19 Nov. 1991, p. 14.

7. *Pagina/12*, 20 November 1989, p. 3.

8. *Pagina 12*, 24 November 1990.

9. Menem, in return, met some of the UCR's demands. Among them: (1) the number of senators per province was increased from two to three with the third senator representing the second largest party (in many provinces the UCR is second only to the PJ); (2) the presidential power to rule by decree was curbed; (3) the new post of cabinet chief (a quasi prime minister figure patterned after the French model) whose appointment is dependent upon congressional approval; (4) the old provision that the president was to be a Catholic was eliminated. Moreover, the Peronists agreed to give greater independence to the judiciary that would be entrusted upon a new institution, the Supreme Council of the Magistrature, to be patterned after the Italian model. However, well into 1999, this last provision was still to materialize since the Peronists kept stonewalling.

10. In the case of YPF shares were also offered on the New York Stock Exchange (21.9 per cent of total shares) and European stock markets (12.5 per cent). Major Argentine investors took 5 per cent and 5 per cent went to small domestic investors.

11. *La Rázon*, 3 October 1985.

12. On Menem's political conservatism see Giussani (1990).

13. *Miami Herald*, 23 April 1990.

14. The Brady Plan was an emergency package devised by US Treasury Secretary Nicholas Brady in 1989. It provided debt relief to debtor countries which showed concrete efforts toward market-oriented reform policies. Contrary to the 'muddling through' and Baker plan approaches attempted under the Reagan administration, emphasizing the full repayment of debt, the Brady Plan acknowledged one of the major points made in the past by debtor countries. That is, forgiveness of part of the debt in order to make repayments possible. Accordingly, the Brady Plan established a 35 per cent debt cut owed to commercial banks. The US, Japan, and some European countries, in collaboration with the IMF, the World Bank, and the Inter-American Development Bank, also

supplied financial assistance for a total of US$30 billion to help the debt rescheduling process.

15. *Pagina/12*, 9 September 1990, pp. 8–11.
16. Interviews with officials from the Ministry of the Economy, Public Works and Services. Buenos Aires, November 1993 and October 1994.
17. For an analysis of the reasons for PEs' steady financial deterioration see Gerchunoff and Cánovas (1995).
18. *Latin American Monitor: Argentina 1991* (London: Business Monitor International Ltd., 1991), p. 44. For instance, the state railways lost annually about $600 million.
19. For Majul, the Pérez Companc group topped the list with $900 million, followed by the Soldati and Benito Roggio groups. Not surprisingly, the Soldati group increased its business by five six times after 1989. Pérez Companc, the largest Argentine conglomerate, doubled its profits. *La Maga*, Buenos Aires, 5 October 1994, p. 4.
20. Interview with Luis Majul. Buenos Aires, March 1995.
21. According to some early surveys, in 1989–91 privatization had a 70 per cent approval rate. *Somos*, 22 July 1991.
22. Edgardo Catterberg, Alfonsín's pollster during the 1983–9 period, admitted that the Radical President failed to appreciate the change in public opinion. When confronted with polls he did not like, Alfonsín downplayed the importance of economic issues, particularly when his administration's policies began to unravel in 1987. He allegedly stated, 'I am going to change the people's mind.' Interview, Buenos Aires, April 1993.
23. World Bank, *OED Précis*, No. 100 (December 1995).
24. Data provided by the Ministry of the Economy, Public Works and Services. The total cost of early retirement schemes during the 1991–94 period amounted to $2 billion financed by the World Bank, the IDB, and the Argentine Treasury.
25. Among them were Arthur Andersen, MacKinsey, Coopers & Lybrand, and Allen & Hamilton.
26. *Pagina/12*, Suplemento Ecónomico, 7 July 1991, p. 2. The privatization receipts were supposed to come from the sale of YPF, SEGBA, ELMA, SOMISA, Ferrocarriles Argentinos, petrochemicals, and ports.
27. Interviews with World Bank and IMF officials. Washington, DC, April 1998.
28. Inspector general Alberto González Arzac was forced to resign; federal prosecutor Oscar Garzón Funes was barred from the supreme court (which Menem 'packed' with loyal justices) from investigating a charge by congressman Moisés Fontela about governmental wrongdoing (Gosman 1991: 246).
29. The Foreign Ministry supported STET's bid as a means of pressing the Italian government, with whom Argentina had signed a bilateral agreement for economic aid worth US$5 billion in 1987. Alsogaray argued that Bell Atlantic possessed superior technology. Prior to this feud, Alsogaray quarreled with Dromi and the foreign ministry on a related issue. A US$135 million loan given by Italy had been scheduled for upgrading the Buenos Aires telephone system. Strings attached to the loan contemplated that 90 per cent of it had to be used to contract two state-owned Italian companies, Italcable and Telettra.

In Alsogaray's view, this could have jeopardized the privatization of ENTel. On the other hand, both Dromi and the Foreign Ministry believed that an exception could be made in order to retain the Italian aid package. In fact, Italian Foreign Minister De Michelis wasted no time in informing his Argentine counterpart that, in the event that Italcable and Telettra were denied the contract, the whole aid package could be terminated.

30. Alsogaray tried her best to save the Bell Atlantic deal. She attempted to convince President Menem to modify some of the contract clauses and to give the North American company some extra time to raise cash. However, in October 1990 Menem publicly undermined her by announcing that, if the Americans failed to produce their debt papers for the partial payment of ENTel North on the due date, they would be disqualified. Ironically, Menem granted to the Italian–French consortium most of the concessions that Alsogaray had sought for Bell Atlantic.

31. *Latin American Monitor: Argentina*, 1991, p. 6.

32. Many of these technocrats had previously worked at the Fundación Mediterranea, a think tank that Cavallo had created in his native Cordoba prior to joining Menem.

33. Interviews with officials of the Ministry of the Economy, Public Works and Services. Buenos Aires, October 1994.

34. In the case of the law privatizing YPF, the government resorted again, as in the case of the State Reform Law, to Congressional ushers as it lacked the necessary quorum to cast the vote in the House of Deputies.

35. *La Nación*, 31 August 1993.

36. See Cavallo's interview in *Clarín*, 14 December 1994.

37. In an article published a year later, Horacio Tomás Liendo, underscored Menem's achievements as follows: 'Luckily, the administration of President Menem has practically solved all the great conflicts that produced the backwardness process that we suffered as a society.' *Pagina 12*, 19 June 1996.

38. Law 24.145 on the Privatization of Hydrocarbons and the Privation of YPF came into effect in November 1992. Law 24.145 established four categories of shares for YPF: Class A for the central government (51 per cent of the total); Class B for the provinces in payment of the royalties due by the central government (39 per cent of the total); Class C for workers' ownership shares (10 per cent of the total); and Class D, being the transformation of Class A and B shares after the sale).

39. Describing this attitude Majul stated, '[These groups] are fascinated with this government because their leitmotif is profit; the more money they earn, the happier they are.' *La Maga*, Buenos Aires, 5 October 1994, p. 4.

40. *Pagina 12*, 6 October 1990.

41. Union bosses received assurances that their control over their union organization and funds would not be jeopardized if they cooperated with the government in diffusing rank-and-file opposition. Interviews with Argentine government officials, Ministry of Labor, Buenos Aires, October 1994. The most ambitious among retraining programs for displaced workers fared poorly, as testified by Martín Redrado in an interview to the *Wall Street Journal*, 2 October 1995, p. R19.

42. The program, also called 'programa de propriedad participada', allowed employees to acquire shares according to the following scheme. The employees: (a) would acquire shares through company dividens over time; (b) would be allowed to name a representative in the privatized company board of directors; and (c) the employee would join the program only on voluntary bases. The problem was that until the shares were fully paid (which in most cases meant no sooner than the year 2000), their management was entrusted upon a trust fund administered by the company's union. See *Noticias*, 16 January 1994, p. 104.

43. *Financial Times*, 2 April 1990.

44. *TELAM*, 14 November 1991.

45. In 1990, DGFM's assets were estimated at US$5.6 billion with annual sales of US$1.2 billion and a work force of 35,000. By 1991, with a cumulative deficit of $700 million, DGFM was the largest drain on the federal budget. *Clarín*, 22 January 1992, p. 18.

46. *Wall Street Journal*, 23 July 1997, p. A18.

47. The importance of having an experienced agency in charge of privatization is explicitly recognized in Glade (1989: 678).

48. This was particularly true of the sale of Aerolíneas Argentinas. The financial scheme proposed by the consortium headed by Iberia presented several parts which were obscure or openly violated financial and property laws (Gosman 1991: 246).

49. Officials of the Ministry of the Economy plainly acknowledged that there was strong reason to believe that private companies had agreed on which PEs each would compete for in order to minimize competition and related costs. Interviews with government officials. Buenos Aires, October 1994.

50. Telefónica's sale earned the state 50 per cent of the projected revenues; YPF's shares were subscribed 15 per cent over the initial floor price. In the case of YPF, the state retained 20 per cent of the company's shares.

51. For instance, some of Dromi's assistants who had designed the privatization bids for the privatization of the highways shortly after the transfer went to work for the very private companies that had won the auctions. Moreover, in the case of the privatization of the television stations, there was strong suspicion that the terms of sale for channels 11 and 13 had been designed to favor the local groups Macri and Clarín respectively (Natale 1993: 102).

52. *Clarín*, 5 November 1994. For a rationalization of the divestiture process in the case of Argentina from the point of view of one of Cavallo's closest aids, see Llach (1991: 214–314).

53. Telephone rates at the time were 50 per cent below those of the United States and Germany and 37 per cent below those of the United Kingdom. Yet it was deemed impossible to demand the payment of international rates to people, like retirees, earning only US$130 a month. See *Buenos Aires Herald*, 25 March 1990, p. 3.

54. While Telefónica was the operating company of the new ENTel South, it owned only 33 per cent of the consortium shares. The remaining shares were divided between Citibank (57 per cent) and Techint (10 per cent).

55. *La Nación*, 6 October 1990.

56. Despite statements to the contrary by Menem, Dromi, González, and María Julia Alsogaray, the administration eventually gave up on the demand by Telefónica

and Telecom to charge higher customer charges than previously agreed (230 austral per unit of time instead of 193 austral). The Argentine currency was the austral until March 1991.

57. Argentina's domestic long distance averaged $0.74 per minute as opposed to $0.21 in Venezuela, $0.24 in Peru, $0.15 in Brazil, $0.21 in Chile, and $0.26 in Mexico. As for international long distance, Argentina averaged $2.66 per minute as opposed to $1.76 in Venezuela, $1.45 in Peru, $1.45 in Brazil, $0.68 in Chile, and $0.88 in Mexico. Data provided by Flemings Securities.

58. *New York Times*, 18 October 1994, p. A7.

59. An appeal court ruling annulled a decree that Cavallo had issued to change telephone rates in 1995, since the only competent institution on the matter was the CNT that the minister had purposely kept at bay.

60. Foreign and domestic investors' bids amounted to US$2.1 billion. About 100,000 small investors, among them Menem, were permitted to purchase shares worth between US$1,000 and US$5,000. After the sale, 60 per cent of the company was owned by the Telefónica–Citibank consortium and 10 per cent by company employees, while 30 per cent was now owned by individual investors and firms. *Latin American Monitor: Southern Cone* (January–February 1992), 979.

61. About 323,000 small investors and 119,026 firms offered a total of US$5.8 billion. *Buenos Aires Herald*, 29 March 1992, p. 18.

62. Between 1995 and 1998 alone, Telecom Argentina and Telefónica had posted net incomes of $1.2 billion and $1.9 billion respectively. Data provided by Flemings securities.

63. Aerolíneas, at the time of its privatization, had posted profits for three consecutive years of about US$30 million. Its fleet (twenty-eight planes) was worth an estimated US$500 million. Aerolíneas also had the lion's share, not only of the domestic market (69 per cent), but also of flights to and from South America (45 per cent), the US (35 per cent), and Europe (38 per cent) (Gosman 1991: 259).

64. In 1987, the Argentine government signed contracts forcing it to clear debts contracted by state-owned companies with commercial banks prior to privatization.

65. Cielos del Sur received 12 per cent, the Zanon Group 18 per cent, and Devi Construciones 9.5 per cent.

66. Iberia officials also complained that the government was breaking its monopoly by giving licenses to charter companies. *Buenos Aires Herald*, 5 April 1992, p. 2.

67. *Buenos Aires Herald*, 1 March 1992, p. 14.

68. Losses amounted to $240 million between June 1992 and June 1993. The following June 1993–June 1994 period resulted in losses of $116 million. *El Cronista Comercial*, 20 October 1994.

69. In describing the Aerolíneas debacle, a commentary by a Buenos Aires daily stated the following. 'The sale of Aerolíneas Argentinas to Iberia is almost a lesson in how not to privatize. The $770 million outstanding in debt equity swap papers became first $272 and then $210 million—around $64 million in real terms with a secondary debt level of 30 per cent. This 30 per cent value cut the other way when it came to reducing the money owed by Iberia—$151 million

allegedly owed the purchaser by the state became $500 million in terms of debt papers. During the negotiations the new owners made much of having to fly without charge those passengers who had paid for their tickets while Aerolíneas was still state-owned, but this factor accounted for only three million dollars—far less than the $11 million for Aerolíneas' notorious free flights. A figure of $151 million was somehow reached by adding more "state debts", notably an inventory difference of $105 million, but even this was not enough so a further $22 million was thrown in during this week's negotiations to finally bring the price for 85 per cent of Aerolíneas down to the $210 (or $64) million' (*Buenos Aires Herald*, 7 July 1991, p. 14).

70. Iberia would later run into deep financial problems of its own. *Financial Times*, 27 October 1994, 1.
71. *Buenos Aires Herald*, 15 March 1992, p. 2.
72. The new owners, in some cases, were allowed to pay the government only several years after charging tolls to users (Natale 1993: 151).
73. *Clarín*, 4 January 1998.
74. Private groups like Pérez Companc and Bridas had subcontracts for oil extraction amounting to about 30 to 40 per cent of total output (Gerchunoff and Coloma 1993: 285).
75. Interview with YPF vice-President Carlos Yanez. Miami, March 1995.
76. Interestingly, once EDENOR and EDESUR started to cut on losses, they found out that the largest debtors were YPF, Telefónica, Banco de Boston, Techint, and the Argentine Senate. *Pagina 12*, 2 and 5 February 1993.
77. Interviews with senior officials at the Ministry of the Economy, Public Works, and Services, Buenos Aires, July 1995 and August 1996. Interviews with World Bank officials, May 1995 and September 1996. All the public officials interviewed had managed directly several aspects of the electricity privatization process.
78. Electricity tariffs between September 1992 and November 1994 dropped as follows: small users −9.0 per cent, medium users −6.2 per cent, large users −7.5 per cent. Only small users under the category T1-R-1 saw an increase. Data provided by national energy regulatory agency ENRE.
79. Post-privatization losses were $52 million in 1992 and $65.8 million in 1993. Profits started to emerge in 1994 ($1.3 million) and 1995 ($46.5 million). Data provided by ENRE.
80. About $30 million a year. *Clarín*, 1 August 1997.
81. Cavallo made the first allegations during the television program 'Key Hour' anchored by journalist Mariano Grondona on 17 August 1995.
82. On Yabram's shady business deals and company ownership see *Noticias*, 27 November 1994, p. 49.
83. Cavallo filed these accusations against Yabram to the Federal Court of Buenos Aires on September 14, 1995.
84. *Financial Times*, 24 September 1995, p. 6. A year later the Minister of Justice, Elías Jassan, was forced to resign as the press disclosed a series of personal phone calls to Yabram cellular phone that he had previously denied.
85. *El Expreso*, a paper close to Menem ran a headline stating 'Cavallo's days are numbered', which was echoed by Ambassador Granillo Ocampo in Washington.

Granillo Ocampo had been Attorney General of La Rioja when Menem was governor of that province.

86. By 1997, Yabram had become the primary suspect for the homicide of a photographer who had taken pictures of him a couple of years earlier. As many former political allies began to distance themselves from him, Yabram found himself increasingly isolated. In late May 1998, he apparently committed suicide as the federal police were about to arrest him. *La Nación*, 16 May 1998.

87. Saúl Liberman, a video-cable entrepreneur, headed the losing consortium. *La Nación*, 1 August 1997.

88. Interview with Prof. Carlos Balbín who legally assisted the legislators who opposed the project in Congress. Buenos Aires, May 1998.

89. Interview with World Bank staff economists. Washington, DC, September 1997.

90. *Financial Times*, 31 July 1998.

91. Data provided by the Ministry of the Economy, Public Works, and Services.

92. World Bank Performance Audit Report, 24 May 1995, p. 24.

93. Ibid., p. 35.

94. Argentina's country risk index dropped from 31.9 points in the first quarter of 1990 to 2.8 points in the last quarter of 1993. The capitalization of the stock market rose from $4.2 billion in 1989 to $44.7 billion in 1996. The average daily trading value quadrupled during the same period (IFC 1997: 129).

95. Ibid.

96. Ibid.

97. *Buenos Aires Herald*, 12 April 1992, p. 18.

98. Of the 280,509 people cut from the government payroll by 1995, 77,000 jobs were transferred to the new owners of former PS and the rest to local government. Data provided by the World Bank.

99. *Clarín*, 17 May 1998.

100. *Clarín*, 17 May 1998 and 22 May 1998.

101. Interview with officers of the Ministry of the Economy, Public Works and Services. Buenos Aires, February 1998.

102. *Clarín*, 17 May 1998.

103. *Clarín*, 22 April 1998.

104. See for instance *Clarín*, 17 May 1998; and *Perfil*, 24 May 1998.

105. In 1994, a survey showed that 84 per cent of the respondents believed the judiciary to be under the influence of the government, while 57 per cent perceived corruption to be one of the most pressing issues affecting the Argentine justice system. Data provided by Gallup Argentina.

106. *Wall Street Journal*, 6 May 1998.

107. The establishment of domestic conglomerates coincided with economic growth during two different periods. The first wave blossomed in the heyday of Argentine agricultural exports during the last quarter of the 19th century. Groups like Bagley (1877), Alpargatas (1883), Bunge & Born (1884), Garavoglio & Zarraquín (1886), and Braun & Madanes (1895) were overwhelmingly concentrated in agribusiness. The second wave of conglomerates were set up during or immediately after World War II at a time in which import substitution industrialization in Argentina was in full swing. These new groups,

including Acindar (1942), Techint (1946), Pérez Companc (1946), Bridas (1948), Arcor (1951), Macri (1952), and Massuh (1957), were concentrated in heavy industry, construction, oil production, and services. The common characteristic of these conglomerates is that they remained firmly under the control of their founding families. These families over time increased their oligopolistic control of key markets in addition to increasing their economic and political clout (Schvarzer 1977: 327). The military regime (1976–83) handsomely rewarded the suppliers of government companies, the so-called *patria contratista*, with highly lucrative contracts. Conglomerates owing large stakes in the petrochemical sector, like Astra, Bridas, Soldati, and Pérez Companc, grew at a spectacular rate during the *Proceso* by overcharging YPF, for the provision of goods and services. The state also awarded contracts to construction businesses like Zorraquín, Loma Negra, Macri, Pérez Companc, and Techint. The thirty largest domestic groups received an additional break in 1982 when the military government acted to avoid the financial collapse of many of them. The then Chairman of the Central Bank, Domingo Cavallo, assumed in the name of the government the bulk of the debts that these groups had contracted abroad, amounting to nearly half of the country's $43 billion external debt.

The restructuring reforms introduced in 1989 further concentrating economic power in the hands of a few foreign corporations and the largest domestic conglomerates. Between 1981 and 1990, the ten largest conglomerates increased their output from $4 million to $7 million, employed 12 per cent of the working force, and owned over sixty of the most important domestic companies. Table 3.9 indicates that, between 1984 and 1992, conglomerates like Techint, Pérez Companc, Bulgheroni, Massuh, Astra, Ladesma, Alpargatas, and Pescarmona climbed rapidly in the national ranking. Conversely, weaker and smaller companies lost ground.

108. *Noticias*, 16 January 1994, p. 104. In the case of telecommunications, salaries rose on average by 45 per cent. The employees who received shares did so at one sixth of the market price. By 1994, the market value of such shares had earned a capital gain of $25,000. World Bank Performance Audit Report, 24 May 1995, p. 21.

109. Interview with Argentine pollster Manuel Mora y Araujo. Dallas, October 1997.

4

Brazil

As in Argentina, the 1989 presidential elections found Brazil in the midst of its worst socioeconomic crisis of this century, with very high inflation, the largest level of foreign debt in the world, capital flight, a large fiscal deficit, increasing poverty and income concentration, and a ballooning domestic debt. To compound matters, the political bickering between the President and Congress, coupled with mounting reports of corruption involving the Sarney administration, brought the country to the point of ungovernability. This, in turn, tarnished the image of the democratic institutions only five years after the end of the military regime (Lamounier 1994). As in Argentina, the stage was set for the emergence of protest candidates. As it was pointed out at the time, 'people are not interested in ideologies, what they really want is something that promises to change everything, government, parties, politicians, the source of their suffering'.[1]

During the electoral campaign the political atmosphere became highly polarized. After the first round two men emerged (in accordance with the 1988 Constitutional provision, if no one wins an outright majority only the two candidates with the largest number of votes are allowed to participate in a run-off). Luis Inácio (Lula) da Silva, a former metalworker and union organizer who was the undisputed leader of the Workers' party (Partido de Trabalhadores, PT), headed the left-wing coalition. Lula's platform was quite ideologically grounded. He refused any privatization and called instead for an expanded role of government intervention in the economy. Lula also supported increases in salaries and social benefits, heavy taxes on the rich, and a moratorium on Brazil's external debt. His opponent was Fernando Collor de Mello, an obscure governor from Alagóas, one of the poorest states in the depressed north-east of Brazil. Although coming from a family well entrenched in Brazilian politics, the young (39 years of age) and flamboyant Collor was considered the long-shot underdog when he first announced his candidacy.[2] Through a subtle television campaign facilitated by the support of Brazil's largest media network (TV Globo), Collor portrayed himself as a political outsider and skillfully exploited popular disgust with politicians.[3] Like Menem, Collor adopted a charismatic style punctuated by slogans like 'whoever steals goes to jail'. He even went so far as to describe himself as a *caçador de marajás*, or hunter of overpaid political appointees and bureaucrats. At the same time, in typical populist fashion, he remained ideologically weak while projecting an image of himself as a savior of the public good, the promoter of modernization and clean government, and the deadly enemy of political corruption; just the type of person people were desperately seeking (Weyland 1993: 6–7). This rhetoric, along with his personal charisma, earned Collor a surprising following among the poorer masses of Brazil's interior. In his pledge to create 'a new Brazil', Collor's conservative populism targeted state intervention in the economy as the culprit of many ills. Market reforms and privatization were often mentioned in his campaign but did not translate into any concrete policy platform (Schneider 1992: 231).

Like any good populist, Collor based his quest for power on his own personal appeal. Although running as the candidate of the National Reconstruction party (Partido de Reconstrução Nacional, PRN), the PRN was merely an electoral machine and played no meaningful role in organizing a mass following in any structured fashion behind Collor's presidential bid (Roett 1992). In fact, the PRN held only four per cent of the seats in the Chamber of Deputies, and its congressmen were an odd group of disgruntled politicians coming from widely different backgrounds. Moreover, from the beginning Collor's brash and arrogant personality clearly showed his unwillingness to share center stage with anyone. None the less, despite their misgivings regarding Collor's true intentions, many conservative politicians and business groups were driven into his camp fearing the possible consequences of a Lula victory.[4] In December 1989, Collor polled 53 per cent of the total vote against Lula's 47 per cent. For the first time in 29 years Brazil had a popularly elected President whose legitimacy could not be questioned.

By the time Collor assumed the highest office in March 1990, there was widespread consensus among the Brazilian political and economic elites that the country was in need of some kind of market reforms and that the federal government had to be downsized to some extent (Sola 1993). However, there was no agreement on the breadth and scope of the reforms to be implemented nor did Collor have a clear mandate to usher a sweeping neo-conservative economic program (Schneider 1992: 231). In the previous chapter we saw that Menem in Argentina lacked such a mandate as well. Still, this did not deter him from using his executive authority to do otherwise. In the case of Brazil, Collor did embark on a neo-orthodox program that, however, was not quite as radical as Menem's.

On the day of his inauguration, with inflation rising out of control, the new President adopted a shock therapy of unprecedented severity in Brazil. The Collor Plan I, as the austerity package was quickly dubbed, had as its immediate objective the halting of runaway inflation. To drastically cut financial liquidity, the administration froze about 80 per cent of the country's financial assets for 18 months and decreed a 45-day price freeze. A new currency, the cruzeiro, was also introduced in place of the novo cruzado. The Plan also called for a sharp cut in the fiscal deficit through a variety of means including new taxes, a crackdown on tax evasion, and the reduction of current expenditures in the public sector. The latter meant the closure of several ministries and bureaucratic agencies, cuts in the government payroll, and the privatization of PEs. In addition, the administration implemented a set of measures aimed at gradually deregulating the economy and liberalizing trade by reducing tariff barriers (this affected consumer goods more than capital and intermediate goods). Tariff reductions had an explicit anti-inflationary goal and were also meant to force greater competition in what was otherwise an economy dominated in many sectors by oligopolistic practices, which flourished under economic protectionism (Abreu and Werneck 1993). Thus, the privatization program was part of the structural reforms accompanying the stabilization plan, but it was mainly conceived as an element of fiscal adjustment rather than a policy in its own right.

Initially, Collor enjoyed a brief honeymoon with Congress. Given the President's popularity and the widespread consensus that the economic crisis required quick emergency actions, the legislative branch, where Collor had no working majority, went along with a flow of executive orders (*medidas provisorias*) used to implement the economic package.[5] On March 15, the administration issued executive order no. 155 setting up the legal framework for the Brazilian privatization program. On April 12, Congress turned it into law by establishing norms and procedures to be followed throughout the privatization process (Law 8.031).[6] The following August, Collor issued a new executive order appointing BNDES as the administrator of the Brazilian Privatization Fund in charge of providing administrative, financial, and material support to the privatization program.[7]

Collor's stabilization plan was successful in the short-run. Inflation dropped from 81 per cent in March to 9 per cent in June. The budget deficit also turned momentarily into a surplus thanks to a sharp increase of tax receipts and the suspension of interest payments on the domestic debt. However, the financial crunch drove the country into a deep recession. Under pressure from Congress and special interest groups, the government was forced to remonetize the economy by granting special credit lines to various economic sectors that bypassed the financial freeze. To make things worse, the transfers mandated by the 1988 Constitution to state and local government prevented the executive from having a tight grip on the money supply. As a result, inflation began to build up again in the second half of 1990. In January 1991, the administration found itself back at square one and was again forced to implement a new stabilization program, The Collor Plan II. Once again, the government decreed a price and wage freeze (the fifth in six years). The following March, Collor announced the National Reconstruction Project, yet another proposal for structural reforms to reorganize and downsize the government bureaucracy, further deregulate the economy, and accelerate the trade liberalization policy. As on previous occasions, the freeze was ultimately unsuccessful and inflationary pressures mounted again in May, leading to the resignation of Collor's first economic team. The new Minister of Economy, Marcilio Marques Moreira, liberalized some prices and raised interest rates to record levels to keep inflation within tolerable levels. However, very positive interest rates worsened the government's domestic debt position while depressing economic activity. Throughout the remainder of 1991, in spite of continuous road blocks posed by Congress against market reforms and fiscal austerity, the administration slowly but steadily pushed forward its deregulation and trade liberalization program. Privatization encountered much of the same problems and the government was only able to carry out its first transfer in October, 18 months after the first announcement of the divestiture program. Moreover, relations with foreign creditors remained strained. Despite his electoral promise to renegotiate the country's external financial obligations, the suspension of debt service payments adopted by Sarney in July 1989 continued under the Collor Plan I. Only in July 1992 did Brazil reach a tentative agreement with the Paris Club group of foreign government creditors for the rescheduling of $11 billion worth of arrearages.

Although progress was made in terms of fiscal balance, inflation continued unabated (Figs. 4.1 and 4.2). International reserves, on the contrary, continued to grow (Fig. 4.3). Uncertainty over the administration's effectiveness in promoting economic stabilization with structural reforms, already widespread until the first half of 1992, increased upon news of a massive corruption scandal directly involving the President. In fact, it was Collor's estranged brother, Pedro, who denounced to a weekly magazine that the President's campaign fund raiser, P. C. Farias, had solicited millions of dollars in bribes from businessmen in return for government contracts and favors since the inception of his administration. Amid these allegations, Congress set up a Parliamentary Commission of Inquiry in June. Its findings first led to Collor's suspension from office in September, forcing Vice-President Itamar Franco to take over, and then to his impeachment on 27 December (Fleischer 1994).[8] For many Brazilians who had warmly welcomed Collor hoping for a new, honest political style, the impeachment was a watershed. However, the very fact that for the first time a President had been removed through the democratic process, rather than a military coup, testified to many the strength of democratic values in Brazil.

Franco, who had been highly critical of Collor's economic policies, considerably slowed down the already slow pace of market deregulation and privatization reforms. Having no power base of his own and being a caretaker president, Franco also was in no position to confront a divided Congress where bold policy initiatives were bound to be stopped. Thus, while the economic team preached fiscal restraint and tried to keep the market reforms initiated under Collor on track, Franco and the Congress pushed for the resumption of growth-oriented but highly inflationary measures.

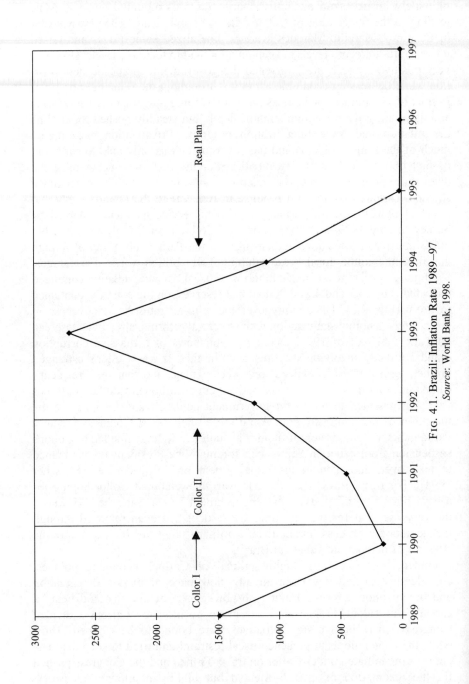

FIG. 4.1. Brazil: Inflation Rate 1989–97
Source: World Bank, 1998.

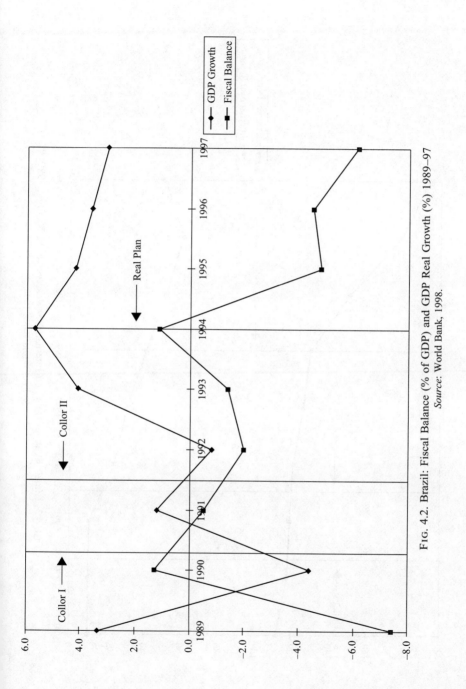

FIG. 4.2. Brazil: Fiscal Balance (% of GDP) and GDP Real Growth (%) 1989–97
Source: World Bank, 1998.

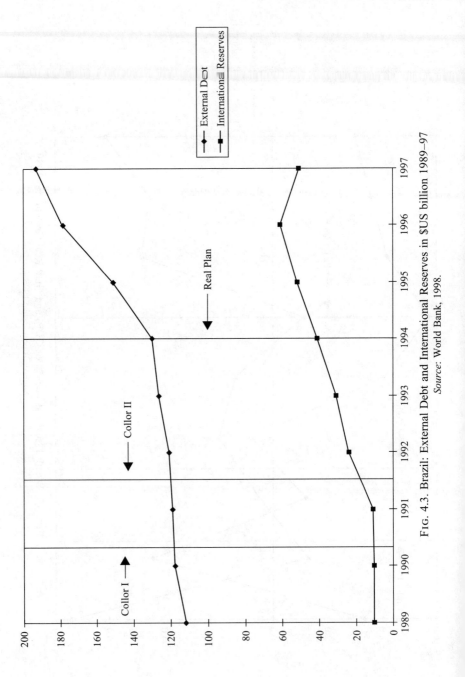

Fig. 4.3. Brazil: External Debt and International Reserves in $US billion 1989–97
Source: World Bank, 1998.

Politics as usual triumphed once more. The profound disagreements between Franco and his economic advisers led to the resignations of the BNDES President and three finance ministers in his first five months in office.[9] It was not until Fernando Henrique Cardoso, a world-renowned sociologist, took the helm of the Finance Ministry in May 1993 that economic policy regained some coherence. In 1993, Cardoso had approved in Congress the sixth major stabilization plan since 1986, the Real Plan. Avoiding the harshness of past attempts that were unlikely to garner congressional approval, Cardoso's first objective consisted in balancing the budget through higher taxes and spending cuts. To do so he had Congress approve the Social Emergency Fund (SEF), an ad hoc measure that allowed the government to draw from funds constitutionally awarded to states and municipalities Second, starting in late February 1994, Cardoso implemented a monetary reform by introducing the *unidade real de valor* or URV, which eventually replaced the cruzeiro as the national currency under the name of 'real' the following July[10] The new currency system fixed the real's exchange rate according to a strict band of fluctuation vis-à-vis the US dollar, in order to bring price stability. Third, the government began to lower tariff barriers in many sectors to promote competition and cut domestic prices.

As for privatization, in late 1994, Franco issued Decree 1.068 aimed at selling minority shares, some of which were in blue chips. This initiative was intended to attract foreign investment to Brazil's stock markets, pave the way for the privatization of key PEs in 1995, and bypass congressional roadblocks.[11] To this end, the Franco administration issued *medida provisoria* 542 creating the Public Debt Amortization Fund. The auction of minority stocks and stocks in excess of what the government needed to keep majority control in specific PEs would go into the fund, which in turn would use these resources to pay off the public debt and finance the fiscal deficit. The Finance Ministry also allowed the entry of private capital into the electricity industry by selling regional subsidiaries of Eletrobrás, whose privatization was not forbidden by the 1988 constitution.

The Real Plan was an instant success. It brought inflation from 2,700 per cent in 1993 down to 5 per cent in 1997 and promoted new growth (Fig. 4.2). Noticeably, rather than hurting the poor and low wage earners, it actually increased their meager purchasing power. According to some estimates, price stability allowed five million people in urban centers to come out of poverty within the first two years from the inception of the Real Plan (Kingstone 1998). These achievements earned Cardoso an instant popularity and allowed him to garner widespread support from the PMDB, the PFL, and his own Brazilian Social Democratic party (Partido Social Democrata Brasileiro, PSDB), a left-wing offshoot of the PMDB, for his presidential bid. In October 1994, Cardoso won in a landslide (54 per cent of the total votes) over Lula, who once more headed the left-wing ticket. Upon taking office in

January 1995, Cardoso announced that his primary goals were to reduce the state role in the economy, bring back foreign investments in key sectors, and increase competition through trade liberalization. Within this context privatization explicitly became a core policy of the market reform agenda and, for the first time, it was made compatible with the macroeconomic goals of the executive. To give credibility to his plans, Cardoso quickly sent to Congress two sets of constitutional amendments. One aimed at downsizing social security, streamlining the federal bureaucracy, and revising the tax code. The other looked for the elimination of monopoly status of PEs in extractive industries (that is, oil and gas) and public utilities. While on the administrative reform front Cardoso met with strong congressional opposition and was able to accomplish very little, he was able to lift most of the constitutional bans thwarting privatization in public utilities and extractive industries in 1996. By 1998, the President had put into place new legislation to set in motion the largest divestiture program in the developing world.

Despite some ups and down, the Cardoso administration made steady progress in consolidating market reforms, while maintaining price stability. Cashing in on these economic results, and capitalizing on his strong popular support at home and international prestige abroad, Cardoso persuaded Congress to pass (May 1997) yet another constitutional amendment allowing him to run for a second consecutive term. According to Cardoso himself, his lifelong main objective had always been to modernize Brazil and making it a more equitable society. To accomplish it, in the 1970s, he had advocated radical ISI policies, but in the 1990s he had come to the realization that ISI was fundamentally flawed and unworkable. Privatization, and other market reforms, he reasoned, had the potential of achieving what decades of wasteful and misguided government intervention could not. Thus, he substituted it for the old development policy model in the hope that it would succeed where ISI had failed.

Willingness

Collor's brief tenure in office makes it difficult to discern to what extent he was a true believer or just an opportunist. The president's conservative populism and his use of emergency measures to extort bribes seem to point in the latter direction. Throughout his political career Collor, like many Brazilian politicians, shifted around several parties only to pursue his personal goals and never gave the impression of being an ideologically driven person. The PRN, for example, was created within weeks of Collor's announcement of his candidacy. 'Modernization', probably the most pervasive theme in Collor's campaign, was nothing new in a country where a score of civilian and military presidents, from Getulio Vargas to Joselino Kubitcheck and Ernesto

Geisel, had used this same theme to justify state-led development policies. The difference with Collor was that he wanted to modernize the country through the adoption of neo-orthodox policies that had become economic dogma in the developed world, a world with which Brazil had always aspired to catch up. Collor realized that if Brazil were not to 'miss the boat' of economic development, it had to conform with the policies advocated by industrialized countries and multilateral lending agencies. Indeed, Collor had often pledged that under his leadership Brazil was going to make the necessary economic strides forward that would finally make it a member of the 'first world'. For some, Collor's determination to foster trade liberalization and economic deregulation was just a matter of public relations 'marketing'.[12] For others, it showed strong signs of the ideological commitment of a late convert.[13] According to Schneider (1992: 227), 'Collor's ideological position was ambiguous and mobile, Brazil lacked a strong ideological right, and the Collor government appeared less intent on destroying the left. In general, the initial planning for privatization manifested little thought for shifting resources to placate opponents and win friends.' In retrospect, it seems plausible that the very pragmatic and ambitious Collor recognized in privatization, and market reforms in general, a means to portray himself as a path-breaking politician who would later be praised as one of his country's most innovative presidents.

Unlike Argentina and Mexico, where privatization was used as a tool to discipline labor, such a motive seemed to be absent from Collor's Plan. Much of the same can be said about popular capitalism. Although often mentioned in the privatization decrees, popular capitalism seemed to respond more to the need to sweeten labor and congressional opposition rather than to an ideological creed and never went beyond the stage of rhetoric. In Brazil, the government used auctions at the Rio de Janeiro and São Paulo stock markets to sell its assets or minority shares, and in some cases some shares were set aside for the general public. However, the largest investors remained private companies and pension funds.

It appears clear from the testimonies gathered by the Parliamentary Commission of Inquiry that Collor substituted state interventionism with market reforms to consolidate his own power. The motives were, however, primarily pragmatic and, as the impeachment proceeding showed, highly dishonest.[14]

The case of Cardoso is quite different. As a left-wing academician, in the 1960s and 1970s he became one of the fathers of 'dependency theory', a school of thought that ascribed Latin America's underdevelopment to the industrialized world's intention to keep developing countries in a state of socio-economic subjugation that was made possible by an alliance of domestic elites with international capital. However, by the early 1990s not only did he downplay his early writings but, as time went on, became one of the most visible Latin American proponents of what may be labelled as market reforms with 'greater equity'.[15] In justifying his change of heart Cardoso stated, 'the realities of international economics have become more complex, interests have become transnational and the State's capacity for intervention in the production of wealth has diminished'.[16] In another speech, he was even more explicit. 'The entry of private capital is no longer a question of ideological preference. It means the difference between carrying out or not carrying out necessary investments.'[17]

Therefore, according to Cardoso's new political thought, to make Brazil a more just society the government had to devote its limited resources to provide better services in education, health, housing, etc. while leaving the task of economic growth to the market forces under the supervision of a state, which was no longer to be an entrepreneur but had to turn itself into an efficient regulator of private activities. So, if Collor's ideological stand remained ambiguous, in the case of Cardoso we see a statesman whose political ideas moved from radical change to moderate, pro-business social democracy. Equally important, Cardoso could convincingly argue to his people that once PEs were in private hands they were better suited to create jobs, investments, and technologically advanced goods/services, and by paying taxes they provided the revenues that would allow the government to attend society's basic needs.

Under Cardoso privatization was not used to discipline labor, and popular capitalism also failed to materialize. It must be noted though that many transfers did allocate usually 10 per cent of shares to employees, and in the majority of cases they were heavily subscribed, particularly in profitable companies with good business prospects like most steel mills and the mining company Companhia Vale de Rio Doce (CVRD) (Table 4.1). As Finance Minister, in November 1993, Cardoso unveiled plans to convert to government pension fund (PI-Paesp), home buyers' fund (PCV), and the severance pay fund (FGTS) into securities, or 'social currencies', for the PEs to be auctioned. In so doing he hoped to swap, via privatization, outstanding federal debts owed to workers. The proposal turned into Law 9.491 in September 1997. Yet again, these were ad hoc initiatives that did not respond to ideologically grounded decisions. In short, of the four elements making up the ideological dimension of willingness, only free market economics as a superior means to state intervention seemed to be shared by Collor and Cardoso, but not by Franco.

Thus, if we set aside Collor's pursuit of personal wealth, several of the pragmatic factors spelled out in Chapter 1 seem to fit the Brazilian case throughout the 1990–8 period. Collor's adoption of the neo-orthodox economic recipe seemed to be dictated by electoral expediency. According to Sola (1993: 154), his market reforms 'catalyzed a series of partial intellectual adjustments on the part of sectors extending well beyond the president's electoral coalition to encompass broader segments of the political and economic elites,

TABLE 4.1. *Brazil: Structure of the Sale Offers 1991–7*

Type of Offer		Company	Offer as % of Total Capital			% Subscribed by Employees	Subscription in $US millions	Employees Subscribing
			Auction	Public	Employees			
Sales in Blocks of Shares	With Public Offer							
Auction of common shares/offer to employees/public offer of preferred shares/auction of preferred shares		Usiminas	37.6 27.9	10.0	10.0	9.6	3.4	17,827.0
Auction of common shares, with offer to employees, followed by offer to general public		Petroflex	80.0	10.0	10.0	10.0	6.6	1,365.0
		Copesul	62.9	9.1	10.0	10.0	30.6	1,409.0
		CSN	65.0	5.8	20.0	11.9	76.0	30,504.0
		Embraer	50.5	10.0	9.9	9.9	9.3	6,036.0
		Meridional	55.4	18.7	8.3	3.8	0.8	
Auction of common shares/offer of preferred shares to employees and general public		Copene	11.8	15.8	3.1	3.1	16.6	4,329.0
Auction of common shares, with offer of common shares to employees		Celma	86.1		10.0	3.0	0.4	342.0
		Fosfertil	78.3		10.0	10.0	4.9	1,971.0
		Acesita	64.0		10.0	10.0	15.1	13,191.0
		Ultrafertil	90.0		10.0	10.0	6.1	1,600.0
		Cosipa	40.0		20.0	20.0	29.4	13,682.0
		PQU	50.0		9.8	9.8	17.6	1,447.0
		Cobra	63.6		19.9			
		Light	60.0		10.0	10.0	237.6	
	Without Public Offer	With Offer to Employees						
Auction of common/preferred shares with offer of common/preferred shares to employees		Acominas	79.9		20.0	20.0	44.3	5,821.0
Auction of common/preferred shares followed by auction of common shares offered to employees		CST	70.9 5.7		12.4	12.4	15.2	6,086.0

TABLE 4.1. *(cont'd)*

Type of Offer				Company	Offer as % of Total Capital			% Subscribed by Employees	Subscription in $US million	Employees Subscribing
					Auction	Public	Employees			
Auction of common shares				Polisul	31.0					
				Acrinor	17.7					
				Politeno	24.9					
				Polialden	13.6					
				Deten	33.5					
				Koppol	49.6					
Auction of common shares followed by auction of preferred shares				PPH	19.0					
				CPC	20.8					
Auction of common shares/offer to employees/public				Salgema	28.3					
				Polipropileno	34.2					
Auction of common shares, with offer to employees, followed by offer to general public				Petrocoque	35.0					
				Oxiteno	15.2					
				Coperbo	23.0					
				Ciquine	31.4					
				Nitrocarbono	19.0					
				Pronor	35.3					
				EDN	26.7					
Sale in One Block	Without Public Offer	Without Offer to Employees	Auction in one block of common/preferred shares	Mafersa	90.0		10.0	9.5	0.1	2,474.0
				Cosinor	89.8		10.0	9.5	1.4	1,106.0
				Piratini	65.2		9.9	0.1	0.0	25.0
				Alcalis	90.0		10.0			

Sale in One Block	With Public Offer	Auction in one block of common shares	SNBP	90.0	10.0			
			Enasa	90.0	10.0			
			Goiasfertil	90.0	10.0	10.0	0.4	676.0
			Caraiba	80.0	20.0	20.0	0.8	907.0
			Lloydbras	79.8	20.0			
			Escelsa	50.0	7.7			
				14.6				
			Meridional	75.6	6.8	3.8	0.8	
				32.8				
		Auction in one block of common/preferred shares	Indag	35.0				
	With Offer to Employees	Auction of common shares	Nitriflex	40.0				
			CBE	23.0				
			Poliolefinas	31.5				
			Arafertil	33.3				
			Polibrasil	25.7				
		Auction in one block of preferred shares	CQR	36.9				
			CBP	23.7				
	With offer to Employees	Auction of common/preferred shares to employees and public offer of common shares remaining from previous offers	CVRD	40/45	5.1	5.1	167.4	34,811.0

Source: BNDES, *Programa Nacional de Destatizacao*, December 1997.

including organized interest groups and members of Congress'. Collor, thus, tried to capitalize on what appeared to be a shifting trend of popular consensus from *dirigismo* to market-oriented policies. This trend had both domestic and international determinants. The miserable failure of the Cruzado Plan no longer made economic heterodoxy a viable alternative while the fiscal crisis of the state took a turn for the worst. More by default than by conviction, many Brazilian elites came to the realization that the fiscal crisis made a restructuring of the state and its increased role in economic development inevitable. Moreover, the 'globalization' of the international economy, with its emphasis on enhanced efficiency requirements, competitiveness, and technological innovation made the old ISI model obsolete (Dupas 1993; Suzigan 1993; Franco and Fritsch 1992). As pointed out by Baer (1993: 4), 'with the changing world—the collapse of communism and the willingness of an increasing number of developing countries to accept market economies—the Collor program to open the Brazilian economy to trade and investment and to privatize a large segment of state enterprises was grudgingly accepted by most sociopolitical groups'. Summing up, the neo-orthodox approach to stabilization was the only coherent option left, despite the fact there was no shared agreement on what form these structural reforms should take.

The overreaching pragmatic factor guiding Collor's privatization plan was the reduction of the government deficit by swapping medium- and long-term domestic debt for shares of PEs and forgoing investments that otherwise had to be made (Castelar Pinheiro and Giambiagi 1993). Abreu and Werneck (1993: 27) synthesized the pros and cons of this approach in Brazil at the time, as follows:

Though it is well established in the literature that selling public assets is a temporary form of financing the public sector deficit rather than a way to reduce it, privatization continues to be seen by many in the Brazilian economic debate as the fast lane to fiscal adjustment. A less objectionable argument views cash proceeds in public assets sales as a way to avoid the issuing of new public debt while real—and slower—fiscal adjustment measures are under way. As not issuing new public debt is seen by most economic agents as eliminating the deficit, inflationary expectations may be positively affected well before the real fiscal adjustment takes place.

Collor's Programa Nacional de Desestatização (PND) presented state divestiture as a means of redefining the role of the state by making it smaller, leaner, more dynamic, and confined to more fundamental tasks than in the past.[18] *Dirigismo* was described as having gone too far and become unfeasible in view of a radically changed macroeconomic situation. More specifically: (1) there was no longer any reason for companies, which started out as private concerns and had no particular connection with government activities, to remain under state control; and (2) the arguments for state intervention in the productive sector no longer applied due to the maturity of the strategic sectors, and to the crisis in public finances that eroded public savings.

The PND enumerated many of the points found in the Argentine case for justifying privatization:[19]

1. Reorganizing the strategic position of the state in the country's economy through the transferring to the private initiative of economic activities unduly exploited by the state sector. Freed from the duty of providing new and increasing investments the federal government will benefit from gains in its global efficiency.
2. Promoting the modernization of domestic industry by forcing competition into the economy.
3. Strengthening domestic capital markets through popular capitalism.
4. Allowing the federal government to concentrate its efforts and resources on social policies like health, education, housing, public safety, and support for research and development.[20]
5. Stimulating investment in areas where the private sector can bring in greater capital and maximize results better than the government.

In 1990, the size of the Brazilian public enterprise sector was considerable. According to a study by the Getulio Vargas Foundation surveying the 500 largest non-financial enterprises in the country, eighty of them belonged to the federal or state government.[21] These eighty PEs accounted for 37 per cent of total gross revenues, 63 per cent of total net worth, and 75 per cent of total fixed assets of GDP (Table 4.2). Their importance weighed heavily in those economic sectors considered as 'strategic' for economic development. PEs had played a monopolistic role in oil (Petrobrás), public utilities (Eletrobrás), telecommunication (Telebrás), and mining. The state also had a considerable market share in other areas like steel production, petrochemicals, and transportation. In 1989, PEs were responsible for 6.8 per cent (of GDP) of the government deficit (Castelar Pinheiro and Giambiagi 1993), although some believed that as much as 70 per cent of such a deficit had to be ascribed to state and municipal enterprises (Castelar Pinheiro and Schneider 1994). Leaving aside the controversy on the real impact of PE losses on the federal government's borrowing requirements, it appeared clear to all that in order to contain costs, like in other Latin American countries, Brazilian PEs' managers had progressively reduced investments. From an average of 4.9 per cent of GDP during the 1980–2 period, investments dropped to 1.9 per cent in the 1989–91 period (Castelar Pinheiro and Schneider 1994: 19). This inevitably resulted in a steep deterioration of services, particularly in public utilities, which strengthened the case for the need to inject private capital through privatization if such services were not to fall apart. Others contended that under private management, provided that old government monopolies be subject to competition, privatization was likely to increase efficiency in the economy, both at the macro and micro level, and cut costs (Abreu and Werneck 1993: Castelar Piheiro and Giambiagi 1993).

TABLE 4.2. *Brazil: Leading Public Enterprises and Largest Companies: Financial Results in 1993**

Sector	Largest Companies (US$ billion)			Public Enterprises (US$ billion)			Participation of Public Enterprises (%)		
	Gross Revenues	Net Worth	Net Assets	Gross Revenues	Net Worth	Net Assets	Gross Revenues	Net Worth	Net Assets
Agriculture	**1.34**	**0.67**	**0.49**	**0.02**	**0.09**	**0.03**	**1.57**	**1.86**	**8.04**
Industry	**135.28**	**73.47**	**74.36**	**49.87**	**40.24**	**54.53**	**36.87**	**54.78**	**73.34**
Mining	20.55	9.88	6.90	18.21	8.47	5.75	88.63	85.72	83.33
Manufacturing	76.22	36.00	29.50	9.62	10.90	13.34	12.62	30.27	45.23
Metallurgy	13.07	10.91	14.20	6.30	7.09	11.62	48.23	64.97	81.83
Chemicals	13.16	8.93	5.12	3.25	3.78	1.71	24.72	42.38	33.37
Printing	0.71	0.20	0.18	0.06	0.02	0.01	8.68	8.66	5.41
Others	49.27	15.94	9.98	0.00	0.00	0.00	0.00	0.00	0.00
Construction	16.19	6.58	1.73	0.00	0.00	0.00	0.00	0.00	0.00
Public Utilities	22.31	21.00	36.21	22.04	22.87	35.43	98.78	99.37	97.85
Services	**52.06**	**41.66**	**25.90**	**20.30**	**33.31**	**21.46**	**39.00**	**79.97**	**82.84**
Commerce	30.69	3.41	2.04	6.33	0.34	0.11	21.63	10.10	5.44
Transportation	5.35	7.35	13.56	2.81	6.64	12.03	52.69	90.34	88.75
Communication	6.83	6.41	7.34	6.70	6.19	7.14	98.20	96.68	97.32
Other Services	9.19	24.47	2.95	4.13	20.12	2.16	45.02	82.22	73.21
TOTAL	**188.68**	**115.80**	**100.75**	**70.19**	**73.64**	**76.02**	**37.21**	**63.60**	**75.47**

Source: Conjuntura Economica, Getulio Vargas Foundation and Pinheiro and Giambiagi (1993)
* The data include the 80 largest federal and state companies and the 500 largest Brazilian companies (private and public companies).

Yet, the Collor administration's main argument in advocating privatization remained the fiscal benefits ensuing from state divestiture.

As in the case of the other countries examined here, privatization was also part of the package to appease the requests of foreign creditors with which Brazil, during the Sarney administration, had a rocky relationship. In fact, under Sarney, Brazil maintained a tough stand in the renegotiation of its external debt. By the end of 1990, Brazil had incurred $10.3 billion in interest arrearages. Through privatization and other market reforms, the Collor administration hoped to recover Brazil's credibility abroad, which was the basis for receiving future loans from the IMF, the Paris Club, and private banks. To signal to the international community that Brazil was serious about changing its economic policies, Collor went so far as to say that his government would privatize one PE a month. In addition, a normalization of relations with foreign creditors was an essential prerequisite to start negotiations leading to debt reduction under the auspices of the Brady Plan. Even though Brazil had been able to negotiate from a much stronger stand point than Argentina and Peru due to its ability to generate large trade surpluses which then were used to finance the external debt with commercial banks without submitting to the harsh conditions of the IMF, it was clear by 1990 that this cat-and-mouse game was, in the long run, counter productive. By contracting short-term loans at very high interest rates, the Sarney administration had progressively diverted important financial resources that could have been used for much needed domestic investment (Sola 1993: 164). Suffice to say that Brazil's short-term debt jumped from $10.9 billion in 1988 to $24.1 billion in 1990.[22]

Whereas in Argentina Menem clearly used privatization to reward supporters from big capital and some sectors of the labor movement, this is not quite as clear in the case of Brazil (Goldstein 1997). Shortly before taking office Collor declared, 'the price of my economic program will be paid by the Brazilian elites, those who already made a lot of money with a development model that benefitted only a handful of people'.[23] Yet the only clear beneficiaries of the administration's market reforms were the President himself, P. C. Farias, and the people involved in the corruption scandal that resulted in Collor's impeachment.[24] Indeed, what stands out in Collor's political style, as opposed to Menem's, was his attempt to isolate the executive from the lobbying effort of traditional power groups and his unwillingness to compromise. A typical case of this behavior was Collor's rejection of the endorsement, during his presidential campaign, of the Federação das Indústrias de Estado de São Paulo (FIESP). Collor charged that FIESP, the powerful business organization of the state of São Paulo representing many of Brazil's most important industrial groups, was merely acting in an opportunistic fashion, trying to please Collor in the event of his victory.[25] Once in office, Collor's selectivity in using trade liberalization and deregulation aimed at undercutting specific business groups, and more specifically those that had thrived under economic protectionism. In so doing, the government hoped to divide those business groups taking advantage of the new policies from the losers, thus weakening the cohesiveness of their interest organizations. The same was true for labor (Weyland 1993).

When Franco inherited the privatization program in September 1992, his willingness to carry it out was very much in doubt. Throughout the first two years of the Collor administration, the vice-President had been an outspoken critic of the administration's neo-orthodox policies and publicly opposed the sale of the steel mill Usiminas. Franco, a nationalist and a long-time supporter of ISI, once in charge found himself at odds and his ministers and advisers had to convince him that structural reforms were inevitable.[26] The privatization process was substantially delayed and thoroughly reorganized.[27] Under Franco, it lost whatever ideological flavor Collor may have given it and was justified only on pragmatic grounds by targeting the deficit reduction. According to the Franco administration, 'privatization looks to contribute toward the reduction of the federal debt, both domestic and foreign, and toward the financial restructuring of the public sector, through the utilization of the resources of these enterprises to reduce the fiscal deficit, or by using the bonds issued by state enterprises in the privatization process'.[28]

Moreover, for Franco and the Congress, which the new President involved in the privatization process, state divestiture was a low priority issue as compared to more pressing problems like inflation, wage indexation, constitutional reform (which was scheduled for 1993 but was later postponed to 1995), and the 1994 presidential elections.[29] Given these problems, Franco privatized only sixteen PEs of the forty-five originally planned, whereas Collor sold eighteen of the twenty-nine slated for divestiture in 1991–2 (Table 4.3).

Under Cardoso, the same pragmatic goals that were conducive to Collor's privatization attempt apply, and in some cases they gained even greater importance. For instance, the fixed exchange rate regime, coupled with trade liberalization established under the Real Plan, made more compelling than in the past the need for large capital inflows from abroad. Privatization could make a significant contribution toward that end by luring foreign investors that had been noticeably scarce up until 1994. Likewise, the Real Plan sustainability hinged upon the maintenance of a low fiscal deficit. Proceeds from state divestitures were deemed crucial to fill dangerous gaps in the government finances during the structural adjustment process. Before closing this section a few words are in order to assess privatization as a means to reward supporters. As noticed earlier, there is no evidence that this was the case under Franco. Collor was in office too short a time to make an assessment, although the sudden large purchase of junk bonds prior to the privatization announcement by the very same banks that ended up purchasing with such means steel, petrochemical, and fertilizer comapnies, raise some questions

TABLE 4.3. *Brazil: Privatization Transactions 1991–8*

Company	Date of Auction	Floor Price (US$ million)	Sale Price (US$ million)	Overprice Paid (%)	Minimum Price in Cash (%)
1. Usiminas—Common shares	Oct. 91	973.2	1,112.4	14.3	
Usiminas—Preferred shares	Nov. 91	264.3	264.3	0.0	
2. Celma	Nov. 91	72.5	90.7	25.0	
3. Mafersa	Nov. 91	18.5	48.4	161.0	
4. Cosinor	Nov. 91	12.0	13.6	13.8	
Subtotal 1991			1,529.4		
5. SNBP	Jan. 92	7.8	12.0	54.4	
6. Indag	Jan. 92	6.8	6.8	0.1	
7. Piratini	Feb. 92	42.0	105.1	150.4	
8. Petroflex	Apr. 92	178.6	215.6	20.7	
9. Copesul	May 92	617.1	797.1	29.2	
10. Alcalis	Jul. 92	78.9	78.9	0.0	
11. CST—Common/pref. shares	Jul. 92	295.4	295.4	0.0	
CST—Common shares	Jul. 92	36.9	36.9	0.0	
12. Nitriflex	Aug. 92	26.2	26.2	0.0	
13. Fosfertil	Aug. 92	139.3	177.1	27.1	
14. Polisul	Sep. 92	56.8	56.8	0.0	
15. PPH—Common shares	Sep. 92	25.1	40.8	62.2	
PPH—Preferred shares	Nov. 92	18.6	18.6	0.0	
16. Goiasfertil	Oct. 92	12.7	12.7	0.0	
17. Acesita	Oct. 92	347.7	450.3	29.5	
18. CBE	Dec. 92	10.9	10.9	0.0	
Subtotal 1992			2,341.2		
19. Poliolefinas	Mar. 93	87.1	87.1	0.0	30.0
20. CSN—1st auction	Apr. 93	1,056.6	1,056.6	0.0	3.8
21. Ultrafertil	Jun. 93	199.4	199.4	0.0	20.0
22. Cosipa—Common shares	Aug. 93	166.3	330.5	98.8	3.8
23. Acominas	Sep. 93	284.8	554.2	94.6	5.0
24. Oxiteno	Sep. 93	53.9	53.9	0.0	5.0
Subtotal 1993			2,281.8		

TABLE 4.3. *(cont'd)*

Company	Date of Auction	Floor Price (US$ million)	Sale Price (US$ million)	Overprice Paid (%)	Minimum Price in Cash (%)
25. PQU	Jan. 94	269.9	269.9	0.0	30.0
CSN—2nd auction	Mar. 94	127.0	127.0	0.0	100.0
26. Arafertil	Apr. 94	10.7	10.8	0.5	10.0
CSN—3rd auction	Apr. 94	83.3	83.3	0.0	100.0
Cosipa—Preferred shares	Jun. 94	7.7	9.6	24.7	100.0
27. Caraiba	Jun. 94	5.0	5.0	0.0	10.0
28. Acrinor	Aug. 94	12.1	12.1	0.0	10.0
29. Coperbo	Aug. 94	25.9	24.9	0.0	10.0
30. Polialden	Aug. 94	16.7	16.7	0.0	10.0
31. Ciquine	Aug. 94	23.7	23.7	0.0	10.0
32. Politeno	Aug. 94	44.9	44.9	0.0	10.0
CST—3rd auction	Oct. 94	6.2	6.2	0.0	100.0
33. Usiminas	Nov. 94	0.7	0.7	0.0	100.0
34. Embraer	Dec. 94	181.5	182.9	0.8	10.0
Subtotal 1994			818.8		
35. Escelsa	Jul. 95	345.0	385.7	11.8	66.9
36. Copene	Aug. 95	253.8	253.8	0.0	10.0
37. CPC—Common share auction	Sep. 95	73.6	73.6	0.0	10.0
CPC—Preferred share auction	Sep. 95	16.5	26	57.4	10.0
38. Salgema—Common share auct.	Oct. 95	48.8	48.8	0.0	10.0
Salgema—Preferred share auct.	Oct. 95	37.9	90.4	138.2	10.0
39. CQR	Oct. 95	0.0	1.7	13,800.0	10.0
40. Nitrocarbono	Dec. 95	29.5	29.6	0.0	10.0
41. Pronor	Dec. 95	62.9	63.5	0.8	10.0
42. CBP	Dec. 95	0.0	0.04	50.1	10.0
Subtotal 1995			973.1		

	Date				
43. Polipropileno—Common share auct.	Feb. 96	67.4	67.4	0.0	10.0
Polipropileno—Preferred share auct.	Feb. 96	13.8	13.8	0.0	10.0
44. Koppol	Mar. 96	3.1	3.1	0.0	10.0
45. RFFSA (Malha Oeste)	Mar. 96	61.2	63.4	3.6	100.0
46. Light	May 96	2,270.9	2,270.9	0.0	70.0
47. Deten	May 96	12.1	12.1	0.0	10.0
48. RFFSA (Centro Leste)	Jun. 96	316.1	316.1	0.0	100.0
49. Polibrasil	Aug. 96	99.4	99.4	0.0	10.0
50. RFFSA (Sudeste)	Sep. 96	870.6	870.6	0.0	100.0
51. EDN	Sep. 96	16.6	16.6	0.2	10.0
52. RFFSA (Tereza Cristina)	Nov. 96	16.1	17.9	11.2	100.0
53. RFFSA (Sul)	Nov. 96	152.2	208.5	37.0	100.0
Subtotal 1996			3,959.8	1.5	22.0
54. CVRD	May 97	2,609.8	3,131.5	20.0	100.0
55. B-Band area 7	Jun. 97		315.0	25.3	100.0
56. B-Band area 1	Jul. 97		2,452.0	341.0	100.0
57. B-Band area 9	Jul. 97		232.0	8.7	100.0
58. RFFSA (Malha Nordeste)	Jul. 97	10.6	14.6	37.9	100.0
59. B-Band area 10	Aug. 97		512.0		100.0
60. B-Band area 2	Aug. 98		1,139.0	141.5	100.0
61. Escelsa	Aug. 97	99.2	119.4	20.3	100.0
62. Tecon 1 (Port of Santos)	Set. 97	92.6	251.1	171.3	100.0
63. Meridional	Dec. 97	155.4	238.7	53.7	100.0
Subtotal 1997			8,405.3		
64. B-Band area 3	Apr. 98		1,327.0	300.0	100.0
65. B-Band area 4	Apr. 98		456.0	30.0	100.0
66. B-Band area 5	Apr. 98		680.0	134.0	100.0
67. B-Band area 6	Apr. 98		305.0	1.4	100.0
74. Telenorte Leste	Jul. 98		2,950.0	0.8	100.0
75. Telecentro Sul	Jul. 98		1,780.0	6.0	100.0
76. Telesp (Sao Paulo)	Jul. 98		4,980.0	64.0	100.0
77. Telesp Cellular (Sao Paulo)	Jul. 98		3,080.0	225.0	100.0
78. Telemig Celular (Minas Gerais)	Jul. 98		756.0	229.0	100.0
79. Telesul Celular	Jul. 98		700.0	204.0	100.0

TABLE 4.3. (cont'd)

Company	Date of Auction	Floor Price (US$ million)	Sale Price (US$ million)	Overprice Paid (%)	Minimum Price in Cash (%)
80. Tele Sudeste Celular	Jul. 98		1,170.0	147.0	100.0
81. Tele Centro Celular	Jul. 98		397.0	91.0	100.0
82. Tele Nordeste Celular	Jul. 98		569.0	193.0	100.0
83. Tele Norte Celular	Jul. 98		162.0	108.0	100.0
84. Tele Este Celular	Jul. 98		269.0	242.0	100.0
85. Embratel	Jul. 98		2,280.0	4.7	100.0
86. Gerasul	Sep. 98		822.0	0.0	100.0
Subtotal 1998			22,683.0		
Total I (1991–8)			42,992.4		
Offers to employees (Total II)			728.2		
Offers to the public					
a. Usiminas	Nov. 91		49.8		
b. Petroflex	Mar. 92		12.5		
c. CSN	Jul. 93		152.4		
d. Copesul	Jul. 94		33.8		
e. Cosipa-1	Sep. 94		70.9		
f. Usiminas international	Sep. 94		480.0		
g. Cosipa-2	Dec. 94		145.3		
Total III			944.7		
Others	Nov. 94	269.8	276.8	2.6	
	Dec. 94	118.5	118.7	0.2	
	Dec. 96	30.4	33.8	11.2	
	Feb. 97	34.1	46.7	36.9	
	May 97	120.2	120.5	0.3	
	Jul. 97	26.3	34.5	31.2	
Total IV		599.3	631.0	5.3	
TOTAL I + II + III + IV			45,296.3		

Source: BNDES, 1998.

of possible collusion between the executive and specific financial institutions. Under Cardoso the picture becomes more complex. The legal tenders for telecommunication and oil concessions were drafted in a way to improve the business opportunities of large domestic groups, which at times had doubtful qualifications in the business. Whether this was done either to appease nationalistic critics, or explicitly reward the administration's supporters cannot be determined with any degree of certainty, but given the cozy relationship existing between politicians and high profile conglomerates like O Globo, Oderbrecth, and Gerdau, to name a few, the suspicion remains strong (Fleischer 1996/7; de Lima 1998).

Opportunity

As in Argentina, the initiation of the privatization program took place under very unstable macroeconomic conditions, which were not conducive to attracting many potential buyers (Abreu and Werneck 1993). However, we saw that in Argentina the government created many incentives to make up for all kinds of difficulties, often in open contradiction with the terms of the public offer and the general thrust of the law regulating state divestiture. One major difference between Argentina and Brazil was the role assigned to private capital. In Argentina very few limits were imposed on foreign investors. In Brazil, the Collor administration lifted the old ban on foreign participation in the acquisition of PEs. None the less, Congress imposed several new restrictions. Diminishing the attractiveness of the Brazilian divestiture program was the fact that the 1988 Constitution gave PEs monopolistic control over oil, gas, and public utilities, which were the most attractive markets for foreign investors. Foreign ownership was limited to no more than 40 per cent of voting shares. The initial privatization law allowed foreigners to eventually acquire majority control of a company only twelve years after the transfer (this requirement was subsequently reduced to two–three years). A six-year waiting period was imposed on foreign capital repatriation ensuing from privatization. In the end, President Franco himself recognized the need for more foreign capital and technology. In 1994, upon Franco's urging, Congress approved an executive-sponsored bill raising the percentage that foreign interests were permitted to hold in privatized companies from 40 to 100 per cent, unless the executive branch would rule otherwise.

Additional factors kept foreigners away. First, the lack of an agreement between Brazil and its creditors on the country's debt, coupled with the already mentioned problems created by political and macroeconomic instability, resulted in a poor country investment rating. This induced many investors to adopt a 'wait-and-see' attitude about privatization.[30] Second, the lack of transparency in the secondary markets for the domestic debt certificates, used as currencies to sell PEs, also scared foreign investors.[31] Third, of the three sectors that the government decided to privatize—steel, fertilizers, and petro-chemicals—only the latter seemed to elicit the interest of foreign investors.[32] Fourth, the bitter dispute raised in Congress by many legislators, opposing foreign participation in the privatization process, added further uncertainty about the reliability of such investments.[33]

All of these problems made the privatization effort dependent upon the interests of a handful of Brazilian groups. Among the most interested parties were those domestic groups that were either in competition with or worked as suppliers of PEs in the sectors mentioned above, with the notable exception of petrochemicals where some private producers were initially against privatization fearing the loss of fat government contracts.[34] The financial sector, which owned a large amount of domestic bonds used to privatize PEs, was also very much interested. However, even these few parties often became reluctant due to the complex ownership of the most palatable PEs up for sale. In fact, in a few cases, some PEs had a substantial minority share in the hands of private owners or local government (Table 4.4). This resulted in a thorny issue leading the government to lengthy negotiations with its private partners, as in the case of the Usiminas and CST steel mills, in order to clear the sale from legal challenges (Mello 1992).

The availability of tenders, both domestic and foreign, became a reality only after the Real Plan stabilized the economy and Cardoso included in the PND the most important PEs. Having weathered the consequences of the 1994 Mexican financial crisis, the Cardoso administration's reform policy had

TABLE 4.4. *Brazil: Changes in Composition of Voting Capital (%) 1991–7*

Main Shareholders of Common Stock	Before	After	Main Shareholders of Common Stock	Before	After
1. USIMINAS			**2. CELMA**		
Siderbras/BNDES	85.3		Federal Government	85.8	
BNDE/opcao minoritarias	9.4	0.6	Pratt & Whitney	10.8	10.8
Nippon-Usiminas	5.0	13.8	FND-Fundo Nacional de	3.3	
Other previous shareholders	0.3	0.3	Desenvolvim.		
Employees		9.6	Other previous shareholders	0.1	0.1
CVRD-Cia.Vale de Rio Doce		15.0	Employees		3.0
PREVI-Caixa Prev.		15.0	Banco Boavista SA		21.4
Func.Banco/Brasil			Banco Safra SA		21.4
VALIA-Fund.Vale de Rio		7.7	Construtora Andrade		
Doce			Gutierrez		21.4
Other Pension Funds (17)		3.4	General Electric do Brasil SA		9.7
Bozano Simonsen		7.6	TELOS-Pension Fund		5.3
Banco Economico		5.7	Individuals		4.0
Other financial institutions		14.9	Banco Bradesco SA		1.8
Steel distributors		4.4	Banco Montreal		1.1
Other shareholders		2.0	SA-Montrealbank		
TOTAL	100.0	100.0	TOTAL		100.0

TABLE 4.4. *(cont'd)*

Main Shareholders of Common Stock	Before	After	Main Shareholders of Common Stock	Before	After
3. MAFERSA			Consorcio PPE		28.8
BNDES System	99.9		Petroquimica Triunfo	0.6	0.6
Previous shareholders	0.1	0.1	Petroflex	0.3	0.3
Employees		9.5	White Martins	0.1	0.1
REFER		90.4	Employees		10.0
TOTAL	100.0	100.0	Public Offer		10.0
4. COSINOR			Fundo Polinvest M Privatizacao-DS		4.6
BNDES System	99.8		Banco Real		4.5
Previous shareholders	0.2	0.2	Banco Economico		4.1
Tronconrdeste Ad. Part. Ltda (Gerdau)		99.8	Banco Bamerindus		2.8
TOTAL	100.0	100.0	Garantia I-Fundo Privat. CP		1.0
			Foreign Capital (26)		4.8
5. SNBP			Pension Funds		7.1
Federal Government	100.0		Others		5.2
Employees reserve		10.0	TOTAL	100.0	100.0
CINCO-Cia. Intern. Naveg. e Comercio		90.0	**10. ALCALIS**		
TOTAL			Petroquisa	92.5	
			BNDES	7.5	
6. INDAG			Cirne (Fargoso Pires Group)		99.9
Profertil	35.0		Employees		0.1
IAP SA	65.0	100.0	**11. CST**		
TOTAL	100.0	100.0	Siderbras	73.9	
7. PIRATINI			CVRD-Cia.Vale de Rio Doce	0.1	15.0
Siderbras	96.2			13.0	13.0
Previous shareholders	3.8	0.7	Ilva	13.0	13.0
Employees		9.5	Employees		8.8
Gerdau		89.8	Bozano Simonsen Group		25.4
TOTAL	100.0	100.0	Unibanco		20.0
8. PETROFLEX			Others		4.8
Petroquisa	100.0		TOTAL	100.0	100.0
Conorcio PIC: Suzano		20.4	**12. NITRIFLEX**		
Norquisa		10.4	Fosfertil	40.0	
Unipar		10.2	Itap	60.0	100.0
Coperbo		10.0	TOTAL	100.0	100.0
Pension Funds		26.0	**13. FOSFERTIL**		
Financial Institutions		2.6	Petrofertil	76.4	
Foreign Capital		0.4	BNDESPAR	11.9	
Employees		10.0	CVRD	11.5	11.5
Others		10.0	COMIG	0.2	0.2
TOTAL	100.0	100.0	Employees		10.0
9. COPESUL			Consorcio Fertifos		68.5
Petroquisa	67.2	15.0	Banco Bamerindus		6.0
BNDESPAR	30.7		Banco America do Sul		1.6
Poliolefinas	0.7	0.7	Noroeste Group		1.0
Polisul	0.2	0.2	Others		1.2
PPH	0.2	0.2	TOTAL	100.0	100.0

TABLE 4.4. *(cont'd)*

Main Shareholders of Common Stock	Before	After	Main Shareholders of Common Stock	Before	After
14. POLISUL			Employees		11.9
Petroquisa	33.4	60.0	Caixa Benef.	9.2	5.8
Ipiranga	33.3	40.0	Empregados CSN-CBS		
Hoescht	33.3		Docenave		9.4
TOTAL	100.0	100.0	Vicunha Group		9.2
15. PPH			Bamerindus		9.1
Petroquisa	20.0		Uniao Comercio Part.		7.7
Petropar	30.0	37.5	(Bradesco)		
Himont	30.0	37.5	Privatinvest		6.3
Oderbrecht	20.0	25.0	Other financial institutions		12.5
TOTAL	100.0	100.0	Other pension funds (26)		2.7
16. GOIASFERTIL			Individuals		0.1
Petrofertil	82.7		Other privatization funds		1.4
BNDESPAR	17.3		Others		11.1
Fosfertil		90.0	TOTAL	100.0	100.0
Employees		10.0	**21. ULTRAFERTIL**		
TOTAL	100.0	100.0	Petrofertil	100.0	
17. ACESITA			Fosfertil		90.0
Banco do Brasil	91.5		Employees		10.0
Previous shareholders	8.5	8.5	TOTAL	100.0	100.0
Employees		12.4	**22. COSIPA**		
PREVI		15.0	SIDERBRAS	99.9	
Fundacao SISTEL		9.2	Anquilla		34.4
Banco Safra/Albatriz SA		8.8	Brastubo		23.0
Banco Real		5.6	Employees		20.0
Banco Comercial Bancesa SA		4.2	Lotten		5.0
Fundacao PETROS		2.2	**(COSIPA** continued) Alamo		2.6
Other Pension Funds		9.7	Particip.		
Foreign Capital		1.8	Others		15.0
Others shareholders		22.6	TOTAL	100.0	100.0
TOTAL		100.0	**23. ACOMINAS**		
18. CBE			Siderbras	99.9	
Monsanto	48.3	48.3	Cia. Min. Part. Industrial		26.8
Unigel	27.8	50.9	Banco SRL		13.4
Petroquisa	23.1		Employees		20.0
Others	0.8	0.8	Banco de Credito		9.9
TOTAL	100.0	100.0	Nacional-BCN		
19. POLIOFELINAS			Mendes Junior		7.6
Petroquisa	31.5		Acos Villares		6.8
Unipar	31.5	31.5	Others	1.0	15.5
Oderbrecht	31.5	62.9	TOTAL	100.0	100.0
Bankamerica	4.4	4.4	**24. OXITENO**		
Hanover	1.1	1.2	Ultraquimica	60.6	69.4
TOTAL	100.0	100.0	Petroquisa	18.5	0.6
20. CSN			Monteiro Aranha	11.3	11.3
Siderbras/Tresury	90.8		Dresdner		8.9
Investors 1st auction		5.3	GBOEX		0.2
Investors 2nd auction		3.5	Others	9.6	9.6
			TOTAL	100.0	100.0

TABLE 4.4. *(cont'd)*

Main Shareholders of Common Stock	Before	After	Main Shareholders of Common Stock	Before	After
25. PQU			**31. CIQUINE**		
Petroquisa	67.7	17.5	Petroquisa	33.2	
Unipar	28.9	30.0	Conepar	33.2	66.4
Banco Industria e Comercio	1.3	2.5	Mitsubishi	27.9	27.9
Bradesco	0.8	0.8	Nisshoiwai	5.4	5.4
Oderbrecht	0.7	0.7	Others	0.3	0.3
EDN Estireno do Nordeste	0.6	0.6	TOTAL	100.0	100.0
Consorcio Poloinvest		13.0			
Employees		9.8	**32. POLITENO**		
Polibrasil		6.8	Petroquisa	30.0	
San Felipe Adm.		6.3	Conepar	20.0	35.0
e Participacoes			Suzano	20.0	35.0
Fundo Privatinvest		4.5	Sumitomo	20.0	20.0
Other pension funds (2)		1.7	Itochu	10.0	10.0
Foreign Capital		0.3	TOTAL	100.0	100.0
Others		5.5			
TOTAL	100.0	100.0	**33. EMBRAER**		
			Federal Goverment	95.2	20.0
26. ARAFERTIL			Banco do Brasil Investimento	4.7	4.7
Quimbrasil	33.3	49.9	Previous shareholders	0.1	0.1
Petrofertil	33.3		Employees		10.0
Fertisul	33.3	50.1	Individual investors		10.0
Others	0.1		Bozano Simonsen Limited		16.1
TOTAL	100.0	100.0	Sistel		9.8
			Previ		9.8
27. CARAIBA			18 Pension funds		9.9
BNDESPAR/BNDES	100.0		Banval CCTVM		2.0
Employees		20.0	Other foreign investors (4)		2.0
Caraiba Metais		80.0	Others		5.6
TOTAL	100.0	100.0	TOTAL	100.0	100.0
28. ACRINOR			**34. ESCELSA**		
Petroquisa	35.0		Eletrobras	72.3	14.6
Rhodia	35.0	48.0	Iven S/A	20.1	45.1
Copene	26.0	48.0	Banco Pactual	1.1	1.1
Unigel	4.0	4.0	State of Espirito Santo	3.4	3.4
TOTAL	100.0	100.0	GTD Participacoes S/A		25.0
			Employees		7.7
29. COPERBO			Prefeituras	1.2	1.2
Petroquisa	23.0		Others	1.9	1.9
Copene	15.4	20.5	TOTAL	100.0	100.0
Petroflex	53.6	71.5			
Gov. Estado PE	5.2	5.2	**35. COPENE**		
Others	2.8	2.8	Petroquisa	36.3	5.6
TOTAL	100.0	100.0	Norquisa	25.7	36.4
			Employees		3.1
30. POLIALDEN			Individual investors		15.7
Petroquisa	33.3		Others	38.0	38.0
Conepar	33.3	66.6	Pension funds (7)		1.2
Mitsubishi	16.7	16.7	TOTAL	100.0	100.0
Nisshoiwai	16.7	16.7			
TOTAL	100.0	100.0			

TABLE 4.4. *(cont'd)*

Main Shareholders of Common Stock	Before	After	Main Shareholders of Common Stock	Before	After
36. CPC			Suzano Resinas Petroquimicas Ltda		49.6
Petroquisa	33.3		TOTAL	100.0	100.0
EPB	33.3	66.7			
Mitsubishi Chemicals	19.0	19.0	**44. LIGHT**		
Nisso Iwai	14.4	14.3	Electrobras	81.6	28.8
TOTAL	100.0	100.0	Others	18.4	10.8
			EDF International SA		11.4
37. SALGEMA			Houston Industries		11.4
Petroquisa	23.2		AES Coral Reef		11.4
Copene	40.3	50.0	BNDESPAR		9.1
EPB	36.5	50.0	CSN		7.1
TOTAL	100.0	100.0	Employees		10.0
			TOTAL	100.0	100.0
38. CQR					
Salgema	49.0	49.0	**45. DETEN**		
Petroquisa	36.9		Petroquisa	35.4	28.4
Apply		36.9	UNA	28.3	35.3
Others	14.1	14.1	UNIPAR	35.3	35.3
TOTAL	100.0	100.0	Others	1.0	1.0
			TOTAL	100.0	100.0
39. NITROCARBONO					
Petroquisa	24.6		**46. POLIBRASIL**		
Petroquimica de Bahia	17.5	19.8	Petroquisa	25.7	
Pronor	57.9	80.2	Shell Consocrcio Mega	25.7	25.7
TOTAL	100.0	100.0	Hipart		8.9
			Polipropileno	47.5	63.9
40. PRONOR			Ipiranga	1.1	1.5
Petroquisa	49.3		TOTAL	100.0	100.0
Petroquimica de Bahia	50.0	99.3			
Others	0.7	0.7	**47. EDN**		
TOTAL	100.0	100.0	Petroquisa	26.7	
			Dow Chemicals	26.7	53.4
41. CBP			Massa Falida Cevekol	13.2	13.2
Petroquisa	23.7		New shareholders	23.7	23.7
Pronor	73.6	73.6	Others	9.7	9.7
BBM	0.5	0.5	TOTAL	100.0	100.0
Atrium DTVM		23.7			
Others	2.2	2.2	**48. CVRD**		
TOTAL	100.0	100.0	Treasury	51.2	15.9
			BNDES	24.8	15.9
42. POLIPROPILENO			Pension Funds	15.0	5.0
Petroquisa	42.8		BNDESPAR/FPS	5.0	5.0
Cia Suzano	30.0	72.8	Investvale	0.0	4.0
Cevekoi	27.2	27.2	Others	4.0	2.0
TOTAL	100.0	100.0	SPE (VALEPAR)	0.0	52.2
			TOTAL	100.0	100.0
43. KOPPOL					
Petroquisa	49.6		VALEPAR composition		
SB Poliolefinas	49.6	49.6	CSN Steel Co.		25.0
Ipiranga	0.4	0.4	Litel Participasoes S/A		39.0
Polipropileno	0.4	0.4			

TABLE 4.4. *(cont'd)*

Main Shareholders of Common Stock	Before	After	Main Shareholders of Common Stock	Before	After
Eletron S/A		17.0	Usinas—Usinas Siderurgicas de MG		20.0
Sweet River Investments Ltd.		9.0			
BNDESPAR		9.0	Cosigua-Cia. Siderurgica da Guanabara		5.3
Investvale		1.0			
TOTAL		100.0	Celato Integracao Multimodal SA		4.3
49. MERIDIONAL			Ultrafertil SA		8.9
Federal Government	100.0		ABS—Empreend. Imob. Part. e Serv. SA		4.7
Banco Bozano Simonsen		100.0			
TOTAL	100.0	100.0	TOTAL		100.0
CONCESSIONS					
1. RFFSA (MALHA OESTE)			**4. RFFSA (TEREZA CRISTINA)**		
Noel Group Inc.		20.0	Banco Interfinance		33.3
Brazil Rail Partners, Inc.		20.0	Gemon Geral de Engenharia e Montagens SA		33.3
Wetern Rail Investors, LLC		20.0			
Bankamerica Intern. Invest. Co.		18.0	Santa Lucia Agroindustria e Comercio Ltd.		33.3
DK Partners		2.0	TOTAL		100.0
Chemical Latin America Equity Association		20.0	**5. RFFSA (MALHA SUL)**		
TOTAL		100.0	Ralph Partner's Inc.		17.5
2. RFFSA (MAHLA CENTRO-LESTE)			Varbra SA		17.5
			Jodori Adm. Empr. e Part Ltd.		17.5
Mineracao Tacuma Ltd.		12.5	Railtex		15.0
Interferrea SA Serv. Intermodais		12.5	Interferrea		17.5
			Brazil Private Equity		11.3
Companhia Siderurgica Nacional		12.5	Brazilian Equity Invetsments II Ltd.		3.0
Tupinambarana SA		12.5	Brazilian Equities Ltd.		0.7
Railtex Int. Holfings Inc.		12.5	TOTAL		100.0
Varbra SA		12.5	**6. RFFSA (MALHA NORDESTE)**		
Ralph Partners I		12.5			
Judori Adm., Empr. e Part. Ltd.		12.5	Taquari Participasoes		40.0
TOTAL		100.0	Companhia Siderurgica Nacional		20.0
3. FFSA (MALHA SUDESTE)			CVRD		20.0
CSN		20.0	ABS Empreendimentos, Part. e Servicos SA		20.0
MBR—Mineracoes Brasileiras Reunidas SA		20.0			
Ferteco Mineracao SA		16.8	TOTAL		100.0

Source: BNDES, *Programa Nacional de Destatizacao*, December 1997.

gained substantial credibility. From mid-1997 through mid-1988, Cardoso exploited his early macroeconomic and political achievements and took full advantage of the renewed interest of international investors looking for new lucrative business opportunities by selling electricity, mining, and telephone companies.

What about a favorable public mood then? As noted earlier, state interventionism became one of the major issues prior to the 1989 presidential elections. All major parties, with the exception of Lula's PT, were by then against it and proposed different recipes toward government restructuring. Privatization became an often mentioned means to that end. By 1990, support had gained momentum among Brazilian elites for the idea that some policy of goverment divestiture was in order. However, unlike Argentina, there were neither opinion leaders nor a conservative party ideologically committed to privatization per se (Goldstein 1997). In other words, no neo-orthodox tide had swept Brazil yet. This is because among the country's elites mixed feelings still existed about the appropriate role of the state, particularly when discussion over the role of privatization moved from the general to the specific. According to Schneider (1992: 232–4);

In a stratified survey of 450 intellectual, media, political, business, and military elites, IDESP probed views on the appropriate sectoral distribution for state enterprises. More than half felt state firms were unnecessary or only somewhat necessary in steel, international trade, computers . . . , and commercial aviation . . . More than half of the same sample felt that state enterprises were very or totally necessary in petroleum, electricity, science and technology, telecommunications, and higher education—areas that were not initially targeted for privatization . . . Beyond the so-called consensus for privatization was a more varied sectoral view among elites of where the state should exist. The Collor program initially conformed these views.

A 1989 survey commissioned by the National Confederation of Industry, sampling different sectors of the business community, showed similar results. Some 67 per cent of the 550 businessmen polled regarded privatization as very important, but 84 per cent still favored BNDES long-term financing. Businessmen seemed to favor trade liberalization and a retreat of PEs in the national economy but still expected the state to provide leadership and cheap financing for Brazil's economic development.[35]

Politicians, on the other hand, still seemed to be anchored to the idea of an entrepreneurial state. In 1993, a congressional study surveyed 74 per cent of the representatives in the Chamber of Deputies and 55 per cent of the senators on whether they agreed that the federal government should keep its monopoly over sectors specified in the 1988 Constitution (petroleum, natural gas, telecommunications, etc.). Only 17.3 per cent favored the end of state monopoly, 40 per cent agreed, and 39.6 per cent agreed but suggested some modifications to open some of these sectors to private investments. When asked if in the upcoming constitutional revision the state should

TABLE 4.5. *Brazil: Public Opinion Poll on the Size of the State in 1993*

The Size of the State Should Be:	%
Strongly reduced	14.0
Mildly reduced	21.0
Mildly increased	19.0
Strongly increased	20.0
Neither reduced or increased	4.0
No answer/don't know	22.0

Source: Companhia Brasileira de Pesquisa e Analise (CBPA), Poll taken in Sao Paulo.

TABLE 4.6. *Brazil: Public Opinion Poll on Products'Quality and Price After Privatization in 1993*

Opinion	Quality (%)	Price (%)
Improve	45.0	39.0
Worsen	11.0	17.0
No change	31.0	31.0
Don't know	13.0	13.0
No answer	1.0	1.0

Source: Companhia Brasileira de Pesquisa e Analise (CBPA), Poll taken in Sao Paulo.

maintain exclusive rights over subsoil resources, an overwhelming 65.4 per cent responded positively.[36]

For the general public, privatization seemed to remain a rather elusive issue. This is not surprising given the fact that, in 1989, 40.9 per cent of the population lived below the poverty threshold (Psacharopoulos *et al.* 1992: 58). A Gallup poll carried out in Rio de Janeiro and São Paulo that same year showed that only 40 per cent had actually heard or read anything about privatization (Schneider 1992). In June 1993, 49 per cent of the respondents of a nationally based survey were against the privatization of Petrobrás, whereas 36 per cent supported it.[37] Other survey results in the city of São Paulo in September of 1993 showed that 39 per cent of the respondents supported state intervention in the economy as opposed to 35 per cent who favored state-shrinking policies (Table 4.5). Yet, when asked about the likely effects of privatization, 45 per cent believed that life quality would improve; 39 per cent also thought that prices would improve too (Table 4.6). In terms of the beneficiaries of privatization, the same sample showed that people favored Brazilian companies overwhelmingly over foreign ones (Table 4.7). In other words, by the time Collor decided to privatize there was no general public consensus

TABLE 4.7. *Brazil: Public Opinion Poll on the Role of Public and Private Capital in Key Sectors in 1993**

Opinion	Domestic Private Capital (%)	Foreign Capital (%)	Don't know/No Answer (%)
Petroleum	53.0	12.0	21.0
Electricity	51.0	6.0	22.0
Water	51.0	4.0	22.0
Mining	50.0	9.0	24.0
Highways	49.0	8.0	23.0
Metrorail	46.0	8.0	23.0
Telecommunications	46.0	12.0	23.0
Steel	51.0	10.0	26.0
Railways	48.0	10.0	23.0
Petrochemicals	48.0	13.0	26.0

Source: Companhia Brasileira de Pesquisa e Analise (CBPA), Poll taken in Sao Paulo.
* Question: What type of enterprises should function in the following sectors?

on the need for such a policy. The average citizen had little or no information about it, while the elites were quite divided among themselves.

Only later on did public opinion trends with respect to privatization become more positive as sectors of the population came to perceive it as a possible solution to the deepening economic crisis (Sola 1993). Indeed, support for it appeared to increase as the debate over the privatization of Petrobrás and Telebrás became more intense. In April 1994, approval ratings for the breaking of the oil and telecommunications monopolies were at 55 per cent and 47 per cent respectively.[38] By 1995, polls commissioned by the leading newspaper Jornal do Brasil indicated that the majority of respondents favored privatization but disagreed with the government use of privatization currencies, preferring instead cash payments. The slow crescendo of the pro-privatization mood can partly be attributed to the fact that while Menem could capitalize on popular dissatisfaction with inefficient PEs in public services to justify his policy, this was hard to do in Brazil where, until the late 1970s, the telephone, electricity, and mail systems performed well. However, the provision of such services began to deteriorate quickly in the early 1990s. By the time the Cardoso administration took office in 1994, it could count on a much greater degree of public support for its divestiture program than any of its predecessors.

As for foreign pressure and financial support, in the late 1980s, in the wake of the failure of the Cruzado Plan the IMF and the World Bank mounted their pressure to convince the Brazilian government on the need to adopt a coherent package of market reforms. To this end the World Bank, even before Collor's election:

organized a series of seminars and conferences. This exchange of ideas generated several reports that were discussed with Brazilian officials and intellectuals for a period of seven months. As a result of this process, the Collor de Mello government was in a position to act rapidly on the reform front in 1990, when most non-tariff barriers were eliminated and the tariff reduction program was instituted. (Edwards 1995: 56–7)

Foreign pressure, however, had little impact on the renegotiation of the external debt. Under Collor's first economy minister, Zelia Cardoso de Mello, relations with the IMF and foreign creditors remained tense but improved under her successor, Marcilio Marques Moreira. However, unlike the Argentine privatization program, Collor's divestiture program did not con- template, in the beginning, foreign assistance from the IMF, the World Bank, the IFC, and the IDB, nor was this assistance sought. The reason for this dif- ferent trend seems to be explained by the Brazilian government's intention to retain freedom of action in the way privatization was to be pursued and avoid charges from left-wing congressmen that the country was giving up its sovereignty to foreign demands. The slow pace and rather limited scope of Brazil's program, as compared to that of Argentina, also made foreign assist- ance a less critical issue. Indeed, in April of 1994, commercial banks waived the pre-condition of a standby accord with the IMF, which had been applied before to Mexico and Argentina, and signed an agreement restructuring $49 billion of Brazil's commercial debt under the auspices of the Brady Plan. This gave Brazil substantial bargaining power despite the fact that the IMF regarded the Franco administration's efforts towards the reduction of the fiscal deficit and inflation as insufficient. However, in October 1994, to ease tensions and meet some of the IMF's demands for reaching a standby agree- ment, President Franco gave the BNDES greater discretion in selling minor- ity stakes in 600 joint ventures with private capital.[39] It is at this time that international assistance for the privatization began to pick up. The World Bank pledged a loan of $400 million in support of the sell-off of some electrical companies.[40] The IFC also promised financial support of approximately $5 bil- lion if Brazil were to push toward the privatization of basic infrastructures in energy, telecommunications, and railways.[41]

In fact, once the Cardoso administration unveiled its ambitious privatiza- tion plans affecting basic infrastructures, the promised IFC funds began to pour into Brazil. Moreover, the World Bank started to play a more active role by assisting Brazil in the privatization of electricity and railway companies, providing structural adjustment loans and technical assistance in both cases.[42] These important developments notwithstanding, even the Cardoso adminis- tration took great pain to diffuse at home any impression that it was under the influence of multilateral lending agencies since this was likely to provoke a nationalist backlash and a loss of support in Congress. In point of fact, after announcing an emergency fiscal program in November 1997, both the

President and his Finance Minister vigorously denied any rumor that Brazil was asking for either financial or technical support from the IMF. In all, none of the three factors shaping the opportunity to privatize was strong enough to tilt the balance in favor of state divestiture under Collor and Franco. Thus, only under the Cardoso administration foreign assistance, and more so the availability of tenders, seemed to play a meaningful role.

Implementation

Government Capabilities

In discussing state restructuring, Sola notes that a country's institutional framework plays a crucial role.

Successful state reform also requires the generation or allocation of organizational resources and concentration of technical expertise, which, in turn, hinges on the ability of competent, specialized, and accountable bureaucracies with a degree of autonomy and insulation from societal pressure. Finally, the ability of elected officials in democratic governments to exert effective control over the 'state machine' is also crucial . . . [However], none of these requirements has been fulfilled in Brazil. (Sola 1993: 161)

Government cohesiveness was a major problem for Collor and even more so for Franco. We have already seen that Franco openly disagreed, while he was Vice-President, with Collor's market reforms. Yet, Collor's problems did not stop there. In general, Collor 'lacked a large, competent team of close aides who were committed to his goals and could help to administer the huge institutional apparatus of the Brazilian state according to his guidelines' (Weyland 1993: 10). The President's first cabinet was quite heterogeneous in terms of ideological leanings and policy preferences. Collor's initial economic team was made up of little-known economists, including his first Economy Minister Zelia Cardoso de Mello, whose qualifications were widely questioned. The failure of Collor's early stabilization policies were later ascribed to Cardoso de Mello's naïve understanding of the crisis (Sola 1993: 156).

In the beginning, the Collor administration entrusted upon the Privatization Committee the authority to design the PND. Directly subordinate to the President, the privatization committee was originally composed of twelve to fifteen members, five of whom were government appointees while seven came from the private sector. The intention was to shelter the PND from lobbies and keep it firmly under government control. The main tasks of the committee were: (1) submitting to the President the companies to be included in the PND; (2) approving the model of privatization and the conditions for the sale of assets; (3) establishing the minimum share price; (4) indicating, when necessary, the creation of special types of shares (i.e. golden shares that allows a government to exercise veto power on corporate management's decisions); (5) crafting guidelines and regulations for the PND; and (6) publishing an annual report about the PND's activities.

The actual carrying out of the PND was left to BNDES, whose President was also the chairman of the privatization committee. The choice of BNDES was a non-controversial one, given the expertise that the bank had acquired in this field in the 1980s and its high standing with both the business community and many politicians of different political leanings. The BNDES's role was: (1) managing the privatization fund; (2) making a public tender for the hiring of consultants and auditors; (3) coordinating and supervising the work of the auditors and consultants; (4) recommending to the privatization committee the general conditions of the sale of assets, including the minimum share price (and other necessary prior adjustments); (5) carrying out the guidelines set out by the privatization committee; (6) putting into operation the decisions made by different levels of government; and (7) carrying out the disclosure of privatization.[43] Under Collor, the President of the BNDES, Eduardo Modiano, a young investment banker, was left with wide powers to act swiftly. Despite the lackluster support from some cabinet members and the opposition of the old guard of the BNDES, Modiano and his team were capable of moving the process along albeit slowly.

After Franco took office the decision-making process underwent substantial changes. Because of the scandal that had brought Collor's impeachment, the privatization program became a prime target of the administration's critics. Being an interim President and in no position to pick up a political fight with Congress on a policy he had openly opposed, Franco put the PND on hold. In mid-December 1992, citing the need to bring greater transparency to the rules used to sell PEs, in order to protect the 'interests' of the Brazilian people, he temporarily suspended the PND. In January 1993, the President announced that the executive would take direct control of the privatization effort. The PND committee was changed and the BNDES President was no longer its chairman. This allowed greater executive control over what PEs were to be sold or to remain under government ownership. Among other things, the executive also reserved for itself the right to: (1) approve the percentage of payment for acquisitions in cash; (2) nominate the members of the privatization committee for congressional approval; and (3) to decide any matter regarding the framework of the PND.[44]

The approach to privatization also changed. Instead of a universal criteria for all transfers that had characterized the Collor administration, Franco switched to a case-by-case method allowing greater flexibility and room for maneuvering.[45] Pension funds, which had been active in the privatization process under Collor, including many belonging to public employees, were temporarily banned from privatization. The following November, the Franco administration issued a new executive order again changing the rules of the game. Under the new scheme, the Finance Ministry gained decisive control over the PND at the expense of the privatization committee, whose decision-making prerogatives were further reduced.

Government cohesiveness behind privatization under Franco severely deteriorated and partly explains why the policy slowed down considerably (Weyland 1997–8). The Economy Ministry that Collor had created in March to centralize the decision-making process was disbanded by Franco and its functions divided between the ministries of finance, industry, and planning, creating multiple jurisdiction problems.[46] As Abreu and Werneck (1993: 40) described at the time, 'in some areas, such as commercial policy, the confusion of attributions among the three recreated ministries is immense and adds considerably to the lack of effectiveness of public administration'.

The general trend of privatization could be described as 'two steps forward and one backward'. Shortly after the suspension of the PND, Franco's first Finance Minister Gustavo Krause resigned in protest. Thereafter, it was quite clear that within the administration there were deep divisions as to how and what to privatize. Modiano's replacement at the BNDES, Antônio Barros de Castro, was more in favor of restructuring PEs rather than privatizing them. He also defended the principle of maintaining government monopolies in extractive industries and public utilities. However, even the reluctant Barros de Castro came into open disagreement with Franco's chief adviser on privatization, José de Castro, who missed no opportunity to call into question the whole policy.[47]

Continuous cabinet reshuffling throughout 1993, either because of new scandals affecting administration officials or disputes between Franco and his ministers, made policy continuity a real challenge. Usually, advocates of privatization in the finance and planning ministries found themselves at loggerheads with the ministries of mines and energy, and communications. The latter, controlling Petrobrás and Telebrás, resisted any privatization because such companies traditionally constituted a huge source of political patronage for the ministers controlling them.[48] The same applies to other ministries whose ownership of PEs was substantial. The split within the Franco administration was thus not based so much on ideological grounds but on the resistance of many ministers and their parties to give up the means sustaining their political clienteles.[49] Minister of Mines and Energy Paulino Cicero and Minister of Communications Hugo Napoleão personified this opposition claiming that Petrobrás and Telebrás were 'national achievements' and 'strategic assets' too sensitive in nature to be entrusted to private concerns. Cicero also became the principal lobbyist of the electric utility companies against Finance Minister Fernando Henrique Cardoso's attempt to privatize them. The mines and energy minister welcomed private companies only in building unfinished hydroelectrical dams and steam plants that the government could no longer finance.

To compound matters, President Franco's ambivalent behavior created uncertainty and confusion among administration officials. In July 1993, only days after the Finance Ministry had announced that the government was to sell its shares in the mining company Companhia Vale de Rio Doce (CVRD) and in Petrobrás Distribudora (gas stations), Franco told a student delegation that such properties were not included in his privatization program. In November, Franco, under pressure from the anti-privatization lobby in his cabinet, delayed by six months the sale of the electrical sector, 'in order to study the best way' to do so.[50] He also started an inquiry into the privatization of the power plant Escelsa for alleged irregularities. Despite these constraints Cardoso, while Finance Minister, managed to keep privatization on course and was able to move forward in some areas. In 1994, the PND incorporated all minority participations held by the public sector (Decree 1.204). In addition, the government lifted the limit on voting shares for foreign ownership and had Congress pass the Competition Law 8.884 in preparation for the privatization of public utilities.

The cohesiveness of the economic team was highest under the Cardoso administration. Although over time Cardoso had to replace some of the most important architects of the Real Plan, he was able to find able substitutes who could manage and give credibility to the administration's market reform agenda. The President also tried to assure a fairly good degree of coordination between the general macroeconomic policies of his government and the PND (Goldstein 1997). To this end, he brought substantial changes to the PND's organization and policy content. In early 1995, the government issued *medida provisoria* 841, replacing the Privatization Committee with the National Privatization Council (Conselho Nacional de Desestatização, CND). The latter was composed of the ministers of planning, treasury, trade and tourism, public administration, foreign relations, and the President's chief of staff. The CND, on ad hoc bases, incorporated the ministers whose PEs were affected and the President of the Brazilian Central Bank when privatization involved financial institutions. Thereafter, the CND assumed the role of setting up policy guidelines for BNDES to carry out while the presidency of the republic retained the power of including or excluding PEs from PND through executive orders. Fundamentally, the rationale behind the creation of the CND was that by involving the most important ministries it was possible to diminish the probability of intra-ministerial squabbles, which had characterized the Collor and Franco administrations, while building support. This is not to say that disagreements were muted as some ministries, resenting the loss of political clout and jobs that the privatization of their firms entailed, dragged their feet (Weyland 1997–8). In point of fact, the outspoken Minister of Telecommunications Sérgio Motta (nicknamed the 'bulldozer'), Cardoso's right-hand man and personal friend, was a source of recurrent controversies within the administration. The most powerful politician in Cardoso's PSDB,

Motta's controversial management of the Telebrás (telephones) privatization and blunt criticisms of key cabinet ministers coming from other coalition parties came close to provoking a cabinet crisis. Internal disagreements also arose from the utilization of sale proceeds coming from the CVRD privatization. These problems notwithstanding, Cardoso was usually able to find the kind of compromise capable of overcoming internal divisions within the CND and moving the divestiture process forward (Galvão de Almeida 1997).

It is also worth noting that under Cardoso the PND became very ambitious in content and scope as it began to affect the core industries of Brazilian economic nationalism, that is, the large utility and extractive companies that Collor and Franco had carefully left out. Cardoso started out his administration by having Congress pass Law 8.987 regulating public concessions, which paved the way for the privatization in electricity, port, and railway sectors. Through a constitutional revision, that same year, he also allowed foreign companies to invest in the oil and gas business.

Moreover, the federal government for the first time made an explicit effort to induce state governments to cooperate in the reform program at the local level. This took the form of state privatizations in exchange for special federal loans disbursed by BNDES to help the depleted finances of the most important states (i.e. São Paulo, Rio de Janeiro, Minas Gerais). The greater cohesiveness and sense of purpose of the Cardoso administration, despite many ups and downs, partially explain why during the 1995–8 period the PND made its most impressive strides.

In terms of technical and administrative capacity, most analysts and pundits agree that BNDES showed a high degree of expertise and professionality in carrying its tasks (Schneider 1992; Goldstein 1997). This achievement, in turn, is credited for the survival of the whole policy despite the shameful demise of the Collor administration and Franco's lack of commitment (Werneck 1993: 27). In a few cases, as we shall see later, some congressmen raised corruption charges regarding the way some PEs were sold, but they were unable to substantiate them. In fact, according to most accounts, BNDES assured a high degree of transparency to the whole process that, while slowing it on many occasions, had the virtue of depriving the anti-privatization lobby of further ammunition to stall the PND.

The Privatization Committee, which under Modiano was staffed with technocrats and qualified members of the business community, lost much of its prestige under Franco since many of its members were appointed following political criteria and had little or no expertise in evaluating the complex matters involved in the divestiture process. Under Cardoso, however, there was a return to a more professional management style. Several ministries in charge of the privatization of their own sector were initially ill prepared to handle large and complex divestiture programs that entailed the development of a modern regulatory framework (i.e. telecommunications, electricity).

Such problems were surely responsible for the slowness with which some important transfers developed, but thanks to BNDES and foreign consultants, both administrative coordination and technical capacity at the ministerial level improved over time. It must also be noted that the Brazilians also took advantage of the experiences of other countries. This induced them to devote more time to the solution of technical and legal problems in order to avoid many mistakes typical of earlier privatization programs in the region.

State institutions also played quite a different role in Brazil as compared to Argentina. As we saw in the previous chapter, Menem acted swiftly to neutralize anti-privatization initiatives from the judiciary and Congress. This approach was unlikely to work in a country like Brazil for several factors. First of all, the 1988 Constitution weakened the authority of the executive by establishing an administrative decentralization process that, in turn, politically and financially strengthened governors and mayors. For instance, the new constitution mandated that one-fourth of federal tax revenues be transferred to state and municipal government, but this important change did not come with an equal transfer of responsibilities (Roett 1997; Rosenn 1998). In fact, the federal government was still held responsible for a host of socioeconomic programs but with substantially less financial resources and political authority to manage macroeconomic policy (Selcher 1998; Weyland 1997–8). Second, the proportional representation, open-list, electoral system sanctioned by 1998 Constitution triggered the proliferation of parties in Congress, forcing an incoming administration to engineer workable legislative majorities pulling together political parties with contending interests. In turn, these parties had substantial veto power on executive decisions since the mere threat of withdrawing their support could spell political disaster for the government's legislative agenda. Third, the electoral system over-represented rural, rent-seeking states from the north and north-east, heavily dependent on government spending and PEs, that made them potentially hostile to market reforms. Fourth, the same system also undermined party discipline as no sanctions existed to prevent legislators from engaging in the old Brazilian tradition of switching party affiliation once elected (Ames 1995; Roett 1997; Smith and Messari 1998). In describing the seriousness of this problem, Cardoso in an interview stated, 'the enemy is not the opposition parties but your own colleague in your own party . . . [the electoral system] destroys any kind of loyalty . . . it destroys the base for democracy in Brazil'.[51] Fifth, the 1988 Constitution established government monopolies in key oil/gas and public utility sectors, which to be lifted required amendments supported by three-fifths of both houses of Congress (Smith and Messari 1998).

Besides having to deal with a strong Congress and local government, and significant constitutional hurdles, a Brazilian President faced a judiciary that, while permeable to political manipulations, enjoyed a fair amount of institutional power in thwarting executive and legislative decisions. Unlike

Mcncm, none of the Brazilian Presidents could take its collaboration for granted. Nor were they able to pack the judiciary with sympathetic judges and federal prosecutors. We saw in the previous chapter that Argentine Chief Justice Rodolfo Barra recognized that his Brazilian colleagues' behavior was instrumental in slowing down the privatization process. In mid-1991 the Supreme Federal Tribunal (STF), the Brazilian Supreme Court, ruled as unconstitutional the system of capitalization of the external debt through privatization, and Collor was forced to back down. Federal courts were also heavily involved in delaying many sales, a trend that Menem discouraged from the beginning in Argentina. Enemies of privatization, both inside and outside government, consistently filed appeals before well-disposed judges to slow down the process from its start. In fact, the first divestiture that went unchallenged was that of Enersul in 1997. However, in most other cases legal battles were bitter and prolonged. The privatization of the electricity distributor Light of Rio de Janeiro was upheld in court for over two years. The CVRD divestiture marked a record 148 law suits, most of which were filed in different parts of the country only a few days prior to the auction to make it hard for the government to appeal.[52] Why could anti-privatization opponents appeal to the STF so freely? Rosenn (1998: 21), succinctly explained in these terms:

The 1988 Constitution created a series of measures that have the potentiality to embroil Brazil's highest court, the . . . STF, in the middle of political controversies with Congress and the President. Articles 102 (a) and 103 . . . permit the President of the Republic; the Procurator General of the Republic; the Executive Committees of the Federal Senate, Chamber of Deputies, or state legislatures, state governors, the Federal Council of the Brazilian Bar Association; any political party represented in Congress; and many syndical confederation or national class entity to bring action directly before the STF challenging the constitutionality of any law or normative act in the abstract . . . During the nine years and nine months that the present constitution has been in force, the STF has received 1,800 direct actions of unconstitutionality, and an average of one new action every two days.

Thus, appeals to the STF and lower courts turned out to be the most powerful means to stop privatization. However, as we shall see in a moment, they proved in the long-run ineffective when they were up against a determined administration, as was the case under Cardoso.

Given this array of obstacles, Collor's strategy to push his market reforms, including privatization, was simultaneously to centralize power as much as possible in the executive branch, while completely shutting down the policy process from the various business and political lobbies that had proliferated under the Sarney administration and had gained privileged access in crafting administrative decisions (Weyland 1997–8). Collor, unlike Menem, lacked a working majority in Congress; however, he thought that being the first elected President in 29 years allowed him some leeway. Thus, he ruled out building a legislative coalition and chose to impose his reforms through unilateral decisions, hoping that Congress would go along. From the start, he made indiscriminate use of *medidas provisórias*, which enabled the executive to act quickly in exceptional circumstances, pending later congressional approval (141 such measures were enacted in 1990 alone). As we saw, the first round of privatization was introduced through a *medida provisória*, which Congress eventually converted into law. As in Argentina, there was no debate about the privatization objectives and the means to accomplish them because Collor wanted to leave Congress completely out of it.[53] However, once the President's honeymoon period was over, Congress began to veto numerous executive orders. Instead of reaching a compromise, Collor simply reissued the same decrees. However, Collor's defiant strategy angered many legislators who appealed to the STF, which at the end of 1990 ruled the reissuing of such decrees as unconstitutional. This decision deprived Collor of a powerful tool to keep his reform program on course. From then on Congress gained control over the legislative agenda at the expense of the executive. Congress's clout received a further boost in the aftermath of Collor's impeachment. Indeed, the need to broaden congressional support prompted President Franco's decision to grant the Senate the power to set the final minimum price of PEs. This initiative mirrored the increased role of the legislature in the country's decision-making process.[54] Given the inability of any given congressional bloc to command a majority in the legislature and the deep splits existing among some of the major parties, it appears clear that granting the authority to rule over sale prices to a divided Senate, while allowing greater scrutiny, made things all the more complicated in terms of implementing a state divestiture policy. In fact, the high degree of independence from their party displayed by many federal legislators often forced the executive to lobby many congressmen individually, but with poor results. Due to these problems, even a conciliatory Franco found it impossible to gain the congressional support needed to speed up the PND. For instance, in mid-1994, the constitutional review abandoned amendments proposed by the Finance Ministry to terminate state monopolies in public utilities and extractive industries. To make things worse, in June 1994 a congressional commission and a federal agency, the Secretaria de Direito Econômico, looked into possible irregularities in the PND.[55] These events combined for a very volatile scenario and negatively affected the process by scaring many investors and undermining the confidence of the PND's committee and the BNDES.

Having learned from Collor's mistakes, Cardoso tried to accomplish many of the same objectives but resorted to bargaining rather confrontation vis-à-vis Congress. Weyland (1997–8: 81) summarized Cardoso's strategy in these terms:

[Cardoso] has systematically sought divergences among the interests of clientelistic politicians, state governors, and business groups, reinforcing those of their demands that coincide with his own reform agenda and compensating demands he cannot satisfy. Cardoso's negotiating strategies differ slightly with each set of potential 'veto players'. In dealing with clientelistic politicians . . . [he] has tried to play their short-term interests off against their long term-goals . . . [he] has offered patronage immediately, as to persuade politicians to accept state-building reforms that seek to limit patronage in the future.

Capitalizing on the widespread support that endorsed his presidential bid in 1994, Cardoso assembled a large (up to two-thirds of congressional seats) yet not very reliable coalition that over time included his own PSDB, the PFL, the PMDB and a host of other smaller parties. The President also appointed prominent members of these and other parties to key posts in his administration as a form of co-optation and payoff. In the beginning, it worked smoothly as Congress passed constitutional amendments abolishing state monopolies in extractive industries and public utilities. However, the legislative approval of new laws and regulatory framework necessary to transfer these sectors to private companies took longer due to internal divisions in the ruling coalition and it cost the President substantial concessions in terms of pork barrel programs and political patronage (Weyland 1997–8; Smith and Messari 1998). As a matter of fact, the largest and most meaningful privatizations did not take place until 1997.

In terms of speed, the PND was noticeable actually for the lack of it up until the large PEs in public utilities and mining began to be privatized in 1997. Collor's original plan had been to proceed quickly since his main concern was maximizing immediate receipts to balance the 1990 budget. The use of *medidas provisórias* to enact privatization was prompted by such a need before opposition against it could organize. However, from the beginning, technical difficulties and political opposition delayed considerably most transfers and Collor's program only began to be operative at the end of 1991, too late to effectively convince private investors of his administration's will and capacity to go through with the policy. Under Franco, the PND almost ran aground and speed became the last one of concerns; instead the emphasis shifted toward proceeding cautiously and making the whole PND as transparent as possible in order to appease critics from all sides.[56]

Political Responses

At the general level, as noted earlier, one crucial difference between Collor and Cardoso was the former's unwillingness to compromise and make alliances with political parties to support his economic policies, including privatization. Collor rose to prominence as a protest candidate. He eventually gained the electoral endorsement of many middle-of-the-road and conservative politicians because he was perceived as a last resort to stop Lula.

Although he had promised to create a center-right party that would support his policy agenda in Congress, once in office he claimed that political compromises would dilute his electoral mandate for 'change' and therefore chose to rule in an autocratic fashion. In other words, he claimed that he knew what was best for the country and expected conservative parties and interest groups to comply with his initiatives. For Weyland (1993: 9), the reasoning behind this approach rested on the conviction that, 'any attempt to base his government on a strong alliance of existing parties would have undermined Collor's cherished personal autonomy and made him vulnerable to the constant pressure of conservative politicians for more government favors ("pork")'. However, unlike in Argentina, the harshness of Collor's economic policies was not followed by any tangible results in the fight against inflation. As a result, by the end of 1990 public opinion polls showed the President's popularity plummeting.

Collor's approach to business was very much the same. Suspicious of their true intentions, Collor kept his distance from entrepreneurial interest groups. As noted by Schneider (1997–8), in the early 1990s Brazil was, along with Colombia, the only large Latin American country without a strong peak business association binding together industry, commerce, and finance. Thus, while some entrepreneurs (and conglomerates) yielded considerable power of their own, collectively they remained weak. Thus, having no peak level organization that could deliver the compliance of their members at the national level, the entrepreneurs' bargaining power as an interest group vis-à-vis Congress and the executive remained very weak (Weyland 1993). Accordingly, Collor reasoned, their support could make little difference.[57] However, Collor, unlike Menem in Argentina, did not even try to make close alliances with the largest Brazilian business groups that individually had considerable socioeconomic clout. FIESP, arguably the best organized and influential interest group in Brazil, had campaigned in favor of state-shrinking policies since the mid-1980s, but Collor simply scorned it and often antagonized it.[58] His refusal to forge alliances with pro-privatization associations actually helped the opposition and other sectors within the business community that in the early 1990s had much to loose from it. Indeed, many feared Collor's economic reforms in general:

The plans to liberalize the economy announced in 1990 and 1991 by President Collor de Mello were, basically, a challenge to the elites' domination of the national economy. But they had always used the rhetoric of the need for greater competition and autonomy for industry in confronting the patrimonial regime over many years. When the new President decided that the Brazilian economy had to be opened to new investment and competition, the private sector began to have second thoughts. (Roett 1992: 167)

The same applies to the most specific case of privatization. Government suppliers and contractors opposed it for fear of losing lucrative federal contracts.[59] As in other countries, even entrepreneurs who did not directly do business with the government had reason to be concerned since many private enterprises had grown accustomed to purchasing inputs from PEs at costs well below those charged in the international market (e.g. in steel, petrochemicals, fertilizers, etc.), resisted privatization because it would end a host of hidden subsidies (Schneider 1992: 226).

The original intent of the Collor administration was to 'depoliticize' the PND and present it as merely a technical means to achieve a short-term goal, i.e. deficit reduction (Schneider 1992: 236). By keeping Congress out of it, as well as pressure groups, Collor's first economic team hoped to avoid confrontation and sell swiftly. The PND's committee did mirror these intentions as the government appointed to it technocrats and corporate representatives sympathetic to privatization. Too busy with more pressing matters, Collor and his first Minister of Economy Zelia Cardoso de Mello delegated to BNDES's President Modiano the task of garnering support for the PND. During his tenure, Modiano energetically fended off opposition within the administration and Congress. He also aired a series of television spots portraying the benefits of privatization in order to build popular support. However, Modiano often seemed to be left alone to fight on too many fronts.[60] For instance, in the case of the steel mill Usiminas, which was regarded as a test case for the government, Collor intervened to support Modiano only two weeks prior to the auction while the opposition to that privatization was in full swing.[61]

Under Franco, privatization was not a priority. Keen on avoiding further controversy on the issue, the new President not only involved Congress in the decision-making process but also allowed for representation in the PND's committee of some critics of privatization. André Franco Montoro, the last of the PND committee's chairmen under President Franco, found himself in a much weaker situation than Modiano. Presiding over a divided committee, and enjoying lukewarm support from Franco, Montoro's authority was constantly undermined by ministers like Cicero and congressional critics. In July 1993, concerned that congressional interference would adversely affect the PND, Montoro warned that he would resign in protest over any legislative decision to block the sale of public companies.[62]

Throughout the Collor and Franco administrations, BNDES remained the governmental institution most engaged in marshalling support for the PND.[63] BNDES's arguments in favor of a meaner and leaner state sector found a receptive audience among many state managers who felt frustrated by the politicians' continuous manipulations of their PEs. By 1990, many managers of BNDES wanted to return to the institution's original mission as a development bank. Indeed they became increasingly frustrated with the constant attacks from privatization critics to the point where many executives were eager to leave the management of the divestiture process to other governmental institutions.

State managers in the steel sector, for instance, faced with shrinking budgets at a time when deteriorated equipment and dated technology were hampering the competitiveness of their enterprises, saw in privatization the only way to save their companies. Usiminas's President Rinaldo Campos Soares explained the large efficiency gains of his company after its privatization in these terms, 'We gained autonomy to define our own goals, [including] reduced time to contract suppliers, the possibility of associating with other companies, greater speed in attending to clients, active participation in financial markets and access to financing barred to state-owned companies.'[64] Even a long-time advocate of state intervention, like former Minister of Mines and Energy Shigeaki Ueki, came to the conclusion that the government should lift its monopoly on petroleum and privatize Petrobrás as the only way left to keep the company competitive.[65] Despite this changing mood among former advocates of economic nationalism and the growing public consensus over privatization since 1990, neither the Collor nor the Franco administrations made any explicit effort to capitalize on them to build support for the PND.

Unlike Argentina, Brazil in the early 1980s did not witness the emergence of a conservative ideological movement committed to privatization and market reforms (Goldstein 1997). Moreover, although most of the largest national newspapers and television networks were behind privatization, Brazil did not experience the emergence of powerful opinion leaders in the media who could shape a political debate on the issue.[66] In general, without any government leadership, the pro-privatization forces, although growing over time, remained disarticulated and incapable of mounting an effective campaign. In fact, aside from Modiano's television campaign to justify privatization, neither Collor nor Franco made any deliberate effort to explain to the public the reason why privatization was not only necessary but also advantageous.[67]

As discussed earlier, only after the Real Plan proved successful in creating the long-awaited economic stability did market reforms generate broad consensus across socioeconomic elites, as well as among 'average citizens'.[68] Capitalizing on his early achievements, Cardoso employed a coalition-building strategy acting simultaneously on several areas. On the public relations front, he proved to be a great communicator by presenting his views in an honest, straightforward manner capable of convincing business leaders and housewives alike. The high popularity levels that he enjoyed during his first term (1995–8) surely helped him to get his message across with people who otherwise may have been skeptical or even opposed.[69] As Finance Minister, and later on as President, Cardoso became his government's most eloquent proponent of privatization. Yet, more importantly, by taking the leadership in the policy debate that ensued, he gave to the PND the credibility and legitimacy that had been missing since 1990. It is also worth noting that not only did Cardoso devote a substantial amount of time to explain to Brazilians why privatization was beneficial to their country, but he also supported it with a large-scale government-sponsored media campaign in highly controversial privatizations like CVRD and Telebrás.[70] By the same token, similar to Menem's practice in Argentina, he used the easy government access to radio and television to put Lula and the left-wing parties opposing the PND on the defensive. On the one hand, Cardoso depicted them as the defenders of small, privileged groups of state workers, and the proponents of irresponsible policies that would bring Brazil back to hyperinflation. On the other, he portrayed himself as a responsible, effective, forward-looking leader whose policies had already borne fruit and were going to bring a bright future for Brazilians from all walks of life (Smith and Messari 1998).

From a legislative point of view Cardoso, unlike his predecessors, developed a clever plan to garner support for privatization from the government bureaucracy and Congress. By dispensing patronage to sympathetic legislators in exchange for votes and by involving the ministries affected by the PND in the decision-making process, he was able to broaden his pro-reform coalition. From the beginning Cardoso set forth a coherent legislative agenda meant to overcome the obstacles to the most important privatizations. The need to tackle the financial crises in Mexico (1994) and East Asia (1997), respectively, and the passage of the amendment allowing his own re-election, made the legislative agenda concerning privatization less of a priority at crucial points in time (Galvão de Almeida 1997). However, the very fact that by 1998 most constitutional obstacles had been removed shows the great strides that Cardoso made when compared to the Collor–Franco period. This was not a small accomplishment if one takes into consideration that, between 1990 and 1994, many members of conservative (PFL), centrist (PMDB), and center-left parties (PSDB), which at one time or another supported the Collor and Franco administrations, had often opposed privatization of PEs for fear that it would put an end to their regional fiefdoms. In fact, in some depressed areas where PEs played a crucial role in the local economy, the sale of PEs put traditional clienteles in jeopardy. Brazilian governors, whose states co-owned several major PEs with the federal government, unlike Argentina, proved to be a strong obstacle to privatization in the early 1990s and exercised a considerable bargaining power in many transactions. For instance in 1993, the fiery governor of Rio de Janeiro Leonel Brizola tried to stop the sale of the Companhia Siderúrgica Nacional (CSN), a symbol of Brazilian ISI created by President Getulio Vargas in 1941, through a court injunction. Once this failed, Brizola threatened President Franco with tough opposition from the PDT in Congress if the auction was allowed, but to no avail. In mid-year, the Governor of São Paulo Luis Antonio Fleury Filho, demanded that privatization of the steel mill Cosipa be suspended until the federal government renegotiated its $300 million debt to his state. Other governors in less prominent states tried similar tactics to gain concessions from Franco with mixed results.

By 1995, save for left-wing parties, most legislators and governors either supported privatization or seemed resigned to its inevitability. What produced this attitudinal change? Much has to do with the fact that politicians began to fear that the Mexican and East Asian crises could quickly extend to Brazil, with potentially disastrous consequences on their ability to get access to government patronage. The executive exploited these fears by putting pressure on Congress to expedite the passage of important legislation affecting privatization. Likewise, many state governors, who had resisted state divestiture, felt even more compelled to act quickly. According to Sotero (1996: 4), 'after January 1995, the risk of financial calamity has transformed hard-core "statists" into born-again "privatists" in state governments throughout Brazil, in a process that is giving new meaning to pragmatism, the only ideology consistently followed by most Brazilian politicians' (Sotero 1996: 4). PEs partly or fully owned by state governments became expendable as the fiscal crisis that governors faced became more acute. Taking advantage of this situation, as argued by Weyland (1997–8), Cardoso traded the governors' short-term needs (obtaining additional financing from BNDES and other federal agencies to close their fiscal gaps) to achieve his long-term goals (the governors' cooperation in the privatization of PEs either completely or partly owned by state government).[71] For example, Brizola's successor in Rio de Janeiro, Governor Marcelo Alencar, used privatization proceeds to clear most of the debt owed to state suppliers. Minas Gerais, Rio Grande do Sul, and Bahia, quickly followed suit. Only São Paulo held out, but by 1998 even its maverick governor, Mario Covas, had grudgingly accepted major privatizations affecting PEs in his own state, including electricity, water, telecommunications, transportation, and Banespa, Brazil's second largest bank.[72]

Likewise, Cardoso could count on much greater business support in the mid-1990s thanks to the changed macroeconomic situation. According to Kingstone (1998: 44):

business groups . . . had to invest in specific adjustment strategies for coping with commercial liberalization. As they have sunk resources into particular strategies, they [became] more dependent on continuing the reform process. Thus, Cardoso, [was] able to draw political support from important social groups that have emerged as either beneficiaries of or at least stake holders in the success of economic reform.

Consequently, rather than ostracizing business organizations, as Collor did, Cardoso tried to forge a strategic alliance with them and even welcomed their attempt to join their lobbying efforts through the Ação Empresarial, which was formed in 1993. In his scheme of things, the development of a peak business organization could actually become a strong supporting base for his reforms. In fact, by 1993 business organizations had come out strongly in favor of the constitutional amendments affecting taxation, social security, and the public administration that Congress grudgingly refused to consider. Many medium- and small-size companies, which were facing the consequences of the trade liberalization policy ushered by the Real Plan, found in market reforms aimed at improving public services, cutting labor costs, and slashing taxation and bureaucratic redtape an important resource to cut costs and remain competitive (Kingstone 1998). Thus, Cardoso's agenda did coincide on key economic issues, including privatization, with that of Ação Empresarial (Schneider 1997–8). In 1996, the President's strategy came into the open when he actively encouraged the leadership of that organization to stage a mass demonstration in front of Congress with the objective of urging legislators to act quickly on constitutional reforms. As a quid pro quo for business support, Cardoso used selective incentives like soft loans for financially troubled companies and tariff protection for others which needed more time to adjust to foreign competition. Moreover, major privatization deals like CVRD, Telebrás, and Petrobrás were structured in a way to assure that domestic capital played a major role in the divestiture process, which surely appeased many entrepreneurs. To make the offers more attractive, BNDES also provided substantial, multi-year financing packages that were needed to defray the high costs in large infrastructure investments like electricity and telecommunications.

As more and more PEs were sold, more companies became part of the process, and so did the number of the employees who were co-opted through stock option deals. Thus, as the ranks of beneficiaries of the PND increased substantially in sheer term, so did its supporting base (Goldstein 1997: 18).

If we now turn to the anti-privatization forces, we can recognize some clear players. Namely unions, left-wing parties, university students, the Catholic Church, and disgruntled members of the ruling coalition. There is also a distinct pattern characterizing their ability to stop the PND. The weaker the administration, such as those of Collor and Franco, the greater their effectiveness. Conversely, once they confronted a determined and strategically skillful President like Cardoso, their obstructionist tactics could delay but not stop a sale.

In 1990, such forces were initially disorganized and heterogeneous, but took advantage of Collor and Franco's ineptitude and were able to lobby successfully. After all, they were preserving the status quo and, given the government's inability to seize the initiative in a decisive manner, it was relatively easy to follow a defensive strategy, particularly in view of the many constitutional and legal provisions besieging the PND.

The most consistent political attacks against the PND came from the left. Within the union movement, as under Sarney, the left-wing confederation CUT was the most active in opposing the privatization process, which it considered to be destroying the 'welfare state' built since President Vargas in the 1940s. The CGT's stance against privatization was less consistent since some of its member unions actually favored it.[73] In 1990, Collor hoped to exploit the rivalries within the labor movement by trying to isolate the CUT from more moderate peak labor organizations, like the CGT.[74] However, the effort was short-lived. Later on, Collor's corruption scandal actually helped labor to set aside its differences momentarily in order to join forces and bring down the President, but union squabbles surfaced again under Cardoso.[75]

Another common issue used by unions to attack the government was the acceptance of domestic-debt papers, or 'junk bonds', as payments for PEs.[76] Such pressure worked for a while. As noted, to address this criticism Franco suspended the use of this type of 'currency' and started to demand cash only instead. Following the same rationale, Franco also created 'golden shares' (although they were selectively used under Cardoso). His administration tried to make other concessions to labor. Among these were setting up training programs for displaced workers, environmental provisions, and the payment of labor-related liabilities (Abreu and Werneck 1993:40). Moreover, Franco abandoned the old emphasis on using privatization proceeds to balance the budget and chanelled them to finance specific social programs.

Another reason why the CUT, more than any other labor umbrella organization, was adamantly against privatization was that its unions were particularly strong in the public sector, which was a prime target of the state-shrinking drive. The interests at stake can be best appreciated if we consider that in 1990 employees of PEs enjoyed job security, higher wages, and better benefits than their counterparts in the private sector (Schneider 1992).[77]

Union militancy against the PND grew in intensity when newly privatized companies began to cut jobs.[78] A typical case used by the CUT was the sale of the highly subsidized Cosinor steel mill in 1991. Its new owner, the Gerdau Group, citing the impossibility of making Cosinor profitable again, closed it shortly thereafter resulting in the loss of thousands of jobs in the already economically depressed north-east where Cosinor was located. Employment losses in four of the largest state steel mills after privatization amounted to over 8,000 jobs (Table 4.8). The same trend took place in other privatized PEs like Celma (aircraft engine repairs) which shed 700 of its 2,300 employees (Castelar Pinheiro and Giambiagi 1993: 27). As layoffs grew so did tensions. In September 1993, an anti-privatization rally in front of the Rio de Janeiro stock exchange, where some PEs were auctioned, turned into violent clashes with the police.[79] Strike activity continued in 1993 when the CSN workers unsuccessfully held out for 32 days.

The tide began to turn clearly against this type of labor tactic in August 1995 when Cardoso ended a five-month long strike by oil workers that had paralyzed the country. Sustained by strong popular backing, Cardoso ordered the Army to take over Petrobrás' refineries. This defining moment not only strengthened Cardoso's authority but irremediably weakened labor, which from that point on fought a losing battle. Although major clashes between union militants and police did occur at the public auction of CVRD in 1997, they did not produce any results. Over time even some employees of

Brazil

TABLE 4.8. *Brazil: Pre- and Post-Privatization Performance*

Company	Debts (US$ million)	Employees	Productivity (t/man/year)	Sales (US$ million)	Profits (US$ million)*
CSN					
Before	2,185.0	19,106.0	n.a.	1,761.0	−314.0
After	873.0	15,772.0	249.0	2,241.0	70.0
Usiminas					
Before	321.0	12,480.0	380.0	1,300.0	59.5
After	504.0	11,036.0	418.0	1,600.0	246.2
CST					
Before	520.0	6,000.0	480.0	565.0	−114.0
After	487.0	4,200.0	740.0	695.0	32.4
Acesita					
Before	220.0	7,375.0	80.0	488.0	−100.0
After	153.0	5,587.0	120.0	592.0	31.4

Source: O Globo, Individual steel mills, *US/Latin Trade* (September 1994)
* Losses are those for the last full year before privatization with th exception of Usiminas.

PEs changed their attitude. The Cardoso administration in some cases weakened the support of the rank-and-file through the use of media campaigns that showed the benefits accrued by workers of privatized companies. Indeed, those who stayed, as in Argentina, experienced substantial increases in salaries. Those who lost their jobs, particularly in large companies like CVRD, the railways, the electricity companies, ports, etc., were offered early retirement, severance payments, retraining programs, and in some cases assistance in looking for another employment.

Among political parties, Lula's PT was ideologically opposed to privatization. The PT's executive council called for the complete suspension of the PND, and its most radical members even went as far as to demand the reversing of those privatizations already completed. However, prior to the 1994 presidential election, the PT began to soften its position in an attempt to diffuse business fears about the consequences of a possible Lula victory. In mid-1994, a PT delegation told international investors in London that, while still criticizing the government undervaluation of assets, Lula was likely to continue the policy in 'non-strategic' sectors by placing emphasis on greater cash receipts rather than debt-conversion papers. The PT's counter-proposal to privatization was to apply private-sector management style to PEs and retain government control over monopolies in petroleum and telecommunications. The PT also supported the participation of private capital in new projects like the Brazil–Bolivia gas pipeline, while maintaining the discrimination of treatment between domestic and foreign companies.[80] By the time the 1998 presidential elections were under way, the PT was campaigning for a full stop to privatization and a thorough examination of the CVRD and other sell-offs because of alleged 'irregularities' that had occurred before the transfer of ownership. The PT also called for foreign companies investing in Brazil to generate new jobs first.[81]

Other left-wing parties, like Leonel Brizola's Democratic Labor party (Partido Democrático Trabalhista), the Socialist party (Partido Socialista Brasileiro), the Communist party of Brazil (Partido Comunista do Brasil), and the Socialist Popular party (Partido Popular Socialista) were all against privatization on ideological grounds, but their small representation in Congress, and deep divisions in terms of common strategy, made their opposition less visible.

Initially, many managers of state corporations, who owed their jobs to political patronage, were equally opposed to privatization since they were likely to lose their jobs.[82] State managers of large PEs who had been appointed because of their political affiliation created formidable coalitions with the ministries under whose jurisdiction they operated in order to avoid privatization. The most skillful at resisting privatization were Petrobrás management and its union. To overcome this opposition, Cardoso changed the company's board and had Congress pass a law to deregulate the industry in August 1998.

That same year, the Petroleum National Agency, the sector's brand new regulator, dealt another blow to Petrobrás's stonewalling strategy by opening to private domestic and foreign companies up to 93 per cent of new oil-producing areas. By 1998 they had lost their battle and the few PE managers still holding their jobs clearly saw their time running out.

The National Conference of Catholic Bishops and the National Students Union were also very critical of privatization because of its negative effects on employment and subsidies for the general public through cheap public utility rates. In an unusual move, prior to the CVRD sale, the Catholic bishops urged Cardoso to suspend the process.

The armed forces, which under the 1964–85 military regime had created a large and deficit-ridden industrial complex geared toward arms production, remained relatively quiet about the PND. For instance, the sale of the Empresa Brasileira de Aeronáutica (Embraer), Brazil's principal producer of military aircrafts whose debt in 1993 amounted to $125 million, raised no major opposition. The only active-duty high-ranking officer who openly denounced Embraer's sale was Brig. Sergio Ferolla, director of the Escuela Superior de Guerra (the equivalent of the US War College). For the most part, criticism remained confined to retired members of the Army and Air Force military clubs who viewed privatization as the undoing of many of the nationalistic achievements of the military period. Along with the CUT and the PT, they believed that 'strategic sectors' of the economy should remain in government hands.[83] However, the hierarchy of the armed forces avoided getting involved in these controversies. More to the point, before the privatization of Telebrás the joint high command issued a communique supporting President Cardoso's claim that Brazil's national security was not being jeopardized if foreign companies were to enter the domestic telecommunications market.

These anti-privatization groups used various forms of lobbying and, in the case of labor, strikes and rallies, to impede the implementation of the PND. As noted earlier, the judicial system played a crucial role in the process. Virtually all major privatizations were challenged in court. Challenges to minimum prices, especially by labor unions, local district attorneys, and some politicians tended to be based upon historical costs, replacement costs, insured value, and constitutional provisions. Some of these challenges were followed by congressional inquiries as well.

Yet some of the most serious and embarrassing challenges to privatization came from within the government coalition. We have already discussed how many pro-government politicians in Congress resented privatization as it threatened the 'pork' with which they fed their political clientele.[84] At crucial moments they left no doubt where their true interests lay. The most typical example was when former presidents Sarney and Franco, as well as prominent members of the PMDB, openly attacked the CVRD sale.

Technical Difficulties

In comparison with the Sarney administration, the PND under Collor and Franco was much more ambitious in nature as it involved larger companies originally created by the government. However, the selection criteria seemed to target PEs that: (1) were no longer considered of strategic importance; (2) posed no regulatory problems; and (3) in many instances, were plagued by financial and management problems (IESP 1993).

By 1990 BNDES had acquired substantial expertise in privatization and could provide the institutional continuity that was absent in Argentina. However, a number of technical difficulties, many of which were unforeseen, added to the bureaucratic and political difficulties discussed above. Some such problems, as in Argentina, stemmed from the poor macroeconomic environment in which privatization took place. Under pressure to push privatization quickly, a top priority under the Collor administration was to unload PEs at almost any price. The initial restrictions on foreign capital further narrowed the government's options. It is not by coincidence that PND began to take off only when such restrictions were lifted and macroeconomic stability ensued.

A set of problems arose from the method used to sell PEs. As noted earlier, the Collor administration used debt-equity conversion schemes meant to swap medium- and long-term domestic debt in return for PEs. Assets were transferred through the auction (complete or partial) of government shares. The granting of concessions in lucrative markets like oil and public utilities did not occur until 1995. In the initial phase of the PND (1990–2) debt-equity swaps in Brazil were used to a much greater extent than in other Latin American countries. According to Castelar Pinheiro and Giambiagi (1993), the reason rested on the need to: (1) write off part of the large public debt that was increasing at an alarming speed; (2) avoid the temptation to use cash revenues to finance current expenditures; and (3) the fear that given Brazil's macroeconomic instability at the time, requiring cash in exchange for shares could jeopardize the financial viability of the PND since private investors would have been highly reluctant to invest large sums for PEs that had to undergo substantial restructuring.

Given that Collor Plan I had frozen the bulk of Brazil's financial assets, the administration chose a rather novel way to get around the lack of funds. As noted earlier, the privatization decree of March 1990 created a number of privatization currencies (or certificates), a type of security traded in the secondary market at highly discounted prices, that potential buyers were obliged to purchase in order to acquire the auctioned shares of state firms. Other currencies used were the domestic debt of state companies and various types of federal bonds. Table 4.9 displays the currencies utilized through 1997 and their share of the total amount that investors paid for PEs.

TABLE 4.9. *Brazil: Means of Payment Used for the Acquisition of Privatized Companies in US$ Million 1991–7*

Sector	Company	Siderbras Debent. SIBR	Privatization Certificates CP	FND Bonds OFND	Securitized Gov. Dep. DISEC	Agrarian Debt Sec. TDA	Foreign Debt Sec. DIVEX	CEF Sec. CEF	Currency (cash)	Not Identified	TOTAL in US$ million	TOTAL (%)
Steel	Usiminas	544.6	323.3	247.9	259.4	65.3	4.4	177.6	495.4		1,941.20	11.0
	CSN	211.0	94.6	32.8	567.2	144.0	1.2	10.3	259.3	7.6	1,495.30	8.4
	Acominas	89.2	6.0	0.1	440.0	23.0		23.3	30.0		598.5	3.4
	Acesita	26.5	74.0	152.0	76.0	111.6	2.1				465.4	2.6
	Cosipa	199.8	4.5		139.0	2.4			240.0		585.7	3.3
	CST	5.2	72.6	7.2	172.2	12.2		77.9	6.2		353.6	2.0
	Piratini	23.6	66.2		10.0	7.0			0.0		106.7	0.6
	Cosinor		15.0								15.0	0.1
	Subtotal	1,100.00	656.5	440.1	1,664.0	365.5	7.8	289.1	1,031	7.6	5,561.50	31.4
Petrochemicals	Copesul	81.9	276.9	60.4	341.1	86.9	7.7	4.8		1.7	861.5	4.9
	PQU	74.5	8.0	0.3	95.2	15.5	0.9	6.8	86.3		287.5	1.6
	Copene	29.0			214.0	0.2			27.0		270.4	1.5
	Petroflex	2.2	154.1	64.0	10.0	3.9			0.4		234.1	1.3
	Salgema	43.5	5.2	0.3	66.9	9.3			14.0		139.2	0.8
	CPC	71.1	0.4		18.1				10.0		99.7	0.6
	Polibrasil				90.0				9.9		99.4	0.6
	Poliolefinas		61.0						26.1		87.1	0.5
	Polipropileno		1.7		71.0				8.1		81.2	0.5
	Pronor				57.0				6.3		63.5	0.4
	Alcalis		4.7		34.0	10.9				32.4	81.4	0.5
	PPH		43.6		0.0		15.3				59.4	0.3
	Polisul	2.2	24.7		6.0	13.1	11.4				56.8	0.3
	Oxiteno				25.0	0.2	25.6		2.7		53.9	0.3
	Politeno				29.0	11.4			4.5		44.9	0.3
	Nitrocarbono				27.0				3.0		29.6	0.2
	Nitriflex		7.6		19.0						26.2	0.1
	Coperbo				23.0				2.6		25.9	0.1
	Ciquine				21.3				2.4		23.7	0.1
	Polialden				15.1				1.7		16.7	0.1
	EDN				14.9				1.7		16.6	0.1

Sector	Item										Total	%
Petrochemicals	Acrinor				10.9				1.2		12.1	0.1
	Deten				6.4	4.5			1.2		12.1	0.1
	CBE				10.9						10.9	0.1
	Koppol				2.8				0.3		3.1	0.0
	CQR				1.4				0.2		1.6	0.0
	CBP				0.0				0.0		0.0	0.0
	Subtotal	304.5	588.0	125.1	1,208.80	155.8	60.9	11.6	209.6	34.1	2,698.50	15.2
Fertilizers	Ultrafertil				159.5	4.9			41.1		205.6	1.2
	Fosfertil	29.4			145.9	6.4		0.3			182.0	1.0
	Goiasfertil	0.2			0.4	12.5					13.1	0.1
	Arafertil				9.7				1.1		10.8	0.1
	Indag	6.8									6.8	0.0
	Subtotal	36.4			315.5	23.8		0.3	42.2		418.3	2.4
Electricity	Escelsa				132.3				387.0		519.3	2.9
	Light Sesa	1.3			626.2	225.7			1,655.60		2,508.90	14.0
	Subtotal	1.3			758.5	225.7			2,042.60		3,082.20	16.9
Railways	Malha Oeste								63.4		63.4	0.4
	Centro Leste								316.1		316.1	1.8
	Sudeste								870.6		870.6	4.7
	Tereza Crist.								17.9		17.9	0.1
	Sul								208.5		208.5	1.2
	Nordeste								14.6		14.6	0.1
	Subtotal								1,491.10		1,491.10	8.3
Mining	CVRD								3,298.90		3,298.90	18.4
	Caraiba				5.2				0.6		5.8	0.0
	Subtotal				5.2				3,299.50		3,304.70	19.0
Ports	Tecon 1								251.1		251.1	1.4
Finance	Merdional	0.1			108.6				12.1	119.4	240.1	1.3

TABLE 4.9. *(cont'd)*

Sector	Company	Siderbras Debent. SIBR	Privatization Certificates CP	FND Bonds OFND	Securitized Gov. Dep. DISEC	Agrarian Debt Sec. TDA	Foreign Debt Sec. DIVEX	CEF Sec. CEF	Currency (cash)	Not Identified	TOTAL in US$ million	TOTAL (%)
Others	Embraer	0.1	0.6	23.3	148.7	19.4			0.1		192.2	1.1
	Celma	55.6	8.4	4.2	6.8	16.0					91.1	0.5
	Mafersa	23.7		25.1							48.8	0.3
	SNBP	12.0									12.0	0.1
	Subtotal	91.4	9.0	52.6	155.5	35.4			0.1		344.1	1.9
	TOTAL I	1,496.0	1,291.4	617.7	4,215.6	806.2	68.6	301.0	8,378.8	161.1	17,337.0	96.6
	in %	8.6	7.4	3.6	24.3	4.7	0.4	1.7	48.3	0.9	100.0	
Minority shares	TOTAL II	0.1	5.3	0.0	51.4	5.2	0.0	0.0	556.5	0.0	618.5	3.4
	TOTAL I + TOTAL II	1,496.1	1,296.7	617.7	4,267.0	811.4	68.6	301.0	8,935.3	161.1	17,955.5	100.0
	in %	8.3%	7.2%	3.4%	23.8%	4.5%	0.4%	1.7%	49.8%	0.9%	100.0%	

Source: BNDES, *Programa Nacional de Destatização*, December 1997.

However some of these currencies, like the Agrarian Debt Notes, the Housing Bank Obligations, the National Development Fund Bonds, and the Siderbras debentures, were commonly regarded as junk bonds, or *moedas podres*. Because all domestic debt securities were converted at face value, critics charged that the government was giving away good companies in return for paper money.[85] Such charges prompted the Franco administration to create new securities and put greater emphasis on cash receipts. Foreign debt notes (Multi-Year Deposit Facility Agreement, MYDFA), on the other hand, played no meaningful role. By the end of 1993, of the $37.5 billion of Brazilian foreign debt only $42 million had been used to purchase PEs. This was quite a disappointment taking into account that, when converted into auction papers, the MYDFAs were accepted at 75 per cent of their face value, which was much higher than their quotation in the secondary market.[86] As a result, privatization currencies progressively lost in importance. Whereas in 1991 they accounted for 98.8 per cent of total income, by 1997 they had dropped to a record low 4.6 per cent.[87]

Another thorny issue was the evaluation of assets. Critics argued that the PND often seemed unclear as to the rules of setting minimum prices for many PEs (Passanezi Filho 1993). In June 1993, the vice-President of the Privatization Committee, João Maia resigned in protest over the low price asked for the shares of Poliolefinas (a low-density polyethylene producer) and CSN. Testifying before a congressional committee, Maia also charged that the price-setting process was flawed by many irregularities that, in his opinion, had cost the federal government $3 billion.[88] Critics also argued that the minimum price floor was often under-estimated purposely in order to sell quickly. On similar grounds, many found it inexplicable that the government sold its steel mills with a net worth of $13.8 billion for a total of only $5.5 billion (Castelar Pinheiro and Giambiagi 1993: 40). Reeling from congressional pressure on this issue, in September 1994, Franco suspended the auction of several petrochemical companies to devise a new method of calculating their minimum price.

To its critics, BNDES and the Privatization Committee responded that the market value of many PEs was much lower than their net worth since many of them had fallen behind in terms of technology, were overstaffed, had not shown a profit for a long time and, in the process, had accumulated large deficits. Montoro pointed out that the steel sector alone had cost the treasury $11.3 billion between 1986 and 1991.[89] As for the controversy over the use of debt equity swaps, the government claimed that by using privatization currencies it could get a higher price for its PEs than would have been possible if requesting cash.

To avoid entirely the complex issues linked to the regulation of monopolistic PEs in public utilities the Collor administration excluded them from the PND list. The initial sale of assets in Brazil primarily targeted manufacturing companies where the government claimed that regulatory measures were not necessary since the simultaneous enforcement of trade liberalization would discipline competitors in the market place. PEs in manufacturing presented also the additional advantage that their shares were already traded in the stock market. Once public utilities and oil/gas industries were finally freed from constitutional impediments, designing transparent and efficient regulatory institutions took a while (electricity 1996, telecommunications 1997, petroleum/gas 1998). Part of the blame rests on the fact that government technocrats, as in other Latin American countries, had to start from scratch, since PEs in previous decades were left to self-regulating themselves. In addition, no real consensus initially existed on whether regulation had to be clearly spelled out prior to privatization. In mid-1996, Elena Landau, the director of the privatization unit at BNDES, resigned. She had insisted on establishing clear regulatory rules before turning the electricity sector to private companies, but her direct superior, BNDES President Carlos Mendoça de Barros, thought otherwise. Eventually, the government created a regulatory agency in 1996, but many details of the regulatory framework were still to be introduced as late as 1998 (Estache and Rodríguez Pardina 1998).

Economic efficiency concerns under Collor seemed to be of secondary importance as a high premium was placed on expediting transactions. Aside from two cases, Celma and Petroflex, BNDES posed no restrictions on the purchase of PEs by their main competitors, customers, or suppliers (Castelar Pinheiro and Giambiagi 1993; de Souza 1999). For example, privatization of the steel sector strengthened the oligopolistic power of domestic groups in that market, since foreign investors were scarce. The Bozano Simonsen Bank, the new private syndicate controlling Usiminas, and the Gerdau Group, came out as the big winners.[90] Gerdau's decision to close the Cosinor steel mill a year after having purchased it, left Gerdau with a monopoly of non-flat rolled steel production, which created a heated controversy. In 1993, fears of market power concentration prompted Mines and Energy Minister Cicero to threaten the lifting of tariffs on imported steel to spur competition. Moreover, as with PEs of mixed ownership in petrochemicals, the government gave preferential treatment to its private partner, hampering competition (IESP 1993: 244).

To overcome the skepticism of private investors when unprofitable PEs were auctioned, the government transferred a substantial amount of the existing company's liabilities to the treasury.[91] Furthermore, unlike Argentina, the largest PEs had to undergo a thorough restructuring process prior to privatization to increase their market value (i.e. Eletrobrás, Telebrás). This turned out to be more costly and time consuming than expected. In 1993, the Privatization Committee reported that the cost associated with putting PEs back into shape exceeded the earnings coming from the auctions.[92] The whole process leading to the privatization of a PE from start to finish, without taking into account the possibility of a failed public auction or legal challenges, averaged 275 days, or more than nine months.[93]

Market failures plagued the PND from the start. Although Brazil could count on relatively large and sophisticated capital markets, in 1993 alone as many as nine auctions were cancelled because most of the shares offered found no takers. The sale of Usiminas, Cosipa, Escelsa (power utility), Lloyd Brasileiro (shipping), and Embraer (aircraft manufacturer), to name a few, suffered several cancellations. Of the thirty-four PEs put on the auction block in 1994, six had originally been scheduled in 1993 and three in 1992. During the 1991–4 period, in spite of some noticeable exceptions, many PEs were sold at minimum price for lack of competition (Table 4.3).[94] In 1995, of seventeen PEs put on the auction block only nine were actually sold. The sale of Banco Meridional, the first financial PE to be privatized, was postponed twice until BNDES was able to restructure its loan portfolio. Things finally began to improve in 1997, as testified by the fact that many companies were sold way above the minimum price (Table 4.3).

Additional problems came from conflicting legislation. The Federal Accounting Court (Tribunal de Contas, an institution similar to the US General Accounting Office) suspended one privatization in the electricity sector because it violated an old law dating back to the mid-1930s. In another instance, the Embraer's sale was once revoked since it lacked the approval required from the Senate.[95] Such problems found some solutions once Cardoso was able to persuade Congress first to terminate old monopoly conditions and later pass new laws streamlining obsolete legislation. I will now briefly examine in some detail the state divestiture under the PND.

Steel. The government decision to divest itself of its steel mills was not a casual one. PEs like CSN and Usiminas had symbolized the heyday of ISI and economic nationalism in Brazil. Thus, the Collor administration hoped that a successful transfer would convince investors of its commitment to privatization. Usiminas, the most profitable of the eight steel mills in government hands, was privatized first after overcoming several problems. The first auction in September 1991 was halted due to a court ruling that restricted the way buyers could pay for shares.[96] A second delay came when the government realized that the legal uncertainties surrounding the sale required a sharpening of the rules governing the transfer. On 24 October 1991, 75 per cent of Usiminas shares were finally sold (94 per cent going to domestic investors and the remaining ones to foreigners). Nippon Steel, the former government partner in Usiminas, retained 15 per cent of shares while company employees acquired 10 per cent. The auction earned the government $1.3 billion. After the sale it became clear that a consortium led by the Bozano Simonsen Bank, acting through several brokerage firms, had gained a majority stake in the company. In 1992, the Bozano Simonsen

Bank became the largest shareholder of the Companhia Siderurgica de Tubarão (CST), a Brazilian–Japanese–Italian venture specializing in slab steel.

The Gerdau Group, which in the early 1980s had gained prominence in the sector by purchasing steel mills like Cimetal and Usibe, seized control of the next two PEs to be privatized, Cosinor and Piratini. As a result of the ownership of Usibe and Piratini, Gerdau achieved a monopolistic position in the production of sponge iron.

The privatization of Cosipa, the other major steel mill, suffered several post-ponements due to financial squabbles between the federal government and the state of São Paulo which owned a substantial share in it. Moreover, investors were wary of the company's liabilities totalling almost $2 billion.[97] Cosipa's problems continued after the sale. In fact, the federal antitrust authorities, started an investigation regarding the true composition of Cosipa's new ownership. The inquiry was triggered by reports that the Bozano Simonsen Bank was behind the syndicate that gained control of 68 per cent of Cosipa.

The other major steel mill, Açominas, went to a syndicate led by the Mendes Junior Group and including the state bank of Minas Gerais and two em-ployees' pension funds. This fact raised the question of whether Açominas had actually been privatized (Açominas is located in Minas Gerais). It also pointed out the intention of individual states to retain some degree of gov-ernment control over privatized companies in order to maintain high employ-ment and investment rates.[98]

The sector as a whole performed well after privatization. By 1994, labor productivity, profit margins, debt exposure, and market expansion im-proved significantly (de Souza 1999). Greater productivity and better man-agement also allowed the steel industry to increase its shares of total exports, thereby making an important contribution to the country's trade balance. The performance was impressive enough to induce Usinor of France, the fifth largest steel producer in the world, to acquire Acesita and CST in May 1998. By 1999, the sector had consolidated around three groups, CSN, Usiminas, and the new entrant, Usinor. Considering the rocky start and the many controversies that it generated, the steel sector divestiture was no small accomplishment.

Petrochemicals. The Collor administration sold Petroflex to a consortium made up of four companies, three of which were direct competitors. Sim-ilarly, a syndicated group of petrochemical producers from Rio Grande do Sul gained control of Copesul. In the case of the Petroquimica União (PQU), the auction failed six times before finally succeeding. The PQU's problems ranged from squabbles over issues like corporate structure to government indecision in setting the sale price of PQU's main raw material, naphtha. The sale of the other PEs in this sector saw the dominant participation of private Brazilian groups, mainly Oderbrecht and Unipar, and to a lesser extent multina-tionals like Monsanto and Hoechst, thus reviving fears of cartel-building.

Fertilizers. In the cases of Fosfértil, Goiásfertil, and Ultrafértil, the new owners were again private competitors. Ultrafértil's first auction was suspended by court order amid charges that the minimum price being sought was too low. With the exception of Arafértil, whose auction failed for lack of private investors, and Nitrofértil which was excluded from the PND list, by the end of 1994 the federal government had virtually abandoned the fertilizer business. The big winner of this divestiture process was the Fortifós group, which after acquiring Fosfértil, gained control of Goiásfertil and Ultrafértil (de Souza 1999). In so doing, Fortifós had gained a dominant position within the market that could only be tamed by foreign imports, which began to pour into Brazil after 1994.

Electricity. The divestiture of the Eletrobrás group marked the turning point of the PND, as Cardoso began to privatize the large public utilities that only a few years before were considered as being untouchable. By 1995, the government could no longer ignore a situation that was becoming critical as power shortages became more and more frequent in urban areas. With Brazil's electricity consumption increasing at a rate of 5–6 per cent annually Eletrobrás, just to meet this demand, needed to invest $30 billion during the 1995–2000 period, an amount of money that it simply did not have nor could be provided by a federal government embarked on a austerity program.[99] The divestiture process was by no means easy as some intricate ownership problems had to be dealt with first. While Eletrobrás's subsidiaries (Furnas, Chesf, Eletrosul, and Eeletronorte) controlled about 50 per cent of power generation and a fifth of its distribution, local states provided 80 per cent of the distribution and 36 per cent of generation (Goldstein 1997: 21).

In April 1995, the CND named a special inter-ministerial committee to come up with a strategy to privatize the sector, which was approved in October. Shortly thereafter, the Ministry of Mines and Energy took the task of executing the report's recommendations that called for the creation of competition in the generation and distribution of electricity (transmission remained under Eletrobrás control) through the breaking up of the vertically integrated federal monopolies, and the development of a clear regulatory framework. Both tasks were to be accomplished prior to privatization. At the end of the year, Congress ended the federal monopoly over electricity so that privatization could begin.

As the emphasis was to privatize distribution first, most of the companies that were sold in the 1995–98 period fell within the state government realm. The first large federal PE to be auctioned was Light of Rio de Janeiro that went to a French-led consortium for $2.2 billion. By October 1998, fifteen electricity companies were sold to investors for roughly $16 billion, of which Eletrobrás accounted for 27 per cent of total proceeds.[100]

For the first time in the PND history, foreign investors played the dominant role leading consortia in association with domestic minority shareholders (primarily banks, pension funds, and manufacturing companies). To lure the latter, BNDES offered over $1.5 billion dollars in short-term credit up 5 to 10 years.[101] Not surprisingly, these privatizations attracted many competitive bids that offered amounts, in most cases, well above the minimum price set by BNDES. Among the most important transactions were Cemig (Minas Gerais, $1 billion), Coelba (Bahia, $1.6 billion), Companhia Norte-Nordeste (Rio Grande do Sul, $1.5 billion), Companhia Centro-Oeste (Rio Grande do Sul, $1.4 billion), and CPFL (São Paulo, $2.7 billion). The positive news was the new private consortia were actively investing hundreds of million of dollars to upgrade the sector's capacity.

However, investors remained weary about the lack of a clear regulatory framework. First, Eletrobrás's intention to hold on to the transmission system was troublesome because, as an investment banker aptly put it at the time, 'potential buyers cannot work out the marginal cost of new investment without knowing what the transmission costs are'.[102] Second, many details of the new rate adjustments were open to questions. Third, the fact that some important decisions affecting separation of integrated activities owned by the states, and the implementation of procedures required an agreement between the federal government and local states further compounded matters (Estache and Rodríguez Pardina 1998).

As expected, in mid-1998 some controversy arose from the decision of ANEEL, the sector's regulatory agency, to fine Light and Cerj $1.8 million after a series of power failures in Rio de Janeiro. The newly privatized companies saw themselves as the victim of overzealous bureaucrats who drew up the rules after the divestiture took place. They also felt as if they were paying for mistakes made under the former PEs which had neglected investments and technological improvements. ANEEL's threat that a recurrence of the same problems could result in some restrictions on the shareholders in future divestitures seemed to materialize investors' misgivings. In 1999, Eletrobrás was planning on transferring to the private sector its subsidiaries in the generation sector whose revenues were expected to net $22 billion.[103]

CVRD. Of all the Brazilian privatizations, that of CVRD was undoubtedly the most controversial and, for Cardoso, it turned out to be the defining moment of his privatization program. In fact, if the electricity privatization already under way at the time, had finally brought momentum to the PND, most domestic and foreign observers considered the CVRD divestiture as the real testing ground about Cardoso's commitment and capacity to move the PND forward.[104] A failure would have seriously undermined Cardoso's credibility and his administration was keenly aware of the high stakes at play. From Cardoso's point of view, the CVRD privatization was not only meant to give a strong signal about the government resolve, but it was also necessary to finance its mounting deficit.

The controversy surrounding the CVRD sale becomes clear once we take into account a few key factors. Getulio Vargas created it in 1942, when he bought out British and US mining companies that had been exploiting the Itabira iron ore deposits. In the decades that followed, CVRD became the flagship of Brazil's state development model. With an estimated value of about $10 billion (the federal government owned a 51 per cent stake), it was consistently a top-ten publicly traded firm in Latin America. Run by a fairly independent and capable management, CVRD was a profitable company. It was the largest producer of iron ore in the world and Latin America's most important gold company. In addition, it was engaged in a wide array of other activities that included copper, aluminum, and paper and wood pulp. With earnings totalling around $1.4 billion in 1996 alone, it was Brazil's most important exporting firm (70 per cent of its production went abroad).[105] Another feature of CVRD was its vertical integration. Besides mines, it owned railways and cargo ships and its 15,500 employees operated in the states of Minas Gerais, Pará, Maranhão, Bahia, Sergipe, Espírito Santo, and Rio de Janeiro. Opposition arguments to the CVRD divestiture were based on a variety of justifications, ranging from economic nationalism, Marxist ideology, to social concerns. Being a symbol of economic nationalism and the source of many needed jobs in several states, particularly in the poor north-east, its divestiture ran against the vested interests of supposedly pro-government state governors and federal legislators. As mentioned earlier, former presidents Sarney and Franco led the charge. They contended that CVRD was run efficiently, produced substantial revenues, played a key role in the country's international export strategy through its large sales, and was an important agent of social development since it used parts of its earnings to fund social projects such as hospitals, schools, and infrastructures in the states where it operated.[106] Some went even further. Paes de Andrade, the President of the PMDB, the largest party supporting Cardoso at the time, filed a law suit to stop the sale. Whereas such politicians took what could be labelled a 'nationalistic' stand, the PT and other left-wing parties attacked the sale from an ideological point of view, claiming that state ownership was the best guarantee to keep society's control over national resources. The Catholic bishops, for their part charged that such an 'indiscriminate' privatization would, 'gravely, and irremediably affect the country's future . . .' and lead to 'increased unemployment, greater disparity between rich and poor, the misery of the excluded, and the consequent violence that devastates society'.[107] Complicating matters was the fact that early on Cardoso's cabinet showed signs of deep-seated disagreements. While some members of the economic team wanted to use the CVRD's proceeds to diminish the government debt, a group led by Motta favored, for political reasons, their re-investment into socioeconomic infrastructure programs.

Technical problems added to the controversy. In the beginning, the government hired two consulting firms to advise on how to handle the sale. Their original estimates of CVRD's worth, which was about $2 billion less than what the government and some investment banks had calculated, stirred in Congress a flair of accusations claiming that the consulting firms were purposely undervaluing the assets. Reports of the discovery of new gold deposits in the Carajas area added further ammunition to the congressional anti-privatization lobby. Some legislators also raised conflict of interest issues with regard to Merryl Lynch, the government chief consultant for CVRD, since it owned the South African brokerage firm Smith Borham Hare that, in turn, worked as a broker from one of CVRD's prospective buyers, Anglo American Co. Using these allegations, the PT asked Congress to set up a Parliamentary Inquiry Committee to look into the facts, but clearly the intention behind it was to derail the whole process.

Yet, the most successful means that slowed the sale and forced its postponement at its first try in April 1997 was a flood of legal challenges in regional courts attacking the constitutionality of the transaction. The most dangerous of these attacks came from the Order of Brazilian Lawyers and some university professors. The Cardoso administration actively fought back the constitutional challenges by asking the Supreme Federal Tribunal to rule quickly on these matters and, after losing a few rounds, in the end was able to overcome all legal hurdles.

On the political front, to appease his critics, Cardoso made several important concessions. In a typically pragmatic decision, he persuaded state governors to cooperate by creating a so-called Economic Reconstruction Fund with half of the proceeds of CVRD's sale, while keeping the rest for debt reduction purposes. The fund would finance infrastructure projects dear to the governors. He also enticed workers by allowing them to acquire 5.1 per cent of shares at a heavily discounted price. As for nationalists, Cardoso tried to placate their ire by requiring the new owners to let BNDES have the right to 50 per cent of new mineral deposits discovered after the sale. The Treasury would retain 'golden shares' for five years allowing it a veto power over ownership changes. In addition, the new owners (a minimum of three partners were required for each bidding consortium) were barred from selling shares for a two-year period (Goldstein 1997).

These political trade-offs were accompanied by a multi-million dollar public relation campaign. It used radio, television, and newspapers and featured some of the most popular Brazilian actors' to advertise the positive aspects of the sale. As part of this multi-pronged campaign, Planning Minister Antônio Kandir, often appeared on the radio Program *Voz do Brasil* to entertain the public's questions regarding the CVRD transaction.

On 6 May 1997, the surprise winner of the auction (45 per cent of voting shares), that took place at the Rio Stock Exchange, was a consortium headed by the Brazilian steel company CSN and integrated by the offshore Opportunity Asset Management investment fund, NationsBank (United

States), and several Brazilian pension funds including Previ, Petros, Funcef, and Funcesp. The new company that emerged from the privatization process, Valepar, paid $3.1 billion, or 20 per cent more than the minimum price. Two more stages were scheduled to a later date, one involving a stock offering to employees (common and preferred shares) mentioned above and a second stock offering of 17–20 per cent of common shares to be held in Brazil and abroad. A year after the sale, provisional data issued by Valepar showed that under private management the company's performance had further improved. In all, the CVRD's privatization was clearly a victory for the administration and strengthened the credibility of the Cardoso administration both at home and abroad.

Telecommunications. The CVRD privatization paved the way for larger divestitures. Telebrás, the country's telephone company, is a point in case. The company was created in 1972 to merge a myriad of small local and long-distance operators that had developed since the turn of the century. Under the military regime, Telebrás was considered a strategic company and received large capital investments to develop new networks across the country and improve technology. Although compared to other Latin American telephone operators, Telebrás performed rather well financially, during the 1980s its ability to modernize its networks declined rapidly (Molano 1997). By the mid-1990s there was substantial agreement among company managers, as well as politicians, that to stay competitive world wide Brazil needed a massive capital infusion in Telebrás that only private investors could provide.

Upon taking office, Cardoso appointed his trusted friend Sérgio Motta at the helm of the Telecommunications Ministry to handle the sensitive transfer of Telebrás. While the government was able to scrap the monopoly status of Telebrás from the Constitution by 1995, it would be not until mid-1997 when Congress sanctioned the general telecommunication law (9.457). The new law established the legal framework for the restructuring of Telebrás, set up the ground rules for the privatization of cellular and fixed telephone service, and defined the new norms to which the private operators would abide. Feuding between Motta, private bidders, and Congress over the solution of complex legal and technical problems related to the regulatory framework further delayed the process. Yet, due to a pent-up demand for 20 million phones, and the large size of its potential market, foreign bidders flocked into Brazil to get a piece of a business some estimated to be worth $100 billion.[108] To help domestic investors compete, as in the electricity sector, BNDES offered them a 50 per cent financing deal at a 7–10 year maturity range.[109] The government started the process by auctioning licenses from the Band-B cellular operators, which presented less problems. From mid-1997 through mid-1998, the government sold nine licenses for $8 billion, or 153 per cent more than it had expected. Indeed, some of the bids went well beyond the government's rosiest expectations. The consortium led by Bell South won the most important license, covering the São Paulo metropolitan area (Area 1), and paid for it a staggering $2.4 billion. The second largest license in the states of Rio de Janeiro and Espirito Santo (Area 3) was awarded a year later to Korea Mobile Telecom. Needless to say, some transactions did not go smoothly. For instance, no bids were received for Area 8 covering Pará, Amazonas, and Maranhão. In another incident, the winning bid for the Southern São Paulo (Area 2), led by the Swedish group Telia, was approved only in early 1998 after a long legal battle that ended up in the STF.

In October 1997, Motta after changing several of the original plans finally announced the Telebrás concession framework. The 27 telecommunications companies making up the Telebrás system were reorganized into 12 'Baby Brás' companies divided into three groups: (1) three regional fixed-line companies; (2) eight A-band cellular operators; and (3) one long-distance company, Embratel. The bidding rules did not contemplate the inclusion of an experienced operator in the winning consortium, which raised the suspicion that the government was trying to help some domestic groups. By the same token though, the Telecommunications Ministry tried to please foreign investors by eliminating the 49 per cent restriction imposed on them in the previous B-Band sale. In addition, the sector's new regulatory agency Agência Nacional De Telecomunicaçoes (ANATEL), required: (1) a 2 per cent fee on net revenues for a 20-year period after the concession expired in 2005; (2) substantial cuts in the price of local, domestic long-distance, and international calls by 2005; (3) a substantial expansion of fixed-line phones (about 9 million by 2001) and their regional coverage, particularly in the scarcely serviced countryside.

Unlike in Argentina, greater emphasis was placed on creating competition almost from the start. Consequently, no buyer was allowed to purchase more than one company in each group and for both fixed and cellular telephony the law contemplated at least two companies vying for customers until 2005 and open competition thereafter. B-Band cellular companies would compete with their A-Band counterparts located in the same geographical area. As for competition in fixed telephony, after the Telebrás privatization the government planned to sell concessions to 'mirror companies' that would be established in 1999. Because such companies were to start from scratch, and would have just 5 per cent of the market initially, bidding rules were expected to be far less stringent.

Understandably, the telephone workers' union attacked the state divestiture contending that the company was profitable. However, their true motive was the fear of losing jobs as the union estimated that up to 54 per cent of Telebrás workforce (roughly 30,000 people) was likely to be laid off. To stop the process, the union and left-wing parties filed a barrage of legal injunctions claiming that the breaking up of Telebrás was unconstitutional on several grounds. Similarly to the CVRD case, law suits and some technical problems (some interested consortia needed more time to study the concession terms and register with the regulatory agency), managed to postpone the sale, but could not stop it. The bombing of two transmission towers and the invasion of BNDES headquarters by Telebrás workers and left-wing students fared no better. Cardoso turned this sterile opposition tactic to his advantage by arguing in public that while his administration was trying to solve the problem of poor telephone service, his opponents were only concerned with defending their special interest even at the cost of sabotaging Telebrás. A clear sign that the public was on the President's side in this battle was Lula's decision to keep a low profile on the issue and stay away from union demonstrations fearing that his involvement could hurt his 1998 presidential campaign.

In the meantime, seventy companies had lined up to bid in the largest auction ever in the developing world, confirming the great interest that Telebrás had generated. In July 1997, as the bids were disclosed the government netted $19 billion, far outstripping the floor price set at $11.6 billion. The São Paulo fixed-line company, Telesp, attracted $4.98 billion by far the largest amount paid for any company included in the PND since 1991. European companies, led by Telefónica of Spain, Portugal Telecom, and Telecom of Italy were the big winners, accounting for 75 per cent of all proceeds. For Cardoso, it was a resounding victory particularly if one considers the financial turmoil already affecting many emerging markets at the time.

Conclusion

In the early 1990s, privatization in Brazil started slowly and was circumscribed to a few, uncontroversial sectors, but by 1998 had gained significant momentum. It was affecting the core industries of the public sector, and was on its way to be the largest divestiture process not only in Latin America but in the rest of the whole developing world.

Whereas the Sarney administration conceived it merely as a policy to contain public sector growth, under Presidents Collor and Franco it came to be regarded as part of a larger program aimed at reducing the size of state intervention in the economy, but it was implemented timidly. However, it was only under Cardoso that privatization moved from being a corollary policy to the adjustment process to becoming the main engine of a new economic development model based upon the preeminence of the market as the best means to foster growth and investments.

Privatization went through a clear evolutionary process in Brazil. In the 1980s, it targeted former private companies that BNDES was forced to acquire to save them from bankruptcy. In the early 1990s its content grew more far-reaching as some of the PEs put on the auction block had been at the core of the ISI strategy from the start, but it was from 1995 on that the largest, most important companies in strategic sectors were included in the PND.

Collor showed greater political commitment to privatization than Sarney, but both willingness and opportunity factors were much weaker than in Argentina, which explains why in Brazil the state divestiture policy never gained the momentum that it did across the border in the early 1990s. Adding to the problem, privatization took place within a poor macroeconomic environment, but while Menem's strong political determination under similar circumstances kept the policy on track, Collor and Franco's weak resolve partly explains the initial lack of progress in Brazil. To Menem, privatization was a means of reshaping socioeconomic power relations in Argentine society. To Collor and Franco, privatization was instead a means of achieving narrower goals. Moreover, judicial intervention in many divestitures, strong congressional opposition, constitutional bans, and restrictions on foreign capital, which were not factors in Argentina, made policy implementation all the more complicated. If to all these factors we then add the impeachment of President Collor, whose association with privatization later negatively affected that policy, one could argue that the very fact that privatization continued at a steady pace was quite an achievement in its own right.

It is also worth noting that, in the early 1990s, Brazilian policy-makers seemed more concerned with using privatization primarily as a tool to cut the fiscal deficit rather than as a means to achieve broader socioeconomic changes. This narrow approach significantly limited the impact of the divestiture program. Indeed, in terms of results, up until 1994 privatization revenues were well below expectations. Whereas early estimates projected a net income of $5 billion yearly, actual results showed a total income of $8.3 billion, of which only 18.6 per cent was in cash. Up until 1994, of the sixty-four PEs slated for privatization in which the federal government was either the sole owner or had majority/minority stakes, thirty-four were sold, five were excluded, and the processing of an additional eleven suspended. The bulk of the revenues came from the steel sector privatization, which accounted for $5.5 billion, followed by petrochemicals with $2.6 billion. Revenues advanced at a steady pace reaching their peak in 1993. The uncertainty surrounding the presidential elections of 1994 was primarily responsible for the lower performance registered that year. Domestic companies (36.6 per cent), banks (25.2 per cent), and pensions funds (13.8 per cent), in order of importance, were the most active players in the privatization process during the Collor–Franco period.

Once again, the picture changed substantially once Cardoso showed a strong commitment to privatization, put together a strong coalition in support, and was able to get rid of all the legal hurdles that had previously forestalled the process. During his first term in office, he transferred to the private sector sixty-two PEs, as opposed to twenty-four during the Collor–Franco period.

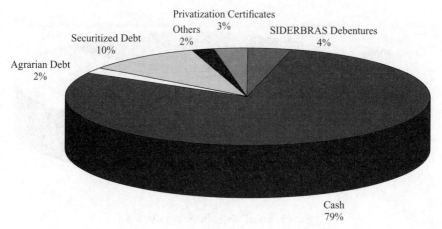

FIG. 4.4. Brazil: Revenues by Type of Payment 1991–8
Source: BNDES, 1998.

Although 1995 and 1996 were disappointing years in terms of both revenues and the number of companies transferred, 1997 and 1998 were characterized by dramatic advances on all fronts. In the latter two years, privatization receipts accounted for 69 per cent of total PND revenues, or $31 billion (Table 4.3). In addition, as opposed to the Collor–Franco period, most of the payments under Cardoso were made in cash, which by 1998 accounted for 79 per cent of all payments (Fig. 4.4). Revenue wise, during the whole 1991–8 period the PND raised $45 billion (Table 4.3). Telecommunications accounted for the largest share of all proceeds with 58 per cent, followed by the steel sector with 12 per cent (Fig. 4.5).

The fiscal impact of privatization was modest at first but became more significant in 1997–8. Passanezi Filho (1993: 3) estimated a deficit reduction of 0.11 per cent of GDP for the 1991–3 period. Another study by Castelar Pinheiro and Giambiagi (1993: 31) calculated the fiscal impact of the PND to be about 0.4 per cent of GDP over the same period. Consistent with other studies on other countries, the same authors argued that the greatest impact of privatization was on foregoing investments. Between 1990 and 1993, according to BNDES, privatization saved the treasury the $1 billion it would have cost had the PEs remained in government hands. In addition to this, it should be noted that savings were made by transferring a substantial amount of PE debt, estimated at $8.1 billion between 1990 and 1997, to the new private owners.[110] Under the Cardoso administration privatization proceeds were usually, but not exclusively used for debt servicing (Goldstein 1997). In 1998, in fact, the government hoped to cover part of the fiscal deficit, estimated to be at 8 per cent of GDP, primarily through privatization revenues.

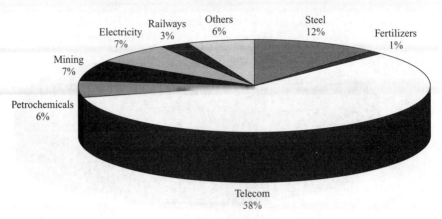

FIG. 4.5. Brazil: Sales by Sector 1991–8
Source: BNDES, 1998.

Unlike other Latin American countries, Brazil has traditionally relied little on foreign direct investments (FDI) as a result of a number of restrictions imposed on foreign capital since the 1950s. In 1996, FDIs accounted for only 8.7 per cent of gross capital formation as opposed to 15.7 per cent in Mexico, 25.7 per cent in Chile, and 22 per cent in Peru. FDIs progressively declined in the first half of the 1990s only to increase in record numbers in the 1996–7 period when they doubled every year.[111] The Collor administration's decision to open up the São Paulo and Rio de Janeiro stock markets, by allowing foreign investors to make direct equity purchases in Brazil, created the basis for large capital inflows later on. In fact, traditionally, Brazilian companies are overwhelmingly controlled by families and multinationals and the vast majority of shares available are 'preferential' or non-voting. To overcome investor skepticism due to this feature of Brazilian capital markets, Collor authorized PEs to be privatized to issue half or more of their equities in the form of voting shares. Foreigners, following a similar pattern in Mexico, immediately invested heavily in large government utilities (i.e. Telebrás, Eletrobrás, CVRD), anticipating their privatization. As a result, whereas the ten largest quoted companies (mostly PEs) in 1989 represented 22 per cent of market capitalization, by 1992 they reached 53 per cent. However, privatization attracted only $353.2 million in foreign investment since public utilities escaped state divestiture and some restrictions on foreign ownership remained in place until 1993. Revenue wise, foreigners contributed only 4.8 per cent of privatization receipts until 1994. The picture changed appreciably once the large public utilities were put on the auction block. By December 1997, their contribution had reached 13 per cent (Fig. 4.6) without taking into account the Band-B and Telebrás privatizations, which

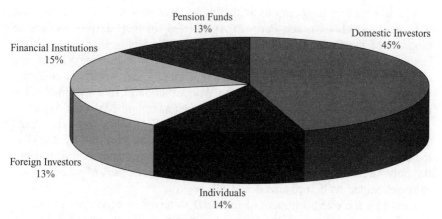

FIG. 4.6. Brazil: Revenues by Type of Investor 1991–7
Source: BNDES, 1998.

were likely to bring that figure up to 18 per cent and higher.[112] In 1996 and 1997, privatization accounted for 27.6 per cent and 29.4 per cent respectively of all foreign direct investments coming into Brazil.[113]

Much the same can be argued for the improvement in the business climate. Several measures initiated under Collor, like trade liberalization, the deregulation of some sectors of the economy, and the integration process with Argentina, Paraguay, and Uruguay played an important role in creating a positive business environment. However, it was only after Cardoso brought inflation under control and gave strong priority to the PND that investors returned to Brazil in large numbers. Such a turnaround proved that, contrary to privatization critics, private investors were interested and were willing to invest in large projects if the government showed the political commitment to expand the scope of the PND. This was demonstrated, for instance, by the stock market capitalization, which jumped from $99 billion in 1993 (before the Real Plan), to $216 billion in 1996.[114] The high quality of the foreign investors who participated in the electricity, CVRD, and telecommunications privatizations, is a further indicator that foreign investors, prior to the mid-1998 financial crisis, looked at Brazil as one of the most important emerging markets in the world.[115] Moreover, the very large investments made by Brazilian industrial groups, banks, and pension funds not only in the privatization process but also in other economic activities after 1994 do point to the fact that Cardoso's reforms had decisively contributed to create a favorable business environment that the country had only last experienced during the booming years of the Brazilian 'miracle' in the early 1970s.

By the same token, although privatization helped in easing relations with commercial banks and multilateral lending agencies, it did not seem to play as much a part in negotiations with foreign creditors as it did in the case of Argentina, Mexico, and Peru. In April 1994, in fact, despite its lack of progress of the PND, Brazil was able to enter the Brady Plan without first having signed a stand-by agreement with the IMF by disbursing $2.8 billion of its reserves to its creditors, a luxury that other Latin American countries could not afford. The assistance of the World Bank and IDB assumed some relevance after 1995, but its magnitude was much more limited than in Argentina and Peru. Only after Cardoso was re-elected in early October 1998, did Brazil aggressively look for an IMF emergency $41.5 billion loan, but by that time the crucial issues in the negotiations were social security and tax reform since the only large PE in government hands was Petrobrás, part of whose assets were scheduled to be privatized in 1999 anyhow.[116]

Although the overall impact of the PND in terms of economic efficiency is difficult to assess since the largest companies were privatized only after mid-1997, some of the sectors transferred early on showed encouraging results. The healthy performance of steel mills once under private ownership is an example of successful privatization. In 1993, Piratini made $1.4 million, the first profit in the company's history. Its new owners also invested $30.2 million in new technology.[117] After years of losses, in 1993 CSN, CST, and Açesita also moved into the black with profits of $70 million, $32.6 million, and $31.4 million respectively (Table 4.8). Usiminas's profits, which during the last year as a PE (1991) had totalled $59.6 million, jumped to $246 million in 1993. Similar improvements were also made in increasing investments and reducing overall debts.

Many companies freed from a web of federal laws were able to renegotiate contracts with suppliers, distributors, and customers (Castelar Pinheiro and Giambiagi 1993) and, in the process, cut redtape and costs. Positive results ensuing from privatization affected the wholesale commercialization of steel and fuels, as well as the road transportation of steel products (Abreu and Werneck 1993: 29). Price controls for steel and fertilizers were lifted and import restrictions and tariffs affecting these products were substantially reduced.

Critics charged that profitability was achieved at the expense of deep cuts in employment levels, which occurred in other former PEs. However, as in the case of CST, the remaining workforce received pay raises of up to 35 per cent.[118] In the case of CSN, expectation of employment and investment growth after the initial restructuring process eased worker–management relations and brought new businesses into the city of Volta Redonda, where CSN is located.[119] The good performance of such companies was also beneficial to workers who were now shareholders in their own companies since the value of their shares, in several cases, appreciated after privatization. As Sola (1993:158) pointed out, 'the expected "winners" and "losers" of privatization have been reversed, since the employees who were entitled to the purchase of shares in the privatized firms have become beneficiaries, albeit indirectly, to the enormous investment potential of the pension funds [investing in such companies]'. Based on these results, in some cases the workforce of former PEs, like in Açominas, Piratini, and some petrochemical companies, openly supported the privatization effort.[120]

One of the best features of the PND over the years was the transparency of its process, at least when compared to other Latin American countries. Although several inquiries were launched to investigate alleged improper behavior by government officials, they came out empty-handed. The high level of scrutiny imposed by the Congress and the courts, either for political reasons or true concern, surely delayed the process, but also prevented that government officials could abuse their discretionary powers as it happened in Argentina. In addition, the insulation of most technical decisions within the BNDES staff, and the strong corporate autonomy displayed by that institution, ensured the continuity of the process while protecting it in many cases from excessive political interference.

The downside of the PND was related to issues similar to Argentina. Under pressure to sell quickly, the Collor and Franco administrations put little emphasis on enhancing competition through privatization. As a matter of fact, in many cases the government allowed domestic private groups to finally acquire their competitors in the public sector like in steel, fertilizers, and railroad equipment (Table 4.4). This decision reduced rather than increased competition, thus offsetting the economic efficiency gains that should have followed from privatization.

As in Argentina, as the scope of privatization expanded, the problem of regulation became more pressing. For instance, in manufacturing, price-fixing cartels made up by large domestic groups and multinationals, like car manufacturers, has been the norm in Brazil. The regulation of cartels has in fact been rather elusive since successive governments actually encouraged their creation by preventing the entrance in protected markets by potential competitors from abroad. Brazil's anti-trust agency, the Conselho Administrativo de Defesa Econômica (CADE), although created in 1962, remained an ineffectual institution since it lacked real independence from the executive branch (Abreu and Werneck 1993). Under the Collor administration there was an attempt to revive regulatory activity on the part of the federal government. CADE's powers were strengthened and the Ministry of Justice created a Departamento Nacional de Proteção e Defesa Econômica (DNPDC) in charge of enforcing antitrust legislation. From 1991 on, both the CADE and DNPDC stepped up their investigations and ruled against one of Gerdau's acquisitions.[121] Once Cardoso began to privatize public utilities, the government committed itself to the creation of clear regulatory frameworks. Similarly to Argentina, Brazil opted for a sector-specific regulatory framework by creating ad hoc agencies in electricity (ANEEL) and telecommunications (ANTEL), in 1996 and 1997 respectively. None the less, many questions about the capacity of such agencies to regulate effectively persisted. In fact, on the one hand the new regulatory regime had the advantage of being sanctioned into a law, which made its repeal much more difficult as opposed to similar legislation enforced via administrative decree that we found in Argentina. On the other hand, particularly in telecommunications, on issues 'related to the regulator's ability to access information, provide efficiency enhancing incentives to the firm, and institute safeguarding mechanisms to protect against expropriation . . . the law falls a bit short of the international best practice' (Goldstein 1997: 98).

In the manufacturing sector, after an initial inquiry CADE seemed to accept the collusive practices emerging in markets like steel, fertilizers, and petro-chemicals. In all these sectors firms were allowed to increase their market power (Castelar Pinheiro and Giambiagi 1993) and in some cases they were able to further vertical and horizontal integration as a result of the PND (de Souza 1999).

Another problem is closely linked to the one just mentioned. That is, the role played by domestic investors within the divestiture process. Until foreign investors entered the process in considerable numbers by 1997, the main players in the PND remained domestic industrial groups, private and public banks, and pension funds often representing interests of government employees. The participation of public pension funds raised questions of the possibility that politicians could still have some leverage in the decision of the new companies since some pension fund managers, like in the case of Previ, are appointed by the executive branch. This is why later on in the process, the participation of such funds to bidding consortia was limited to 25 per cent of voting shares (Goldstein 1997). Moreover, the preponderance of banking institutions in many transactions raised the suspicion that the financial–industrial nexus so created could plant the seeds for the emergence of very powerful bank-dominated conglomerates that could heavily influence political decisions in the future to the detriment of competition and transparency in the market place.

Although employees began to subscribe to the companies' shares offered to them in increasing numbers as privatization gained momentum after 1996, true popular capitalism did not materialize since the general public remained at the margins of the process. As a result, public auctions, which were the primary means used to transfer ownership, catered almost exclusively to the interests of institutional investors rather than small ones. The government use of public auctions, which accounted for 91 per cent of all revenues, was to lure a substantial pool of large investors to maximize revenues (Fig. 4.7). In turn, institutional investors demanded control over the assets being privatized. The relatively small size of the Brazilian capital markets and the lack of strong provisions safeguarding small shareholders also offered doubtful prospects to individual investors. To remedy this situation, the Cardoso administration

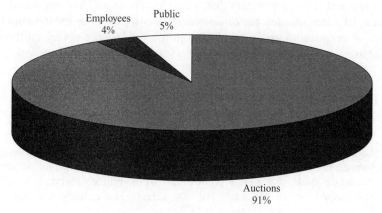

Employees
4%

Public
5%

Auctions
91%

FIG. 4.7. Brazil: Type of Offer 1991–7
Source: BNDES, 1998.

set up special credit lines through BNDES for people interested in buying shares and planned to launch international public offers to privatize Petrobrás. None the less, even if these measures were to meet with strong public response, analysts expected their overall impact to be negligible.

Summing up, as Cardoso's second term began in 1999, the PND had achieved considerable results, although much later than in other Latin American countries, primarily because under his presidency it had found the strong political leadership necessary to overcome the opposition of a large number of vested interests that had dragged down the policy under Collor and Franco. In the second half of the 1990s prospects had also considerably improved. Brazil's economic and political elites had finally realized that a large but weak government apparatus only exacerbated the fiscal crisis; and it was no longer capable of effectively guiding the development process. Within this context, many recognized privatization to be a necessary policy to make the state smaller but more efficient. Others were persuaded by the looming financial crisis they were confronting. Long-time opponents among clientelistic governors not only conceded the point, but were actively privatizing at the state level. By early 1998, state governors had privatized companies for an estimated $19 billion and were offering many more at such a rate that they often undercut one another as well as the PND, since potential bidders could choose among many attractive deals.[122] The year 1999, despite the Real's devaluation and the worsening of the fiscal deficit situation, promised to be a good one as BNDES planned to raise $2 billion through the sale of its remaining 25 per cent share in CVRD and an additional $5 billion in the auction of its 31 per cent stake in Petróbras.

Lastly, from a broader perspective, one of the PND's most important accomplishment was to signal to domestic socioeconomic groups, multilateral agencies, and foreign investors that, albeit slowly, Brazil had embarked on a process of economic reform of far-reaching consequences for the country's future. It produced a profound change in the way people perceived the role of the state and its responsibilities vis-à-vis society as a whole.

Endontes

1. *Latin American Regional Reports: Brazil Report*, 6 July 1989, p. 2.
2. Fernando Collor de Mello's grandfather, Lindolfo Collor, was a prominent minister during the Getulio Vargas regime in the 1930s. His father, former Senator Arnon de Mello, was a close political ally of the military regime in the 1960s and helped launch his son's political career. The military first appointed Fernando as mayor of Alagóas in 1979.
3. Collor's family owned the most important media conglomerate in the state of Alagóas, with ties to TV Globo.
4. A notable exception was Ulysses Guimarães, the leader of the PMDB, the largest party in Congress, who wary of Collor's demagoguery decided to throw his support to Lula.
5. *Medidas provisorias* are executive orders whose enforcement is valid for three months, but can be reissued and altered in content. The President can use them to solve problems deemed 'urgent' and 'relevant' to the national interest. After a month such *medidas provisorias* are either converted into a law by Congress or, with its tacit consent, they can be re-issued.
6. Congress approved an amended version of the executive order with a vote of 370 to 90.
7. The same decree (99.463) listed the first ten PEs and eighteen shareholdings in the privatization program. Later on, three other executive orders were issued including ten more companies and seventeen shareholdings in the privatization program.
8. According to the congressional investigation, Farias was Collor's designated negotiator in charge of arranging corrupt deals with businessmen and politicians, collecting money, and then depositing it in phantom accounts at the disposal of the President, cabinet ministers, and government bureaucrats. In this way, Farias disbursed a total of $32.3 million, of which $6.5 million went directly to Collor's family. With the President's blessing, Farias acted as the gray eminence behind the throne. While holding no official position in the administration, he set up a parallel government that was in charge of the most important decisions. Senado Federal, Relatório Final da Comissão Parlamentar de Inquérito de Senado Federal (Brasilia, March 1993).
9. In March 1993, upon quitting, the President of BNDES publicly accused the government of 'egregious incompetence'.
10. The SEF was eventually renewed by Congress in 1995 and 1997.
11. Some blue chip shares that were sold affected Banco do Brasil, Vale do Rio Doce, Biobras (pharmaceutical), CBV Nordeste Industria Mecanica, Itautec (electronics), Eletrobras, Petrobras, and Salgema (chemicals), to name a few. In

companies like Eletrobrás and Petrobrás sheltered from privatization by constitutional provisions, BNDES planned to sell voting stocks in excess of the 51 per cent required to retain majority control. In other PEs where such restrictions did not exist, the amount of stocks up for sale was greater.

12. Interview with Senator Antônio Carlos Magalhães (Brasilia, April 1995).
13. Interview with the Brazilian ambassador to the United States Paulo Tarso Flecha de Lima, Miami, November 1994. Interview with Eduardo Modiano, Rio De Janeiro, November 1998.
14. Collor's goal was to use market reforms to create a financial empire of his own through the abuse of public office. The strategy consisted not only of remitting some of the profits of corrupt practices abroad but, more importantly, '. . . accumulation of capital and property that could guarantee to the new millionaires respect among entrepreneurs, economic power, and a place in the market' (Krieger *et al.* 1992: 126). In their effort to create a financial empire, Collor and Farias concentrated on three sectors: aviation, mining, and the media. Again, so-called economic reforms were used to this end. The privatization of the airline VASP was awarded to Wagner Canhedo, thanks to the illicit funds provided by Farias who already owned a number of private jet companies. Involvement in media ventures reflected the President's wish that he have a mechanism to publicize his political plans in the future. To this end, Farias proceeded with the purchase of several broadcasting companies and newspapers.
15. For an analysis of Cardoso's change of heart see *The Economist*, 2 April 1994, p. 39.
16. Speech delivered in New York City on 23 October 1995 at the World Statesman Award.
17. *New York Times*, 12 November 1994, p. C2.
18. The same logic was later reiterated under the Franco administration. Franco's chairman of the PND, André Franco Montoro Filho, stated quite clearly that, 'we are working steadily and surely toward reorganizing the role of the State. In order to do so, it must put an end to its role as an entrepreneur' (*Obrecht Informa*, May/June 1994, p. 13).
19. Banco Nacional de Desenvolvimiento Econômico e Social, *Brazilian Privatization Program: Brazil Company Handbook*, special edition (Rio de Janeiro: IMF editora, 1991).
20. On this point Montoro was quite explicit, 'Imagine deciding whether it is better to earmark $1 billion to modernizing the companies or the national health programs.' Ibid.
21. Getulio Vargas Foundation, *Conjuntura Econômica*, August 1991.
22. World Bank, *World Tables 1993* (Baltimore: World Bank and Johns Hopkins University Press, 1993), p. 147.
23. *Veja*, 14 February 1990, p. 73.
24. Senado Federal, *Relatório Final da Comissão Parlamentar do Inquérito do Senado Federal* (Brasilia, March 1993).
25. *Folha de São Paulo*, 25 January 1990, p. A-11.
26. Interviews with congressional staffers in charge of privatization legislation, Brasilia. October 1993.

27. Mr. Daniel Dantas, director of Banco Icatu, one of Brazil's largest banks, explained Franco's slow approach in these terms, 'I think Itamar [Franco] realizes he has no alternative to privatisation but wants the process to be too perfect. He wants to do it in such a way that nice buyers come who pay the government a lot of money and make no layoffs' (*Financial Times*, 15 September 1994).

28. Banco Nacional do Desenvolvimento Econômico e Social, *Programa Nacional de Desestatização: Relatório de Atividades*. Brasilia: May 1993, p. 7.

29. Interview with David Fleischer and Luiz Pedone Brasilia, October 1993.

30. Interview with David Moreira São Paulo, August 1993.

31. Interviews with domestic bond traders São Paulo, October 1993.

32. Interview with BNDES officials in charge of the privatization process, Rio de Janeiro, August 1993.

33. Ibid.

34. Interview with investment bankers Alberto Ortenblad Filho and Guido Padovano, São Paulo, October 1993.

35. Confederaçao Nacional de Indústria, *Competitividade e Estratégia Industrial: A Visão de Leres Industriais Brasileiros* Rio de Janeiro, 1990.

36. Data collected by the Departamento Intersindical de Assesoria Parlamentar. Estado de S. Paulo, 20 June 1993, p. 13.

37. Ibid.

38. DataFolha, April 1994.

39. *O Estado de São Paulo*, 30 October 1994, p. B6.

40. *Latin American Monitor: Brazil*; February 1994, p. 4.

41. *Gazeta Mercantil*, 22 November 1994, p. 1.

42. In June 1996, the World Bank disbursed $700 million for the railways restructuring prior to privatization. World Bank, Press release No. 96/66/LAC.

43. In any given privatization, one consulting firm was in charge of appraising the value of PEs and proposing the minimum price sale. A second one would recommend potential problems in the transfer, identify potential buyers, and indicate the best model possible to carry out the transfer. The executive office retained the authority of establishing the minimum sale price for a PE. Banco Nacional de Desenvolvimiento Econômico e Social, *Brazilian Privatization Program: Brazil Company Handbook*, special edition (Rio de Janeiro: IMF editora, 1991).

44. For a complete list see Decree no. 724.

45. Under these new provisions, the upper management of each PE was allowed to participate in the evaluation process.

46. Franco's decision was dictated by the need to create additional ministerial posts to satisfy the demands of the parties supporting his administration in Congress (Abreu and Werneck 1993).

47. *Latin American Regional Reports: Brazil*, 11 February 1993, p. 4.

48. *O Estado de S. Paulo*, 15 August 1993, p. 8.

49. Former Petrobrás President, Benedicto Moreira, stressed that his major problem in office was to resist political pressure of all kinds. He described Petrobrás as 'a fort like in cowboy movies, surrounded by indians from all sides' (ibid., p. 7).

50. *Brazil Watch*, 22 November–6 December 1993, p. 8.

51. *Financial Times*, 28 October 1997, p. 17.
52. *Financial Times*, 30 April 1997, p. 13.
53. Interview with members of the Brazilian Congress Brasilia, October 1993.
54. *Medida provisória* no. 327.
55. A congressional inquiry headed by Senator Amir Lando suspected that, while head of BNDES, Modiano had favored some industrialists and banks involved in the privatization program who later rewarded him with high-ranking appointments in their organizations.
56. *O Estado de S. Paulo*, 15 August 1993, p. 8.
57. On the weaknesses of industrial associations see Leigh Payne 1994.
58. On FIESP's strength vis-à-vis other interest organizations in Brazil see *Veja*, 29 July 1992, pp. 78–9.
59. Law 2.300, for instance, strictly regulated PE purchasing orders, which were usually limited to domestic companies.
60. Modiano not only faced strong attacks by anti-privatization advocates but also from people within the cabinet. In May 1992, he weathered political pressure calling for his replacement when criticized for not moving privatization through fast enough. Some congressmen wanted his and other BNDES jobs in exchange for political support for the administration. Interview with Eduardo Modiano, Rio De Janeiro, November 1998.
61. Interview with David Moreira, São Paulo, August 1993.
62. *O Estado de S. Paulo*, 4 July 1993, p. 8.
63. However, a minority of BNDES officials, particularly from the older generations, who grew up under the aegis of ISI, resisted privatization. Interview with BNDES officials, Rio de Janeiro, August 1993.
64. *US/Latin Trade*, September 1994, p. 97.
65. *O Estado de S. Paulo*, 15 August 1993, p. 7. Collor's Minister of Infrastructure Ozires Silva, a nationalist himself, came to the same conclusion regarding the SIDERBRAS (steel) holding company (Schneider 1992: 230).
66. Interviews with Antônio Carlos Seidl and Fabio Paim, economic editors of Folha de São Paulo and O Estado de São Paulo, São Paulo, April 1995.
67. Interview with Senator Antônio Carlos Magalhães, Brasilia, April 1995.
68. *Miami Herald*, 13 August 1995, p. 1, 6K.
69. *Veja*, 4 March 1998.
70. *Miami Herald*, 24 April 1997, p. 16A.
71. The financial burden of state government comes mainly from overstaffing. Years of patronage politics and clientelism drove Brazil's major states, such as São Paulo, Rio de Janeiro and Rio Grande do Sul, to spend on payroll around 70/80 per cent of their budgets. *Financial Times*, 13 February 1998.
72. The federal government swaped the state's debt obligations to Banespa, which amounted to over $24 billion, for its privatization to be managed by BNDES. *Latin American Monitor: Brazil*, April 1998, p. 7.
73. However, another minor labor organization, Força Sindical, openly supported the privatization process.
74. *Istoé Senhor*, 26 September 1990, pp. 20–23.
75. In early 1995, some Brazilian unions also launched a sleek television campaign tying the collapse of the Mexican economy of December 1994 and the

difficulties experienced by Argentina shortly thereafter privatization and other market-oriented reforms.

76. A typical case of these junk bonds was the Agrarian Debt Bond on which the government had stopped paying interests many years earlier.
77. Despite the privatization drive, unions in many PEs were able to negotiate much higher salary hikes than in the private sectors, testifying to their lobbying power. In 1993, the Franco administration seemed to have lost control over salaries in the PE sector. With seven ministers in the economic area being replaced in the first half of that year, PE managers and union leaders had de facto set up their own wage policy. Salary expenses in 1993 were expected to exceed yearly inflation by 10 per cent. *Gazeta Mercantil*, 3 June 1993, p. 1.
78. *Classe Operaria*, 17–30 May 1993, vol. 69, no. 102, p. 12.
79. One such demonstration took place 10 September, 1993 when workers belonging to the CGT and students clashed with police in Rio de Janeiro while the government was auctioning the last steel mill Açominas.
80. *Folha de São Paulo*, 3 April 1995, p. 7.
81. *Latin American Regional Reports: Brazil*, 2 June 1998, p. 2.
82. *Brazil Watch*, November 22–December 6, 1993, p. 7.
83. Interview with military officers, Brasilia, August 1993.
84. *O Estado de S. Paulo*, 15 August 1993, p. 8.
85. Junk bonds sold quickly. While at the end of 1992 their total value in the market was about $6 billion, in mid-1993 only $2.2 billion worth of junk bonds were available. As such securities became scarce, discounts began to fall sharply, from a high of 65 per cent to 30 per cent in June 1993. For an argument against the sell-out charge, see Abreu and Werneck (1993: 28).
86. In July 1991, the MYDFA were traded at 34 cents per dollar. None the less, 'many banks resisted accepting the official 25 per cent discount rate since they would be legally compelled to write-off their assets' (Abreu and Werneck 1993: 28).
87. Data provided by BNDES.
88. *Latin American Regional Reports: Brazil*, 8 July 1993, p. 6.
89. *US/Latin Trade*, September 1994, p. 85.
90. Usiminas in 1993 produced 60 per cent of Brazil's flat-rolled steel and 100 per cent of the steel plates. Gerdau controlled 40–45 per cent of the non-flat-rolled steel market. *Business Latin America*, 20 September 1993, p. 3.
91. Some estimates that $3 billion in company debt transferred to the private sector. *Latin American Monitor: Brazil*, June 1994, p. 5.
92. The sale of the first 18 PEs cost the government $3.2 billion plus a loss of dividends of $127 million. *Latin American Monitor: Brazil*, September 1993, p. 4.
93. BNDES, *Programa Nacional de Destatização*, December 1994.
94. The steel mill Açominas was sold for 90 per cent over the minimum floor price.
95. Interview with Minister Carlos Atila, President of the Federal Accounting Court, Brasilia, April 1995.
96. *Wall Street Journal*, 3 October 1991.
97. *Latin American Monitor: Brazil*, August 1993.

98. *Brazil Watch*, 27 September–11 October 1993, p. 16.

99. *Financial Times*, 2 October 1997, p. 5.

100. Elaboration on data provided by BNDES.

101. *Lagniappe Monthly on Latin American Projects & Finance*, April 1988, p. 3.

102. *Wall Street Journal*, 13 May 1997, p. A 16, and *Financial Times*, 2 October 1997, p. 5.

103. Data provided by BNDES.

104. *Financial Times*, 30 April 1997, p. 13.

105. *Latin America Monitor: Brazil*, April 1997, p. 5.

106. Between 1980 and 1996, CVRD spent $169 million on those programs. *Miami Herald*, 24 April 1997, p. 16A.

107. Ibid.

108. *Latin American Monitor: Brazil*, August 1997, p. 6.

109. *Lagniappe Monthly on Latin American Projects & Finance*, August 1998, p. 2.

110. Data provided by the BNDES.

111. *Latin American Regional Reports: Brazil Report*, 2 June 1998, p. 5.

112. *Citicorp Privatization Update*, 16 June 1997.

113. *Latin American Regional Reports: Brazil Report*, 7 July 1998, p. 4.

114. International Finance Corporation (1997: 133).

115. *Financial Times*, 31 July 1998, p. 7.

116. *Financial Times*, 9 October 1998, p. 1.

117. *US/Latin Trade*, September 1993, p. 83.

118. Ibid.

119. *Exame*, 29 September 1993.

120. Interview with Márcio Ferreira Verdi, General Coordinator of Management. Ministry of Planning Brasilia, April 1995.

121. Interview with Milton Seligman, Executive Secretary, Ministry of Justice, Brasilia, April 1995.

122. *Latin American Economy and Business*, May 1998, p. 16.

5

Peru

The Peruvian presidential election of mid-1990 took place amidst the worst crisis that the country faced in this century. The factors characterizing the economic debacle closely mirrored those previously analyzed in Argentina and Brazil in 1989, only to a worse degree. According to an official statement (COPRI 1993: 8–9):

Between 1985 and 1990 prices increased twenty thousand times. The economy underwent the second longest-running hyperinflation recorded for any country in this century. . . . The country was isolated from the international financial community . . . [debt] arrears were above $14 billion (70% of total debt). Peru had been declared ineligible by the World Bank and the Inter-American Development Bank. Export figures were 40% lower than in the previous decade . . . In July 1990 international reserves were a negative US$50 million. The state was broke.

What made Peru's crisis much more dramatic than the previous two cases was the level of political violence. The country was in a virtual state of civil war and a state of emergency was enforced in two-thirds of the national territory affecting half of the Peruvian population. Ten years of guerrilla warfare claimed the lives of over 26,000 people and caused damages estimated at $22 billion.[1]

Alan García, whose charisma, youth, and promises for a better future had raised high hopes among different sectors of Peruvian society upon taking office in 1985 (much like Alfonsín and Sarney), became a lame duck president by the end of his term (at the time the Peruvian constitution prevented a consecutive second term). Like his Argentine and Brazilian counterparts, his political image was in complete disrepute by the time he left office. In early 1989, public opinion polls in metropolitan Lima put García's support at no more than 10 per cent. His dismal performance from the start dumped the electoral chances of APRA's next presidential candidate, Luis Alva Castro. However, the crisis did taint the credibility of opposition parties as well. By mid-1990, traditional parties were generally perceived as inept and corrupt. The left-wing coalition that put up the strongest challenge to García in 1985 became plagued by internal rivalries and split into two different tickets. As stressed by Dietz (1992: 251), 'The inability of the parties that dominated electoral politics during the 1980s to cope with the protracted and deep economic crisis . . . greatly weakened them and contributed to the emergence of maverick, anti-establishment candidates and movements that play on the voters' desperation.' A typical example of this trend was Mario Vargas Llosa. A world-famous novelist who spent most of his adult life in Europe, Vargas Llosa was, by his own admission, a political dilettante who entered politics in 1987 to protest García's nationalization of domestic banks. Although in his youth he had openly sympathized with Communism and Fidel Castro, by the late 1980s Varga Llosa's political leanings espoused the tenets of free-market economics and state-shrinking. In February 1988, Belaunde's AP and the other major conservative group, the Popular Christian party, joined forces with Vargas Llosa's 'Liberty' movement giving birth to the center-right electoral coalition called the Democratic Front, or FREDEMO. In 1989, FREDEMO finished a close second in the Lima municipal elections, boosting its prospects for the 1990 presidential contest.

In fact, in early 1990, all opinion polls gave Vargas Llosa a comfortable lead over his closest presidential contender. Some analysts even forecast that he would win an outright majority in the first round of balloting, which would have spared him a run-off with his closest challenger.[2] However, as the presidential campaign came to a close, Vargas Llosa's lead evaporated. This was partly due to his abrasive style and poor management of public relations. Perhaps more importantly, Vargas Llosa's disclosure of his harsh shock therapy to combat hyperinflation, which contemplated deregulation, privatization, the elimination of government subsidies, and massive layoffs in public administration, while consistent with the ideological creed of neo-conservative thinkers, scared away many early supporters (McClintock 1994). In a country where 60 per cent of the population was estimated to live in absolute poverty such plans, no matter how good their intentions, only promised more misery in the short-run.[3]

Such fears were exploited by another maverick, Alberto Fujimori, an unknown political entity until two months prior to the elections. The son of poor Japanese immigrants, Fujimori was an agricultural engineer by training who went into teaching immediately after graduation. He eventually became Chancellor of Peru's National Agriculture University in the second half of the 1980s. During this period Fujimori acquired some public exposure by hosting a talk-show on public-policy issues which, while hardly watched in Lima, had some following throughout the countryside (Jochomovitz 1994: 260). When he entered the presidential race (he never held public office prior to 1990) with a budget of a few thousand dollars, even his own family was quite skeptical.[4]

Fujimori's presidential ambitions were backed by Cambio '90, a small party that he helped create in 1989, and the Peruvian evangelicals who were key in providing organizational and mobilization skills to the campaign of the former university professor.[5] The alliance with the Protestants cost Fujimori, a practicing Catholic, the enmity of the Catholic bishops who eventually found themselves in the embarrassing position of endorsing Vargas Llosa, a well-known agnostic (Klaiber 1990).

Fujimori portrayed himself as an independent, moderate candidate escaping the extremism of Vargas Llosa's conservative agenda as well as that of the left-wing candidates. In typical populist fashion, he was short on specifics but very apt in devising catchy slogans like, 'honesty, hard work, and technology'. In three weeks his support jumped from 5 per cent in public opinion polls to 24 per cent of the actual vote cast in April, finishing only three percentage points behind Vargas Llosa, thus forcing a run-off election. Pitted against Vargas Losa, Fujimori put his contender on the defensive. He outrightly rejected FREDEMO's austerity package, promising instead to adopt a gradual, supply-side approach to economic stabilization. This meant emphasizing government investment and development projects in order to promote new jobs and economic growth. By the same token, he also pledged to resume negotiations with foreign creditors only if the latter were willing to make major concessions in the rescheduling of Peru's onerous debt.

Another peculiarity of Fujimori's was his ability to turn his minority status, as a Japanese-Peruvian, to his advantage. Peruvian society historically has been divided into rigid racial lines, within which small groups of white elites have dominated the majority of the population of mestizo and indigenous background, commonly referred to as *cholos*. In the second round, Fujimori was the object of racial attacks. Some of Vargas Llosa's supporters openly charged that his opponent's loyalty was to Japan rather than Peru, but these insinuations backfired.[6] Many *cholos* saw in Fujimori's very physical appearance and humble background something with which they could identify. He did exploit this fact during his tours in the countryside and in Lima's shanty towns by portraying himself as a 'Peruvian like you'. All of a sudden he became an honorary *cholo* (Werlich 1991). By contrast, Vargas Llosa's appeal remained confined to middle and upper-middle class Peruvians. Unsurprisingly, Fujimori won by large margins in *cholo*-dominated urban and rural areas, which comprised the bulk of the electorate (Dietz 1992: 251). When the final tallies were tabulated, Fujimori came out with 62.5 per cent of the vote against Vargas Llosa's 37.5 per cent, capturing twenty-three of Peru's twenty-four departments (McClintock 1994: 306).

As had been the case for Menem, Fujimori had neither a clear idea of the magnitude of the crisis he was about to confront nor did he have a plan to tackle it. In the few weeks before assuming power (July 28), Fujimori travelled to the United States and Japan trying to obtain desperately needed financial assistance.[7] Those countries (along with Spain, United Kingdom, France, Germany, and Canada) promised to provide Peru with a bridge loan worth $1.7 billion to pay arrearages due to the IMF and the World Bank. However, this help came at a stiff price. In Washington, Fujimori was told that he had no alternative but to enforce a drastic stabilization program together with sweeping structural reforms and resume foreign debt payments under the close supervision of the IMF and the World Bank (Dietz 1992: 252).

In August, Fujimori's economic team developed a market-oriented plan that went far beyond what Vargas Llosa had proposed. By comparison, the plan was much tougher than the ones previously adopted by Menem and Collor. It also represented a complete repudiation of Fujimori's electoral promises. The plan was so radical in content that it was dubbed 'Fujishock' (Salcedo 1990). Prices and salaries in the private sector were liberalized whereas the prices charged by PEs rose steeply to generate profits since the government was no longer attending to PE financial needs. At the same time, the government proceeded to substantially cut public employment and many subsidies. All exchange controls were eliminated as were the existing restrictions on investment, capital flows, imports, and financial markets. Sharp cuts also affected social programs. Tariffs were simplified and reduced first to three and later to only two rates (COPRI 1993*b*: 10). In the beginning, noticeably absent from the government agenda was any specific reference to privatization.

To alleviate the consequences of such measures on the poorest sectors of society, the government raised the minimum wage fourfold and set up a $400 million poverty relief program. None the less, the consequences of the 'Fujishock' were felt immediately. According to Werlich (1991: 82), the plan, 'brought Peru its steepest one-day price increases in the twentieth century. The cost of gasoline soared 3,000 per cent. . . . Electric rates quintupled, and the charge for water in Lima rose more than eightfold. The price of most food staples jumped 300 to 400 per cent.' As expected, the 'Fujishock' had a positive effect on inflation, which dropped from 397 per cent in August to 23.7 per cent in December. However, it also had a devastating economic impact, furthering the recession and worsening poverty levels since many subsidies to support the poor were drastically cut. According to official estimates, by the end of 1990 only 10 per cent of the economically active population in metropolitan Lima was adequately employed while real wages fell 19.4 per cent for the year (IDB 1991: 145).

As in Argentina in 1989, Fujimori's about-face in economic policy brought a profound change in the ruling coalition. The President's party, Cambio '90 held only one-fourth of the seats in Congress, thus requiring an expansion of the support base if any legislation was to be passed. After the election, it was clear that many among Cambio '90's small business and evangelical groups became quite displeased with Fujimori's shift to the right. Undeterred, the President appointed a cabinet of 'national unity', whose members came from different political backgrounds and whose primary feature was the conspicuous absence of Cambio '90 representatives, who thereafter played no meaningful role in the decision-making process.[8] Although three ministers came from left-wing parties, the bulk of the appointments went to independents and conservative politicians. With the FREDEMO alliance dissolved and

Vargas Llosa gone to his self-imposed exile in Europe after the election, it was relatively easy for Fujimori to co-opt the political right given that he was actually implementing the very policies for which conservatives had campaigned.[9] At the same time, the President forged an iron alliance with the military (Kay 1995; Cameron and Mauceri 1997). He demoted the leadership of the national police, claiming that it was corrupt, and put the armed forces in charge of the war against terrorism. This ended a long-standing dispute over which institution, the police or the military, was best fitted for that mission.

To enact his reforms, Fujimori followed the same pattern already observed in Argentina and Brazil. Upon his inauguration, the President told the country that he had inherited a 'disaster' from Alan García which required immediate action. Under pressure, the Peruvian Congress delegated to the executive the power to legislate on sensitive policy areas using constitutional articles 188 and 211 for a limited time. Under these conditions, the President was very effective in implementing his policy agenda swiftly (McClintock 1994: 310). As in Menem's Argentina, the executive tried to prevent the main opposition party, APRA, from obstructing the government's legislative agenda by threatening to investigate the corruption scandals that allegedly had taken place under the García administration.[10] He also 'attacked legislators as "professional demagogues", judges as "jackals" and the Catholic Church as "medieval and recalcitrant"' (McClintock 1994: 308).

By combining arguments based on the economic crisis and terrorist emergency, and by intimidating political opponents Fujimori, during his first year-and-a-half in office, had Congress readily approve executive-sponsored legislation. One such bill created the *rondas*, or peasant militias, which were part of the administration's strategy to fight terrorist insurgency in rural areas (Palmer 1994). When support was in doubt, like in the case of the sensitive issue of strengthening US involvement in Peru to combat cocaine production, Fujimori simply signed a treaty with Washington in May 1991. In so doing he completely bypassed Congress, which was required to ratify it. To strengthen his executive authority, Fujimori also thoroughly reorganized the intelligence services, placing at the helm Vladimiro Montesinos, a former army captain with a dubious past who quickly became the gray eminence behind the throne.[11]

In February 1991, the President appointed Carlos Boloña, a conservative economist, to head the Ministry of Economics and Finance (Ministerio De Economia y Finanzas MEF). In the 22 months of Boloña's tenure the basic goals of IMF-supported stabilization program, signed by Peru in September 1991, remained in place and were actually pursued with even greater vigor than even the IMF had demanded (Gonzales de Olarte 1996). In 1992, Peru's GDP shrank by 2.7 per cent but inflation declined to 57 per cent annually, international reserves (which were at times negative in 1988) rose to

$2.5 billion, tax collection increased to 10 per cent of GDP, and foreign investment jumped to $360 million (COPRI 1993*b*: 12–13). At the same time, substantial strides were made in terms of slashing the budget deficit, lowering tariff barriers, and reducing redundant public employment. In March 1992, Peru paid back $1.76 billion to the IMF and the World Bank with the support of a bridge loan from the US Treasury and Japan's Export-Import Bank. The clearing of arrearages paved the way for a three-year loan from the IMF's Extended Facility Fund, which in turn cleared the way for further loans from the World Bank and the IDB. In 1995, the World Bank extended to Peru a five-year credit facility worth $2 billion, while the IDB provided $350 million in low-interest loans for infrastructure programs.[12] Yet more importantly, it is under Boloña that privatization took off after March 1991 when the President issued an executive order (DS 041) regulating the process of restructuring and downsizing twenty-three PEs. The following September in accordance with the legislative powers delegated to him by Congress, the President issued executive order 674. One of its most important provisions was the creation of the Commission for the Promotion of Private Investment (COPRI), whose explicit mandate was the planning and execution of an ambitious divestiture program to be completed by the end of Fujimori's first term in 1995. However, privatization proceeded slowly as tensions began to build up again between the President and his foes both within and outside Congress. As the time under which Fujimori could enact laws through the powers delegated by Congress was about to expire, the President accelerated his legislative agenda. In the last month of 1991 he pushed through a marathon of executive orders, 126 in total. Many of them pertained to policy areas for which he had no mandate to legislate under article 188 (McClintock 1994: 311). In early 1992, Congress held a special session that amended or repealed twenty-eight executive orders. One of the most important amendments regarded the exclusion of the mining sector from the list of PEs to be privatized.[13]

On April 5, claiming that the legislators' narrow interests were putting national security at risk, Fujimori, with the support of the military, staged a coup by closing Congress, dismissing half of the Supreme Court, and suspending the constitution.[14] Most analysts tend to agree that Fujimori had no desire to negotiate with Congress and was just looking for an excuse to rule as he saw fit.[15] The coup effectively muted most organized opposition at home while receiving strong popular support. However, the government encountered unexpectedly strong criticism abroad. An estimated $400 million left the country and foreign governments and multilateral lending agencies stopped the disbursement of financial aid.[16] This sudden drop in financial resources made privatization all the more attractive. It could generate an independent source of income to bridge the fiscal gap in a more stable manner than short-term financial capital flows (Indacochea 1993: 68).[17] It is at this point that

Fujimori accelerated privatization plans. He put more PEs on the auction block and promised to reach complete state divestiture by 1995, hoping that in so doing he could regain confidence abroad (Burneo 1993: 29; Pinzás 1993: 7). In September 1992, Peru signed an accord with the IMF calling for the privatization of seventeen PEs by year's end, a goal that was not achieved. The following November, under pressure from the United States, the European Economic Community and some Latin American nations, the President convened a new Constituent Congress staffed by government backers.

Some sales were carried out in 1992 and continued at a greater pace in 1993 and 1994, although with less rapidity than originally planned. Aside from some technical and macroeconomic problems, part of the reason for the slow progress rested on the fact that the government's greatest concerns progressively shifted toward political goals. The capture of Shining Path leader Abimael Guzmán in September 1992 meant a severe blow to terrorism, and consequently enhanced Fujimori's public image. Strengthened by this success, the President concentrated his efforts on the approval of a new constitution aimed at strengthening executive authority and allowing him to run for a second consecutive term. The need to build public support for the President's political agenda inevitably resulted in increasing pressure upon Boloña to 'print money, grant subsidies and privileges to economic interest groups, and use foreign reserves to finance private and public-sector credit', forcing the minister to quit (January 1993). In Boloña's own words, it became impossible to serve 'a government with an eye on opinion polls and short-term popularity'.[18] In October 1993, a new constitution containing the provisions mentioned above barely passed a national referendum. None the less, its approval eased relations with the United States and multilateral agencies, which resumed their financial aid. At the end of 1993, government backers controlled Congress, allowing the President to ease his authoritarian stance.

By early 1995 Fujimori seemed to be firmly in control. The guerrilla movement appeared to be in disarray. The economy was also on its way to recovery posting strong growth rates, while inflation dropped to only one per cent a month (Figs. 5.1 and 5.2) and the fiscal deficit turned momentarily into a surplus between mid-1993 and mid-1994. The foreign debt rose in absolute terms, but so did international reserves (Fig. 5.3). With Peru back in good standing with the international financial community, both international lending and foreign capital returned in large amounts. Between the last quarter of 1994 and the first quarter of 1995 the privatization process slowed down considerably only to resume after Fujimori's re-election in April 1995. Although the President was no longer talking about complete state divestiture by year's end, the privatization process, despite several delays and setbacks, continued at a steady pace with a major transfer in electricity taking place by the end of that year (Edegel).

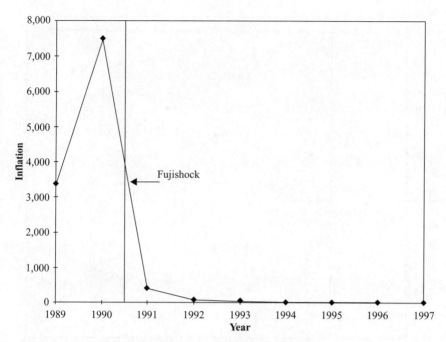

FIG. 5.1. Peru: Inflation Rate 1989–97
Source: World Bank, 1998.

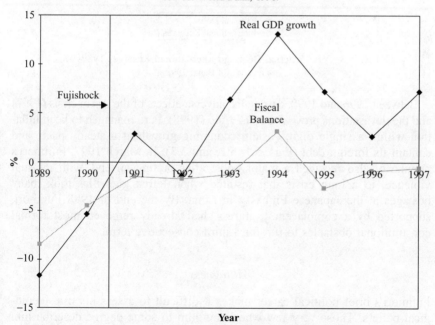

FIG. 5.2. Peru: Fiscal Balance (% of GDP) and GDP Real Growth (%) 1989–97
Source: World Bank, 1998.

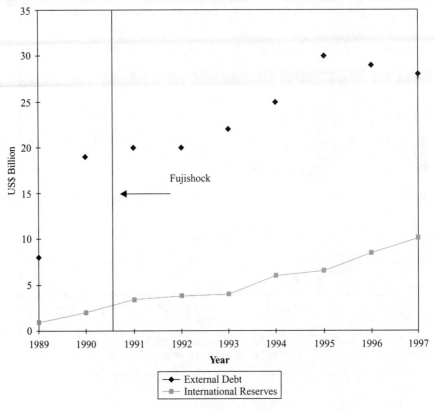

F IG . 5.3. Peru: External Debt and International Reserves 1989–97
Source: World Bank, 1998.

Between 1996 and 1998, despite the adverse effects of the Asian crisis (1997) and the devastations provoked by *El Niño* (1998), Peru managed to keep inflation within a single digit, sustain economic growth at a steady pace, and contain its foreign debt (Figs. 5.1, 5.2, and 5.3). In March 1997, Fujimori's popularity also received a major boost after putting an end, with unusual violence, to a long crisis that resulted when leftist guerrillas took many hostages at the Japanese Embassy in Lima. By the end of 1998 Fujimori, supported by a complacent Congress, had already removed most formal constitutional obstacles to run for a third consecutive term.

Willingness

Fujimori's brief political career makes it difficult to assess his true ideological beliefs. Those very few who know him to some degree describe him as a very reserved man with an ambiguous if not obscure personality whose life-time motto was, 'first act, then speak' (Jochamovitz 1994: 243). In the 1970s, Fujimori had sympathized with the left and particularly with Castro's brand of Communism after a brief teaching experience in Cuba in 1978. Later, in his successful attempt to become university chancellor, Fujimori lured the support of left-wing student and staff organizations to defeat his conservative contender.

His presidential campaign revived old themes stressing government intervention in the economy through development projects and other conventional supply-side economic policies. It is clear that, at least in early 1990, privatization had no affinity with Fujimori's ideological standings nor did he regard market economics as superior to state intervention. In fact, during the presidential campaign Fujimori rejected the privatization of PEs in strategic sectors and claimed that their losses could be cut simply by improving their management.[19] It is not accidental then that while in Argentina and Brazil market reforms were accompanied by privatization, although in varying degrees, the draconian Fujishock did not contemplate any privatization at all. Far from being a natural reformer, Fujimori was highly skeptical at best with regards to the need for privatizing. In the aftermath of the Fujishock, the President began to talk vaguely about the need for restructuring PEs prior to their sale. By late 1991, he became persuaded only after prolonged discussions with his closest advisers including Boloña, and representatives from the IMF, the World Bank, and the IDB, on the need for a complete state divestiture.[20] Still, in 1991 only two PEs were sold for a mere $2.6 million (Table 5.1).

In the years that followed, Fujimori used much of the ideological rhetoric to justify his state divestiture program, but it is quite clear that such arguments were dictated more by convenience rather than conviction. In fact, 'true believers' of the neo-orthodox approach in Peru often reiterated their suspicion that Fujimori's support for market-oriented policies was contingent upon his continued popularity.[21] These suspicions were strengthened again when the President, prior to the 1995 elections, unexpectedly accepted the proposal of his main presidential contender, Javier Pérez de Cuéllar, to postpone the privatization of Petroperú, which he had declared to be unavoidable only a year earlier. This decision was apparently dictated by Fujimori's concern over public opinion polls showing declining support for privatization (Fig. 5.4). The rhetoric seemed then to be changing again as the privatization of strategic companies was put into question.[22]

Privatization, along with a host of deregulation measures, was indeed used to discipline and intimidate labor unions, but this was more a function of practical rather than ideological considerations. Since the Velasco years, Peruvian organized labor in both urban and rural areas had increased in numbers and organizational skills which, depending on the economic sector, gave

TABLE 5.1. *Peru: Privatization Proceeds 1991–7*

Company	Sector	Date	Revenues (US$ million)	Investment Commitment
Sogewiese Leasing	Finance	Oct. 91	1.08	
Minas Buenaventura	Mining	Jul. 91	1.51	
Subtotal 1991			2.59	
Minera Condestable	Mining	May. 92	1.29	
Banco del Comercio	Finance	Jun. 92	5.37	
Gas Stations	Hydrocarbons	Dec. 92	39.32	
Enatru Buses	Transport	Aug. 92	11.07	
Inasa	Fishing-Shipyard	Jul. 92	0.81	2.00
Quimpac	Industry	Jul. 92	6.56	
Solgas	Hydrocarbons	Aug. 92	7.55	5.00
Minpeco	Mining	Sep. 92	4.10	
Hierroperu	Mining	Nov. 92	120.00	150.00
Quellaveco	Mining	Dec. 92	12.75	562.00
Subtotal 1992			208.82	719.00
Aeroperu	Transport	Jan. 93	25.41	30.00
Renasa	Industry	Jan. 93	2.93	
Petromar	Hydrocarbons	Feb. 93	200.00	65.00
Sudamericana de Fibras	Industry	Jul. 93	1.00	
Ecasa	Services	Jul. 93	14.66	
Ertur Arequipa	Transport	Aug. 93	0.25	
Eretru Trujillo	Transport	Aug. 93	0.23	
Banco Popular (Bolivia)	Finance	Nov. 93	6.15	
Petrolera Transoceanica	Transport	Nov. 93	25.25	
Cerro Verde	Mining	Nov. 93	35.45	485.30
Envases Sanmarti	Industry	Nov. 93	1.90	
Conversion Lima	Industry	Dec. 93	2.70	
Flopesca	Fishing	Dec. 93	0.78	
Subtotal 1993*			337.40	580.30
Chillon	Industry	Jan. 94	6.50	2.00
Cemento Yura	Industry	Feb. 94	67.10	5.00
Cerper	Services	Feb. 94	1.40	
Entel/CPT	Telecomm	Feb. 94	1,391.43	1,800.00
La Granja	Mining	Mar. 94	1.00	475.00
Lar Carbon	Industry	Apr. 94	1.25	
Chao Lands	Agriculture	Apr. 94	2.50	
Ilo Copper Refinery	Mining	Apr. 94	66.63	20.20
Cartavio	Industry	Apr. 94	4.40	1.00
Shares in Banco Nac.	Finance	Apr. 94	0.57	
Cementos Lima	Industry	Jun. 94	103.29	
Epsep (assets)	Fishing	Jun. 94	1.00	
San Antonio de Poto	Mining	Jun. 94	2.42	
Edelnor	Electricity	Jul. 94	176.49	150.00
Edelsur	Electricity	Jul. 94	212.12	120.00
Interbanc	Finance	Jul. 94	51.00	20.00
Sindicato de Inv. y Admon.	Services	Aug. 94	4.72	
Nuevas Inversions	Services	Sep. 94	2.56	

TABLE 5.1. *(cont'd)*

Company	Sector	Date	Revenues (US$ million)	Investment Commitment
Minera Tintaya	Mining	Oct. 94	277.00	85.00
Cajamarquilla Refinery	Mining	Nov. 94	193.00	50.00
Planta Chicama (Pescaperu)	Fishing	Nov. 94	8.90	
Cemento N. Pacasmayo	Industry	Dec. 94	19.60	
Pescaperu Chimbote	Fishing	Dec. 94	5.90	
Emsal	Industry	Dec. 94	13.90	
Pescaperu Mollendo	Fishing	Dec. 94	5.10	
Subtotal 1994			2,619.78	2,737.30
Pescaperu-La Planchanda	Fishing	Jan. 95	10.25	
Ertsa Puno	Transport	Jan. 95	0.15	
Pescaperu-Atico	Fishing	Jan. 95	7.50	
Tourists Hotels	Tourism	Jan. 95	36.16	22.90
Compl. Agroind. Chao	Industry	Jan. 95	8.80	
Entel Peru-Employees	Telecomm.	Jan. 95	19.70	
EPSEP-Assets	Fishing	Feb/Nov. 95	5.18	
Pesq. Grau-Compl. Paita	Fishing	Feb. 95	6.70	
Yacimiento Berenguela	Mining	Mar. 95	0.04	0.76
Tourists Hotels	Tourism	Mar. 95	17.50	4.24
Banco Continental	Finance	Apr. 95	255.70	
Cahua Generator	Electricity	Apr. 95	41.80	
Pesquera Samanco	Fishing	Jun. 95	4.70	
Cementos Norte Pacasmayo	Industry	Jun. 95	56.10	
Viviendas de Ilo, Mineroperu	Mining	Jul. 95	1.20	
Holding Continental	Finance	Aug. 95	32.00	
Lima Norte (Edelnor)	Electricity	Aug. 95		
Fertisa	Fertilizers	Aug. 95	3.10	
Pescaperu Norte Supe	Fishing	Aug. 95	5.60	
Siderperu (real estate)	Industry	Aug. 95	1.86	
Edegel	Electricity	Oct. 95	524.40	182.95
Enafer (real estate)	Railways	Oct. 95	0.24	
Cesur	Industry	Oct. 95	33.30	5.00
Epersur	Fishing	Nov/Dec. 95	0.70	
Ede-Canchay	Electricity	Dec. 95	10.30	
Subtotal 1995*			1,098.31	215.85
Empresa Minera del Centro	Mining	Jan. 96	0.21	
Siderperu	Industry	Feb. 96	188.80	30.00
Epersur	Fishing	Apr/Jun. 96	1.10	
Ede-Chancay	Electricity	Apr. 96		
Maquina Papelera Paramonga	Industry	Apr. 96	16.10	
Epsep	Fishing	May/Aug. 96	0.28	
La Pampilla	Oil	Jun. 96	180.50	50.00
Egenor	Electricity	Jun. 96	228.20	15.80

TABLE 5.1. *(cont'd)*

Company	Sector	Date	Revenues (US$ million)	Investment Commitment
Edecanete	Electricity	Jun. 96	8.60	
Telefonica del Peru (shares)	Telecomm.	Jul. 96	1,239.05	2.00
Centromin-Antamina	Mining	Jul. 96	20.00	2,506.50
Pescaperu Chimbote Sur	Fishing	Jul. 96	6.50	
Pescaperu Supe Sur	Fishing	Jul. 96	5.80	
Luz del Sur/Edegel	Electricity	Aug. 96		
Petrolube	Oil	Aug. 96	18.90	
Refineria de Ilo	Fishing	Aug. 96	0.80	
Industrial Cachimayo	Industry	Oct. 96	6.22	137.70
Etevensa/EGEC/Egenor	Electricity	Oct. 96		
Pescaperu Chancay	Fishing	Dec. 96	5.75	
Luz del Sur (shares)	Electricity	Dec. 96	162.48	
Pescaperu Huacho/ Callao N.	Fishing	Dec. 96	19.01	
Subtotal 1996*			2,626.96	2,742.00
Electro Sur Medio	Electricity	Feb. 97	51.28	
Yauliyacu	Mining	Feb. 97	8.05	110.20
Centromin-El Perro Ciego	Mining	Feb. 97	1.05	
Radio Panamericana	Telecomm.	Feb. 97	16.00	
Plesulsa	Industry	Mar. 97	1.16	
Modulo Trupal Paramonga	Industry	Mar. 97	14.60	
Pescaperu Tambo	Fishing	Apr. 97	5.80	
Pescaperu Callao Refiney	Fishing	Apr. 97	0.87	
Mineroperu-Las Huaquillas	Mining	May. 97	0.84	1.90
Mineroperu-La Granja	Mining	May. 97	7.00	25.00
Pescaperu-Ilo Sur	Fishing	May. 97	7.50	
Enata	Industry	May. 97	0.87	
Empresa Minera Mahr Tunel	Mining	Jul. 97	127.78	60.00
Pescaperu Tambo de Mora N.	Fishing	Aug. 97	0.10	
Enata (real estate)	Industry	Aug. 97	0.55	
Tierras Chavimochic	Agriculture	Aug. 97	0.24	0.06
Subtotal 1997			243.69	
TOTAL			7,137.55	4,063.69

Source: *Informativo COPRI*, 1997.
* Includes revenues from concessions, transfers, and capitalizations not shown in this table.

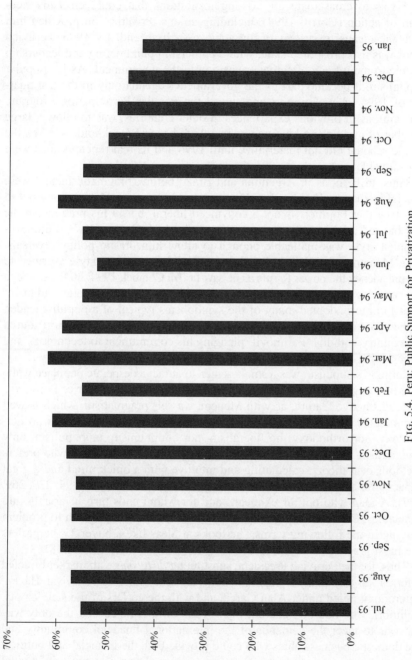

Fig. 5.4. Peru: Public Support for Privatization
Source: Apoyo, polls taken in Lima 1994–5.

it considerable bargaining power. It is clear that from the start that Fujimori's goal was to emasculate all existing institutions that could curb his freedom of action (Gorriti 1994), including unions. Privatization provided him with the means to systematically achieve such an end. By 1995, Peruvian labor was in a prostrated state, with membership plummeting and leadership unable to mount any effective opposition to the government. As for popular capitalism, it became part of the government's agenda only in the last quarter of 1994 when Fujimori announced the Popular Participation Program. The aim, as in previous experiences in other countries, was to allow a large number of middle and low-income people to become stockholders.[23] Yet, the whole scheme did not materialize until 1996 and its real repercussions were questionable, as we shall see later on.[24]

Thus, in Peru, as in Argentina and Brazil before, pragmatic factors were crucial in shaping Fujimori's willingness to privatize. As Boloña aptly put it, 'It's true that Fujimori is not a convinced liberal, but in his pragmatism he has backed a [privatization] programme that has seen results.'[25] Fujimori's populist style was malleable enough to allow him drastic policy reversals. Like Menem and Collor before him, Fujimori's messianic style ascribed to the presidency the power to rule as he saw fit (McClintock 1994: 304). Although not nearly as charismatic as Menem and Collor, during his campaign and thereafter Fujimori adopted many of the symbolisms typical of a populist leader. If the 'productive revolution' was Menem's favorite theme, Fujimori toured the country with his 'Fujimovil' pledging his commitment to technology and honesty, but hardly moved beyond that.

Fujimori's populism was a smokescreen to attract a desperate populace while avoiding any clear commitment. Setting aside political rhetoric, Fujimori's most distinctive feature, as with Menem, was his pragmatism, which is well documented. In an interview, the President bluntly stated, 'there is no heterodoxy, nor orthodoxy; no liberalism, nor communism, or populism, only pragmatism'.[26] Fujimori consistently portrayed himself as a man who prefers methods over theory, calculating and intuitive with a quick mind and a great capacity for adapting to changing circumstances (Jochamowitz 1994: 239, 269, 277). A man who optimizes means and for whom ends turn invariably into timetables. One of his biographers described Fujimori's approach to problem solving in the following terms, 'he looks at ideas like a buyer . . . he prefers the most practical over the idealistic ones' (Jochamovitz 1994: 278).

Thus, for the Peruvian President, substituting *dirigismo* with market-oriented reforms was essentially a pragmatic issue, an issue of political survival. Having heterodoxy failed under Alan García and with the coffers of the state empty, Fujimori, who had no coherent plan of his own, realized that the only way out was to meet the demands of the international financial community and the domestic business elites who could provide both the financial and political support to rescue the country from its collapse. For a pragmatic individual like Fujimori switching from state-led development to neo-orthodoxy was not a problem as long as his change of heart could bring tangible benefits.[27]

The first two years of Fujimori's stabilization policies concentrated on achieving the following macroeconomic goals (COPRI 1993*b*: 1):

1. Peru's reinsertion into the international financial community,
2. Creating a free and competitive market through the dismantling of tariff barriers,
3. Luring back foreign investment,
4. Enhancing the competitiveness of the domestic market in order to better compete in international trade,
5. Obtaining an Extended Fund Facility with the IMF,
6. Restructuring the country's debt payments with the Paris Club's creditors and reducing Peru's external debt under the auspices of the Brady Plan.

That pragmatic factors were the driving force behind Peru's privatization was stressed by COPRI's Executive Director Carlos Montoya (1992: 53) when he stated, 'the philosophical debate [over privatization] ended a while ago'. Although the privatization program came into play later in Peru, if compared to Brazil, it was part of a much more radical vision of state reform. Fujimori's team began from the premise that the private sector was much better suited than the state for promoting economic development. COPRI's (1994: 24) official statements in this regard left no doubt:

1. The restructuring seeks to direct the State's resources towards a better fulfillment of its essential responsibilities of providing adequate health, education, justice, security, and basic infrastructure.[28]
2. The private sector is accorded the responsibility of producing the goods and services demanded.

Privatization served as the means through which the state would pass on the entrepreneurial initiative to the private sector. Thus, similarly to Menem, Fujimori and his economic team aimed at complete state divestiture arguing that there were no 'sacred cows'. To give a clear signal to domestic and foreign investors the President reiterated time and again that, by the end of his term, he would have sold 'all or nearly all PEs'.[29]

In more detail, privatization was instrumental for the government (COPRI 1993*b*: 26) in: (1) increasing both domestic and foreign investment; (2) earning income in foreign exchange; (3) increasing employment levels; (4) generating growth in aggregate production; (5) satisfying people's demand for quality goods and services; (6) increasing competition; and (7) creating the basis for fiscal revenues.

Although Montoya repeatedly stressed that the government's goal in privatizing was not financial gain but rather the redefinition of the state role in the economy, in practice, as in the previous two cases, the greatest incentive behind state divestiture was to cut fiscal losses and rationalize state operations (Burneo 1993: 41; Indacochea 1993: 63). According to Minister of Mines

Peru

TABLE 5.2. *Peru: Real Price Index of PEs' Services (July 1985 = 100)*

Service	Units	1985 July	1987 December	1989 December	1990 March
Drinking water	20 m3	100	96.8	48.8	17.9
Domestic Kerosene	Liter	100	25.2	34.8	17.3
Electricity	100 kw/h	100	48.4	19.4	6.5
Telephone	150 Ilds	100	87.2	40.9	7.4

Source: Kuczynski, Pedro Pablo and Flipe Ortiz de Zevallos, *Respuestas para los 90s*. Lima: Apoyo, 1990

and Energy Daniel Hokama, 'It [took] an enormous effort to rationalise public companies, reduce staff and make them viable for sell-off.'[30] Although small in comparison to the state sectors of Argentina and Brazil in terms of absolute numbers, Peruvian PEs played an important role in the domestic economy.[31] They accounted for 15 per cent of GDP, 28 per cent of total exports, 26 per cent of total imports, and employed between 2.0 per cent and 2.6 per cent of the economically active population (between 170,000 and 200,000 people), with assets (excluding financial institutions) estimated to be $5.5 billion (Alvarez Rodrich 1992: 21; Kuczynski and Ortiz de Zevallos 1990: 30).[32] The state sector had monopoly control over electricity, oil, communications, gas, and had substantial market shares in mining (35 per cent), foodstuff, and fishery production (Burneo 1993: 23). However, by the time Fujimori assumed office, Peruvian PEs were in a state of prostration and were plagued by many of the problems observed in other countries, i.e. chaotic growth, lack of clear goals and priorities, little cooperation among themselves and other bureaucratic organizations, inadequate government supervision and internal controls, a cumbersome decision-making process, continuous managerial turnover, overstaffing, corruption, and political meddling (Kuczynski and Ortiz de Zevallos 1990: 30; Alvarez Rodrich 1992: 23; Burneo 1993: 18–20; Indacochea 1993: 56–57). Non-financial PEs's current account earnings shrunk from 25.3 per cent of GDP in 1985 to 12.4 per cent of GDP in 1988 (Kuczynski and Ortiz de Zevallos 1990: 31). This trend, as noted in Chapter 2, was heavily dependent upon the steep deterioration of the real prices charged by PEs, which took place in the second half of the 1980s (Table 5.2). By 1988, the losses of Peru's top PEs amounted to an estimated $2.7 billion (Table 5.3). In July 1991, 'Eleven of the country's 12 largest companies were owned and operated by the state. Heavily overstaffed, protected from international competition and often incompetently managed by the recipients of political favors, the companies . . . were costing a bankrupt nation $2.5 billion a year.'[33] Through privatization the government not only expected to receive badly needed revenues but hoped to

TABLE 5.3. *Peru: Net Revenues or Losses of the Principal Non-Financial State Companies in 1988 (US$ Million)*

Company	Amount
Petroperu	−1,334.7
Electroperu	−45.7
Electrolima	−15.2
Centromin	−70.1
Mineroperu	−156.8
Tintaya	5.8
Entel	−11.0
Aeroperu	−21.6
CPV	−714.3
Siderperu	−31.6
Sociedad Paramonga	2.0
Pescaperu	5.4
Enci	0.7
Ecasa Sedapal	−54.5
Rest	−290.3
TOTAL	−2,713.0

Source: Kuczynski, Pedro Pablo and Flipe Ortiz de Zevallos, *Respuestas para los 90s*. Lima: Apoyo, 1990.

create the basis for future ones since the new private owners were going to pay those taxes that many PEs had long stopped honoring (COPRI 1993*b*: 10).

As in Argentina, after taking office the government began to charge high prices while letting many PEs in public utilities deteriorate in performance in order to build popular consensus for their sell-off (Burneo 1993: 9).[34] Since PEs were undercapitalized and chronically lacking steady cash flows, privatization was perceived as the only way to modernize run-down infrastructures and meet consumer demands, which would save the government a lot of money at a time of severe budgetary constraints (Alvarez Rodrich 1992: 15). As a COPRI (1993*b*: 16) document put it, 'given the incapacity of the State to invest, the decision is whether we would like to have services or not'.[35] As noted above, privatization was regarded by administration officials as a key element to improving resource allocation. State divestiture, it was argued, enhanced economic efficiency since former PEs would become more productive and competitive once under private control because they had to obey the iron laws of the market. Government officials also saw privatization as a means to enhance professional standards in the private sector as a result of increased competition with foreign firms (COPRI 1993*b*: 16).

Additional factors encountered in the two previous cases, like the improvement of the business climate, did play an important role. With Peru's

TABLE 5.4. *Peru: Prices of the Latin American Financial Debt in the Secondary Market, 1985, 1986, 1989 (Cents per dollar in nominal value)**

Country	1985 July	1986 July	1989 July
Argentina	60	63	13
Brazil	75	73	21
Colombia	81	80	64
Mexico	80	56	40
Peru	45	18	6
Venezula	81	80	36

Sources: Kuczynski, Pedro Pablo and Felipe Ortiz de Zevallos, *Respuestas para los 90s.* Lima: Apoyo, 1990.
* Auction price.

country-risk rating at an all-time low, a radical privatization program was a tangible way to lure otherwise wary foreign and domestic investors. The situation was dramatic as can clearly be seen from the value of the government debt paper traded in international markets, which shows how Peru was in a much worse position than Argentina and Brazil (Table 5.4). Foreign investment in 1991 had been a meager $108 million (COPRI 1993*b*: 9). For Minister Hokama, attracting foreign investment through privatization was an initiative vital to reviving key economic sectors like mining, where Peru holds a comparative advantage to other Latin American countries, and telecommunications and transportation, both of which were lucrative markets that had been lagging behind technologically for lack of investments.[36] Strengthening domestic capital markets via privatization was also a motive to implement the policy, but appeared to be a minor one.

To what extent Fujimori used state divestiture to reward supporters remains unclear since there is little evidence to back up such a possibility. Unlike Menem, the Peruvian President did not ally himself with big domestic economic groups and instead dealt with them from a position of strength. He appeared to owe few favors to the traditionally powerful in Peru, thus, 'giving him a free hand in policy-making.'[37] His decision to overturn the sale of Aeroperú (see later), first awarded to a domestic consortium but later sold at a second auction to Mexican investors, would seem to give support to the previous statement. Perhaps, his aloof approach may have been based on the rational calculation that, being Peruvian investors too small to play a meaningful role in the large scale privatizations to come, he could afford to keep them at an arm length. In the end, Fujimori, albeit reluctantly, perceived privatization as a necessary means to alleviate the state finances for which there was little, if any alternative (Wise 1994: 94).[38] After all, government officials argued, many PEs would close anyway (COPRI 1993*b*: 11).

Opportunity

When privatization was announced in 1991, it began within a very adverse investment environment (in many ways worse even than in Argentina in 1989), due to the complications added by the terrorist threat. As a financial newsletter stated at the time, 'Who will invest in this terror-infested, low exchange-rate, hugely high interest-rate, volatile environment?' (quoted from Wise 1994: 94). However, the Fujimori administration turned a bad situation into one of opportunity (Indacochea 1993: 67). Despite the chaotic situation in which the country found itself in 1990, Peru's vast and untapped mineral resources made it a prime candidate for investments in this sector.[39] The fishing, oil, and telecommunication industries could also represent good deals for investors. Arguing that only through foreign capital could such sectors be revitalized, the government (unlike Brazil but similar to Argentina) moved quickly to revamp existing legislation (Indacochea 1993: 66). The Foreign Investment Promotion Act established non-discriminatory treatment toward foreign investors. Foreigners were allowed to invest in almost all economic sectors and repatriate all profits and capital equipment as they saw fit. The Private Investment Growth Act protected domestic and foreign entrepreneurs from sudden changes in the rules of the game and established a system of dispute resolution. This provision also applied to privatized companies. Peru subscribed to a number of international accords, including the Agreement for Constitution of the Multilateral Investment Guarantee Agency (a World Bank institution), the Investment Insurance with the Overseas Private Investment Corporation, and the Convention on the Settlement of Investment Disputes.

Moreover, trade reforms, like the already mentioned reduction of the number of tariffs to essentially two (15 per cent and 25 per cent) and the substantial cut in port related service duties and costs, were aimed at facilitating investments in capital equipment and bring efficiency into the economy through increased competition. A simplified tax system and the complete liberalization of foreign exchange transactions were all measures geared in the same direction. The government also scrapped previous labor codes and replaced them with new ones that made the labor market more flexible and better suited to business needs. In addition to these initiatives, the Fujimori administration began to reform legislation in a number of key economic sectors. The government substantially deregulated the financial system, lifted restrictions on foreign participation in banking, gave Peruvians and foreigners equal access to domestic loans, and permitted the creation of private management pension funds. The Agrarian Reform Act was revoked and a new law was enforced promoting private investment in agriculture and agroindustrial activities. The administration also lifted all restrictions on fishing activities and investments in the mining sector as well.[40] The government monopoly over oil exploitation and marketing was gradually phased out.

In terms of a favorable public mood, Vargas Llosa's crusade in the late 1980s set the stage for a heated debate over market reforms, including privatization (Alvarez Rodrich 1992; Cameron 1994). Even prior to the 1990 elections many conservative analysts advocated that the state should abandon all productive activities and concentrate only on the provision of basic services, defense, and justice (Portocarrero 1992*b*: 66). Actually, for some, a de facto privatization of many areas traditionally ascribed to state intervention had been taking place since 1988 as many businesses flourished to make up for the deterioration of public services, like in education and mail delivery (Webb 1991). It is also clear that many among the Peruvian elites had come to the conclusion that such a policy was a *sine qua non* condition to rescue the country from its disastrous situation. If indeed Fujimori's victory can be easily interpreted as a vote against Vargas Llosa's radical proposals, it is also true that the hard-core FREDEMO supporters represented the most influential elements of Peruvian society. For instance, the bulk of the private sector endorsed Vargas Llosa's presidential bid and, in varying degrees, his reform agenda. Thus, in Peru we find a stronger ideological right than in Argentina and Brazil. Its opinion leaders, namely Vargas Llosa and Hernando de Soto, dominated the political debate almost unopposed until early 1990 and were instrumental in paving the way for Fujimori's subsequent policies (Durand 1997). The new President, a man quite keen on public opinion trends, could not escape survey research data indicating unequivocally that the country's socioeconomic elites, who had voted against him but whose consent he needed to rule, were still supporting market reforms even after Vargas Llosa's defeat.[41] For instance, a public opinion poll commissioned in 1990 found that 65 per cent of its sample favored privatization and 92 per cent favored the opening up of the economy (Kuczynski and Ortiz de Zevallos 1990: 33, 26). Another survey showed that the great majority of those interviewed believed that private companies paid more taxes, contributed more to the country, were more efficient, and were less corrupt than PEs (Fig. 5.5). Later polls, taken in March 1994, unequivocally showed that support for privatization increased with socioeconomic status (Fig. 5.6).

In the previous paragraphs, we saw foreign pressure on Fujimori to promote privatization. Such pressure was exercised not only through threats but came also accompanied with tangible incentives, both financial and technical. The World Bank and the Japanese government gave Peru technical assistance grants worth $30 million and $3 million respectively in order to hire foreign and domestic consultants to prepare the privatization of PEs. In fact, depending on the PE, consulting fees, promotion programs, and other expenditures linked to a transfer totalled, in some cases, up to $2 million.[42] The United Nations Development Programme (UNDP) provided technical assistance and administered foreign assistance funds to guarantee transparency (COPRI 1993*b*: 8). Some foreign governments provided additional financial assistance

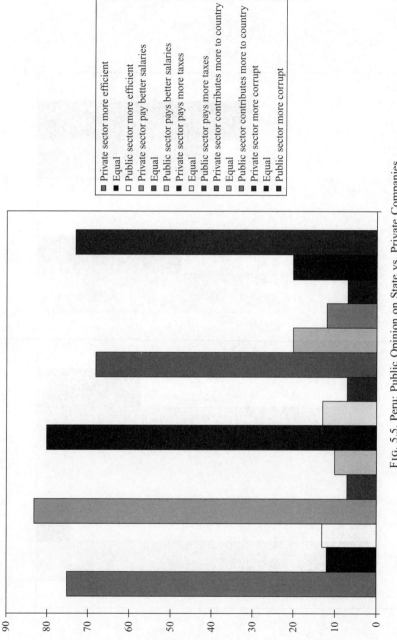

Legend:
■ Private sector more efficient
■ Equal
□ Public sector more efficient
■ Private sector pay better salaries
■ Equal
■ Public sector pays better salaries
■ Private sector pays more taxes
□ Equal
■ Public sector pays more taxes
■ Private sector contributes more to country
■ Equal
■ Public sector contributes more to country
■ Private sector more corrupt
■ Equal
■ Public sector more corrupt

FIG. 5.5. Peru: Public Opinion on State vs. Private Companies
Source: Kuczynski and de Zevallos (1990).

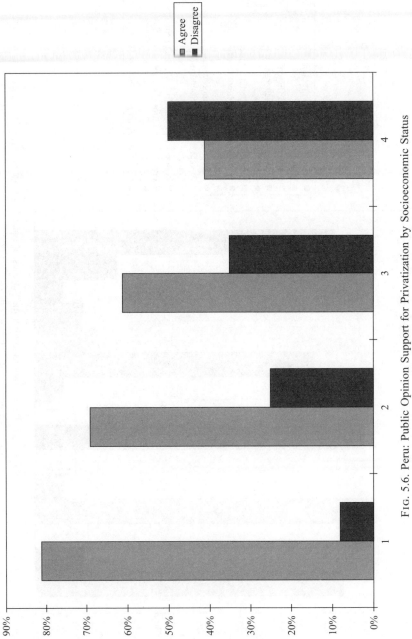

FIG. 5.6. Peru: Public Opinion Support for Privatization by Socioeconomic Status
Source: Apoyo, polls taken in Lima in March 1994 (from left to right highest to lowest income quartile).

either through long-term loans or ad hoc donations. The World Bank and the IDB also helped technically and financially in supporting early retirement schemes.

Summing up, by the time the privatization program was announced, a favorably disposed public mood and foreign support were present. Although initial conditions were extremely negative, the Fujimori administration seized the initiative and made a deliberate effort to turn things around by creating a number of incentives appealing to investors, particularly foreign ones.

Implementation

Government Capabilities

The cohesiveness of the Fujimori administration was very strong. More so than under Presidents Belaunde and García, the decision-making process under Fujimori was extremely centralized in the executive branch and the President consistently showed an almost obsessive, hands-on style regarding even the most obscure details. Fujimori's authoritarian style mirrored his tendency to trust only a handful of close associates, among whom members of the Japanese–Peruvian community were highly visible.[43] According to some analysts, until mid-1998, all major decisions, including privatization, were made by the President in consultation with his 'kitchen cabinet' made up of the President's brother; Mr Montesinos, the head of the intelligence forces; General Nicolás de Bari Hermoza Ríos, the Army commander; and, occasionally, a few ministers.[44] Fujimori made no excuses for his autocratic style, which he justified in the following terms, 'I think most people want a strong executive power which exercises its mandate to the fullest, that uses all its faculties to achieve important objectives. Here there is a chairman of the board or a general manager who controls, supervises, prosecutes and tries to ensure things go well.'[45] At the time a foreign newspaper described the President in these terms, 'Fujimori practices a very personal style of rule, he likens himself to a Japanese corporate boss, not a politician, and takes pride in micro-managing ministers, whose budgets he tracks down in detail on a personal computer.'[46]

In the economic realm, first Boloña, and later on Camet and Jorge Baca adopted the same economic philosophy at the MEF, which assured a fairly good level of policy continuity over a prolonged period of time. Although Camet and Baca seemed to be more willing than Boloña to tolerate Fujimori's pressure to ease certain aspects of macroeconomic policy to help him weather specific political circumstances, their effort to preserve monetary stability and continue market reforms, including privatization, remained steady over time.

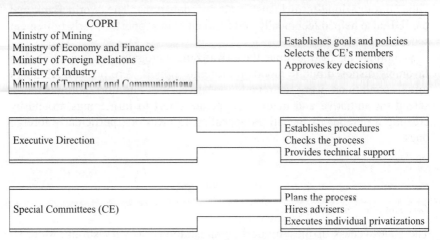

FIG. 5.7. Peru: Organization of Privatization Process
Source: COPRI, *Privatization Report*, 1994.

As for COPRI, the privatization agency, it was completely dependent upon presidential approval for any sale but, by the same token, was sheltered from the pressure of other institutions like Congress and the judiciary as well as interest groups. COPRI's board of directors, appointed in November of 1991, was staffed by the ministers of energy and mines, economics and finance, foreign affairs, industry, and transportation and communications (Fig. 5.7). An executive directorate, first headed by Carlos Montoya, a Peruvian business consultant who had worked on the privatization of Aerolíneas Argentinas, was then entrusted with the responsibility of guiding, managing, and coordinating the privatization process. The micro-management of individual privatizations was assigned to ad hoc committees, or CEPRIs, which came into effect in February 1992.[47] While working in close association with COPRI's executive directorate, each CEPRI had some degree of discretion in organizing and carrying out the transfer of the PEs assigned to it.[48] This also implied hiring auditors, consultants (technical, financial, and legal) and investment bankers when considered appropriate (COPRI 1993*b*: 6). Thus, the Peruvian privatization process tried to take advantage of previous experiences. For instance, in its general organization, it opted for a flexible approach to privatization based on specialized, ad hoc committees, rather than using a standard model as done by Collor in Brazil.[49]

However, unlike Brazil, which could count on the long-time expertise developed by BNDES, Peru (like Argentina) found itself ill-prepared to design and carry out a far-reaching privatization program. As observed at the time:

Part of the problem is the lack of a large team to push economic reform forward. Only a handful of people is helping [the] . . . minister of economy, a much smaller group than those who pursued reform in Mexico, Argentina, or even Bolivia. The small size of the group has also hindered implementation of legislation already passed —the government's labour law reform is an example—because there is nobody to draft the rules'[50]

To overcome these objective difficulties, the Fujimori administration recruited most of COPRI's staff from the private sector. Several IMF and World Bank missions also helped in advising the Peruvian government.[51] Even so, the Peruvians had the smallest staff working on privatization in comparison with Argentina and Brazil.[52] The absence of a well trained technical staff at the lower levels of the public bureaucracy was even more acute.

Although, as we have seen, the decision-making process was highly centralized, issues concerning bureaucratic cooperation did arise. It was not uncommon to hear discrepancies among ministers regarding the goals and means of privatization affecting their areas. Nor did all CEPRIs seem to abide by the same strategies, plans, priorities, and criteria (Alvarez Rodrich 1992: 36). Consequently, occasional conflicts arose between individual CEPRIs and COPRI's executive directorate on the issues just mentioned, which were invariably resolved in favor of the latter.[53]

In terms of state institutions, Peru presented the most overt effort by an executive to eliminate political opposition to its reforms. Fujimori's boldness in closing Congress and purging part of the Supreme Court and lower courts which stood in the way of his agenda shows a strong dose of arrogance and disregard for the democratic process (Cameron 1994). In November 1991, while addressing the country on television, the President left no doubt as to his true intentions with regard to the opposition within and outside Congress when he stated, 'Nothing, nobody can stop the government's program.'[54] It is this aggressive approach that led some analysts to the conclusion that, 'to an even greater degree than García, President Fujimori governed as a dictator—even prior to his assumption of dictatorial powers in April 1992. Whereas on most decisions García was constrained at least somewhat by his political party, Fujimori was not' (McClintock 1994: 307). Indeed, despite much fanfare in portraying himself as a new brand of leader, 'in Fujimori's authoritarian streak many [saw] the stamp of the traditional Latin American leader'.[55]

As noted earlier, in the beginning all important legislation regarding market reforms was enforced through executive orders, which were issued on several occasions even in open violation of the powers that Congress had delegated to the executive.[56] All these structural reforms were eventually incorporated into the new constitution ratified by the Constituent Assembly in late 1992, thus preventing any further legislative debate. In fact, more so than in Argentina and Brazil, the Fujimori administration purposely avoided any debate about the criterion according to which privatization was to be pursued (Alvarez Rodrich 1992: 38; Pinzás 1993: 7; Gonzales de Olarte 1994: 13).

The Supreme Court and lower courts after the self-coup of 1992 were staffed with people sympathetic to the government's political agenda, very much like in Argentina. When, for instance, in 1997 three members of the Constitutional Tribunal objected to Fujimori's intepretation of the 1993 Constitution that he could run for a third consecutive term, he dimissed them by the stroke of a pen.[57] Understandably, this type of behavior discouraged the opposition from going to court to challenge COPRI's decisions. The Congress ensuing from the self-coup, dominated by Cambio '90 and the Nueva Mayoría (an independent group), both supporting Fujimori, also posed no threat to the government's agenda. A congressional commission in charge of economic matters was allowed to oversee the implementation of market reforms but, as in Argentina, it was relegated to monitoring functions and had no veto powers.[58]

As Alvarez Rodrich pointed out at the time, the President, 'has been good at destroying the bad; but he has been less effective at creating something to take its place'.[59] However, this is not completely accurate. During his term Fujimori did pay particular attention to the strengthening of one institution, the national intelligence, not merely to fight terrorism but also to keep his political foes in check through intimidation.[60] It is no accident that in a public opinion poll carried out in Lima, people ranked Mr Montesinos, the intelligence services chief, as the most powerful man in the country after the President.[61]

Speed was a primary concern in the Peruvian privatization program. As Montoya (1992: 54) acknowledged, one of COPRI's top priorities was to transfer:

the most important companies as quickly as possible. This did not mean that [such companies] were the first to be transferred, because the process, which is the most important thing, takes time. However, we gave priority to the important companies . . . and accomplish through it a more profound privatization process yet. We do not see strategic companies that should stay in government hands.[62]

COPRI's hastiness in rushing privatization through as quickly as possible was dictated, similarly to the Argentine case, by the need to earn credibility with foreign investors, comply with the agreements subscribed with multilateral lending agencies, outpace political opposition, and obtain badly needed cash receipts (Pinzás 1993: 7).

Political Responses

Peru's case, in terms of political responses, presents some of the features also encountered in Argentina and Brazil. On the one hand, like Menem, Fujimori during the 1990 campaign promised to revive redistributive policies only to enact Vargas Llosa's neo-orthodox recipe in an even harsher form. However, while Menem was quite skillful in creating a new conservative coalition behind his reforms to replace the center-left parties and unions that had supported his presidential bid in 1989, Fujimori only actively sought a close alliance with the military. The Peruvian center-right parties against which he had run, but whose program he implemented, had no other option but to support Fujimori and go along with his agenda. Although early in his first term the President gave some members of AP and other conservative parties cabinet posts, it became clear as time went on that his intention was to attract their voters. Indeed, as the major parties were rapidly losing mass popular appeal by the time he assumed office in 1990, Fujimori did not have any reason to create formal alliances. Instead he proceeded to diffuse the class-based polarization that had characterized Peruvian society under the traditional party system in order to enhance his own standing before the electorate. As time went on the Peruvian President, like Menem in Argentina, managed to bring together a disparate electoral support encompassing both upper and lower social classes by defeating inflation and terrorism, resuming economic growth, and dispensing ad hoc compensations to specific groups of voters who suffered the most as a result of the implementation of market reforms (Stokes 1996; Roberts and Arce 1998). The retention of the electoral support among the poor was in fact achieved through anti-poverty programs to ameliorate their dismal status. The *Fondo Nacional de Compensación y Desarrollo Social* (FONCODES) created in 1991, and the *Instituto Nacional de Infraestructuras Educativa y de Salud* (INFES) poured hundreds of millions of dollars into highly visible and politically manipulated programs aimed at enhancing Fujimori's re-election prospects in 1995 and again in 2000. Such programs were centralized within the presidency and well publicized in the media to project Fujimori as the sole benefactor of the needy. As Fujimori had expected, this strategy paid high dividends in his re-election bid in April 1995, when he won an outright majority (64.4 per cent) at the first round of balloting, leaving his toughest contender, Pérez de Cuéllar, with only 21.8 per cent.[63] Not surprisingly, the areas that FONCODES and INFES had targeted later displayed strong electoral support for the President (Roberts and Arce 1998; Weyland 1998).

Moreover, from a personality point of view, Fujimori had a poor attitude toward compromises of any kind. He simply expected opposition parties and interest groups to comply with his reform agenda. As his former minister Carlos Amat y León aptly put it, 'Fujimori does not have a mind-set to work through consensus' (Jochamowitz 1994: 297). However, unlike Collor in Brazil, Fujimori could count on the military's support in his feud with an opposition front made up by traditional parties and organized labor that, by 1991, was quite divided within itself and held in low esteem by the public (McClintock 1994: 310). In fact, not only did the self-coup of April 1992 encounter no resistance, but thereafter it had the effect of debilitating even more organized opposition to the President. The opposition's weakness along with his success in fighting inflation and terrorism explain why Fujimori, despite the lack of solid party backing and grass-root support, was able to win re-election in April 1995. He captured an outright majority in Congress, by then reduced to only one chamber following the enactments of the 1993 Constitution, as his movement Cambio '90/Nueva Mayoria gained 67 seats against 53 for the opposition.[64]

The President's disregard for party politics was quite evident when, in commenting on the unexpected wide margin of his 1995 electoral victory, he stated:

I hereby affirm that today political parties ended. The government works without political parties. It is a direct democracy where the executive is in contact with the people without the mediation of political organizations that here, like elsewhere, have failed. This is a model that has proven to be efficient in solving problems, a democratic model that I would not be surprised, modesty aside, if it were reproduced in other countries.[65]

Interestingly enough, although the privatization process in Peru started slowly, it went largely unopposed until the mid-1990s (Pinzás 1993: 8). The various delays and setbacks privatization suffered were due primarily to exogenous factors and the indecisiveness of the President, at different points in time. This explains why Fujimori did not bother to create a pro-privatization coalition or to explain to the public why privatizing was good business for the country.[66] Moreover, even the most credible opposition leader, the independent Javier Pérez de Cuéllar, while arguing that the government should improve the performance of PEs before deciding to privatize them, was not opposed to the policy in principle.[67]

As the 1995 election drew to a close, and the privatization of Petroperú became a campaign issue, Fujimori, like Menem, tried to please voters by earmarking privatization revenues to combat poverty and build public infrastructure. In March 1994, the IMF agreed to let the Peruvian government use up to $876 million from privatization revenues for the ends mentioned above.[68] Such revenues came in very handy during the 1995 electoral campaign to fund Fujimori's public works.[69] In typical populist fashion, the President personally inaugurated hundreds of schools, water supply projects, bridges, and so forth, 'with an eye on the television cameras, the other on his popularity ratings'.[70]

Fujimori's lack of an actual public relations effort can also be explained by the fact, as noted earlier, that Vargas Llosa had already prepared the ground for acceptance of privatization as a necessary measure (Durand 1997). Large and medium-sized business groups, which had embraced Vargas Llosa's reform agenda, became strong supporters of Fujimori's policies after he took office. Peru's National Confederation of Private Entrepreneurial Institutions (Confederación Nacional de Instituciones Empresarias Privadas, CONFIEP), the peak business organization in the country, repeatedly endorsed the government's efforts. One of CONFIEP's past Presidents, Jorge Camet, eventually replaced Boloña at the helm of the MEF, testifying to Fujimori's willingness to intensify ties with domestic capital (Wise 1994: 99). In fact, it appears clear that Fujimori's approach to business was more like that of Collor rather than Menem, in that the Peruvian President avoided forging any overt alliance that would limit his freedom of action. Indeed, aside from the appointments of some of its members to cabinet posts, CONFIEP did not seem to have any institutional input in the administration's economic program.[71] In general, there was little criticism of the President from businessmen.[72] Some remained fearful that Fujimori's pragmatism could induce him to resort to populist measures for electoral reasons. Others thought that actually Fujimori's reforms were not going far enough, fast enough. As for privatization, CONFIEP advocated that some of its revenues be utilized to promote exports and to finance the elimination of administrative taxes.[73] None the less, despite being relegated to a minor role, CONFIEP and large economic groups were quite appreciative of Fujimori's ability to defeat terrorism and bring economic stability (Kay 1995). Thus, it avoided any serious confrontation with the government.

APRA, AP, and the Popular Christian party, the traditional parties of Peruvian politics, failed to develop any credible opposition, let alone alternative, to Fujimori's policies. As a result, none of the candidates of such parties for the 1995 presidential elections were able to garner even 5 per cent of the total vote required to retain legal status, which some interpreted as a clear sign of their eclipse.[74]

If party opposition was ineffectual, so was that of unions, at least until 1995, due to a variety of reasons. First, the government lost no time in resorting to massive layoffs to break strikes in PEs where workers opposed privatization (Pinzás 1993: 8). The same fate was shared by many state managers, for example in Petroperú and mining PEs, when they resisted the way their firms' restructuring process in preparation for privatization was handled.[75] Second, strikes proved ineffective as a bargaining tool since the deep recession caused by the Fujishock brought demand to an all-time low in PEs operating in the public utility and manufacturing sectors. Third, the fact that the private sector was itself laying off workers in the aftermath of the Fujishock acted as a deterrent against strike activity in many PEs, since many workers saw no alternative to their jobs were they to lose them because of a union walkout. Fourth, in 1993, when the economy began to recover, unions faced a new situation. The need to survive in a market that was increasingly more competitive led many employers to improve productivity (by using idle capacity and acquiring new technology) and cut costs (by laying off redundant workers), thus further deterring workers from strike activity.[76] Not surprisingly, according to Minister Hokama the number of strikes in 1992 dropped to their lowest level in ten years. Fifth, new legislation deregulating the labor market also gave a severe blow to the union movement.[77]

To swallow the bitter pill, like in Argentina and Brazil, the government set aside in some cases 10 per cent of available shares from PEs being privatized for workers and management but such a program only worked in a few PEs. In most cases, though, shares were undersubscribed (Table 5.5). In fact, this was little compensation for those who lost their jobs. Between 1991 and 1994, the government cut the workforce in PEs from about 140,000 to 50,000 people. In Centromin alone total employment went from 18,500 to 13,000 people.[78] In many cases, employees were fired outrightly, but in others the COPRI and individual PEs, as a form of incentive, set up early retirement schemes (Table 5.6). Later COPRI, under the advice of the World Bank and the UNDP, studied the possibility of retraining redundant workers; but due to the lack of funds, things remained at the planning stage up until 1995.

The labor leadership was also slow in grasping how things had changed (Balbi 1997). Many union leaders were ideologically committed to full employment at any cost, when it was quite clear to all that many PEs were overstaffed and badly in need of drastic restructuring both in terms of management and labor utilization. The tough stance by some union leaders toward privatization actually played into the government's hands. Both the administration and the television networks and printed media sympathetic to Fujimori portrayed unions in the public sector as having contributed to the economic disaster of the García administration through their unrealistic demands. Union leaders were charged with preserving the privileged status of public employees at a time when everyone was asked to make sacrifices. This anti-labor campaign thoroughly discredited the unions from the public sector in the eyes of a large strata of public opinion, which saw layoffs as a necessary cost involved in government restructuring (Pinzás 1993: 8). As in Argentina, unions in the public sector were left completely isolated in their quest for survival.

Only in 1996 did labor opposition begin to experience some success in slowing down the government's privatization effort, as workers of Petroperú and Centromin went into prolonged strike activities. In the case of Centromin, the union's task was in part helped by a drop in the international prices for copper and gold, which negatively affected the sale of several of Centromin's mines. As for Petroperú, its union Fenpetrol staged several strikes in early 1996 to protest the layoff of 1,250 workers at the Talara refinery, and coupled with other strikes by miners and health-care workers. Yet, what helped Fenpetrol in the following years was that many of the political and strategic concerns linked to the war with Ecuador that had stalled its sale in 1995 continued. Thus, only a handful of assets were sold thereafter despite repeated government promises that a complete divestiture was just a matter of months.

TABLE 5.5. *Peru: Employee Participation in the Privatization Process 1991–7*

Company	Activity	Date of Sale	Sale Price (US$ thousand)	Shares Transferred	Number of Employees	% of Shares Bought by Employees	Sale Price to Employees (in soles)
Quimpac	Chemicals	Jul. 92	6,064.1	100%		7.4	405.3
Enatruperu	Urban transport	Jul./Aug. 92	11,066.5	452 buses	1,450	100.0	11,066.0
Solgas	LPG distribution	Aug. 92	7,331.2	100%		4.1	215.4
Hierroperu	Mining (iron ore)	Nov. 92	120,000.0	100%		1.6	1,944.80
Aeorperu	Transport	Jan. 93	54,000.0	72%		7.2	2,312.40
Ertur Arequipa	Urban transport	Aug. 93	248.8	63 buses	185	100.0	248.7
Eretru Trujillo	Urban transport	Aug. 93	225.5	68 buses	155	100.0	225.5
Petrolera Transoceanica	Oil Cargo	May 93	25,175.0	100%	Assets		71.2
Cerro Verde	Mining (copper)	Oct. 93	37,000.0	Concession		8.4	3,088.70
Cerper	Sanitation	Feb. 94	1,601.0	100%		10.0	160.1
Interbanc	Finance	Jul. 94	51,000.0	100%		9.5	4,832.9
Emsal	Salt producer	Dec. 94	14,680.0			5.0	730.0
Ertsa Puno	Urban transport	Jan. 95	151.0	12 buses + assets		100.0	151.2
Entel Peru	Telecommunications	Jan. 95		9.6 million shares	1,954	100.0	19,800.0
Holding Continental	Finance	Aug. 95	4,000.0	2.1 million shares	1,178		
Vivienda de Ilo, Mineroperu	Mining	Jul. 95	1,200.0	100%	50	100.0	
Lima Norte (Edelnor)	Electricity	Jul. 95	9,200.0	24 million shares			
Siderperu (real estate)	Industry	Jul./Aug. 95	1,500.0	Assets			
Siderperu	Industry	Feb. 96	2,600.0	Shares		3.5	
Ede-Chancay	Electricity	Apr. 96	114,000.0	Shares		0.7	
Luz del Sur/Edegel	Electricity	Aug. 96	104,000.0	114 million shares			
Etevensa/EGEC/Egenor	Electricity	Oct. 96	47,000.0	86 million shares	308		

Source: Informativo COPRI, 1997

TABLE 5.6. *Peru: PE's Employment Reduction Ensuing from Privatization 1991–7*

Company	Employees Prior to Privatization	Employees who left without incentives	Employees who left with incentives	Employees in Aug. 91	Estimated workforce after privatization	% of reduction ensuing from privatization
Mineroperu	5,000	1,100	500	3,300	3,300	34.0
Centromin	18,500	2,000		1,500	1,500	91.89
Tintaya	1,500		200	1,200	1,100	26.67
Hierroperu	3,200			3,200	1,500	53.13
Siderperu	5,600		1,500	4,100	2,600	53.57
Paramonga	4,500	200	300	4,000	2,500	44.44
Petroperu	9,700	450		9,250	7,250	25.26
Pescaperu	3,720		620	3,100	2,910	21.77
Enci	3,100	100		3,000	1,000	67.74
Ecasa	4,300	400	1,660	2,300		100.00
CORPAC	3,893		331	3,562	2,692	30.85
Entel	10,400	363	1,539	8,498	6,200	40.38
Aeroperu	2,160	135	25	2,000	1,650	23.61
Sima	1,500	150		1,350		100.00
Electroperu	2,400		950	1,450	1,450	39.58
Enafer	5,996			5,996	3,496	41.69
CPV	1,350		200	1,100	100	92.59
Banco de la Nacion	9,800		1,400	8,400	7,000	28.57
Banco Continental	5,800	400	400	5,000	3,000	48.28
Banco Hipotecario	1,500		350	1,150	650	56.67
Interbanc	3,000		400	2,600	2,000	33.33
Banco Popular	3,700		1,000	2,700	2,300	37.84
Banco Agrario	5,500		2,000	2,500	2,500	54.55
Banco de Vivienda	1,350		200	1,150	625	53.70
Banco Industrial	3,450	1,250		2,200	1,600	53.62
Banco Minero	1,600	108	1,314	178	70	95.63

Source: COPRI, 1997.

The Shining Path and other guerrilla organizations, which were of course against everything the Fujimori administration represented, were unable to sabotage the 1995 elections, contrary to their promises. With most of their leadership behind bars and calling for the end of the armed struggle, the guerrilla movement lost much of its credibility and retreated to remote areas where they could do little to disrupt economic activity.[79]

In all fairness, some academic think-tanks, the newspaper *República*, and the weekly magazine *Caretas*, were among the steadiest critics of the administration's privatization policies. However, their misgivings seemed to have no effect on the way the divestiture process developed. Moreover, Fujimori and Montesinos showed in general little tolerance for criticism when it exposed the administration's most hidden flaws. In 1997, the government withdrew Peruvian citizenship from Baruch Ivcher, an Israeli-born business-man, whose television station had produced damaging investigative reports implicating government officials. Subsequently, the Fujimori administration made ample use of tax audits to intimidate its critics.

The military, as noted earlier, was the only institution whose support Fujimori courted to consolidate his power. To do so, he divided and conquered it by marginalizing those officers who resisted the President's politicization effort while rewarding those who accepted his patronage. Systematically, Fujimori began to retire opposing officers while lifting all restrictions on tenure limits, which allowed him to keep loyalists in place as long as he saw fit. General Hermoza Ríos, who sided with the President, played a pivotal role during the 1992 coup, and made sure that the military squarely backed the President at crucial times (Kay 1995). Then, when Fujimori felt strong enough and sensed that Hermoza Ríos's support within the military had decreased, he forced him into retirement in mid-1998 and replaced him with an officer close to Montesinos. In so doing, Fujimori eliminated the pos-sibility that the military, the only institution still possessing a fair degree of autonomy, could challenge his authority.

This does not mean that members of the military stood idle during the President's first term with respect to what was to be sold off. In October 1994, the Minister of Defense Victor Malca Villanueva publicly asked for its involvement in deciding which PEs were to be privatized. This meant includ-ing a representative of the armed forces in COPRI. However, Fujimori quickly replied that the military was already being consulted before decisions were made and the whole issue was dismissed.[80] In effect, the military took a low profile on privatization. Fujimori had already rewarded the armed forces in many ways. Early on, he granted them complete jurisdiction over the fight against terrorism and openly defended them against charges of brutality raised by human rights organizations, foreign governments, and the press. In late 1995, the government approved a broad amnesty absolving military and police personnel of all possible charges in their fight against subversion. Moreover,

Fujimori also provided new military equipment and financial incentives in the form of lucrative contracts to carry out large public projects to the Army Corps of Engineers, in unprecedented quantity.[81]

Military concerns about privatization began to truly materialize as a result of the border conflict between Peru and Ecuador in January 1995. Even pro-government analysts who had been supportive of the state divestiture process began to question the privatization of Petroperú, since that company produced special fuels for military purposes that were likely to be discontinued under private ownership. Privatization critics also added that since Petroperú had begun its restructuring in 1992, the company's performance improved significantly, leading to profits of $29 million in 1992, $85 million in 1993, and about $200 million in 1994.[82] Thus, the argument went, not only was Petroperú a company of strategic importance but also one that could generate important revenues if well managed, which were good reasons to keep it under government ownership. As the conflict escalated in intensity so did such misgivings. Sensing the shift in momentum, the President temporarily halted the privatization of Petroperú, which was originally scheduled for December 1994. After Fujimori's re-election, the government opened a 'technical debate' regarding the privatization of Petroperú but, as Hokama clearly pointed out, the only thing that was going to be discussed was the best way to sell the company, not whether the PE should be sold in the first place.

The uneasiness created by the conflict with Ecuador also raised the question of the increasing involvement of Chilean investors (Chile, along with Ecuador, has traditionally been Peru's main foe) in the privatization process of sectors that all of a sudden became again of 'strategic importance'. As a result, plans for the concession of several ports to Chilean businessmen were cancelled. Further questions were also raised about some companies awarded to Chilean investors like those handling oil tankers (see below) and electricity distribution.[83] As these concerns became widespread within the pro-government press as well, Fujimori addressed them in a typical pragmatic fashion, as we shall see later in the case of the electricity sector. This spared the President from forcing an issue that could break a relationship with the military that since 1990 had been mutually beneficial. In turn, the top brass of the armed forces did not attack the President overtly, preferring to settle matters behind close doors.

Technical Difficulties

As was the case in Argentina, Peru did not have a government agency with a considerable amount of expertise in privatization. This lack of experience resulted in a slow, and at times, rocky start which hampered the early efforts of the Fujimori administration in state divestiture. Montoya himself publicly acknowledged that the initial optimism was unwarranted and that the government overestimated its capacity to handle sales. As with the previous two cases, as Montoya admitted, the government decided to transfer the most important PEs as quickly as possible.[84] However, the pressure to sell quickly, virtually at any cost, put less emphasis on other considerations that proved crucial. COPRI's goals often appeared unclear, eventually compounding technical problems both before and after the transfer (Pinzás 1993: 8; Burneo 1993: 37; Gonzales de Olarte 1994: 13). Contrary to official statements, it did not look as if COPRI had a clear criteria in setting up the timetable regarding which PEs were to be privatized first (Indacochea 1993: 69). Although initially the idea was to start by privatizing large PEs, in reality due to technical problems rather than any adherence to macroeconomic theory the first divestitures involved small companies. Fujimori himself well synthesized the various problems that delayed the privatization process:

The first is that some of these public companies required some adjustments to be made by the state in order to sell a more profitable company. Point two, privatizations require large resources because each one of the medium-sized and large state companies had very heavy liabilities in the way of debt and excess personnel. Third, legislation did not permit adequate privatization. We, therefore, had to introduce modifications to the laws which related to the functioning of these companies within the framework of a market economy. Fourth, nobody was going to invest in Peru while there was terrorism—nobody—particularly foreign companies. The larger companies which are the most profitable—telecommunications and electricity—would have sold but at very low prices. Shares in the telephone company a year and a half ago cost 40 centavos; today [September 1993], the price is seven soles.[85]

Indeed, financial problems were serious. Of the 250 PEs the government owned in 1991, only 217 remained after some consolidations. The government had majority stakes in most of them. When the privatization program started, 58 companies were in a state of liquidation or were closed, leaving only 159 PEs in operation, 60 of which were very important.[86] However, most of the latter group had large debts, which made it difficult to sell them. In many successful cases, the government had to clear these debts prior to the transfer.[87] In other cases, this was more difficult. For instance, one factor complicating the sale of Petroperú was the debt of several of its subsidiaries, like AIGE, which alone had liabilities of $176 million.[88]

The managerial restructuring of many PEs turned out to be a thorny issue. The initial intention of COPRI was to sell whenever possible without restructuring, but when it was clear that no takers would come forward COPRI was either forced to close the company or embark on a drastic cost-cutting reorganization, mostly by shedding labor, to make the firm a good investment prospect. Coincidentally, the financial performance of PEs like Aeroperú, Banco Popular, and Peruinvest, among others, deteriorated after their privatization was announced (Alvarez Rodrich 1992: 46). To put them back into shape, however, took more money and time than initially expected, leading, as in Argentina and Brazil, to postponements of several deadlines. Another issue forcing restructuring was the pollution affecting many of Petroperú's oil fields as well as the mines controlled by Centromin. Many foreign companies interested in Petroperú's refineries and Centromin's mines had stricter environmental rules than the Peruvian government and were scared away by the amount of pollution they found. An internal study by COPRI estimated that clean-up operations in Centromin alone was going to cost up to ฿00 million.[89] Although plans were at an advanced stage to devise an environ-mental program, only in April 1995 was the government able to secure some funds from the IDB ($350,000) and the Norwegian government ($500,000) to clean up the Mantaro valley.[90]

The problem of overcoming skepticism from foreign investors was serious. Peruvian entrepreneurs were active in the purchase of small-and medium-sized PEs (Table 5.7), but for large companies in need of sophisticated technology foreign capital was essential. Because of Peru's tarnished reputation, COPRI's officials had to travel abroad on numerous occasions to lure investors' inter-est. For example, Hokama asserted that Peru was able to charge much less for the same type of mines than its neighbor Chile due to the country's high risk rating.[91] As the country's macroeconomic and political situation improved, the trend began to reverse itself, with larger and more serious foreign firms coming to Peru looking for business than had initially been the case.[92] Foreigners at times formed consortia with local groups, although this was not required by law, as had been the case in Argentina.

In terms of methods, COPRI primarily adopted public auctions to: (1) sell shares; (2) sell assets; and (3) award concessions. Direct negotiations took place whenever public auctions failed. However, while Argentina, and more so Brazil, accepted different types of government domestic and foreign debt as currencies, Peru did so only on five occasions up to mid-1996.[93] There were several factors limiting debt-equity swaps. First, creditor's lawsuits and Peru's lengthy negotiations to reschedule its foreign debt made it difficult for the Fujimori administration to get waivers from creditors to buy back its com-mercial debt on the secondary market and use discounted debt for privatiza-tion currencies. Second, many foreign investors expressed an unwillingness to purchase Peru's debt titles fearing that their bid might be unsuccessful, and they would get stuck with them.[94] Third, ironically as Peru's debt value appreciated steeply over time, going from $.04 in 1990 to $.57.5 in 1998, the use of debt titles became less attractive for investors since they had become too expensive.[95] Fourth, Fujimori himself was very reluctant to use debt-equity swaps; partly because public opinion polls showed that the majority of the people surveyed were against (Alvarez Rodrich 1992: 41). Using cash pre-vented the opposition from accusing him of 'selling out' the public property, as had happened in Argentina and Brazil. Another of Fujimori's concerns was that such transactions were highly volatile and easy prey for financial speculations.[96] In the end, Hokama announced that COPRI was not going to use debt-equity swaps for the sale of Petroperú.[97]

TABLE 5.7. *Peru: Comparison Between Base and Sale Price 1991–7*

Company	Date	Base Price (US$ million)	Sale Price (US$ million)	Shares Transferred in %	Type of Sale	Buyer
Sogewiese	Jun. 91	1.00	1.10	15.00	LSE*	25 buyers
Minera Buenaventura	Jun. 91	2.30	1.51	9.20	LSE	50 buyers
Minera Condestable	May 92	2.20	1.29	80.20	LSE	Serfin Group
Banco del Comercio	Jun. 92	5.40	5.37	59.00	LSE	Carlos Manrique (CLAE) and Bankers Trust
Gas stations	Jun/Dec. 92	25.00	39.32	100.00	Public auction	Local investors
Enatru buses	Jul. 92	13.00	11.07	452 buses	Public auction	Employees
Inasa	Jul. 92	1.70	0.81	89.35	LSE	Arinco and employees
Quimpanc	Jul. 92	6.00	3.86	60.00	LSE	Institutional investors
			2.10	32.66	LSE	Institutional investors
Solgas	Aug. 92	6.10	7.33	100.00	LSE	Inter Gas, Grunter, Eternit, Ostusar, Transporte Cural, Lima Gas
Minpeco	Sep. 92	5.50	4.10	100.00	LSE	Kibo Group (Brazil)
Hierroperu	Nov. 92	22.00	120.00	100.00	International auction	Shougang (China)
Quellaveco	Dec. 92	9.00	12.00	Concession	Public auction	Aerovias de Mexico, Serminco and Dora Zapata de Papini
Aeroperu	Jan. 93	41.00	54.00	72.15	Public auction	Foreign investors (Shell, Chilean Co., etc.)
Renasa	Jan. 93	2.20	2.93	92.90	LSE	Institutional investors
Petromar	Feb. 93		200.00	Concession	International auction	Petrotech International Co. (USA)
Sudamericana de Fibras	Jul. 93	1.00	1.00	30.14	Public auction	Mittlenwald (Uruguay)
Ecasa	Jul. 93		14.66	100.00	Public auction	SUNAD
Ertur Arequipa	Aug. 93		0.25	63 buses	Public auction	Employees
Eretru Trujillo	Aug. 93		0.23	68 buses	Public auction	Employees
Banco Popular-Bolivia	Nov. 93	3.50	6.15	100.00	Public auction	Financiera de Credito del Peru and others
Petrolera Transoceanica	Nov. 93	21.50	25.18	100.00	Public auction	Glenpoint Enterprises Inc. (Panama) and Ultragas (Chile)

TABLE 5.7. (cont'd)

Company	Date	Base Price (US$ million)	Sale Price (US$ million)	Shares Transferred in %	Type of Sale	Buyer
Cerro Verde	Nov. 93	30.00	35.00	Concession	Public auction	Cyprus Minerals (USA)
Envases Sanmarti	Nov. 93	1.90	1.90	100.00	LSE	Envases Nishli
Conversion Lima	Dec. 93	0.70	2.70	100.00	LSE	Empresa Industrial Suizo Peruana
Flopesca	Dec. 93		0.78	100.00	Public auction	Paita
Chillon	Jan. 94	3.40	6.50	Assets	LSE	Rubini Group
Cementos Yura	Feb. 94	30.00	67.10	100.00	Public auction	Gloria Group
Cerper	Feb. 94	1.60	1.40	100.00	Public auction	Drokasa
Entel-CPT	Feb. 94	546.00	1,391.43	35.00	Public auction	Consorcio Telefonica Peru led by Telefonica de Espana
La Granja	Mar. 94		1.00	Option rights	Public auction	Camblor Inc. (Canada)
Lar Carbon	Apr. 94		1.25	10.93	Public auction	Cementos Lima
Ilo Copper Refinery	Apr. 94	65.00	65.00	100.00	Public auction	Southern Peru Copper Co.
Cartavio	Apr. 94	6.60	4.40	100.00	LSE*	Fierro Group
Cementos Lima	Jun. 94	76.3	103.27	48.89	Dutch auction	Different investors
San Antonio de Poto	Jul. 94		8.63		Public auction	Local consortium Begsa and Andes Co.
Edelnor	Jul. 94		176.49	60.00	Public auction	Inversiones Dismillima
Edelsur	Jul. 94		212.12	60.00	Public auction	Consortium of Ontario Hydro (Canada) and Cilquinta (Chile)
Interbanc	Jul. 94		51.00	99.90	Public auction	International Financial Holdings
Sind. Inver. y Admin.	Aug. 94		4.72	4.33	Public auction	Association comprised of SIA and Cementos Lima
Nuevas Inversiones	Sep. 94		2.56	4.69	Public auction	Association of NISA and Cementos Lima
Minera Tintaya	Oct. 94		277.01	100.00	Public auction	Magna Copper Co Global Magma Ltd. (USA)
Cajamarquilla Refinery	Nov. 94		193.00		Public auction	Consortium of Cominco (Canada) and Marubeni Co. (Japan)
Planta Chicama (Pescaperu)	Nov. 94		8.90		Public auction	Sindicato Pesquero
Pescaperu Chimbote	Dec. 94		59.30		Public auction	International Fish Protein
Emsal	Dec. 94		14.68		Public auction	Quimica del Pacifico

Pescaperu Mollendo	Dec. 94	5.10		Public auction	Sindicato Pesquero
Pescaperu La Planchada	Jan. 95	10.25	12 buses + assets	Public auction	Employees and Productos Pesqueros Peruanos
Ertsa Puno	Jan. 95	0.15		Public auction	Employees
Pescaperu-Atico	Jan. 95	7.50		Public auction	SIPESA
Tourist Hotels	Jan. 95	17.50	Assets	Public auction	
Compl. Agroind. de Chao	Jan. 95	8.80	Concession	Public auction	Promotora Mercantil
Entel Peru-Employees	Jan. 95	19.70		Preferred shares	Employees
Epsep-Assets	Feb/Nov. 95	5.18	Assets	Public auction	Andina de Desarrollo, Frigorifico de Huaraz, Andimar (employees)
Pescaperu Grau-Compl. Pita	Feb. 95	6.70	Assets	Public auction	Pesquera Hayduck
Yaciminetos de Berenguela	Mar. 95	0.00	Option rights	Public auction	Keppes, Cassiday & Associates (USA)
Banco Continental**	Apr. 95	255.70	60.00	Public auction	Banco Bilboa Vizcaya (Spain) and others
Cahua Generator	Apr. 95	41.80	60.00	Public auction	Sindicato Pesquero del Peru
Pescaquera Samanco	Jun. 95	4.70	100.00	Public auction	Casamar
Cementos Norte Pacasmayo	Jun. 95	56.10	100.00	Dutch auction	Individuals
Vivienda de Ilo, Mineroperu	Jul. 95	1.20	100.00	Public auction	Employess
Holding Continental	Aug. 95	32.00		Public auction	Employees
Lima Norte (Edelnor)	Aug. 95			Public auction	Employees
Fertisa	Aug. 95	3.10	Assets	Public auction	Sudamericana de Fibras
Pescaperu Norte Supe	Aug. 95	5.60	100.00	Public auction	Productos Pesqueros Peruanos
Siderperu (real estate)	Aug. 95	1.86	Assets	Public auction	Pacifico S. Wong, employees
Edegel	Oct. 95	524.40	60.00	Public auction	Edegel Inc (USA), Inverandes (Argentina), Wiese, Grana y Montero
Enafer (real estate)	Oct. 95	0.24	Assets	Public auction	Incasur, Asociacion Comerciantes Minoristas Exterior Mercado Cent.
Cesur	Oct. 95	33.30	100.00	Public auction	Consocreio Gloria
Epersur	Nov/Dec. 95	0.70	100.00	Public auction	Consorcrio Uniagro, Inversiones El Pacifico
Ede-Canchay	Dec. 95	10.30	60.00	Public auction	Inversiones Distrilima

TABLE 5.7. *(cont'd)*

Company	Date	Base Price (US$ million)	Sale Price (US$ million)	Shares Transferred in %	Type of Sale	Buyer
Empresa Minera del Centro	Jan. 96		0.21	Concession	Public auction	Grupo Bonaventura
Siderperu	Feb. 96		188.80	96.46	Public auction	GS Industries Inc. (USA), Wiese, Stanton Funding (USA), employees
Epersur	Apr./Jun. 96		1.10	100.00	Public auction	Pesquera Hayduck
Ede-Chanchay	Apr. 96			0.72	Public auction	Employees
Maquina Papelera Paramonga	Apr. 96		16.10	100.00	Public auction	Abitibi Price (Canada)
Epsep	May/Aug. 96		0.28	Assets/Vehicles	Public auction	El paicifco EIRL, Frigorifico de Jaen, Frigorifico de Celendin, Wiese
La Pampilla	Jun. 96		180.50	60.00	Public auction	Respol (Spain), YPF Argentina, Mobil (USA), Crana y Montero, Wiese
Egenor	Jun. 96		228.20	60.00	Public auction	Dominion Energy (USA), Marc T. Cox (USA), Thomas Farrel
Edecanete	Jun. 96		8.60	100.00	Public auction	Luz del Sur
Telefonica del Peru (shares)	Jul. 96		1,239.05	65.00	International auction	Institutional investors
Centromin-Antamina	Jul. 96		20.00	Concession	Public auction	Inmet Mining Co. and Rio Algom Ltd. (Canada)
Pescaperu Chimbote Sur	Jul. 96		6.50	100.00	Public auction	Pesquero Mistiano
Pescaperu Supe Sur	Jul. 96		5.80	100.00	Public auction	Pesquera del Pacifico Centro
Luz del Sur/Edegel	Aug. 96				Sale of pref. shares	Employees
Petrolube	Aug. 96		18.90	100.00	Public auction	Mobil (USA)
Refineria de Ilo	Aug. 96		0.80	100.00	Public auction	Pacific Oil
Industrial Cachimayo	Oct. 96		6.22	100.00	Public auction	Empresa Yura
Etevensa/EGEC/Egenor	Oct. 96				Sale of preferred shares	Employees

Enterprise	Date	Price	% / Type	Method	Buyer
Pescaperu Chancay	Dec. 96	5.75	100.00	Public auction	Pesquera Nemesis
Luz del Sur (shares)	Dec. 96	162.48	100.00	International auction	Institutional investors
Pescaperu Huacho/Callao N	Dec. 96	19.01	100.00	Public auction	Pesquera Maria del Carmen, Pesquera Esmeralda, Del Mar, Pacific Oil
Electro Sur Medio	Feb. 97	51.28	98.20	Public auction	Consorcio HICA
Yauliyacu	Feb. 97	8.05	99.81	Public auction	Gubins
Centromin-El Perro Ciego	Feb. 97	1.05	Concession	Public auction	Gubins
Radio Panamericana	Feb. 97	16.00	100.00	Public auction	Delgado Parker
Plesulsa	Mar. 97	1.16	100.00	Public auction	Consorcio Coril
Modulo Trupal Paramonga	Mar. 97	14.60	100.00	Public auction	Empresa Manufacturera de Papeles y Caryones
Pescaperu Tambo	Apr. 97	5.80	100.00	Public auction	Servicios Tecnicos EIRL
Pescaperu Callao Refinery	Apr. 97	0.87	100.00	Public auction	Pesquera Alonso
Mineroperu-Las Huaquillas	May. 97	0.84	100.00	Option rights	Vegsa/Andescorp
Mineroperu-La Granja	May. 97	7.00	100.00	Option rights	Cambior Inc. (Canada)
Pescaperu-Ilo Sur	May. 97	7.50	100.00	Public auction	Pesquera Rubi, Pesquera Hayduck
Enata	May. 97	0.87	100.00	Public auction	Tabacalera del Sur
Empresa Minera Mahr Tunel	Jul. 97	127.78	100.00	Public auction	Volcan Compania Minera
Pescaperu Tambo de Mora N.	Aug. 97	0.10	Assets	Public auction	Pesquera Maria Milagros
Enata (real estate)	Aug. 97	0.55	Assets	Public auction	Alberto Ortega, Municipalidad de Jaen, Negocios Intercontinentales
Tierras Chavimochic	Aug. 97	0.24	Assets	Public auction	Small investors

Source: COPRI, *Informativo COPRI*, 1997.
* Lima Stock Exchange.
** Base price was not available after April 1995.

As in Argentina and in Brazil, COPRI established quantitative and qualitative targets in some public utilities. Some CEPRIs demanded investment requirements in the mining sector, but this was not done on a consistent basis, as many PEs were sold without such clauses. Yet, some observers doubted the government's ability to make sure that such provisions be respected.[98] Unfortunately, such prediction turned out to be true in several cases. The most typical one was the Chinese Shougang Co., which acquired Hierro Peru in 1992. Although Shougang had pledged, in the transfer agreement, to invest $300 million in three years, by 1996 the funds actually disbursed were only $35 million. This led to lengthy renegotiations between the government and the private company. In 1996, Shougang settled for $137 million of new investments to be completed by 2000, although many remained skeptical that even that reduced target would be actually met.[99] In 1997 and 1998, as a result of falling prices for many privatized mines, several companies, like Cambior and Inmet Mining of Canada and Anglo American, decided to drastically reduce their projected investments.[100]

Market failures were frequent, derailing many transfers. On several occasions the government simply was unable to privatize for lack of offers. The gold deposit Yauricocha was put up for sale three times before being sold in late 1997. Even then, there was only one bidder. In other cases, COPRI approved the sale despite receiving only one offer. A typical case among others (Cerro Verde, Ilo Refinery, Envases Sanmarti) was the sale of the concession for the B-Band cellular service outside of Lima. In May 1998, after several postponements, the only bidder that qualified, GTE of the United States, decided to withdraw. At the last minute, the US-Peruvian consortium made up by BellSouth and Tele 2000 (which had failed to qualify) was urged by the government to make a last-minute offer, which was only $100,240 over the $35 million minimum price.

Another problem was that domestic entrepreneurs proved unable to participate in complex privatizations requiring large capital and sophisticated technology, leaving foreigners as the only option (Portocarrero 1992). Yet, even when foreigners seemed to be the solution to the problem, occasionally they faded away. The Mexican company Peñoles inexplicably pulled out from la Oroya smelting complex in August 1998, after placing the winning bid ($185 million) only a few months earlier.

On at least four occasions, transfers were marred by clear irregularities according to COPRI's own account (Minpeco, gas stations, Petrolera Transoceanica, Banco del Comercio). The government also made last minute changes in the rules, in open violation of the terms of sale, to rescue a privatization, as it was the case in the just mentioned B-Band case as well as in Solgas, Banco del Comercio, and Aeroperú. In other cases, failures resulted from exaggerated base prices (Minpeco, Petrolera Transoceanica, Solgas, Cementos Lima, and Cartavio), forcing the government to underestimate prices in later auctions. However, this did not seem to matter much, since COPRI's President candidly stated, 'we are going to sell, no matter what the price'.[101]

Severe constraints were also posed by the Lima stock exchange at the outset of privatization. In 1990, the stock market value was $800 million, or 2 per cent of GDP. By mid-1997, though, it had reached a capitalization of $19.5 billion, a dramatic increase that financial experts ascribed to the privatization program (Cabello and Shiguiyama 1998: 32, 39). In fact, privatization helped the stock market develop by bringing in large capital inflows from abroad (in 1996 foreign investors accounted for 22 per cent of trading volume) and substantially expanding the number of stocks offered. Privatized companies such as Telefónica del Peru, Luz del Sur, and Cementos de Lima became trend-setting blue chips in the Lima market. To facilitate the process, as had happened in Argentina, the government enacted in 1991 a new law aimed at protecting the rights of both domestic and foreign investors, creating market regulations conforming to international standards, and forcing quoted companies to disclose their financial status. For its part, COPRI designed a two-pronged approach that tried to make the Lima stock market part of the process when sizable PEs were involved. In the first stage of the privatization, the controlling stakes of a given PE were awarded to the strategic investor that would take over management. In the second stage, the remaining shares still in government hands were offered to both institutional investors as well as small ones through a popular capitalism scheme called *Participación Ciudadana*. The first company to experiment this scheme was Cementos Norte Pacasmayo. Cabello and Shiguiyama (1998: 35) reported that between 1994 and 1995, the government sold 17 per cent of the company to 18,400 small investors, many of whom were first time shareholders. The same authors also estimated that privatization, through the selling of shares in one form or another, was responsible for 400,000 new domestic retail investors.

None the less, popular capitalism failed to really take off as advertised. As mentioned earlier, the pool of potential investors was to begin with limited. The public's poor understanding of financial markets and lack of trust in this type of investment instrument did not help either. Moreover, on occasions, governmental exigencies pushed the *Participación Ciudadana* into a low priority as it happened in 1996. In July of that year, to diffuse popular opposition against the sale of 23.6 per cent of its remaining shares in Telefónica del Peru, the government planned to offer to the public a sizable amount. However, due to strong international demand, at the last minute the government decided to substantially cut the amount set aside for small domestic investors (a record 263,000) who had already placed advance orders. The event turned out to be an embarrassment for Fujimori as it clearly showed where his true priorities rested.[102]

Deregulation was another technical issue that sprang up from the process. As in other Latin American countries, monopolistic/oligopolistic conditions were pervasive in Peru due to the small size of the economy and the limited access to technology (Gonzales de Olarte 1994; Boloña 1996). However, it soon appeared clear that COPRI paid little attention to the possibility of monopolistic/oligopolistic markets ensuing as a result of privatization. The Comité de Libre Competencia (CLC), the regulatory institution that the government created for this purpose, started to operate late and quite ineffectively. In the case of monopolies transferred to the private sector, for example in the telephone and electricity sectors, regulatory agencies began to effectively operate only after privatization and, despite their much vaunted independence, they were actually staffed with people linked to the government and the new private owners.

As regulatory problems began to surface in the second half of the 1990s, and criticism became more and more widespread with regard to the high prices charged by new monopolies in public utilities, the Fujimori administration tried to remedy the situation in a piecemeal fashion. In the electricity sector for example, Congress passed a new amendment to the existing law in November 1997 that, without consulting the new owners of power companies, gave the government 'golden shares' to veto any changes of ownership that were believed to jeopardize national security. Fujimori justified the change in the rules of the game with the fact that two of the largest electricity operators in Peru, Endesa of Spain had acquired an important share in Enersis of Chile since privatization, possibly creating problems of vertical and horizontal integration. The sector's regulatory agency also began to assert a more aggressive stance on tariff rates, which prompted private companies to complain that the executive branch was appeasing popular dissatisfaction with electricity charges for political, rather than technical reasons.[103]

In the telecommunications sector, changes in existing contracts were less abrupt, as the government and Telefónica del Peru agreed to end the monopoly status of the Spanish-owned company a year ahead of schedule. Under heavy pressure to deregulate the sector, the government offered Telefónica a three-year reprieve to lower tariffs if profits rose after the opening of the market to new competitors. For its part, the telephone company pledged $2.5 billion in new investments to be completed by 2002. I will now turn to a brief analysis of the most important privatizations by sector.

Transportation. In this sector, the privatization of the national airline Aeroperú was an example of improvisation and flawed procedures. A few hours prior to the auction the government issued a legal ruling through which Aeroperú would continue to be the national airline for eight more years, a period during which the government granted exclusive concession to international routes, the company's most valuable assets. The winner of the first auction was Naviera Santa, a domestic consortium, but its closest competitor, Aeroméxico, presented an appeal charging that Naviera Santa had actually not complied with all the prerequisites. COPRI accepted the appeal and a week later nullified the auction. In January 1993, COPRI made a new call for tenders in which Aeroméxico won the bid for 72 per cent of Aeroperú's shares paying $54 million (after deducting debts it came down to $25.4 million), which was about $13 million above the minimum price. Naviera Santa, whose bid was about $9 million lower, charged COPRI of unfair practices, but to no avail.

In the case of urban transportation, the government sold the assets through a public auction to the employees (Table 5.5), who set up several new companies. However, the lack of regulation after privatization, while increasing the availability of services, also led to chaos since the new companies chose the routes they found most profitable while ignoring others. As a result, too much competition in few routes led to worse traffic conditions and diminishing returns for some firms.[104]

Telecommunications. The privatization of Entel-CPT (Empresa Nacional de Telecomunicaciones-Compañía Peruana de Teléfonos) was the single most important of all transfers up to 1998 in terms of revenues and future investments. The government's overreaching goal was the improvement of telephone service and the increase in the number of lines installed. To monitor the compliance with investment requirements, the government created a regulatory agency (Organismo Supervisor de la Inversión Privada en Telecomunicaciones, OSPITEL). On 28 February 1994, COPRI auctioned off 35 per cent of Entel, 20 per cent of the government's share in CPT, and a share capital increase to reach 35 per cent. The winning consortium led by Telefónica of Spain offered $1.39 billion in cash for the government's shares, and $610 million in additional capital subscription for CPT, that is, four times the floor price set at $525 million. About 10 per cent was offered to employees and the remaining 55 per cent was to be placed through offering shares to the public. Telefónica pledged to install 1.1 million lines in five years and to connect every village with more than 500 people, which required $1 billion in investments.[105]

The sizeable difference between the government's initial price and Telefónica's offer raised some questions. Critics argued that this indicated the flaws in COPRI's evaluation methods and that the government, in its quest to sell quickly, was actually 'selling out' attractive companies. COPRI responded that Entel-CPT was part of Telefónica's strategy to acquire a dominant role in South America (already having large stakes in Argentina, Chile, and Venezuela) and was therefore willing to pay any price. To back up this argument Montoya pointed out that the second largest bid offered by the US GTE was for $850 million, close to the government's estimate. After taking over the company, Telefónica used $320 million, of the $610 million allocated to CPT, to clear debts and embarked on an ambitious investment plan totalling $2 billion that was carried out by the end of 1998. The company also reduced total employment from 12,000 to 8,900 people, which partly explains why productivity per worker also increased since privatization.[106]

None the less, the government pointed out that early results were positive not just because of greater investments, increased number of lines installed, reduced time of installation, and overall better service than before but also because had the company remained in public hands, all these improvements could not have occurred for lack of resources. In July 1996, Telefónica del Perú's good performance induced the government capitalize on it and sell 23.6 per cent of its shares in the company through an international public offer, the fourth largest at the time in Latin America. It earned an impressive $1.2 billion and led to a sudden, although momentary upsurge of the Lima stock exchange.

Mining. In this sector the record was quite mixed. The sale of the first firm in 1991, Compañía Minera Condestable, was marred by administrative irregularities. The company was sold at a very low price (just over a million dollars), despite the fact that it was a profit-making enterprise. Moreover, its buyers were a group that had never been involved in mining.

Minpeco (Minero Perú Comercial S. A.), the PE in charge of marketing for the mining sector, constituted a special case. In 1991, Minpeco had sales totalling $400 million, with one of its associates, Minpeco USA, accounting for $178 million. COPRI decided to sell Minpeco USA for $4 million and liquidate the rest of the company. To some, this operation seemed to be lacking transparency. By the end of 1991, Minpeco USA owed Minpeco S. A. of $4.1 million. But by the time it was privatized in 1992, the situation had reversed itself, with Minpeco S. A. suddenly owing the debt to its affiliate for that amount. For Indacochea (1993: 73–4) the coincidence that the sale price was $4 million did not seem fortuitous.

The COPRI in mining presented Hierro Perú's privatization as a success story. In 1992, Hierro Perú was in a deep crisis of decapitalization, which forced COPRI to undergo a thorough restructuring process. To cut costs, the government, with World Bank support, set up plans to shed 1,600 out of 2,400 jobs, through an early retirement program and the elimination of several company services. In November 1992, the company sold for $120 million, five times the base price of $22 million (Table 5.7). The new owners took over $41.8 million worth of debt and pledged in $150 million investment in three years (Table 5.1). Oddly enough, the winning bid came from another state corporation, Shougang Co. of China. Shougang's large offer was explained by the strategic importance that Hierro Perú had for the Chinese government, both in terms of production geared toward its domestic needs and as a first step to enter the Latin American market. However, on the negative side, COPRI failed to monitor the promised investments, both in terms of quality and quantity. The little investment made by the company appeared to be of poor quality and, as noted earlier, Shougang had to renegotiate its investment pledge in 1996. Moreover, since privatization, working conditions and labor relations worsened, leading to several strikes after 1994.[107]

The main state holding company, Minero Perú, sold several assets, including mines like Cerro Verde (copper), the Ilo copper refinery, Cañariaco-Jehuamarca/La Huaquillas (copper and gold), La Granja (copper), Colpar-Hualatán-Pallacochas (gold ores), and San Antonio de Poto (gold). In the case of Cerro Verde, about nineteen companies qualified for the auction, but the only one that actually made an offer was Cyprus Minerals Co., which eventually paid $37 million and pledged $485 million in future investments. For the Ilo copper refinery, COPRI needed two auctions. The first did not draw any interested parties since investors thought the price was too high. In the second one, only one bidder came forward, Southern Perú, which was declared the winner. A contract between Southern Perú and Minero Perú assured the former that it did not have to bargain over ore price in the uncertain context of bilateral monopoly (bilateral monopoly is a market in which just one seller faces only one buyer). For the most part, the PEs belonging to Minero Perú were transferred (either through concessions or sales) according to pledges of large investments and/or with an option to buy the company.

The privatization of Centromin, a holding company controlling seven mines in the central Andes, was troubled by several setbacks through 1998. Part of the problem rested on its large deficit which in 1991 amounted to $140 million. In 1992, through job cuts (the workforce alone dropped from 23,000 to 13,000 people) and more rational production strategies, Centromin returned to profitability.[108] About 24 firms registered for its auction. COPRI asked for $280 million in cash, $60 million in debt titles, and $240 million in investment commitments. However, at auction time in January 1994, no buyers came forward. As noted earlier, the heavy pollution affecting Centromin's mines scared many investors away. Moreover, Centromin's mines, due to their isolation, offered their workers a number of services like hospitals, schools, transportation, etc., that private corporations were unwilling to subsidize. By 1998, the Centromin mines were still up for sale.

Electricity.   Privatization in this sector was based upon the Law of Electrical Concessions through which the government established a system of regulated prices permitting investment in the generation, transmission, and distribution of electricity. The law forbade that these three activities be in the hands of the same company to avoid monopolies. Companies could also challenge tariffs before the Committees of Economic Operation of the System (Comités de Operación Económica del Sistema, COES). The COES was created to plan and coordinate the operation of the system and is staffed with the managers of the generating and transmission companies that are interconnected.

Electrolima and Electroperú were the generating and distributing companies in the electricity service. Both of them were restructured to conform to the new legal framework, paving the way for privatization. Electrolima was divided into three units: Edelnor (distribution), Edelsur (distribution, later

renamed Luz del Sur), and Edegel (generation). The two distribution companies were privatized in July 1994. A consortium headed by Endesa of Spain,
Chilectra and Enersis of Chile, and Cosapi of Peru paid $176 million for
the controlling stake in Edelnor. Chilquinta of Chile and Ontario Hydro of
Canada purchased Luz del Sur for $212 million. Luz del Sur's employees
also bought the 10 per cent stake made available to them.

The government sold Edegel in October 1995 to Endesa of Chile (controlled by Enersis) and the US Energy Power Development for $424 million
plus $100 million in secondary market debt papers. This constituted the largest
sell-off that year. In 1996, the government sold the last of the large electricity companies, Egenor, for $228 million. By then, most transactions affected
small regional companies and remaining shares of privatized companies still
in government hands.

Oil and Gas. The law of hydrocarbons set the legal frame for this sector's
privatization. The government lifted fuel price controls and eliminated the
government monopoly status in this sector. Petroperú held a monopoly in
fields such as oil exploration, production, refining, transportation, distribution (through pipelines), storage, and marketing. Given the complexity of
Petroperú's ventures, COPRI decided to sell them in separate transactions
corresponding to specific business activities. The first units to be sold were
gas stations, storage facilities, and small refineries for a total of $272 mil-
lion. These divestitures were primarily chosen because they were considered
to raise little controversy. In fact, when larger, more visable companies were
put up for sale, resistance grew appreciably. As a result, the remaining oil
fields and refineries, which were also the most important and set to be
transferred by the end of 1995, remained in government hands well into 1998
due to the opposition factors examined above.

The privatization of gas stations was marred by many problems. In some
cases, auctions were nullified for lack of bidders. In others, the winners delayed
their payments and some were actually jailed for having failed to pay the
government. Critics initially charged that the indiscriminate fuel price liberalization allowed the new private owners to make very high profit margins
that indicated collusion practices. The condition of the gas stations was very
poor and there was no control over gasoline quality. Over time, however,
according to COPRI, many gas stations improved the quality of their service
and increased the number of services offered.[109]

The sale of Petrolera Transoceánica (oil cargo fleet), a subsidiary of
Petroperú, also created controversy. The first auction failed since no bidders
showed up. The second one adjudicated the company to a consortium apparently based in Panama, but which was allegedly a cover for some Chilean
investors and the Peruvian group Wiese. COPRI was also criticized for selling
the company at a price, $25 million, considered by critics to be too low given
that the fleet's worth, according to some estimates, was about $24 million,

and it operated in a monopolistic market, which made it a highly profitable operation (Indacochea 1993).

Solgas S. A. was another case where the government sold a profitable PE for a price regarded as too low. COPRI earned $7.5 million from its sale, about 52 per cent over the base price, but its value was about $10 million. Additionally, the Solgas S.A.'s privatization was highly controversial because the government, days before the auction, changed the regulatory framework by creating entry barriers, thus consolidating the monopolistic power of the new private owners (Indacochea 1993: 96–7).

Unlike the cases discussed above, Petromar's privatization went smoothly. It was carried by an international auction, which imposed greater transparency. Petrotech International (United States) won the concession rights for Petromar, paying $200 million in cash and pledging an additional $65 million in investments.

The privatization of La Pampilla refinery in mid-1996 provoked the strongest opposition yet that the government encountered in this sector. In the end, the company was sold but the oil and gas sector privatization languished thereafter. The debacle of the Camisea natural gas development project in 1998, when Shell and Mobil after long negotiations with COPRI pulled out from what was estimated to be Peru's largest investment ever at $2.7 billion, was a devastating blow for the Fujimori administration at a time when foreign capital inflows were most needed due to the growing balance of payments deficit.

Manufacturing. In this sector, the most important PEs sold were in cement, chemicals, paper, and ship building. The most important qualms again regarded COPRI's transfer methods and, in some cases, the base price it charged. Cementos Lima was the largest PE sold in this sector ($103 million). It also represented the first experience of a sale targeting exclusively portfolio investors (sixty-five investors from seven countries). The offering in the United States raised by itself $82 million (Cabello and Shiguiyama 1998:36).

Quimpac had inventories worth $2 million, debts for $4 million, and assets estimated at $18 million. However, COPRI set the floor price at $3.9 million. As in many other cases, COPRI failed to disclose the methodology used to reach such an estimate. In the end, only one bidder came forward offering $6.5 million.

The Industrias Navales S.A. (Inasa) also had problems with the base price. This time, COPRI sold the PE at 58 per cent below the minimum requested (Table 5.7). Nevertheless, COPRI decided to award the company claiming that the market established the price, despite the fact that this reasoning seemed at odds with the lack of competition since only one bidder came forward. Moreover, unlike other privatizations, no strings were attached as far as enhanced productivity and competitiveness were concerned (Indacochea 1993: 97–8).

The Complejo Industrial Paramonga included several PEs, some of which were producers of paper, cardboard (Envase Sanmarti, Conversión Lima, and Chillón), and chemicals (Cartavio, PVC cloro-soda). COPRI set up a timetable whose main criteria was to sell companies that were producing monthly operating deficits of $2 million. For one of these PEs, Envases Sanmarti, the only company that offered the minimum price won. In the case of the Conversión Lima, two bidders competed in a stock auction that generated four times as much as the amount set as the floor price (Table 5.7). The Chillón company sale, on the contrary, was postponed after the failure of the first auction, but on the second try it received twice the amount sought (Table 5.7). Cartavio's sale turned out to be a disappointment as COPRI obtained for it only $4.4 million instead of the $6.6 million it estimated the company was worth (Table 5.7). The PVC's privatization was suspended since no investors showed interest.

Banking.   The transfer of the government-owned banks took off with a shaky start, but finished on a positive note. The first financial institution to be sold was the Banco del Comercio, the first PE to be transferred through public auction at the Lima stock exchange. Again, here we have another example of how the rules of the game were changed at the last minute, without clear goals or planning. The CLAE group seized control of the Banco del Comercio, but it appeared that this was a flawed transaction from the start since CLAE did not comply with the prerequisites of the Peruvian banking law. Coincidentally, the same day of the auction, the government issued a ruling that excluded the Banco del Comercio from the existing banking law and authorized the purchase of an amount of shares 15 per cent higher than the bank's capital. Additionally, COPRI did not require the new owners to present an investment plan, targets to improve competitiveness, or guarantees.

A second case of blunt miscalculation involved the Banco Popular, generally regarded as one of the most poorly handled cases of the privatization process. First, COPRI made a mistake when it included the Banco Popular in its first group of PEs to be privatized without having issued a legal framework to this end, causing a lack of confidence, withdrawal of deposits, and the suspension of debt payments. Second, the indiscriminate process of early retirements and layoffs disarticulated the bank's management and its service to the public. Third, the Central Bank of Peru injected $30 million into the Banco Popular to keep it afloat until its transfer, an initiative that required a change in the legal framework of the sale. Indeed, changes were made even shortly before the sale. Understandably, several auctions failed miserably either because there were no bidders or because when they did appear they did not comply with COPRI's prerequisites. Finally, in 1993, COPRI decided to dissolve the bank with the exception of one of its subsidiaries, the Banco Popular-Bolivia, which was sold for $6.5 million that year (Indacochea 1993: 85–9).

The next bank privatization, Interbanc, was comparatively speaking less problematic and produced better results. COPRI awarded Interbanc in July 1994 for $51 million. Although critics argued that this price was too low, COPRI responded that the new owners' pledge of $20 million in future investments did make up for any possible short-fall.

The last bank privatized, Banco Continental, was by far the most successful. Of the five consortia that participated in the auction, the winner was the one led by the Spanish Bank Bilbao Vizcaya which offered $255.7 million, of which $195.7 million was in cash and $60 million in debt titles. This amount was twice that set by the minimum floor. This sale also ended state involvement in banking, which had aroused so much controversy particularly under Alan García.

Conclusions

Fujimori's privatization program started relatively late, but its aim, complete state divestiture, was as far reaching as Menem's was in Argentina. However, while Menem by 1998 had practically sold most PEs, Fujimori's program after gaining momentum between 1994 and 1996 lost steam thereafter. In late 1998, important companies such as Centromin and Petroperú were still far from being sold and their divestiture seemed to encounter more technical difficulties and political resistance than earlier expected.

These problems notwithstanding, the rather quick design and implementation of the privatization program can be explained, as was argued earlier, by the fact that both willingness and opportunity factors did coincide at the right time. Although the process was flawed with poor planning, cancellations, administrative irregularities, and postponements, Fujimori pushed it through as he saw fit. To his critics the President replied, much as Menem did, that the country simply had no option and, in a few years, the policy was instrumental in earning Peru much needed revenues and international confidence.

There is little doubt that privatization did have several positive results. It brought into the state coffers roughly $7.1 billion (Table 5.1), the bulk of which was paid in cash. Of the 250 PEs controlled in 1991, by January 1998 about 106 (42 per cent) had been sold, including 11 whose privatization was only partial. About 18.4 per cent had been or were to be liquidated, while the remaining 40 per cent was on process of being privatized. The lion's share of the revenues came from telecommunications, with 40 per cent of the total, followed by mining with 20 per cent (Fig. 5.8). Revenues, which were negligible in the first year (1991), climbed steadily in 1992 and 1993, and surged dramatically between 1994 and 1996. It must be underscored, though, that the sale of telecommunication and electricity companies accounted for the bulk of the revenues in the latter period. Foreign companies, as expected, played

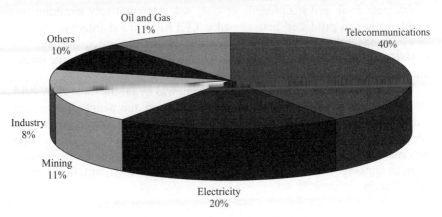

FIG. 5.8. Peru Revenues by Sector 1991–7 (%)
Source: Informativo COPRI 1997.

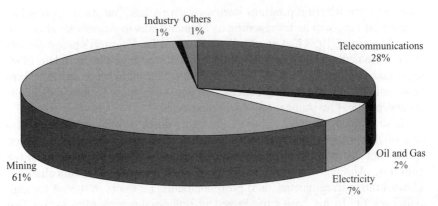

FIG. 5.9. Peru: Investment Pledges by Sector (%)
Source: Informativo COPRI 1997.

a pivotal role accounting for roughly 84.4 per cent of total revenues. Taking into account the disastrous macroeconomic and political environment of the early 1990s, this was no small accomplishment. Workers' participation was, on the contrary, negligible as it constituted only 1.3 per cent of total revenues. In terms of methods, public auctions accounted for 87.9 per cent of the money earned, followed by auctions through the Lima stock exchange and international public offers with 8.6 per cent.

The privatization program accounted for the bulk of foreign investment. Investment commitments, totalling an impressive $4 billion, reached their peak in 1996 (Table 5.1). Mining accounted for 61 per cent while telecommunications was a distant second with 28 per cent (Fig. 5.9). The most active investors by country were, in order of importance, Spain, the United States, Chile, and Canada.

This positive trend also had a positive impact on the general business climate. The Lima stock exchange experienced the arrival of new foreign investors, which gave new confidence to domestic economic groups. Some of them began to look for additional financing by having their companies going public, which in turn diversified the market by providing more choice. Privatization, along with other market reforms, helped the country to improve its credit-worthiness abroad as evidenced by the steep appreciation of the Peruvian debt in international secondary markets, which is a clear sign of investor confidence. Indeed, as a sign of changed times, the prestigious US rating agency Moody's Investors Service listed Peru bonds and notes for the first time in early 1996.

In terms of the fiscal impact, it is impossible to ascertain its amount since COPRI did not disclose the amount of money spent to restructure PEs nor the costs associated with the preparation of each sale (in a few cases the new private owners also took over outstanding debts of former PEs). However, as with the Argentine and Brazilian cases, the hidden impact of privatization was on foregoing investments to the private sector; investments that the government could no longer finance. Privatization revenues were used to finance Peru's current account deficit, which increased appreciably as a result of the opening of the economy to foreign imports. Such revenues were also important in strengthening Peru's foreign reserves, which rose to $10 billion in 1997 (Fig. 5.3).

The Fujimori administration, amidst difficulties, was able to make important strides towards the renegotiation of its foreign debt. Within this context, privatization played an important role since the IMF and creditor banks demanded it as part of the structural reform needed to enter long-term debt rescheduling agreements. Peru started by clearing arrearages with the IMF and the World Bank and by rigorously meeting the macroeconomic targets agreed upon with the IMF. In May 1993, Peru successfully restructured its arrearages with the Paris Club's creditors. In March 1997, Peru closed a deal under the auspices of the Brady Plan, which allowed it to slash its outstanding debt by $5.3 billion. The World Bank and the IDB announced plans to fund part of the $1 billion that Peru needed to pay its creditors to enter the Brady Plan.

The government was also able, despite the brief period that had elapsed since the beginning of the privatizations program, to point to some success stories in the companies it had transferred to the private sector. Under the new owners, in 1994 Aeroperú posted its first profits in twenty years and also increased on time departures from 17 per cent to 88 per cent. Between 1993 and 1994, the airline's share of the domestic and international markets rose by 5 per cent and 20 per cent, respectively. Significant improvements in productivity were also made by Cemento Yura, Tintaya, Enatru, Sudamericana de Fibras, Paramonga, Chillón, Envases Sanmarti, and Conversión Lima. In the case of Solgas S.A., a consumer survey showed that 90 per cent of the customers were satisfied or very satisfied with the company's improvements since privatization.[110]

Privatization was also instrumental in helping the government eliminate overstaffing in the public sector and, most certainly, a lot of the corruption within it. The combination of the restructuring process affecting many PEs and the sale of others also helped in slashing the PEs' deficit from 4.1 per cent of GDP in 1990 to only 0.5 per cent in 1991 (Portocarrero 1992: 67).

Politically speaking, as in Menem's Argentina, the adoption of privatization turned out to be a positive move for Fujimori, as his stunning re-election victory in 1995 proved. His campaign was based on the popular approval of his market reforms. Actually, his fellow Peruvians seemed to agree that the country was better off than when Fujimori took office in 1990 and that, as the President had argued, he was the best man to finish the job. After the electoral contest, Fujimori could 'claim, with justification, that business and the military [were] by no means his only supporters'.[111] His much criticized brand of authoritarian reformism did triumph at last, pointing to the fact that people were more preoccupied with terrorism and inflation, than with democratic government, something which, some could argue, had never truly existed in Peru.

Privatization, coupled with the deregulation of the labor market, also helped in emasculating the power of one of Fujimori's greatest opponents, unionism. By 1998, leaving aside the strong union opposition still existing in Centromin and Petroperú, it seemed clear that most critics were not questioning the policy *per se* but rather its criteria and the way it was being carried out. Such a scenario would have been inconceivable in 1990, which provides some dimension of how dramatically Fujimori's policies had changed the nature of the political debate in Peru.

However, many of the problems encountered in Argentina and Brazil could also be found in the Peruvian privatization process. Selling under pressure resulted in many situations that went against several of COPRI's very tenets. These included administrative irregularities in the sale procedures, sudden changes in the legal frameworks, and the cancellation of many auctions.

Moreover, although Montoya and his successor after 1995, Jorge González Izquierdo, announced that COPRI's aim was not merely to complete sales but also to ensure the success of the venture once in private hands, post facto, it appeared clear that the government often paid scant or no attention at all to problems of competition and efficiency (Indacochea 1993: 72). In most instances, privatization of public utlities took place without an effective regulation being in place prior to the transfer affecting markets that remained monopolistic in private hands. Nor did the CLC seem very effective in enforcing anti-trust legislation. Even in those few cases where regulatory agencies were created, many cast doubts about first, the political independence of such agencies and second, their ability to regulate effectively (Gonzales de Olarte 1994: 15). The sudden changes in the rules of the game for the electricity sector seemed to confirm such misgivings. There were also deep concerns about the capability of the government to effectively monitor the actual implementation of the investment plans to which many private groups had committed themselves.

Such issues were also tied to the transparency of the whole process, which despite COPRI's statements, was far from clear (Indacochea 1993: 71). First, there was no independent government agency or institution that could effectively detect possible irregularities both at the planning and implementation stages of a given transfer. Second, often there was a complete absence of information on the methods used to calculate the assets and price of a PE up for sale and the criteria adopted for selecting consulting firms. Third, on numerous occasions, the award contracts remained mysteriously secret to the public. Fourth, the expenditures involved in the sale were also never disclosed for public scrutiny. Fifth, when the press found out that privatization revenues had been deposited in foreign accounts abroad, Fujimori declined to disclose where these accounts were located claiming that there were security reasons involved, without giving further explanation. Sixth, there were strong suspicions of manipulation of privatization revenues for personal use. For instance, in 1992, the executive issued a number of decrees allowing the office of the presidency to use COPRI funds in order to purchase computer equipment. Eventually, the executive gave this equipment to Jaime Yoshiyama, COPRI's President before Daniel Hokama, for his own electoral campaign for Congress (Burneo 1993: 58). Seventh, there were reported cases of collusion where some members of individual CEPRIs and government consulting firms ended up buying or working for the privatized companies.[112] Indeed, there were no clear rules for COPRI and CEPRI staff members regarding conflicts of interest that could prevent them from working for or owning privatized companies, which on occasion did occur.

Who won after all? Surely foreign and domestic investors came out from the privatization process as the big winners. The upper middle class also benefitted from better public utility services that they could afford. PEs' unions and their workers were the biggest losers. Only those workers that were able to retain their jobs after privatization enjoyed better salaries and some shares of their companies. Those who were laid off were left facing a very uncertain future and joined the ranks of the already large number of people working in the informal economy.

In spite of the administration's promise, there was little evidence that the government had effectively reallocated resources to improve education, health, and the judicial system in order to fulfill its primary responsibilities.

The judicial system remained in shambles, as did health care. Funds in education were spent on physical rather than human resources. Only a handful of tangible improvements could be seen in basic infrastructure like roads, bridges, and water supplies, often funded with foreign aid and built to maximize electoral results prior to elections.

In conclusion, from a pragmatic standpoint, Fujimori did achieve most of his initial goals. However, from a more theoretical perspective, there were substantial discrepancies between COPRI's rhetoric and the actual execution of many privatizations. Their causes rested on the lack of clear planning and priorities. The goal seemed to be divesting and let the market economy take care of economic growth. Nor there was any evidence that privatization had strengthened the state and its institutions in their fundamental tasks. Yet, as most analysts agree, strong capitalist economies do need strong institutions to facilitate business operations, on the one hand, and protect individual rights from market abuses on the other. In the case of Peru, the absence of long-term planning and institution building was, unfortunately, the direct result of Fujimori's one-man approach to problem solving. As Hunt (1996: 49) pointed out:

long-term growth requires a consistent development model. Consistency requires a strong state that will ensure continuity and therefore credibility. The Peruvian state as currently constituted is too weak to give assurance that it can maintain its policy line—neoliberalism—or any policy line. Therefore, Peru has not yet found a viable development model that gives prospect for sustained growth.

These misgivings notwithstanding, by the end of his second term Fujimori could claim victory on all fronts, while his critics, no matter what the substance of their arguments, seemed completely powerless.

Endnotes

1. *Financial Times*, 29 September 1993, p. 1.
2. As in Brazil, the Peruvian electoral law for President requires a run-off election if no candidate reaches 51 per cent of the popular vote.
3. *Financial Times*, 29 September 1993, p. 1.
4. Fujimori was regarded by many as an outsider even within the Japanese–Peruvian community in Lima. *La República*, 6 January 1991.
5. Cambio '90 started out as a movement made up by businessmen and professionals to sponsor Fujimori's plans to become a senator. His most noticeable representative was Máximo San Roman, a self-made man coming from a mestizo background who made a fortune in manufacturing small backery equipment.
6. During World War II, the Japanese community in Peru was the object of widespread harassment. Many of its members were actually deported to the United States and their property was confiscated.

7. Economist Hernando de Soto, a former associate of Vargas Llosa's before a split during the 1990 presidential campaign, and UN Secretary General Javier Pérez de Cuéllar, allegedly played an important role in helping Fujimori's effort to re-establish good relations with multilateral agencies and private banks.

8. Cambio '90 only accounted for thirty-two out of 180 representatives in the Chamber of Deputies, and fourteen out of sixty senators. Many Cambio '90 legislators left the party and became independent after Fujimori's move to the right (Webb and Fernández Baca 1991: 1032).

9. *Latin American Regional Reports: Andean Group*, 7 March 1991, p. 2.

10. *Caretas*, 22 April 1991, p. 13.

11. *Financial Times*, 29 September 1993, p. 1; Gustavo Gorriti, 'Fujimori's Svengali', *Covert Action*, no. 49 (Summer 1994), pp. 4–59. Montesinos was expelled from the military for leaking intelligence information to foreign countries in the mid-1970s. Later, he became a successful lawyer and gained the national spotlight for defending alleged drug dealers. He became one of Fujimori's most trusted advisers during the second round of the 1990 elections.

12. *Latin American Monitor: Andean Group*, July 1995, p. 8.

13. However, the hottest issue in dispute concerned executive orders with regards to counter insurgency. This legislation suspended most civil rights and provided the military with wide discretionary powers.

14. In an interview, Fujimori justified the coup in these terms, 'One of the biggest problems was violence, which advanced—not because Sendero Luminoso had any merit—but because the state was so inefficient. This produced the rupture of April 5 last year. That was a break with the previous system and now we want a normal situation from what is evidently a period of transition. The changes proposed include some important reforms concerning the legislature and the judiciary. We are seeking a more efficient Congress and judiciary less dependent on political party interests, less subject to manipulation and corruption. These are fundamental reforms, without which we would continue to suffer political instability' (*Financial Times*, 29 September 1993, p. 1).

15. *Peru Report*, 7 May 1992, p. 3.

16. Fujimori himself admitted that negative reactions from abroad were stronger than he had anticipated. *Financial Times*, 29 September 1993, p. 1.

17. Another policy triggered by the financial squeeze was the fiscal reform.

18. Both quotes are from the *Latin American Regional Reports: Andean Group*, 28 January 1993, p. 2.

19. *Página Libre*, 21 May 1990.

20. Interview with Manuel Romero Caro, editor of the business newspaper *Gestión*, Lima, April 1995.

21. *Financial Times*, 29 September 1993, p. 1.

22. Interview with Manuel Romero Caro, Lima, April 1995.

23. *Perú económico*, 'Para todos: Difusión de la propriedad', 17/6 (June 1994), pp. 2–3.

24. The potential benefit of popular capitalism in Peru were expected to be limited from the start. For instance, while in Chile the government financed workers' stock acquisitions at zero interest, Peru, with a per capita income much lower

than its neighbor, did not. This, in turn, made it impossible for many people to acquire shares. *La República*, 9 July 1994, p. 16.

25. *Financial Times*, 29 September 1993, p. 1.

26. *Expreso*, 6 November 1991.

27. Fujimori was used to about-face changes. After being elected university chancellor with the vote of the center left, he managed campus with the support of the right (Jachomowitz 1994: 239).

28. Jaime Yoshiyama, first President of COPRI, declared that with the exception of health, education, and infrastructures, everything was up for sale. *Semana Económica*, 23 December 1991, p. 5.

29. *Financial Times*, 29 September 1993, p. 1.

30. *Financial Times*, 29 September 1993, p. 3.

31. Instituto Nacional de Estadística e Informática, 'Estadísticas de las empresas estatales no financieras 1984–90', Lima, November 1991.

32. About 60 per cent of assets belonged to Petroperú, Electroperú, and Entelperú. In 1990, the state owned or had minority shares in 47 financial companies. Of these, the state fully owned eight, had majority shares in thirty-five, and was a minority shareholder in the remaining four (Kuczynski and Ortiz de Zevallos 1990: 30).

33. Ibid.

34. Investments in PEs declined from an average of 4.3 per cent between 1981 and 1985 to 1.6 per cent (of GDP) between 1986 and 1989 (Alvarez Rodrich 1992: 24).

35. In 1983, PE capital expenditures represented 5 per cent of GDP but by the end of the 1980s they had dropped to 1.5 per cent (Kuczynski and Ortiz de Zevallos 1990: 31).

36. COPRI, 'The Turn of Peru', *COPRI Special Supplement*, Lima, May 1993.

37. *Financial Times*, 29 September 1993, p. 1.

38. Interview with José Bazo Luna, manager of the CEPRI in charge of the sale of state-owned banks. Lima, August 1994.

39. According to some estimates only 10 per cent of Peru's mineral wealth was exploited in 1992. *Financial Times*, 29 September 1993, p. 6.

40. The state reserved for itself, however, special rights over some areas of exploration.

41. Interview with Augusto Alvarez Rodrich, Lima. August 1994. On Fujimori's concern for public opinion data, see Jachamowitz (1994: 277–8).

42. COPRI, 'The Turn of Peru,' *COPRI Special Supplement*, Lima, May 1993, p. 15.

43. Jorge Yoshiyama became President of Congress, Daniel Hokama took over the powerful Ministry of Mines and Energy, and Santiago Fujimori, one of the President's brothers, was appointed his special adviser.

44. Interview with government pollster and presidential adviser Augusto Alvarez Rodrich. Lima, August 1994.

45. *Financial Times*, 29 September 1993, p. 1.

46. *The Economist*, 19 February 1994, p. 44. However, foreign diplomats in Lima told this author that the image that the President wanted people to believe was

quite inaccurate since Fujimori had virtually no control over the day-to-day operations of even high-ranking bureaucrats.

47. Officially, CEPRI members were drafted from the private sector based upon their expertise and professional achievements in the sector being privatized. However, the selection criteria was never disclosed. Upon closer scrutiny, it appeared that a common feature of several COPRI officials was that they had been classmates of Yoshiyama in the Escuela de Administración de Negocios para Graduados (ESAN). Interview with Alejandro Indacochea, professor of accounting and finance at ESAN. Lima, April 1995.

48. By the time privatization came into full swing, some 40 CEPRIs were in operation. On CEPRI autonomy, Montoya stated, 'the special committees . . . operate with autonomy but not complete independence. They have guidelines to follow, and must meet COPRI's timetable and objectives'. COPRI, 'The Turn of Peru', *COPRI Special Supplement*, Lima, May 1993, pp. 13–15.

49. Peruvian teams travelled to Argentina, Brazil, Chile, and Mexico to study privatization experiences in those countries.

50. *Financial Times*, 29 September 1993, p. 1.

51. Ricardo Lago, the country economist for Peru in the World Bank, is regarded as having played a significant role in crafting the initial stabilization policies for the government. Luis Valdivieso, a Peruvian staffer at the IMF, later sent to Lima during Boloña's tenure, was very influential in economic policy making. Other Peruvian staffers of the IMF and World Bank returned to their country on brief leaves of absence to help the Fujimori administration in different capacities. Multilateral agencies and foreign governments also set up special funds to pay for newly recruited people coming from the private sector (the regular civil service salaries were so low that nobody of any ability would have accepted them). For instance, Luis Cortavarría, the banking superintendent, was recruited from Coopers & Lybrand. As for privatization, the World Bank sent Marcelo Antinori, an Argentine expert, to Lima upon the request of Yoshiyama. However, the 'advice' of the multilateral agencies was given in an 'informal' way and its common thought among pundits and analysts that the program was designed in Lima, not in Washington.

52. COPRI could count on 30 people, including drivers, and all the CEPRIs had a staff of about 100 people. Interview with COPRI officials, Lima, April 1995. In Argentina and Brazil the same staffs numbered several hundreds.

53. Interview with COPRI officials. Lima, April 1995.

54. *Latin American Regional Reports: Andean Group*, 19 December 1991, p. 3.

55. *Financial Times*, 29 September 1993, p. 1.

56. The DL (decree law) 674 of September 1991, setting up the legal framework of privatization, was approved by the Court of Constitutional Guarantees in February 1992.

57. The 1993 Constitution established that a President could run for a second but not a third consecutive term. Fujimori's contention was that his first election did not count since it happened before 1993. Thus, his 1995 election had to be counted as his first term.

58. Interviews with Kurt Burneo and Alejandro Indacochea. Lima, April 1995.

59. *Financial Times*, 29 September 1993, p. 1.
60. *El Comercio*, 6 April 1991.
61. Ibid.
62. Montoya went as far as to say that, 'the idea is to privatize, on average, one public enterprise per month'. *Expreso*, 23 May 1992.
63. Data provided by the Jurnda Nacional de Elecciones.
64. In conceding defeat, Pérez de Cuéllar acknowledged, '[I] recognize that the people have preferred to reward the defeat of terrorism and hyperinflation although they have not earned, at the same time, a democratic future with social development.' *El Comercio*, 10 April 1995. Indeed, a May 1995 public opinion poll showed 79.9 per cent of the people surveyed approved the President's policies, up from 70.5 per cent in the month of April. Data provided by APOYO.
65. Interview with CNN reported in *El Comercio*, 11 April 1995.
66. Interview with Manuel Romero Caro. Lima, April 1995.
67. *El Comercio*, 30 August 1994.
68. Interestingly, the large proceeds from privatization started in 1994 and, with the IMF blessing, they became available just in time for the 1995 re-election campaign when they were channelled into the FONCODES and the Fund for the Promotion of Private Investments.
69. *La República*, 6 August 1994, p. 6.
70. *The Economist*, 19 February 1994, p. 44.
71. Interview with CONFIEP's President Arturo Woodman Pollit, Lima, August 1994 and CONFIEP's past President Rafael Villegas Cerro, Lima, April 1995.
72. Peru's private fishing lobby criticized the sale of Pescaperú in separate companies, claiming that the country's plant capacity already exceeded the quantity of fish available for processing. *Financial Times*, 26 August 1994, p. 24.
73. See Woodman's inauguration speech in *El Comercio*, 4 March 1994, p. 74.
74. *Latin American Weekly Report*, 20 April 1995, p. 169.
75. Jaime Quijadria left Petroperú in protest in 1994.
76. It is estimated that the private economy lost about 250,000 jobs between 1990 and 1994. Data provided by Kurt Burneo.
77. Interviews with Carlos Monge (Centro Peruano de Estudios Sociales) and Javier Mujica Petit, director of Centro de Asesoria Laboral del Peru, Lima, April 1995.
78. Data provided by Kurt Burneo, Lima, April 1995.
79. In September 1993, Guzmán and the majority of the Shining Path leadership publicly asked their followers to give up the armed struggle. In the Spring of 1998, the security forces captured Pedro Quinteros, one the remaining prominent leaders of the organization.
80. *El Comercio*, 22 October 1994, p. 4a.
81. This decision aroused the strong protest of private engineering companies, traditional recipients of such contracts, which saw their business severely affected. Some pundits interpreted this fact as a means for Fujimori to reward the Army for its support. Interview with Gustavo Mohme Llona, director of the newspaper *La República*. Lima, April 1995.
82. *Actualidad Económica*, no. 157, August 1994, pp. 9–11.
83. *Actualidad Económica*, no. 162, March 1995, pp. 12–13.

84. Things proceeded quickly as can be testified by the fact that, according to Montoya (1992: 54) the privatization strategy was devised in only four months (from November 1991 to February 1992).
85. *Financial Times*, 29 September 1993, p. 1.
86. COPRI, 'The Turn of Peru', *COPRI Special Supplement*, Lima, May 1993, p. 12.
87. *El Comercio*, 18 September 1993, p. 9b.
88. Interview with Alejandro Indacochea, Lima, April 1995.
89. Interview with COPRI's officials. Lima, April 1995.
90. *Latin American Weekly Report*, 18 May 1995, p. 211.
91. COPRI, 'The Turn of Peru', *COPRI Special Supplement*, Lima, May 1993, p. 25.
92. Interview with COPRI's officials, Lima, April 1995. See also the *Langiappe Monthly on Latin American Project & Finance*, January 1998, pp. 27–8.
93. Debt-equity swaps for privatization were established through Law 26250 of November 1993.
94. Interview with COPRI's officials. Lima, April 1995.
95. *Financial Times*, 15 November 1994, p. 7. Data for 1998 provided by Flemings Securities.
96. Ibid.
97. *El Comercio*, 25 November 1993, p. 6a. The government decided to use a complex five-point criteria in selecting which PEs would be sold through debt-equity swaps. See Montoya's interview in *El Comercio*, 6 March 1994, p. 1f.
98. Interview with foreign diplomats. Lima, April 1995.
99. *Latin American Monitor: Andean Group*, October 1996, p. 9.
100. *Lagniappe Monthly on Latin American Projects & Finance*, April 1998, p. 5.
101. *Semana Económica*, 1 June 1992, p. 4.
102. *Latin American Monitor: Andean Group*, August 1996, p. 9.
103. *Lagniappe Monthly on Latin American Projects & Finance*, December 1997, p. 4.
104. Macroconsult, 'Evaluación preliminar del proceso de privatización', Lima, mimeo, June 1994, p. 8.
105. *The Economist*, 5 February 1994, p. 70.
106. *Perú económico*, no. 2, February 1995, p. 3.
107. Kurt Burneo, 'Privatización de Hierro Perú: Exitosa para quien?' *Opinión*, Lima, 11 April 1994.
108. COPRI, 'The Turn of Peru', *COPRI Special Supplement*, Lima, May 1993, p. 16, 26.
109. *Perú económico*, February 1995, pp. 14–15.
110. *Perú económico*, February 1995.
111. *Latin American Weekly Report*, 4 May 1995, p. 190.
112. These cases involved Minera Condestable and Electrolima. Interview with Kurt Burneo. Lima, April 1995.

6

The Theory and Practice of State Divestiture

Privatization is a very complex policy that, by its very nature, affects and is affected by a variety of interrelated political and economic factors. Through the model set out in the first chapter, I have focused on the dynamic interrelationship binding these factors together both at the decision-making and implementation stage. Although our sample was limited to only three countries, the model seems to explain very well why privatization did not materialize in the 1980s, and conversely, why in the 1990s state divestiture occurred relatively quickly in Argentina and Peru whereas in Brazil it did not gain strong momentum until the second half of the 1990s.

As hypothesized by the model, privatization did take place when both willingness and opportunity coincided and the presidents in charge displayed a strong leadership role in pushing the policy forward both at the decision-making and implementation stage. When willingness *and* opportunity were absent, chances were doomed from the start, as the experience of the 1980s testifies. In fact, we have seen that, although there were very good reasons to privatize in that decade, very little happened. Instead, governments responded to signs of economic crisis indecisively, partly because they were unable to perceive the magnitude of the problem. Alfonsín, Sarney, Belaunde, and García were politicians whose culture was rooted in the ISI tradition and believed that a strong state was still essential to overcome the mounting economic problems that affected their countries. The little privatization that some of these presidents timidly attempted was primarily meant to raise revenues in order to bridge the fiscal deficit. Thus, privatization was meant as a short-term remedy, not as part of a comprehensive adjustment plan. The opportunity dimension also failed to materialize in the 1980s. In the middle of that decade all three countries met with brief success in attempting heterodox stabilization plans. The heterodox approach tried to control inflation through wage and price freezes and monetary reform without resorting to budget cuts that, it was assumed, could have had a negative affect on employment and investments. Its initial success, however, created the illusion that quick-fix solutions were still readily available. Politicians continued to believe that the 'entrepreneurial state' development model could still be pursued through relatively minor changes. By the same token, all the presidents mentioned above did not see an opportunity to privatize since the macroeconomic environment discouraged private investment and most political parties and interest groups actively opposed a profound redefinition of the role of the state in the economy. Politics as usual ensued but with disastrous effects as the failure to respond to crises in the mid-1980s led to a worsened scenario by the end of that decade. In all fairness, only Alfonsín, by the end of his term, seemed to have realized that some kind of privatization was in order but, by 1988, whatever opportunity he had early in his term had vanished.

The Nature of the Crisis: Hyperinflation. In Chapter 1, one of the main questions was 'How does privatization get on the government agenda?' Part of the answer rests on the nature of the economic crisis. What I found is that socioeconomic crises of unprecedented magnitude are positively related to both the willingness and the opportunity to privatize. To be sure, an economic crisis is neither a necessary nor a sufficient condition *per se* to spur privatization. Again, the experience of the 1980s speaks for itself. Rather, what seems instead to be crucial is the intensity of the crisis. When a lingering crisis turns into hyperinflation, the chances for radical reforms, including privatization, improve tremendously. In fact, by most accounts, it was the socioeconomic chaos provoked by hyperinflation that induced Menem and Fujimori to opt for radical remedies against which they had campaigned only weeks before taking office. This is consistent with previous findings (Grindle and Thomas 1991) that saw policy reform as emerging in response to national crises. Indeed, as pointed out by Williamson and Haggard (1994: 563–4), 'crises have the effect of shocking countries out of traditional policy patterns, disorganizing the interest groups that typically veto policy reform, and generating pressure for politicians to change policies that can be seen as have failed'. In Brazil, on the contrary, the inflationary crescendo built up more gradually and postponed the sense of urgency among policy-makers.[1]

Ironically, the economic crisis is not an inhibiting factor for policy reform, as it was assumed in the 1980s by many politicians and analysts alike. It seems then clear that an unprecedented crisis opens for a president a *political* window of opportunity to break the impasse, introduces drastic changes, and puts privatization foes on the defensive. As pointed out by former Polish Finance Minister Lezsek Balcerowicz (1994), if the socioeconomic crisis reaches a point of no return, it creates the conditions for 'extraordinary politics'. In the 1990s, privatization in Argentina and, to a lesser degree, in Peru and Brazil respectively, was no longer meant as a short-term remedy but as part of market reforms aimed at shrinking the role of the state in the economy, as well as at redefining power relations among the most important political and socioeconomic actors of the countries here examined. Thus, as Williamson and Haggard (1994: 565) aptly put it, 'the worst of times give rise to the best of opportunities for those who understand the need for fundamental economic reform'.

This point brings us back to what was argued in the beginning of Chapter 1, and was reiterated consistently during my interviews with politicians, technocrats, economists, and business people. That is, in the end privatization is shaped by political rather than economic considerations. As long as a president is skeptical about it, it hardly gets off the ground; and even when it does, political factors, let alone economic ones, are likely to undermine its implementation. Politicians must be convinced that privatization can yield greater political and economic advantages than the 'politics as usual'. Menem, Fujimori, and to a lesser extent Collor, despite the many constraints they faced, still had the ultimate word on policy decisions and, unlike their predecessors, came to the conclusion that the best strategy was to embark on a privatization effort. In varying degrees, these three presidents reasoned that the potential payoffs outweighed the drawbacks. Capable technocrats were there in the 1980s but found themselves dealing with politicians either too afraid or simply unwilling to promote market reforms. Menem, Fujimori, Collor, despite their populist past (and later on Cardoso), recognized that profound reforms were no longer avoidable and that, as noted above, if the gamble paid off they could turn a dismal initial situation into one of opportunity for future gains. Their intelligence was to appoint good technocrats and delegate to them (in varying degrees of latitude) the authority to implement market reforms. As Bates (1994: 30) noted, 'technocratic power and good policy may well go together . . . but the former does not cause the latter. Rather, the relationship is the result of the decision of politicians to delegate political power to otherwise powerless experts so as to secure economically superior public policy.'

Leadership. This, in turn, takes us to the other factor that I identified as being crucial to sustaining a privatization policy from start to finish: leadership. Consistent with previous studies on policy reforms, I found that the stronger the leadership of the President in supporting the policy, the greater its rate of success in terms of speedy execution. In this regard, there is little doubt that Menem proved to be the most politically skillful and consistent President of all. Despite the strong opposition that he encountered within his own party and the constant feuding within his cabinet ministers, the Argentine President showed a remarkable sense of purpose. Menem's strong leadership made it possible for privatization to survive three different economic teams and a series of embarrassing corruption scandals. More so than the other presidents, Menem made privatization the focal point of his market reform agenda, which would explain his insistence in the face of occasional setbacks. Fujimori, on the contrary, was initially reluctant to push for privatization. Although he supported it, such a support was at times subordinated to short-term political considerations. For instance, privatization was substantially slowed down during the border conflict with Ecuador in 1995. Critics argued that where Chilean bidders were involved (i.e. ports and electricity) they could pose a national security threat since Chile has been a traditional foe of Peru and an ally of Ecuador. Fujimori appeared quite sensitive to Pérez de Cuellar's criticism (his main contender in the mid-1995 elections) that the scheduled privatization of strategic sectors like ports and petroleum were against the national interest. Fearing a loss of popularity, the Peruvian President basically put on hold the whole process until he won a second consecutive term. In the last quarter of 1995, with Fujimori firmly in control of a congressional majority, the privatization resumed although at a slower pace than before. Thus, political exigencies seemed to dictate Fujimori's support more so than was the case for Menem.

Collor de Mello, who actually was the only one of the three who had campaigned on a vague market reform platform, once elected proved to be the least consistent of all. Eduardo Modiano, the President of BNDES who spearheaded Collor's privatization policy, had often to count on his own ability to lobby Congress, interest groups, and the media, since he received scant support from the Finance Ministry and the Presidency. In Collor's priority list, as it was the case in the early stages of the first Fujimori administration, the anti-inflationary program absorbed most of the Brazilian President's energies, which relegated privatization to an issue of secondary importance. Only when the policy appeared to be derailing in Congress did Collor come out openly to support Modiano's efforts. The corruption scandal involving the President, which began to unravel in mid-1992, was the final disruptive element that almost sank the whole policy. Collor became embroiled in a nasty and time-consuming fight against Congress and the Supreme Court to prevent his own impeachment, leaving Modiano more isolated than ever at a time when the anti-privatization lobby multiplied its attacks. Support for the state divestiture program was even shakier under Vice-President Franco, who assumed the presidency after Collor's impeachment at the end of 1992. Having been an open critic of privatization while he was Vice President, Franco found himself in the awkward position of continuing a policy that, despite its many critics, had gained the endorsement of relevant political and business sectors. As time went on, Franco became convinced that many of the scheduled sell-offs had to be completed, but he proceeded very cautiously. Lacking a clear majority in Congress and faced with more urgent issues, Franco did not want to usher in new privatization plans that could have alienated him from some potential supporters. Therefore, he involved Congress in the privatization decision-making process and weakened the institutional authority of Montoro, who in the meantime had replaced Modiano as the technocrat in charge of the whole policy. As a result, Montoro found himself working on much shakier ground than his predecessor. He could not rely on the unequivocal support of his President when it counted the most. Moreover, he had to chair a privatization committee in which he had to argue with new members appointed by Franco (for political reasons) who opposed the policy. To complicate matters, he often ran into heated disputes with the Finance Ministry that often objected to some of his decisions.

It was noted in Chapter 1 that some scholars have suggested that a specific type of leadership is linked to successful policy reform: the visionary leader with a sense of history. Piñeira (1994) made this point by stressing the key role played by General Augusto Pinochet who, in his quest to reshape Chilean society, stood by the harsh market reform policies designed by his economic advisers regardless of their unpopularity. However, unlike demo- cratically elected leaders, Pinochet was a dictator and could afford taking the time and the political risks involved. Could any of the Presidents that under- took privatization in the 1990s still be labelled as visionary leaders? All of them envisaged for their country a great future under their statesmanship, but the only one who comes close to Pinochet's example is Menem. The Argentine President repeatedly talked about changing the course of history. More so than Fujimori and Collor, he made good on his promises, even though privatization went against the Peronist tradition as well as Menem's personal stance prior to 1989. The difference between Pinochet and Menem is that, while the former profoundly believed in the creation of a long-lasting con- servative regime, Menem was more concerned with his place in 'history', rather than the means to achieve that place. It was Menem's pragmatism that convinced him that market reforms were the right formula in the 1990s, not ideology. Much of the same can be argued for Fujimori, a self-proclaimed no-nonsense leader. Yet what distinguishes the Peruvian President from his Argentine counterpart is that it took Fujimori longer to embrace market re- forms, including privatization, wholeheartedly. In Collor's case, as testified by the 1992 impeachment procedure against him, it is evident that he was more interested in creating a financial empire by taking advantage of his office than in what was good for Brazil. Cardoso's case is quite different. Once he became convinced that market reforms and privatization were the only pos- sible solutions to overcome Brazil's economic problems, he embraced them with unusual vigor and sense of purpose. He then proceeded to pull together what had been until his election a very disorganized pro-reform coalition and kept it united through several crucial political tests. Moreover, what dis- tinguished Cardoso from his predecessors, as well as from Menem and Fujimori, was his ability to articulate in front of audiences of any kind why privatization was beneficial to society. Taking into account the fact that he faced much stronger institutions than was true in Argentina and Peru, Cardoso's coalition building effort was quite remarkable.

In the first chapter I also stressed that the style in which leadership is exercised is critical. Clearly Menem, Fujimori, Collor, and Cardoso displayed very different styles, which account for the different success encountered by their divestiture programs. Menem, Collor, and Cardoso, while retaining the power to make the financial decision, delegated substantial authority to their respective economic teams in terms of policy design and implementation. In Argentina Menem established a competitive system within his cabinet to provoke debate so that he could learn more from discussions. However, by the same token, he also delegated a lot of authority to his economy ministers. This was particularly true of Domingo Cavallo who, due to his competence and strong support from business, foreign governments, and multilateral agencies, excelled in Menem's competitive system and usually prevailed over cabinet opposition to his plans. As a matter of fact, Cavallo became a virtual economic czar who centralized all economic decisions. This, in turn, enabled Cavallo to design probably the most coherent and speedy divestiture program of the three cases observed. None the less, even a strong personality like Cavallo had to reckon with Menem, a very astute politician whose skills proved time and again critical to keeping the privatization program on track. Indeed, even the closest of Cavallo's associates recognized that no major privatization, or market reform for that matter, could be implemented without Menem's consent. Collor and Franco also were delegators but often, when feeling the pressure of political opposition, tended to run into open conflicts with their economic advisers thus resulting in a revolving door of technocrats. Cardoso's style was also characterized by the delegation of a substantial amount of authority to his ministers. Yet, he was much more prone to consensus building, and displayed great skill in overcoming the many differences existing among contending factions within his cabinet. Fujimori, on the contrary, adopted a 'hands on' style, which led him to be involved in the micromanagement of several policies, including privatization. Unlike his Argentine and Brazilian colleagues, Fujimori relied on the teamwork and the wisdom of a small group of advisers. This style, while giving coherence to the government policies, on occasions, turned out to slow down privatization as the President and his staff were simply overworked.

The Decision-Making Process

Willingness. Let us now turn to a discussion of how the model explains the different degree of success that the various administrations had in deciding and rapidly implementing their state divestiture policies. As discussed earlier, the decision to privatize was shaped by both willingness and opportunity. In turn, I argued that willingness was the result of mixed motives that we divided into ideology and pragmatism.

In the three countries studied ideological factors were, at best, secondary in affecting the decision to privatize. This finding is consistent with previous research on reform policy (Williamson 1994b). As noted earlier, of all the Presidents, only Collor campaigned on a vague market reform platform, whereas Menem and Fujimori were actually against it before taking office. The philosophical tenets upon which privatization is based were alien to the political background of all the Presidents observed. None the less, although the Argentine and Peruvian Presidents were far from being 'true believers', they turned out to be quick learners. Once in office, they embraced the rhetoric of market economics as a development strategy superior to state-led capitalism. Cardoso instead converted prior to his election and campaigned on a market reform agenda but appeared to be equally committed to it during his first term.

It is also unlikely that the emasculation of labor power was perceived as an ideological issue, as was the case for Pinochet and Thatcher. Rather, privatization was used as a means to discipline labor in the public sector, which was traditionally a privileged group within the union movement and resisted any move toward change. Menem was elected in 1989 with the crucial aid of labor and maintained political alliances with the most important sectors of the labor movement (in the private sector) by the time he was re-elected in 1995. On that occasion, he promised to 'pulverize' unemployment through a new public infrastructure program and other social policies benefitting the working and middle classes. Collor, and more so Franco and Cardoso, while not sympathetic to the unions, were far from being hostile to them on ideological grounds. Only Fujimori seemed to have a deep-seated antipathy for unionism. Yet again, this is not enough to argue that such an attitude was ideologically grounded.

Popular capitalism, despite official documents and public speeches, had no true ideological dimension to it. In all the three countries it was tried selectively and usually when large PEs were at stake, often to overcome political resistance.

As for workers' participation in the process, steps were taken in each program to allow workers to acquire shares of their companies, although gain this was done for a minority of PEs. None the less, this effort seemed to respond more to public relation and strategic considerations. Shares were offered as a means to soften employees' opposition to privatization. In many cases they were largely undersubscribed as employees did not find them to be a good investment. Furthermore, workers' participation programs appeared to many as a mere façade, an impression that was strengthened by the often poor and disorganized effort that government officers made to 'sell' the idea.

It was then political pragmatism that was instrumental in bringing about state divestiture. Among pragmatic factors, as I explained before, hyperinflation stands out as being probably the most crucial. Having more gradual approaches to economic stabilization (such as the heterodox experiments of the 1980s) failed, no alternatives were left to policy-makers other than implementing those market reforms advocated by the IMF, the World Bank, the US government, and the international financial community. It is important to underscore that, at the peak of the crisis, some factors carried more weight than others. Namely, the use of privatization revenues to finance the fiscal deficit and the balance of payments. Moreover, as governments began to prioritize their expenditures and areas of intervention in the economy, privatization became an essential policy in rationalizing the state sector by divesting those service and manufacturing operations that were no longer perceived as strategic. In this regard Menem's approach was the most radical as he began to sell off, right from the beginning, large companies in the service sector. In Brazil, initially, the bulk of the privatization effort affected manufacturing companies as they were less controversial. In addition, some sectors like petroleum and telecommunications, which were sold rapidly in Argentina, could not in Brazil simply because the 1988 constitution forbade it. Only after President Cardoso took office in 1995 did the Brazilian Congress give the green light for the participation of private investments in those areas. Peru's case falls in between. As in Brazil, privatization started with manufacturing and mining companies but did not gain momentum until the national telephone company was transferred to Telefónica of Spain in 1994. However, it took almost two years until the next large divestiture, involving some assets of the oil company Petroperú, would resume. As noted earlier, this delay was largely due to Fujimori's electoral exigencies in 1995.

A second set of factors, like the improvement of economic efficiency, the modernization of the domestic economy (by allowing foreign companies to take over former state monopolies and bring along badly needed modern technology), and the improvement of the business climate, were also important, but not as critical, particularly in the early stages of the stabilization effort. In fact, in the beginning, the immediate concern was to raise cash and cut costs. Efficiency considerations came into play later in the privatization process. The reason was twofold. First, as the economy began to stabilize, there was less anxiety and more time for careful planning than had earlier been the case. Second, critics correctly pointed out that many sales in all these countries ended up by transferring monopolies from the public to the private sector or by strengthening existing oligopolies without assuring an adequate protection of consumers and investors. Thus, economic efficiency became an issue as the initial hastiness gave way to greater public scrutiny.

Privatization as a means to improve the business climate was important in Argentina, Peru, and in Brazil under Cardoso. In Argentina, Menem repeatedly stated in several interviews that one of his main goals upon taking office was to create good relations with the business community, both domestic and foreign, which had deteriorated significantly in the last two years of the Alfonsín administration. In this regard, Menem took a very active role as we shall see in a moment. Fujimori adopted much of the same rationale as under his predecessor, García, government relations with the business community were even more antagonistic than in Argentina. In July 1987, García's decision to nationalize private banks turned the entire private sector against him such that, by 1988, it was openly calling for García to resign. In the case of Collor, privatization was also to set the stage for an improvement in government relations with business. However, this intention was undercut by other measures introduced by the Collor Plan I. In fact, the plan not only introduced the privatization program but, in order to combat inflation, also froze the bulk of the country's financial liquidity (about 80 per cent) held in the short-term, 'overnight' market, or in personal savings accounts. Squeezed out financially, many businesses protested the measures. To make things worse, Collor's authoritarian, confrontational style vis-à-vis his critics, contributed to exacerbating rather than improving the business climate. Under Franco instead, the low priority placed on privatization did not seem to have any appreciable impact in this regard. Cardoso instead understood from the start the importance of privatization as a key factor to convince the business community that he was serious about market reforms and, despite some initial difficulties, had Congress pass key legislation as a preliminary step to overcome investors' initial skepticism.

The use of state divestiture as a means to reward supporters shows mixed evidence. It surely was the case in Argentina. Menem courted the endorsement of big domestic business from the beginning. Many of the Argentine conglomerates had been thriving from the 1950s on thanks to inflated government contracts and industrial production subsidies. Dismantling the entrepreneurial state was threatening to such interests, but Menem was skillful in proposing as a compensation mechanism the sale of state enterprises under very favorable conditions. As a matter of fact, the first privatizations in telecommunications and air passenger cargo required that consortia be formed among foreign companies that would take over management and provide new technology, international banks that held debt-equity papers to be used as part of the payment, and domestic groups that had the political connections and knew the market.[2] In other cases, like the highways, only domestic conglomerates came forward as they had already pre-arranged the terms of sale with government officers behind close doors. It is no coincidence then that in the first round of privatizations, between 1990 and early 1991, the participation of domestic conglomerates reached its peak and that during this time the whole process was marred by contract irregularities, charges of corruption, and collusion between government officials and business representatives. According to Majul (1994), who conducted extensive interviews with the leaders of some of the most important Argentine conglomerates, there was a direct relationship between the amount of business that these groups obtained through privatization and their 'donations' to Menem's campaign fund. When in the first quarter of 1995 Argentina suffered a massive capital flight (about $8 billion) in the wake of the Mexican financial crisis of December 1994, the same conglomerates came to Menem's help by subscribing $1 billion in government bonds as a public gesture of support. By 1996, the symbiosis between political and economic power reached levels last seen in Argentina in the 1930s, when big landowners ran the country to their own benefit.

In Brazil, on the contrary, support from the key interest groups did not develop under Collor. While Menem created compensation mechanisms for key interest groups to build support, Collor refused to do that. The only beneficiaries of his policy were people who would submit to the corruption scheme engineered by his campaign manager, P. C. Farias. Cardoso's style was quite different. Since his inception he tried to organize business support for his reforms to overcome congressional resistance. He also made sure that Brazilian businesses could play a large role in his most important divestitures, although there is no clear evidence that this was done in order to forge a privileged alliance between his administration and specific domestic conglomerates as it was the case in Argentina.

As for Peru, there is no clear evidence either of wrongdoing or of an explicit government attempt to reward supporters. If indeed Fujimori's policies favored private capital, the Peruvian President made a point of not identifying himself too closely with a domestic business community that had squarely supported Vargas Llosa in the 1990 Presidential elections.

Of all the pragmatic factors, the strengthening of capital markets through privatization was probably the least relevant. Although the capital markets of Argentina, Brazil, and Peru literally boomed in the mid-1990s thanks to the inflow of foreign capital and the return of domestic capital taken abroad during the 1970s and 1980s, only a handful of important transfers were carried out through the placement of shares at the local stock exchange. The country that most often used this method was Brazil, which had the largest and most sophisticated capital markets in Latin America. In general, Argentina and Peru, aside from some international public offers, opted for public auctions. The reasons are simple. First, to lure investors, it was fundamental to guarantee them the management control of the companies they were going to acquire. Second, despite some reforms to make local stock exchange operations transparent, insider trading remained prevalent in all these countries, which alarmed small investors. Thus, government officials concluded, it was safer to sell companies through auctions than using public offers that, had investors not shown up, would have been an embarrassment.

Opportunity. In all three countries privatization programs were launched under adverse macroeconomic conditions. However, there were still investors willing to take their chances. The general rule of thumb to explain business interest in state divestiture rests on the nature of the company up for sale. On the one hand, tenders were more likely to come forward when PEs operated in lucrative markets characterized by either monopoly or oligopoly conditions. Telecommunications, electricity, and oil in all these countries attracted most of the attention. In Brazil, steel and petrochemicals companies found buyers among their private competitors and suppliers. On the other hand, companies that were deficit-ridden and did not appear to have good prospects for quick investment returns were hard to sell. The cancellation or postponement of several sales were not only due to technical difficulties but often to the lack of interested buyers.

Of course, governments were not mere passive sellers. The Menem and Fujimori administrations tried hard to overcome the objective obstacles posed by the dismal macroeconomic conditions they inherited by creating good opportunities for entrepreneurs. Argentina and Peru moved quickly to lift old restrictions on foreign investments: unlike in the past, foreigners were allowed to invest in whichever sector they pleased without any limitation on ownership rights. Equally important, domestic and foreign investors were given equal treatment before the law, while previously local entrepreneurs had enjoyed greater privileges. Incentives came also in the type of PEs that the government chose to sell. As already discussed, Argentina and Peru put on the auction block companies in natural monopolies that were likely to generate immediate returns. In the case of the telephone company in Argentina, the Menem administration increased tremendously tariffs prior to privatization and included in the sale contract clauses that assured the new private owners over a sixteen per cent profit in the first year after the transfer.

The Argentine and Brazilian governments gave additional incentives in the form of debt-equity conversion schemes. By accepting debt-equity instruments as a form of payment instead of cash (as it was the case in Peru), potential investors could make huge savings since the quotation of these equities in the secondary market at the time was at an all time low. As much as the Argentines and Peruvians moved aggressively to lure buyers, the Brazilians proceeded more cautiously, which partly explains the lack of enthusiasm among investors when Collor unveiled his privatization program. For instance, Argentina and Peru tried to diffuse foreign investors' concerns by renegotiating their external debt with creditor banks and the IMF, which decreased their country-risk rating. On the contrary Brazil, under Collor and Franco, continued to have serious disagreements with its creditors, thus fueling the skepticism of many foreign investors regarding the chances of market reforms and keeping them out of the country. Moreover, while restrictions on foreign ownership were progressively eased, they remained substantially higher than in Argentina and Peru.[3] The constitutional ban against the sale of state monopolies in the sectors most attractive to foreigners, like telecommunications and petroleum, further limited the appeal of the Brazilian privatization process. Strong congressional opposition to any constitutional change on this matter added to the general sense of uncertainty regarding the future of the whole policy. It is thus not by chance that, compared to Argentina and Peru, foreign participation in the state divestiture program was significantly less important in Brazil until Cardoso had Congress pass new legislation eliminating discriminatory rules against foreign investors and government monopolies in oil and public utilities.

A favorable public mood among important sectors of society existed in Argentina, and to a lesser degree in Peru, but not in Brazil. In the first two countries the debate over privatization had heated up by the late 1980s. Alsogaray and Angeloz in Argentina, and Vargas Llosa in Peru, emerged as powerful opinion leaders who persuaded important domestic constituencies that state divestiture was unavoidable. The disastrous state of PEs in public services in these two countries also created a fertile ground for privatization advocates. People had simply had enough. Public opinion surveys taken in urban areas showed that in both countries people favored privatization. In Brazil, on the contrary, public services had deteriorated but still performed well enough for many people to see no reason to sell them. Moreover, left-wing parties and trade unions scared off many people by arguing that privatization would invariably lead to higher tariffs and result in the beginning of the end for many social benefits acquired by the working and middle classes since the 1950s. Furthermore, in Brazil there did not exist the kind of articulate and forceful opinion leaders present in Argentina and Peru. Brazilian socioeconomic elites began to displaying the same kind of consensus witnessed in Argentina and Peru on privatization only in the mid-1990s, which coincided with the election of a determined President like Cardoso who made it a top priority of his reform agenda.

Certainly, one may argue that it is disputable that a consensus existed in the first place. After all, Menem and Fujimori were elected in their first attempt by campaigning against it. Does then a well disposed public matter? Sachs (1994: 505) argued that, 'in deep crises, there simply is no consensus to build upon, only confusion, anxiety, and a cacophony of conflicting opinions'. This is because, in Sachs's view, radical policy reforms are too controversial, they provoke fear among the public about the unforeseen consequences, and the public itself does not really know what the true content and benefits of the policies are. This kind of a scenario, Sachs concluded, is not conducive to consensus building and Presidents and technocrats alike should not waste precious time in that direction. In general, in a situation of acute crisis, it is rare that consensus exists. However, what tends to explain the difference between Argentina and Peru, on the one hand, and Brazil, on the other, is the degree to which large strata of society were convinced that fundamental changes were necessary. In the former two countries this was the case earlier than in Brazil. We shall see later that this helps explaining why, privatization encountered much less opposition in Argentina and Peru than in Brazil.

There is considerable agreement among both practitioners and analysts that foreign aid is crucial for successful reform policy. As Sachs (1994: 504) succinctly stated it, 'the market cannot do it all by itself, international help is critical . . . Aid is crucial because reforms are inherently very fragile. There is typically little consensus on what should be done, pessimism is rife, and the reformers' hold on power and policy tenuous'. My own findings do confirm that external aid was positively associated with the decision to privatize and the more foreign help was involved, the greater the chances that privatization would be sustained over time. All three countries faced external pressure to stabilize their economies and honor their debt commitments. There is little doubt that this was the case in Argentina and Peru. In both countries foreign aid came in the form of conditionality. Financial assistance came forward but was made contingent upon the enforcement of structural adjustment policies that invariably made privatization a top priority. In the stand-by agreements that the Menem and Fujimori administrations signed with the IMF, state divestiture always occupied a significant role as it was often used to finance the fiscal deficit. The IMF worked as a broker of the international financial community, by negotiating with each country the terms upon which financial help was disbursed. The World Bank and the IDB in both Argentina and Peru provided technical assistance and funds. Through these institutions' loans, Argentina and Peru hired foreign consultants to assist the government in designing their privatization programs. In addition these same institutions routinely sent technical missions of experts to these countries for specific projects. Moreover, they also provided funds for early retirement programs. In the case of Peru, the United Nations Development Agency also got involved (in Argentina its role was negligible due to disagreements with Cavallo) by managing the funds of the privatization receipts. The Paris Club and foreign governments, primarily the US, and some member states of the European Union, also disbursed important loans for the reform process as a whole.

Foreign aid seemed to have been critical in making Menem and Fujimori swallow the bitter pill of economic austerity. By the end of the Alfonsín and García administrations external financing had virtually come to a halt. The return of foreign aid to these countries strengthened the prestige of the President and their teams domestically because, as Menem and Fujimori argued, without it their respective countries could have hardly survived. As in Turkey and Poland before, external help strengthened reformers at home; but there is more to it than that. External pressure was for instance instrumental in allowing Cavallo to win political battles within Menem's cabinet on numerous occasions. In August 1995, some Peronist legislators tried to alter the content of the bill privatizing the mail system that was being debated in Congress. The changes were meant to openly favor a powerful domestic businessman personally tied Menem and some key ministers. To stop this not-so-covert move, Cavallo denounced the scheme to the press. Eventually, an angry Menem halted the debate of the bill as the US Embassy, foreign investors, and multilateral agencies openly supported Cavallo fearing that an eventual cabinet crisis would ensue leading to the minister's resignation. Given that Cavallo was widely credited for Argentina's successful market reform policies, the international community reasoned that he was, for the time being, their best guarantee for those policies to be carried out in a competent manner.

Brazil, again, did not fit this pattern. In mid-1989 Sarney had declared a de facto moratorium on debt interest payments, which angered the international financial community. Collor's election led to some optimism that the impasse on the external debt negotiations could be broken and payments be resumed. None the less, no real progress was made under Collor to negotiate a stand-by loan with the IMF. Things did not improve much with Franco either. In March 1994, the IMF refused to endorse a $2.1 billion stand-by loan. This prevented the US Treasury to issue a zero coupon bond that Brazil needed for a Brady-type deal to renegotiate $52 billion owed to commercial banks. The IMF simply considered Franco's stabilization policies as not going far enough and as such cast doubt over the effectiveness of Brazil's privatization program. In the meantime, precious time was wasted. Brazil reluctancy to submit to the IMF's demands prevented Collor, and later Franco, from using foreign assistance for its privatization program. In fact, foreign assistance in Brazil was noticeable for its absence. The state divestiture program remained largely a domestic affair. Whether or not this fact is positively correlated to its initial lack of progress, as compared to Argentina and Peru, remains an open question. Most likely, foreign financial institutions would have pressed Brazil to make changes in the breadth and scope of the divestiture program, changes that Brazil was not willing to make at the time. In fact, giving in to the IMF demands was likely to force budget cuts totalling $1 billion.[4] This would have meant the cancelling of the international financing of large PEs, whose expenditures constituted a heavy burden on the government deficit. However, doing so would have affected the 'pork' of too many powerful interests in Congress that Franco could not alienate. In the end, Brazil could afford to avoid an agreement with the IMF because it could finance additional loans from commercial banks by using its large trade surplus (although at very high interest rates). Argentina and Peru simply could not. Only in the Fall of 1998 did Brazil ask the IMF for its financial assistance, but by that time the largest privatization transactions had been completed. Summing up, compared to its neighbors, foreign aid for privatization was not a vital issue for Brazil until the financial crisis of November 1998 due to the stronger bargaining position that it enjoyed vis-à-vis multilateral agencies and commercial banks.

Implementation

Government Capabilities

Government cohesiveness is positively related to the implementation of privatization. Likewise, whenever privatization was an integral part of a comprehensive program, as was the case under Menem, Fujimori, and Cardoso, rather than a piecemeal one, as under Collor and Franco, it became a high government priority and was implemented with greater vigor. A clear example of this can be found in Argentina. In the first year and a half of the Menem administration privatization was the cornerstone of Menem's stabilization program but was plagued by cabinet squabbles (i.e. the Ministry of Public Works in charge of privatization and the Economy Ministry), resulting in a series of embarrassing feuds over who was in charge of what. With the appointment of Domingo Cavallo as new Minister of the Economy, the whole situation turned around dramatically. Cavallo made privatization compatible with the macroeconomic target of his Convertibility Plan, whereas before, as in Brazil, state divestiture and economic stabilization were entrusted to different ministries and seemed to proceed on different, and often colliding tracks. Moreover, with Menem's blessing, Cavallo centralized all economic decisions under his authority, thus turning his department into a super ministry as it was never seen before. The Ministry of Public Works was merged with the Economy Ministry and the implementation of the privatization process became directly dependent upon Cavallo. The minister brought about 200 trusted advisers and technical staff, many of whom had worked with him at his Fundación Mediterranean in Cordoba. These people were placed in the most sensitive places of the Ministry of the Economy, Public Works, and Services and faithfully carried out the plans that Cavallo laid out. The situation that was so created allowed an unprecedented degree of coherence in both the formulation and implementation of economic policy, and played a crucial role in the rapid implementation of the privatization program.

In March 1990, the Collor administration moved quickly in what seemed to be a bold attempt to create a strong cohesiveness in the cabinet. The President cut the number of cabinet ministers from thirty-two as existed under Sarney to twelve. This was widely interpreted as a sign that Collor wanted to exercise a strong hand in policy making. Moreover, the finance, planning, industry, and trade ministries were merged into a new 'super ministry'—the Economy Ministry, foreshadowing what happened a year later in Argentina. The privatization committee, in charge of state divestiture, was made dependent directly upon the President. Key positions in all these government jobs were awarded to young, relatively unknown economists who had served under Collor when he was governor of Alagoas, like Economy Minister Zelia Cardoso de Mello. Notwithstanding these bold moves to make the economic team cohesive and strengthen its authority, almost from the start disagreements surfaced among cabinet ministers and members of the economic team. As the Collor I and later the Collor II stabilization plans failed, such disagreements exacerbated leading to a score of resignations. The technical qualifications of Zelia Cardoso de Mello and her team became increasingly a matter of controversy, putting President Collor on the defensive and eventually forcing him to sack his Economy Minister in May 1991. Her replacement was the Brazilian Ambassador to the United States, Marcilio Marques Moreira, a diplomat who enjoyed the respect of the domestic business community and international creditors. However, even Marques Moreira, despite his pledge to continue market reforms, could not do much, particularly in the face of the corruption scandal that involved the President starting in mid-1992, which paralyzed the administration. After Franco took office, the economy ministry was disbanded and its functions spread among ministries that had been previously merged. As a result, the decision-making process became more cumbersome and diffused. Government cohesiveness also deteriorated, as Franco's cabinet represented a wide range of interests often in conflict with one another when it came to privatization. In sum, whatever coherence and centralized authority that existed under Collor deteriorated appreciably up until Fernando Enrique Cardoso was appointed as Finance Minister toward the end of the Franco administration. This helps explain the snail's pace that the state divestiture process took from between 1993 and 1994. Once elected President, Cardoso greatly improved the cohesiveness of his own cabinet. Although some of the technocrats who had helped him designing the Real Plan eventually left, he was able to replace them with people who shared the same economic philosophy and commitment to market reforms.

In the case of Fujimori, government cohesiveness was strong. Fujimori, and his 'kitchen cabinet' seemed to be more involved in micromanagement decisions than their counterparts in Argentina and Brazil. As in Brazil (under Collor) and in Argentina (beginning with Cavallo), the Economy Ministry was entrusted with wide powers to manage the economy. In spite of the fact that several economy ministers were at the helm of macroeconomic policies, as was the case in Argentina, the general thrust of the stabilization policies did not change. The privatization program in particular, was entrusted upon COPRI and made directly dependent upon the executive branch. Under the leadership of Montoya, who was COPRI's director for nearly four years, the program moved along steadily, although it remained vulnerable to presidential vetoes. Thus, both the government in general, and the economic team in particular, appeared to be more cohesive under Menem, Fujimori, and Cardoso, than under Collor and Franco. This, in turn, resulted in a greater support from the executive to the economic team carrying out the privatization program, which gave the latter the political muscle to resist the lobbying of interest groups, the legislature, and critics within the cabinet.

Technical and administrative capacity at the time the privatization programs were launched in all these countries was in general weak. Only BNDES in Brazil already had experience in state divestiture programs, as a few were carried out under Sarney. In Argentina and, more so in Peru, there were no special agencies or ministries having staffs capable of tackling the economic and legal issues involved in the transfer of assets to the private sector. The rather sloppy way in which privatization was carried out prior to Cavallo is partly the consequence of the lack of expertise from the Ministry of Public Works, and Services that was responsible for it. Invariably, in all these countries, foreign consultants were hired to advise on technical matters. In Argentina and Peru, as we noted earlier, these consultants were often paid through loans from multilateral lending agencies. The same agencies also provided direct technical assistance in all these countries but Brazil where, at least during the Collor period, the BNDES spearheaded the whole process. Through trial and error, as time went by, in each country usually (but not always) both the technical and administrative performance of government officers improved significantly. Many professionals were hired locally away from the private sector. A typical case was Montoya in Peru. The same applies to Argentina where the size of the technical staff devoted to privatization within the Ministry of the Economy, Public Works, and Services expanded rapidly after Cavallo took over as the number of PEs on the auction block reached its peak between 1992 and 1994. In terms of organization of the whole process, a similar pattern took place in Peru where, however, the Peru adopted a more decentralized at the micromanagement level than Argentina and Brazil. In fact, the individual CEPRIs were a more flexible administrative unit, made up primarily from private sector representatives. Once a company was sold, the CEPRIs would cease to exist. Thus, generally speaking, the Brazilian and Argentine governments counted more on their own bureaucracies than Peru did.

Bureaucratic cooperation turned out to be a crucial issue. Often administrative decisions took more than expected to be implemented in all of these countries. Whenever the decision-making process was ambiguous and diffuse, squabbles and delays ensued. For instance, in the first phase of the Argentine program, Dromi ran into several harsh disagreements with the then Minister of the Economy, Erman González, and the trustee of the ENTel telephone company, María Julia Alsogaray, which created a situation of confusion and anxiety among bidders. Bad experiences like these later convinced Menem to grant Cavallo the authority to centralize all decisions under his authority and to downgrade several ministries into undersecretariats to simplify and quicken the whole process. In the case of Brazil, particularly under Franco, the multiple jurisdictions and actors involved in the final decision slowed considerably state divestiture. Even in Peru, where a highly centralized decision-making process was instituted from the start, occasional disagreements would occur between the COPRI and individual CEPRIs, with the latter being invariably overruled.

Strong executive authority was positively associated with the implementation of state divestiture. On this matter Nelson (1994: 473) observed that in many developing and post-communist countries the, 'initial macroeconomic stabilization measures and the first (often very major) steps toward deregulation and opening up the economy have typically been taken rather autocratically, by executive decree, with legislature pressured to act quickly to provide pro forma approval'. This is precisely the case in all three of our examples, as privatization was enforced through executive orders in its early stages. The method chosen was, however, a little different in style rather than in content. In Argentina, Menem had Congress delegating to him emergency powers to legislate without any supervision. This was accomplished by using carrot and stick tactics with the main opposition party, the Radicals. Menem simply threatened Congress that had the legislature resisted his plans, he was going to enforce them through executive orders anyhow. Having left office six months ahead of schedule in complete disgrace, Alfonsín and his Radicals were incapable of mounting a credible opposition, no matter how outrageous Menem's methods were. Having done so would have amounted to political suicide. Thus, in less than two months after taking office, Menem enforced the legal mainstay of his market reforms, namely the State Reform Law and the Law of Economic Emergency, by the stroke of a pen. In Peru, Fujimori was even bolder. In April 1992, he closed the Congress and thereafter legislated by executive orders until a friendlier legislature was elected in 1993 under a new constitution that broadened executive powers. By that time, the traditional Peruvian parties were more in disrepute than in Argentina, and Fujimori's supporters won a comfortable majority in the new congress making authoritarian measures no longer a necessity. In Brazil, Collor tried much of the same, but with much less success. His administration set in motion the privatization program through an executive order shortly after his inauguration. However, Collor faced a much stronger Congress than did his Argentine and Peruvian colleagues. Nor did he have a political party with the large representation in Congress that Menem enjoyed. Collor's political movement had only 7 per cent of the seats in the House of Deputies. In such a situation, some kind of political engineering to build coalitions was a must. Had he been a skillful negotiator like Menem the President could have actually exploited the deep divisions existing among the many parties represented in the federal legislature to his advantage. Instead, Collor antagonized his enemies. As a result, paradoxically, he brought together political parties that otherwise would have been on different sides of the debate but ended up joining forces as they perceived Collor's authoritarianism an even greater threat. In the end, the legislature stopped Collor's abuse of executive orders by vetoing them and successfully appealing to the Brazilian Supreme Court, which severely constrained the administration's room for maneuvering thereafter. Cardoso, on the contrary, made coalition building his first priority. Having learned from Collor's mistakes, he engaged in a complicated strategy contemplating short-term payoffs appealing to congressmen and governors in return for their support regarding privatizations that otherwise would have never got off the ground. While his efforts were often costly for the federal treasury, and took some time to accomplish, by 1998 only the oil sector was still left to be divested.

A similar pattern took place with respect to the independence of the judiciary. Menem, a few months after being elected in 1989, packed the Argentine Supreme Court. Fujimori simply ousted those justices he did not trust. These measures turned out to be of fundamental importance in sheltering the reform agenda from legal challenges. In fact, as we saw in Argentina, when a federal prosecutor tried to stop the very first privatization until charges of irregularities could be cleared, the Supreme Court took away the case from the investigating magistrate and ruled in no time in favor of the government. At the federal court level, both Argentine and Peruvian Presidents made use of their prerogative to appoint judges and state prosecutors to key positions. Those magistrates who were inherited from previous administrations that did not follow the executive's wishes often resigned in disgust or were simply fired as in Peru. Again, Brazil's case was the exception to the rule. As noted, the Supreme Court's ruling on the unconstitutionality of Collor's reissuing of the same executive orders once they had expired, prevented the President from adopting the strategy employed by the other two heads of state. Likewise, the Brazilian Supreme Court proved to be more independent than in Argentina when it disallowed the system of capitalization of the external debt through privatization. In the face of these reversals Collor could do little as had he tried to change the court's composition in his favor he would have created a political storm. The lower courts were also less susceptible to political manipulations. Unlike Argentina where the judges and prosecutors are nominated by the President and ratified by the Senate, following in the United States model, in Brazil appointments are made through competitive examination following the French model. Although this is not to say that the federal judiciary is not politicized in Brazil, it is not as easily manipulated like in Argentina. Even Cardoso, who ultimately prevailed in pushing controversial privatizations like CVRD and Telebrás, had to spend a lot of time and energy to come up with a strategy that would prevent court injunctions to stop the divestiture process at every step of the way. Moreover, in Argentina and Peru, there was a clear attempt to eliminate, or at least emasculate, governmental institutions that could perform administrative inquiries.

In short, while Cardoso was a dedicated democrat who tried to work within the boundaries of the rule of law, Menem, Fujimori, and Collor shared a similar authoritarian style towards problem solving. The preservation of fundamental democratic principles was for them an expandable nuisance. Keeping an appearance of constitutionality was desirable but not necessary. The reason then why the Argentine and Peruvian privatization programs moved along rapidly in their first phase, as opposed to Brazil, had much to do with the capacity of Menem and Fujimori to neutralize the checks and balances of the legislative and judicial branch of government. Later on in their terms, both Presidents acted less aggressively as their respective parties through new congressional elections were able to gain enough seats to control the legislative agenda and pass reforms in a democratic way. In Brazil this was never the case. The importance of this point cannot be emphasized enough. In Argentina in 1995, for instance, things began to change. Although inflation dropped to record lows, a deep recession ensued and the economy registered negative growth (−4.4 per cent of GDP). This trend was coupled with an unprecedented 17.4 per cent of unemployed.[5] Peronist legislators began to openly oppose the bills that Cavallo sent to Congress. Government officials close to the economy minister openly admitted that by 1995 the political climate had changed. Congress had become more belligerent and was trying to regain some of its prerogatives and force the government to negotiate its policies.[6] In July 1996, following yet another squabble, Menem decided to sack Cavallo, a decision that not only encountered the support of Congress but also that of public opinion.[7]

In Chapter 1, we saw that some analysts believed that successful reform was possible if technopols, or technocrats with wide political authority, were put in charge of economic policy. Only in the case of Argentina can we regard Cavallo as fitting the definition of a technopol. In Brazil, Fernando Enrique Cardoso, when he became Finance Minister, came close to have some of Cavallo's prerogatives. Coincidentally, under Cardoso's leadership Brazil launched its first, comprehensive, and very successful stabilization plan in decades.[8] However, once Cardoso became President he did not allow the emergence of a technopol among his ministers. In the case of Peru, Boloña, Fujimori's second economy minister, tried to assume a strong profile but when he disagreed over the President's plan to put greater emphasis on social spending and job creation in preparation for his re-election bid of 1995, he had to quit. Thus, in Peru, the market reforms, including privatization, continued despite some hiccups, casting doubts on the need of a technopol at the helm. So, while such a figure is surely desirable, the evidence presented by our country sample leads to inconclusive results.

The political science literature, on both developed and developing countries, emphasizes the fact that the time to introduce controversial economic reforms is immediately after a new administration takes office. The so-called honeymoon hypothesis postulates that the public will be more willing to tolerate the sacrifices imposed by new policies at the beginning rather that at the end of a given government. 'Presumably', as Williamson (1994*b*: 20) contended, 'this honeymoon will be longer, and the scope for profound change greater, the deeper was the proceeding crisis.' Speed is therefore essential. The experiences of the countries in this book do confirm it. Furthermore, they also show that the faster and the more comprehensive privatization was, the more momentum it gained. Argentina is a typical case in point. Brazil, like Argentina, made privatization part of its stabilization program from the beginning under Collor. However, it was not nearly as comprehensive nor did it move as fast. In Peru, Fujimori stabilized the economy first and privatized later and more gradually than in Argentina.

The importance of speed is that it helps in preventing political opposition to mobilize. Its drawbacks are, particularly when a government has little experience in state divestiture, higher chances that technical mistakes may occur and assets be undervalued. Moving slower can produce more careful planning and economic performance down the road but not necessarily better prices if the international market crowds out or take a nose dive as it happened in the second half of 1998. The tradeoff between the political risks involved in moving gradually, on the one hand, and revenues and efficiency concerns is a difficult one. This is a point to which I shall return later. From a general standpoint, what seems clear is that the bolder and the quicker a stabilization program contemplating privatization was, the faster the economy returned to growth. Argentina and Peru experienced higher growth levels in the first half of the 1990s than Brazil. A similar pattern can be seen in Eastern Europe.

Political Responses

Nelson (1990*b*) argued that when political opposition is either discredited or disorganized policy reforms are easier to implement. This statement holds true in our cases. In Argentina and Peru both opposition parties and unions were quite discredited. Brazil, instead, presents a more complex picture. Public opinion polls did show in the late 1980s that people were quite disillusioned with political parties. However, as weak and divided political opposition was to Collor in Congress, it was still capable of slowing down his reform process even prior to his impeachment. This points to the fact that a situation where the opposition is discredited and divided does indeed help, but in order to swing the balance a President should take advantage of such weaknesses to form, early on, a political coalition that can prevent privatization foes to regroup. However, a policy like privatization, which takes many years to bring to completion, needs in the long run if not consensus, at least a substantial amount of public support. Bresser Pereira (1993: 351), who was Finance Minister under the Sarney administration, made this point explicitly: 'economic reforms need political support. And political support depends on the seriousness of the crisis and the sensitivity of society to economic disarray. Lack of political support for my economic plan was clearly the central problem. I did not get support from my President, nor from my party, nor from the broader society.'

In this regard, as we already discussed, presidential leadership did make a difference. Menem, Cardoso, and to a lesser extent Fujimori, were able to put together political coalitions that cut across party lines and socioeconomic groups and were ultimately capable of overcoming patential opposition. We did see how Menem won support by compensating big business for lost revenues by framing a privatization scheme that initially favored the most important domestic conglomerates. Furthermore, the pro-market reform political right was completely co-opted as the President began to implement the very policies that the conservative UCD had advocated. In a very astute move, Menem appointed to some important positions in his administration the UCD's most visible leaders; many of whom, by 1995, decided to join Menem's party. The labor unions in the private sector, which had little to lose from privatization, joined the presidential bandwagon in return for government special treatment when it came to the administration of social security and health care funds managed by the unions. Menem also saw to it that union leaders in the public sector that were willing to cooperate would obtain for their workers early retirement programs, stock options, and other forms of hidden pork-barrel benefits. In this way, Menem was capable of isolating the most recalcitrant unions in the public sector that were opposing privatization. When such unions split from the CGT and called for the same general strike that had brought Alfonsín to the bargaining table, they failed miserably.

The privatization of the large military-related manufacturing sector (DGFM) encountered seemingly little opposition from the armed forces. Menem obtained the compliance of the armed forces to a state divestiture program that would have been unthinkable only a few years earlier. His strategy in this regard was twofold. On the one hand, he pardoned all those military officers sentenced or still awaiting verdicts on human rights violations, an issue that led to three military uprisings under Alfonsín. On the other, he promised (but often did not comply) to use part of the privatization revenues coming from DGFM for the purchasing of military equipment and the increase officers' salaries, which had deteriorated precipitously after 1983. Having lost much of its political clout as a result of the disastrous results of its direct rule in the 1976–83 period, the military had little choice but to cooperate.

Menem also mounted an effective pro-privatization campaign through the media. To this extent, he received the enthusiastic endorsement of some of Argentina's most important talk show hosts, who not only gave the President free air time but even organized public rallies to counter the demonstrations of anti-privatization unions. The printed media was also generally well restrained in its criticisms as Menem, time and again, threatened to withdraw government advertising from newspapers that were too hostile, like the center-left *Pagina 12*.[9]

In Peru, Fujimori sought the alliance of only one institution, the armed forces. He needed them not only to fight terrorism but also to silence opposition parties. This became plain in 1992, when with the military's help he practically staged a coup that sent home the legislature and curtailed civil

liberties. Fujimori's authoritarian style was not conducive to coalition building. He made that plain when he stated, 'we must not be dogmatic and impose
the so-called democratic system' and that the proper way to deal with Peru's
crisis was, 'to fix it with a machete'.[10] The President was greatly helped
by the very fact that the general public perceived opposition parties and
labor as the very cause of the disastrous state of affairs that the President had
inherited in mid-1990. When opposition parties, like APRA and the United
Left, tried to rally support against Fujimori's coup, they found out that a good
part of the public opinion actually sided with the President and many others
were just indifferent. After that, traditional opposition parties continued to
lose voters. The labor movement, once extremely active and well organized,
saw its membership falling equally fast. Public opinion surveys showed that
the militant and strike-prone approach of the unions in the 1980s led many
people to believe that the labor movement did bear heavy responsibility in
bringing the country into an economic paralysis. Thus, by the early 1990s,
political opposition lacked the legitimacy necessary to attack the President.
In addition, in the public eye it was also ineffective because, as in Argentina,
it had no credible alternative plans to the President's agenda. The privatization process' slow start thus should not be attributed to an articulate opposition front but rather to Fujimori's initial indecisiveness and short-term
political calculations, particularly after he decided to run for re-election. The
Peruvian President's task, in terms of gathering public consent was also facilitated by the very fact that big business and most of the media had espoused
Vargas Llosa's market reform agenda by the late 1980s. Only the weekly
magazine *Caretas* and the daily *La República* consistently criticized the
government, but to no avail. The only time when the state divestiture program began to be seriously questioned was in the aftermath of the border
dispute with Ecuador in January 1995. At that time, the military began to
show its own concerns which gave the unions some unexpected ammunition
to revive their efforts that up until then had been frustrated. However, by the
end of that year, despite mounting strike activity by oil workers to prevent
Petroperu's sale, the privatization effort continued, albeit at a lower pace, since
Fujimori was not constrained by electoral considerations anymore and the
conflict with Ecuador was over. In sum, privatization in Peru did not require
much of a coalition-building effort because the potential foes to the policy
were much more politically debilitated than in Argentina.

Brazil presents us with the opposite case of Peru. Like Fujimori, Collor
had little inclination toward compromise as he was afraid that any initiative
in that direction would severely limit his freedom of action. Collor, similarly
to Fujimori, simply expected Congress and interest groups to go along with
his policy initiatives. However, this could be done in Peru, where parties
and interest groups were extremely weak, but not in Brazil. Using the

'machete' was not an option for Collor. For example, opposition parties in Congress were divided and could not come up with an alternative policy plan but still retained a significant power to stop the President's legislative agenda, as actually happened. Congress in Brazil could not be simply shut down for failing to collaborate. The presence of many parties in the federal legislature made the task of engineering a working majority difficult, but Collor devoted little effort in that regard leading to the exacerbation of relations between the Presidency and the Congress. Potential allies like the PMDB (centrist) and the PFL (conservative), which had supported Collor's election, asked for more saying in the way the President was going to make decisions but were rebuked. On the left, the PT, Brizola's Democratic Labor party, the Socialists, and the Communists, were squarely against privatization. In view of the much greater powers enjoyed by the Brazilian Congress, as compared to both Argentina and Peru, Collor's confrontational style proved a costly mistake. One may argue that, given the divided nature of the Brazilian legislature, Collor had little option but to act unilaterally to get things done. Indeed, if it is true that the Brazilian electoral system allows for the proliferation of parties, it is also true that President Fernando Enrique Cardoso, facing many of the same challenges was able to win important concessions from Congress in the way of privatization and economic liberalization in 1995.

Much of the same rationale applies to the labor movement. Unlike in Peru, Brazilian labor had become stronger in the 1980s and was a main force in pushing the military out of power in 1985. During the rest of the decade the most radical and independent labor confederation, the CUT, was so politically relevant as to become the backbone of the PT that eventually, under Lula's leadership, it contested the presidency in 1989 and 1994. By far and large, although divided into rival organizations, Brazilian labor was in a much stronger position than in Peru, and its opposition to the state divestiture program grew in intensity and effectiveness under Franco.

In terms of the business elites, they were quite divided and the potential support that Collor could have garnered from those who endorsed state divestiture was not exploited by the President. As Roett (1992: 119) explained:

with the failure of Collor Plan I, and the announcement of Collor Plan II in early 1991, the level of tension between the government and the business class rose dramatically. From the government's viewpoint, the business community was unwilling to make the sacrifices needed to guarantee the success of liberalization. The business sector's position was that the government did not know what it was doing with—or to—the economy.

The military that represented a potential foe to state divestiture remained, for the most part, at the margin of the political debate. Much greater opposition came from local governors, student organizations, and even high-ranking members of the Catholic Church, all of whom played no meaningful role in Argentina and Peru.

The only active supporters of privatization were the BNDS, some prominent state managers, and a large part of the media. However, in the latter case, no prominent opinion leaders emerged to fill in the vacuum left by the lack of government leadership in organizing a pro-privatization lobby. In short, the greater complexity of the Brazilian political scenario, coupled with the strength of the Congress and key interest groups, would have required a clear strategy to build support for the policy. Under Collor and Franco this was sorely missing and a divided opposition was able to effectively slow down the implementation process not so much for its greater skills but rather for the ineptness of the government. As noted earlier, it was only after Cardoso ushered his first presidency that a dramatic turnaround did take place as he was capable of putting together a large, although heterogenous and not always reliable, political coalition that was capable to put the anti-privatization forces on the defensive.

Technical Difficulties

On this score, Argentina, Brazil, and Peru encountered many common problems that often slowed down the privatization process more than political opposition did. The methods chosen were often flawed leading to results that differed considerably from what proponents of privatization had envisioned. The general approach was, particularly in the beginning, 'sell at any price'. Upon acknowledging that things had gone wrong in many cases, a top COPRI officer, who did not want to be identified for obvious reasons, told me in an interview, 'Sir, macroeconomic theory is one thing, reality here was another, we did what we had to do even though this often meant going against the book.' Let us now turn to the main technical problems that we encountered in the field research.

The lack of experience was particularly noticeable in the beginning of each process. This was clearly evident in Argentina and Peru where small staffs of technocrats were overworked and ill prepared to manage the complex technical and legal issues involved in the divestiture of large PEs. As time went by, many of the initial problems were overcome thanks to the assistance of foreign consultants contracted out by or coming directly from the World Bank, the IDB, and the UNDP. BNDES in Brazil fared somewhat better due to its previous experience on the matter but still had to rely on outside consultants. Even then some problems arose. In 1996, BNDES disqualified the consortium Itajuba (led by Booz Allen and Morgan Stanley) that was expected to handle the privatization of the transport and mining conglomerate CVRD. The Brazilian government had originally planned to award the contract in

January of 1996 so that the privatization process could be concluded by the end of that year. However, as Itajuba offered less than the minimum floor price, the bid was suspended. When Itajuba appealed the decision in court, the CVRD privatization suffered a further delay at the expense of the very consultants who were expected to speed up the process.

Market failures were common across countries. On many occasions no buyers came forward, forcing the postponement of the auction. This usually happened with smaller companies marred by high deficits and little prospect for high returns on the investment. In other cases governments were faced with only one bid. Under such circumstances, when hard-pressed, governments decided to sell in spite of clear rules that called for at least two competing offers. The typical example was Aerolíneas Argentinas. There were also instances when offers that had been originally accepted were later disallowed as the private groups turned out to fall short of the technical and financial requirements spelled out in the contract of transferring the assets.

The inadequacy of domestic financial markets further narrowed the options of selling methods in all these countries. Brazil, which among the three had the largest and most sophisticated stock markets, was able to carry out several sales through the San Paulo and Rio de Janeiro stock exchanges, but there were also instances when public offers also found no interest among investors. In Argentina, the only major public offer involved the oil giant YPF, whose shares were also placed in the New York and London markets. Similarly, Peru whose capital markets were the smallest, did pursue that avenue only in a handful of occasions when large PEs were put on the auction block.

The evaluation of assets was a thorny issue in the largest sales. Each government, at one point or another, found even companies in natural monopolies, which potentially could yield high profits, hard to assess in terms of price. This is because almost invariably PEs tended to have large financial debts, were overstaffed, undercapitalized, and lagged behind in technology. Therefore, it was not unusual that potential buyers engaged in behind-the-scene negotiations with the government to bring down the asset value of PEs, which constituted the main criteria in fixing the minimum floor price. Opposition groups denounced the low prices that the government charged on many occasions. The usual accusation was that the government's jewels were sold at bargain prices. The response to this politically damaging charge varied. In Argentina, in the first phase of the privatization program, the government used as payment a combination of cash and debt-equity instruments. In this way Menem wanted to show that the revenues from PEs were utilized partly to reduce the country's foreign debt. In Brazil, Collor used much of the same rationale and turned government domestic debt instruments into privatization currencies. In both instances, this attempt backfired. In Argentina, the scheme forcing banks and service or manufacturing companies to create business ventures ended in the collapse of several consortia. This is because the consortium's partners did not trust one another or simply were unable to put up the needed cash and debt equity papers. After Cavallo took over the Economy Ministry such a sale method was abandoned. In Brazil, the fact that several of the privatization currencies were junk bonds outraged the opposition, later forcing President Franco to devise a new strategy where cash receipts would acquire a significant role. It is likely that these early experiences convinced Fujimori, who started privatization later than Menem and Collor, to adopt cash receipts only for the most part.

The indiscriminate way in which privatization took place, on several occasions, brings up the second issue: deregulation mechanisms (Pinzás 1993). In Peru, the transferring of natural monopolies into private hands occurred without creating regulatory agencies prior to the sale. The Fujimori administration, arguing that the setting up of regulatory agencies could be later used by intervention-prone governments to unravel the market reform agenda, adopted a general regulatory regime that left little room for interpretation, similar to that of the Chileans in the 1980s. This approach, according to one analyst (Tenenbaum 1995: 3), 'is appealing because it is perceived as the regulatory equivalent of going on "autopilot", but it is likely to work only when a government has a clear idea of the industry structure it wants, moves quickly to this structure, and then does not change its mind'. The problem in Peru was that the Fujimori administration did not seem to have a clear idea on what kind of industry structure it wanted and, not surprisingly, the regulatory legislation was rather broad and loose as well, leaving much room for interpretation.

In Argentina, under Dromi's tenure, regulation was actually regarded as a potential factor hindering privatization. The contracts transferring monopolistic companies in air passenger cargo, telecommunications, and highway transportation carefully left regulation vague. Only after Cavallo took over the privatization process did regulation become somewhat of a concern. None the less, the only sector that saw the creation of a regulatory agency prior to its privatization was the mail system. Many sectors kept being regulated by undersecretariats depending directly on the Ministry of the Economy. By 1996, only a handful of agencies seemed to be working according to relatively high standards in terms of professionality and transparency, namely the electricity and gas regulatory agencies.

In Brazil, the government avoided the privatization of public services asserting that it would have taken too much time to devise a proper regulatory framework. As a result, the Collor and Franco administration sold PEs in steel and petrochemicals asserting that in such sectors regulatory problems would not surface. This was wishful thinking. As a matter of fact, private producers bought out their public competitors strengthening their oligopolistic market shares. This de facto situation resulting from privatization led the World Bank, which supported the process, to assess its unintended consequences. The basic and disturbing question is, 'If the industry became more concentrated, would there be a predisposition to greater protection, particularly non-tariff barriers such as quotas, voluntary export restraints, and anti-dumping actions against other producers?'[11] While it is too early to respond with any degree of certainty, there are signs in the steel sector, in both Brazil and Argentina, that this is a likely scenario.

That regulation of monopolistic markets became a crucial issue in Brazil as later underscored by governmental officials. In January 1996, the BNDES President, Luiz Carlos Mendonça de Barros justified the slow progress toward the privatization of telecommunication and electricity companies with the need to prepare a careful, well-designed regulatory framework, which was still to be fully worked out by 1998.

Why then this was not a concern in the early 1990s? What appeared clear from the interview process is that the emphasis of government regulators of privatized sectors was primarily on meeting investment targets, rather than enhancing the quality of service. One example illustrates this point. During an interview, the chairman of one of the most important regulatory agencies admitted that the bulk of the private companies competing with the public corporation in mail delivery were actually owned by the same person, Alfredo Yabram, a businessman very close to President Menem. Yabram was, at the time, the front runner to win the auction of the public mail system since Congress had tailored a privatization bill whose clauses made impossible from an other investor but him to compete. Upon being asked if, as a regulator, it was his duty to first force Yabram to sell the companies in which he had front men and then proceed with privatization, the government official replied, 'That is a political question [sic]; all I care about is to set up a maximum price for a provision of a given service in my sector. That's it!' What was behind this rather puzzling response was that Yabram's close ties with Menem and many powerful legislators made him an untouchable shortly before his apparent suicide in 1998.

There is an additional problem with regulation, even when a government is serious about it, and that is the lack of experience in this field in all these countries. In the case of Peru, for example, a foreign diplomat who knew the issue well believed that the Fujimori administration did not have the capacity to regulate effectively. Similar comments were expressed privately in Brazil by high-ranking officials in the Ministry of Justice and the Tribunal de Contas.[12] Even in countries where legal frameworks are reasonably sophisticated, problems are serious. According to Devlin (1993: 176): 'the problem is not so much the lack of formal systems—they are often quite sophisticated and imaginative, as in the case of the Chilean electricity sector—but rather that they are emerging with little or no track record and apparently weak or non-existent enforcement systems.'

On the Pros and Cons of Privatization

In the previous pages we saw how Menem and, to a lesser extent Fujimori, rushed market reform policies so swiftly and decisively that they were able to defeat political opposition. By 1998, in Argentina and Peru, most of the opposition parties agreed upon the general direction of the reform agenda while limiting themselves to mandates for greater transparency in the privatization process and greater emphasis on social policies. In Peru, left-wing parties became completely isolated and unable to present a credible alternative. As for labor leaders, they were surprised by Menem's and Fujimori's changes and appeared increasingly resigned to conforming to the new rules, thus accepting privatization as inevitable. In 1998, Argentina was close to completing its last round of privatization, while Peru was seemingly preparing to embark into major transfers within the petroleum and mining industries. In both countries, market reforms had triumphed, a fact that was unthinkable only ten years earlier. Brazil, that had for long lagged behind precisely because of political opposition, once Cardoso managed to convince the legislature to go along with his plans, made great strides. By 1988, Brazil had become the Latin American leader in privatization revenues with the sale of public utilities and a host of manufacturing and mining companies.

This brings us to a first preliminary conclusion. Williamson and Haggard (1994: 573) suggested that when a legislature is against market reforms, 'the ability to sustain reforms depends on the development of mechanisms to bypass the legislature'. Menem and Fujimori clearly understood this precept from the start and acted upon it. Unfortunately, the mechanisms they used were far from being truly democratic. This why the title of this book is 'Privatization South American Style'. Coups, in the case of Peru, and the emasculation of the checks and balances of the democratic process, as happened in Argentina, would have been unthinkable in Western Europe or North America. However, Menem and Fujimori consistently replied that had they abided by pure democratic procedures nothing could have been accomplished. So is there an incompatibility between freedom in the markets and freedom in the polity of developing countries? In Pinochet's Chile, his economic advisers, the so-called 'Chicago boys', seemed to believe so. Muñoz (1991: 170) synthesized their philosophy in these terms:

Economic freedom achieved through the market is extended to other decisions by reducing the role of political institutions (particularly the state) and taking decisions back to the individual. However, what if the voting processes are imperfect and, in addition individuals are not rational in the ways that market allocation requires? If socialist ideas have crept into the minds of individuals, the argument goes, rational behavior cannot be expected, at least not until the superiority of the new, free-market principles have been widely demonstrated. Hence, authority must be strong and vigilant and democratic decisions must be postponed.

Understandably, walking the fine line between getting the job done and going by the book is complex and risky. Given the situation of extreme crisis that Menem and Fujimori faced, and knowing the intense conflict plaguing their societies when it came to shouldering the sacrifices of economic reform, one reluctantly has to admit that in the short run some unilateral decision-making style is hardly avoidable. However, and it must be emphasized, emergency powers are exactly what they are meant for, emergencies. Once the economy is stabilized, democratic forms of conduct should be the norm. Unfortunately, power and success are seductive and, by 1996, Menem and Fujimori seemed to believe that a strong hand was still in order. Interestingly, their fellow citizens seemed to agree. Indeed from a political standpoint, regardless of the means used to achieve their goals, the market reform gamble paid high dividends for Menem and Fujimori. Both were re-elected in 1995 in a landslide primarily because they were capable of accomplishing economic stability and growth. This confirms earlier findings by Williamson and Haggard (1994) who argued that reform policies that in the beginning encountered strong opposition eventually gained widespread support as they brought about tangible results. While in Argentina and Peru people questioned their Presidents' true commitment to the democratic process and honest government, they did recognize their achievements. Cardoso, whose democratic credentials are not in doubt, was re-elected in 1998 precisely because he had brought economic stability to an inflation-plagued country, not because of his achievements on social issues. Collor's policies, on the contrary, were ineffective on all fronts and when his corruption scandal broke out, Brazilians went to the streets and put pressure on a reluctant Congress to impeach him.

In general, public opinion in Argentina and Peru was supportive of privatization, a trend that grew in intensity in Brazil as well by 1998. However, in Argentina, people were also very critical of the way privatization was being carried out. The biggest complaints were: (1) poor execution; (2) corruption associated with some sales; (3) lack of real gains for the country; (4) unemployment; (5) lack of control over privatization; and (6) in some cases poor public services under private ownership (Mora y Araujo 1993: 319). With regard to the latter point, people of the upper-class neighborhood of Recoleta in Buenos Aires grew tired of the frequent interruption in power service, and in 1994 hung up a banner reading, 'SEGBA: Return, We Forgive You', in reference to the old state power company.[13] Moreover, in Argentina, 59 per cent of those interviewed in 1993 believed that the government did not have the capacity to monitor private companies in the service sector.[14] Not surprisingly, several sectors of society demanded that the government play a strong role in the control and regulation of newly privatized companies. People's fear was that the private companies were reaping the benefits of the market reforms without delivering on their promises for efficiency and customer satisfaction. Thus, the consolidation of reforms like privatization requires not just positive results in the short term but, most importantly, positive results in the long term to gain public acceptance. This is because, as time goes by, people's expectations increase and their leaders are held to higher standards of performance. Ushering in harsh state divestiture programs is a huge task, and people can overlook authoritarian means, but consolidating them requires a much more refined, consensus-minded political style than in the early stages of market reforms.

There is another issue at stake when considering the political dimension of privatization. Some have argued that politicians should not tell the electorate, while running for office, of their true intentions. Instead, they should deceive people, promising easy, painless solutions, but once elected they should freely interpret their mandate. The rationale behind this approach is that people are risk averse. They will never vote for a program that promises blood and tears but offers no assurances that it will turn around the situation in a relatively short period of time (Przeworski 1995). This seems to be the case with Menem and Fujimori, both of whom ran as populists only to change their policies by 180 degrees once in office. Similar cases can be found in Bolivia, under President Victor Paz Estensorro in 1985, and in Venezuela under President Carlos Andrés Pérez in 1990. Yet in the Argentine and Peruvian cases it is hard to demonstrate that Menem and Fujimori knew well in advance that they would implement harsh economic measures. The available record and the interviews I carried out during the field research suggest the contrary. Moreover, not all these cases ended in success, as the Venezuelan experience demonstrates. What seems to be important is not so much whether a President, purposely or not, deceived the electorate but rather whether his policy led to tangible, positive results (Sachs 1994). As Williamson and Haggard (1994: 586) pointed out, 'electorates respect decisive and effective government and . . . they will reward liberalization efforts'. Argentina and Peru bring support to this assertion. In both countries the traditional right, vitriolically opposed to Menem and Fujimori prior to the beginning of their first term, enthusiastically endorsed them when they ran for re-election in 1995.

Moreover, the study shows some support for the hypothesis that administrations with strong labor support, paradoxically, are more successful in implementing market reforms than could be the case under right-wing governments. Menem's Argentina, again, is a case in point. Oddly enough it took a Peronist President to unravel many of the social welfare and industrialization policies that Perón initiated in the 1940s. This is not an isolated instance. The socialist Prime Minister of Spain, Felipe González, adopted in the 1980s market reforms that he had opposed a decade earlier and in doing so he drafted the support of labor. In France, starting in the mid-1980s, President François Mitterrand did much the same.

Economically, privatization brought much-needed cash into the state coffers of all three countries and had a positive impact on the fiscal balance of at least Argentina. It also contributed to easing relations with multilateral agencies, luring foreign investors, and improving relations with private lenders. In Brazil the macroeconomic impact began to be felt only when the large PEs began to be sold after 1996. In terms of efficiency gains, however, it is too early to assess the impact of privatization since most PEs have been in private hands for a brief period and there are problems in assessing trade-offs and the impact of externalities. What seems to be sure though is that, as expected, a lot of privatized companies are now generating hefty profits. This is particularly true in oligopolistic markets, like those in telecommunications (Argentina and Peru), petroleum (Argentina), and steel (Brazil).[15]

While the public sector's unions were the biggest casualties of privatization, the winners were invariably domestic and foreign companies that took advantage of the opportunity for consolidation of their oligopolistic positions in some of these countries' economic sectors. Consumers invariably experienced price increases in public services transferred to the private sector. Yet such increases not always resulted in improvements for the service provided. Popular capitalism, as an Argentine privatization official candidly admitted, remained primarily a nice slogan devised to make the policy look good, but it was not actively pursued. The impact of privatization on incomes is also very difficult to assess but in the short-run they were necessarily negative as most companies were overstaffed and related jobs had to be considerably shed (Lawton 1995). The troublesome consequence was, as admitted by Cavallo himself, that many of those who lost their jobs through privatization in the public sector did not find suitable employment thereafter.[16]

What appears clear is that compensation mechanisms for potential losers, as argued by Haggard and Webb (1992) are closely associated with the rapid implementation of privatization programs. In Argentina, such compensations, targeting big domestic conglomerates, were overt.[17] In other words, Menem bought out some of the country's most important rent-seekers. Thus, at least in the Argentine case, Bates' (1994) hypothesis that economic reform in general is a means to change the groups for which the economic system is set up, rather than an effort to promote an open economic system, seems to be confirmed. This raises some troublesome questions regarding the true nature of privatization in these countries. Vargas Llosa, the Peruvian privatization zealot, evaluated the results of state divestiture in Latin America in rather dark and alarming tones:

What principally happened with the privatization efforts in Peru, Mexico, and Argentina does not differ much from the transfer of State monopolies into the hands of the large private entrepreneurs. This contradicts the moral reasoning behind privatization: opening the markets and beginning the competition that will lead to the process of wealth creation . . . privatization was used simply to inject fresh money into a bankrupt State through the corrupt sale of assets to the friends of the political leaders. Privatization should be, on the contrary, the key element toward social and economic reform. It should allow people to participate in the system and give them [economic] independence.[18]

Transparency and Regulation.   Two major issues raised above deserve some discussion here, as they will be the center of the academic debate in the next decade due to the fact that they deal with the consequences of privatization. The first is transparency. As Devlin (1993: 169–70) pointed out:

Transparency improves social welfare because it reduces possibilities for corruption, collusion and the misuse of inside information, all of which permit privileged gains from the sale of public assets. It can also be complementary with many other object-ives. Since transparency opens the process for more public scrutiny, errors can be checked more easily and fairer evaluations can be made as to whether the govern-ment's stated objectives—regarding the privatization process as well as its end pro-duct—are being reasonably fulfilled. The closer results are to objectives, the more likely it is that privatization will have a 'happy ending' for the firms, the govern-ment, and the general public, which in turn reduces the risk of policy backlash. Transparency also enhances the efficiency of the 'learning by doing' process which is an inevitable part of any government's privatization programme. An enhanced flow of information will obviously also contribute to overall market efficiency and price maximization.

However, all too often in the cases examined here transparency was sorely missing, particularly in Argentina and Peru, where the emasculation of the judiciary and other independent institutions made many feel uncomfortable. As even a pro-government analyst underscored, 'the abuse of decrees of *need* and *urgency* from the part of the executive bring about worrisome ques-tions . . . Between the importance and the urgency, society (and the govern-ment) . . . must give top priority to the consensus over the importance of the changes introduced [by the economic reform program]' (Bour 1993: 263–4). This sentence, written to describe the situation in Argentina, could be easily applied to Peru and Brazil. In all three cases, policy makers reasoned that, 'privatization should be implemented with less concern about the correct way to do it and more emphasis on getting it done quickly'.[19]

Moreover, the need to act quickly, regardless of the cost, is no justification for macroeconomic mismanagement and collusive practices, both of which took place in these countries. Speed has more to do with political than eco-nomic reasons. As Devlin (1993: 170) underscored, 'most of the objectives that commonly drive privatization processes are not necessarily enhanced by speed; indeed many of them, such as productive and allocative efficiency, credibility, government revenue, catalytic effects, etc. . . . can be seriously compromised by a hasty privatization process'. Modiano, the former head of Collor's privatization program, went even further stating: 'one can always choose urgency, make bad shareholder decisions, leave significant debts pending, reduce the minimum price, etc. These, however, are not good recipes for a successful privatization programme. Indeed, they are detrimental to the principles of fairness transparency, as well as to the public wealth (represented by the assets being sold off).'[20] For example, those PEs that were transferred under time pressure, like Aerolíneas Argentinas and ENTel Argentina, were plagued by technical and legal problems and marred by suspicions of corruption. In justifying the poor government record in these two cases, a senior Argentine official flatly stated that those were, 'political privatizations'. In Argentina, as well as Brazil and Peru, whenever the government tried to rush sales, transfers were invariably problematic in one way or another, as it had been the case in Chile during the late 1970s (Hachette and Lüders 1993; Bitrán and Sáez 1994).

Moreover, the need to act quickly seemed often an excuse to cover up for illegal practices. Lack of transparency resulted in alleged cases of wrongdoing, ranging from the sale of privileged information to outright bribes, which failed to be investigated simply because of the heavy government influence in the judiciary, particularly in Argentina and Peru. In Brazil, where in the wake of Collor's impeachment Congress was under pressure to investigate alleged corruption cases in the privatization process, a special commission found evidence of collusion but its findings never led to criminal investigations for lack of political will.[21] In Argentina, where the press denounced repeated cases of corruption involving Menem's inner circle, all cases were dismissed by sympathetic judges.[22] Clearly, this was not just a problem in Argentina. An analysis of the privatization process in Mexico during President Carlos Salinas de Gortari points to a similar pattern:

[The August 1995] scandal involving fugitive former AereoMexico President Gerardo de Prevoisin and the ruling *Partido Revolucionario Institucional* (PRI) offers the first proof that nouveau-riche Mexican businessmen—many favored in government privatization auctions—pumped millions of dollars into the PRI's campaign war chest for the 1994 federal elections. The PRI spent more than 90 centavos of every peso that political parties paid out during the August 21 contest, winning the presidency and majorities in both houses of Congress. Rumors of multi-million dollar donations from privatization kingpins or their newly acquired companies began with reports that ex-President Carlos Salinas hosted a 'millionaires' banquet' on February 23, 1993 to ask the entrepreneurs to organize businessmen into groups donating $25 million each to the PRI. Salinas confirmed that the dinner occurred, but denied asking for million-dollar donations. The latest scandal (AeroMéxico) shows otherwise.[23]

The press uncovered another major scandal when it found out that the private owners of the former telecommunication state monopoly paid to Salinas's brother Raúl $50 million for a 'venture capital fund'. Subsequently, the justice department of Mexico traced $300 million in Raúl Salinas' bank transfers to foreign banks. 'If the President's brother starts depositing millions of dollars at a time, you should certainly suspect that he did not make it from any legitimate business,' said Tom Cash, a former senior US Drug Enforcement Administration official.[24]

One of the most troublesome aspects of these corrupt practices is the damage they wreak on public support for market reforms required for economic growth and investment. This is the case in Brazil, for example, where anti-privatization lobbies successfully slowed down the privatization process by associating it with the demise of President Collor.

The second issue has to do with regulation. With anti-trust legislation either weak (Brazil) or simply non-existent (Argentina and Peru), privatizing under monopolistic/oligopolistic conditions raises serious doubts about the establishment of a true market economy, as Vargas Llosa's statement stressed before. As reported by the *Financial Times*, describing the Argentine situation after privatization, 'the importance of effective regulation has become paramount: a perception that newly-privatised utilities are using their monopoly positions to exploit the public could damage the government and its economic programme severely'.[25] Indeed, it seems that the creation or strengthening of monopolistic/oligopolistic markets under private ownership was at best a marginal concern in all these countries. Actually, as I already mentioned in the case of Argentina, the lack of a clear regulatory scheme in many sectors was a deliberate government action as part of the incentive package to lure investors, i.e. Aerolíneas Argentinas, ENTel, and gas companies. For instance, the Argentine Consumer Protection Law 24.240 of 1995 did not apply to privatized companies. Complaints and legal charges against them were the jurisdiction of the regulatory agencies. This provision did not seem accidental. In fact, once regulatory agencies were set up, after privatization, they found it difficult to effectively monitor the private operators of public services.[26] This occurred for two main reasons. First, the contract of transfer contained loopholes allowing the private companies to resist controls. Second, many agencies had little information about the way public services operated and private companies often withheld such information. When some regulatory agencies tried to defend consumers, private companies went on the attack charging that such agencies should instead 'harmonize' consumer interests with 'the rights of the private operators of public services'.[27] On one such occasion, Menem sided with the private telephone companies and reduced the prerogatives of the National Commission of Telecommunications by assigning some of them to the undersecretariat for telecommunications, which depended upon the executive branch. However, in all three countries, clashes between private companies and regulatory agencies were more the exception than the rule. In fact, regulatory agencies often went along with the executive wishes since most of their members were political appointees.

These facts do not invalidate the theoretical premises upon which privatization stands. However, they do indicate, in varying degrees, the extensive shortcomings of such policies if preliminary steps for economic deregulation and political transparency are not taken. The divestiture process often did not lead to greater competition, but merely reassigned rents to the private sector without any regulatory structure for the supervision of the new monopolies' operations. The concern here is that there are not sufficient safeguards against the kinds of collusion and abuses that might give a small group of companies a stranglehold on the markets they dominate. Neo-orthodox economic theories do justify privatization as it increases economic efficiency through competition. The more competition, the better, and I fully agree with it. Yet when markets tend to be natural monopolies or become oligopolies for a variety of reasons, government regulation is necessary precisely because it guarantees competition by thwarting collusion practices (Rose-Ackerman 1992; Galal *et al.* 1994; Ramamurti 1996; Levy and Spiller 1996). What we need is not the old-style regulation that in the past allowed governments to impose arbitrary controls on the economy and reward special constituencies. What we need is instead a new-style regulation.

Private investment requires a new-style regulation that is limited, transparent, and 'lets managers manage'. The choice between [old-style and new-style regulation] is ultimately a pragmatic one. If a country really wants private investment in [i.e.] its powers sector, it has no choice but to adopt a new regulatory system that keeps promises and exercises self-restraint. . . . Regulation, then, is simply a system that allows a government to formalize its commitments to protect consumers and investors. (Tenenbaum 1995: 1)

So far, at least in the countries examined, there has been little effort to promote new-style regulation. Yet, if no effort will be made in this direction, it is hard to see how true competition can emerge under the present monopolistic or oligopolistic conditions characterizing many important sectors in Argentina, Brazil, and Peru. If the issue will not be resolved, it may become a political, as well as an economic, hot potato in the years to come. Fortunately, by 1998 it was clear that the World Bank and other multilateral institutions had recognized the urgency of the problem and they were actively encouraging countries that were embarking on privatization to address early on regulatory issues. Brazil, for instance, tried to create competition in the telecommunications sector prior to state divestiture. By the same token, countries that had privatized earlier, like Argentina and Peru, were facing the task of how reconfigure existing legislation in the face of regulatory failures.

Conclusion

Summing up, the presidents who privatized, consistent with our analytical framework, did not do so out of ideology. They took from the privatization philosophy what was convenient to them and ignored the rest. While the official rhetoric was to make the government leaner and meaner, there is little evidence to support the argument that the state is now performing better in its essential tasks (i.e. education, defense, justice, etc.) than it did before. Privatization, presented as a key means to free the markets from undue government interference and corruption, was pursued through little or no debate and rather unilateral means (delegated laws and executive orders). Instead of leading to greater government transparency and private sector accountability to consumers, it resulted in little of both. Privatization can indeed play a major, positive role both politically and economically and people are likely to support it when they perceive tangible benefits associate with it. What matters is that such a policy be implemented according to clear rules, which too often were either ignored or overtly violated in the countries I examined here. As Vargas Llosa warned:

With the type of privatization that is pursued at the moment, the principal benefits of [economic] growth favor exclusively a very small elite. This is a big mistake because in ten years we will have a contrary reaction against the free market and privatization. Populism will again find a propitious round in Latin America. . . . The only way to avoid this effect is to assure that the market takes its roots in the practical life of the majority of the population. Otherwise, everything is reversible, because the economically underprivileged population will not believe in the market as an instrument of progress.[28]

During seminars and conferences I often heard the question, 'are privatization, and market reforms in general, reversible?' The question is not as academic as it may seem. Market reforms in Argentina, Brazil, and Peru occurred under the leadership of men who belonged to parties or political movements that, at one time or another, promoted state intervention. When Argentina hit the skids and plunged into a deep recession in 1995, many Peronists, including the governor of Buenos Aires who, after Menem is the most powerful politician in the country, attacked head-on Cavallo's market reforms and urged the President to resume the old-fashioned, free-wheeling spending policies of the past. However, market reforms have come too far in Argentina and Peru to be reversed, at least in the short term. As Przeworski (1991) hypothesized, they have produced a 'big bang' effect that has burned too many bridges. Too many vested interests have been created in the process to allow a quick return to the past. Cavallo's Convertibility Plan, for example, very much as in Poland, worked effectively to restrain the easy spending habits typical of a populist party like the Peronists. Domestic and foreign investors do believe today that neither Menem, nor Fujimori, nor Fernando Enrique Cardoso have the will to rescind privatization. As Bates (1994: 32) pointed out, 'should a politician violate the economic interests of those upon whose political support he depends, he would increase his chances of losing power'. Cavallo's ability to prevent Menem from manipulating the privatization of the mail system, which I described earlier, is a typical example.[29] Bates was indeed quite correct when he argued that, 'politicians can costlessly dispose of unprotected academic advisers; they cannot do so, however, if those academics have become associated with a policy that is highly prized by powerful interests'.

However, coherent, sound policies need to survive their masters to be sustained over time. This requires the creation of institutions capable of assuring the continuation of such policies over time, by sheltering them from pork-barrel politicians who are likely to manipulate them would they be given a chance. Pinochet in Chile, before withdrawing from power, created an independent central bank and engineered an electoral system that could make it impossible for his political enemies, once in power, to reverse his policies. Unfortunately, Chile remains an isolated case in Latin America. Central Banks remain highly dependent upon the executive and the checks and balances of the democratic process are likewise tenuous, particularly in Argentina and Peru. These two countries, and to a lesser extent Brazil, have made great strides to reform their economies, but such reforms have been confined to the economic realm. Unless they are accompanied by political reforms that promote an efficient and independent judiciary, a legislature that is responsive to its citizens rather than specific lobbies, and a more self-restrained, and transparent executive branch, Vargas Llosa's warning may not sound too unrealistic after all. In the years to come, if market reforms are truly to succeed as economic theory postulates, they should be matched by an equal effort to spread wealth and strengthen the democratic process. There is nothing inherently wrong with free-market policies as some left-wing critics argue. Rather, it is the lack of transparency that demands scrutiny and action. As St Augustine reasoned, 'States without Justice are but bands of thieves enlarged.'

Endnotes

1. That even the most sophisticated observers of economic trends were still unwilling to concede that their country was slipping into a situation similar to its Argentine and Peruvian neighbors was clear to me during an interview I had with a former chairman of the Brazilian Central Bank in August of 1988. When I raised this possibility, the interviewee disdainfully replied that there was no chance that Brazil would fall into hyperinflation. By the end of 1989, consumer prices had increased by over 1,860 per cent.
2. That the main task of domestic conglomerates in this type of trilateral consortium was to take care of the 'political side' of the negotiations with the government was confirmed to me, quite candidly, by the chief public relation officers of one of Argentina's largest groups in an interview. Buenos Aires, November 1995.
3. The process started with the Collor Plan I and continued through 1996 when Congress approved a motion allowing foreign companies to control majority shares in the mining sectors.

4. *Latin American Monitor: Brazil*, April 1994, p. 4.

5. *Latin American Regional Reports: Southern Cone*, 28 December 1995, p. 5.

6. Interviews with officers from the Argentine Ministry of the Economy, Public Works and Services. Buenos Aires, November 1995. Se also the *Financial Times*, 20 April 1993, p. 17.

7. According to an opinion poll taken by Huho Haime & Asociados, 62 per cent of the respondents supported Menem's decision while only 20 per cent opposed it. *Pagina 12*, 28 July 1996, p. 4.

8. In early 1996, monthly inflation recorded its lowest level since 1958.

9. *Christian Science Monitor*, 22 September 1993, p. 3.

10. Douglas W. Payne, 'Ballots, Neo-Strongmen, Narcos and Impunity', *Freedom Review* (January–February 1995), p. 28.

11. Ying Qian and Ronald C. Duncan, 'Privatization, Concentration, and Pressure for Protection: A Steel Sector Study', *World Bank Working Papers*, Washington, DC, March 1993.

12. Interviews held in Brasilia, April 1995.

13. *New York Times*, 18 October 1994, p. A7.

14. Data provided by SOCMERC, Buenos Aires.

15. Telecom of Argentina reported profits of $50 million in the first half of 1993 and $150 million in 1992. Telefónica of Argentina posted a $150 million profit during the same time span in 1993. *Financial Times*, 9 August 1993, p. 15.

16. *El Nuevo Herald*, 25 March 1996, p. 4B.

17. See also the *Wall Street Journal*, 13 September 1996, p. A11.

18. *Clarín*, 17 November 1993, p. 18.

19. Woodrow Wilson Center. *Noticias* (Spring). Washington, DC, 1991.

20. Statement delivered by Eduardo Modiano at the Seminar on the Politics and Economics of Public Revenues Expenditures, sponsored by the World Bank and the Ministry of Economics, Brasilia 10–12 June, 1992.

21. Commissão Parlamentar Mista de Inquérito, Relatório no. 3, De 1994-CN, Brasilia, National Congress, 21 July 1994.

22. Interview with journalist Hétor Ruiz Núñez. Buenos Aires, March 1995.

23. *Mexico Weekly Fax Bulletin*, Mexico City, 14 August 1995. Early warnings of such scandals were reported earlier by the *Miami Herald*, 26 September 1993, p. 27A.

24. *Miami Herald*, 25 March 1996, p. 6A.

25. *Financial Times*, 27 May 1993, p. 3.

26. The only two exceptions are the electricity and gas regulatory agencies.

27. *Clarín*, 22 March 1995, p. 26.

28. *Clarín*, 17 November 1993, p. 18.

29. Eventually, Menem dismissed Cavallo in August 1996 but, in the process, the privatization of the post office had become such a hot controversy that the government had to postpone it.

References

Abreu, Marcelo and Rogério Werneck (1993). 'Privatization and Regulation in Brazil: The 1990–1992 Policies and the Challenge Ahead', Working Paper no. 300. Pontifical Catholic University of Rio de Janeiro.

Acuña, Carlos H. (1994). 'Politics and Economics in the Argentina of the Nineties (Or Why the Future No Longer Is What It Used to Be)', in Smith *et al.* 1994: 75–102.

—— and William C. Smith (1994). 'The Political Economy of Structural Adjustment: The Logic of Support and Opposition to Neoliberal Reform', in Smith *et al.* 1994: 17–66.

Adam, Christopher, William Cavendish, and Percy S. Mistry (1992). *Adjusting Privatization: Case Studies from Developing Countries.* London: Currey, Randle, and Heinemann.

Alvarez Rodrich, Augusto (1991). *Empresas Estatales y Privatización: Cómo reformar la Actividad Empresarial del Estado en el Perú.* Lima: Apoyo.

—— (1992). 'Situación y perspectivas de la privatización en el Perú', in Portocarrero 1992*a*: 13–50.

Ames, Barry (1987). *Political Survival: Politicians and Public Policy in Latin America.* Berkeley: University of California Press.

—— (1995). 'Electoral Rules, Constituency Pressure, and Pork Barrel: Bases for Voting in the Brazilian Congress', *Journal of Politics* 57 (May): 324–43.

Armijo, Leslie (1991). 'Private Capital for the Public Good or Surrender of the National Patrimony? Debating Privatization in Four Semi-Industrial Countries and the Washington Policy Community', paper prepared for the XVI International Congress of LASA. Washington DC, 4–7 April 1991.

—— (1992). 'Policymakers' Motives to Privatize, with Illustrations from Recent Experience in Argentina, Mexico, Brazil, and India', paper prepared for the XVII International Congress of LASA, Los Angeles, 24–7 September 1992.

—— (1998). 'Balance Sheet or Ballott Box? Incentives to Privatize in Emerging Democracies', in *The Problematic Relationship between Economic and Political Liberalization*, ed. Philip Oxhorn and Pamela Starr, pp. 161–202. Boulder: Lynne Rienner.

Austin, James, Lawrence Wortzel, and John Coburn (1986). 'Privatizing State-Owned Enterprises: Hopes and Realities', *The Columbia Journal of World Business* 21, (Fall): 51–60.

Azpiazu, Daniel (1998). 'La élite empresaria y el ciclo económico. Centralización del capital, inserción estructural y beneficios etraordinarios', in *La Económia argentina a fin de siglo: fragmentación presente y desarrollo ausente*, ed. Hugo Nochteff, pp. 47–68. Buenos Aires: Eudeba/Flacso.

—— and Adolfo Vispo (1994). 'Algunas enseñanzas de las privatizaciones en Argentina', *Revista de la CEPAL* 54 (December): 129–47.

Babai, Don (1988). 'The World Bank and the IMF: Rolling Back the State or Backing its Role', in *The Promise of Privatization*, ed. Raymond Vernon, pp. 254–85. New York: Council of Foreign Relations.

Baer, Monica (1993). *O Rumo Perdido: A Crise Fiscal e Financiera do Estado*. São Paulo: Paz e Terra.

Baer, Werner (1993). 'Introduction', in *Brazil and the Challenge of Economic Reform*, ed. Werner Baer and Joseph Tulchin, pp. 1–8. Washington DC: Woodrow Wilson Center Special Studies.

Balbi, Maria Rosa (1997) 'Politics and Trade Unions in Peru', in Cameron and Mauceri 1997: 134–51.

Balcerowicz, Leszek (1994). 'Poland', in Williamson 1994a: 153–77.

Barber, James (1992). *Presidential Character: Predicting Performance in the White House*. Englewood Cliffs, NJ: Prentice Hall.

Barham, John (1991). 'Argentine Defense Ministry Pressed to Sell', *Privatization International* (November).

—— (1992). '$650m Telecom Argentina Offer This Month', *Privatization International* (March).

Bates, Robert (1991). *Beyond the Miracle of the Market*. Cambridge: Cambridge University Press.

—— (1994). 'Comment', in Williamson 1994a: 29–34.

Belaunde Terry, Fernando (1994). *La conquista del Peru por los peruanos*. Lima: Minerva.

Béliz, Gustavo (1986). *Menem, Argentina hacia el año 2000*. Buenos Aires: Galerna.

Bello, Richard, and David Shiguiyama (1998). 'Peru's Privatization Program 1990–96', in Lieberman and Kirkness 1998: 32–41.

Bianchi, Andrés, and Takahashi Nohara (eds.) (1988). *A Comparative Study between Asia and Latin America*. Tokyo: Institute of Developing Economies.

Bienen, Henry, and John Waterbury (1989). 'The Political Economy of Privatization in Developing Countries', *World Development* 17: 617–32.

Bitrán, Eduardo and Raúl Sáez (1994). 'Privatization and Regulation in Chile', in *The Chilean Economy*, ed. Barry Bosworth, Rudiger Dornbusch, and Raúl Labán, pp. 329–77. Washington, DC: The Brookings Institution.

Blake, Charles (1994). 'Social Pacts and Inflation Control in New Democracies: The Impact of "Wildcat Cooperation" in Argentina and Uruguay', *Comparative Political Studies* 27/3 (October): 381–401.

Blanco, Eduardo (1993). *Aerolíneas Argentinas Arrodillada*. Buenos Aires: El Otro Mundo.

Boeker, Paul (ed.) (1993). *Latin America's Turnaround: Privatization, Foreign Investment, and Growth*. La Jolla: Institute of the Americas.

Boloña, Carlos (1996). 'The Viability of Alberto Fujimori's Economic Strategy', in Gonzales de Olarte 1996a: 183–264.

Borón, Atilio (1991). 'Los axiomas de Anillaco. La visión de la política en el pensamiento y en la acción de Carlos S. Menem', in *El Menemato*, ed. Borón, Atilio *et al.*, pp. 122–89. Buenos Aires: Letra Buena.

Bortz, Jeffrey (1987). 'The Dilemma of Mexican Labor', *Current History* 86, 518 (March): 105–8, 129–30.

Bös, Dieter, and Wolfgang Peters (1991). 'Privatization of Public Enterpises: A Principal–Agent Approach Comparing Efficiency in Private and Public Sectors', *Empirica* 18/1.

Bour, Enrique (1993). 'El programa argentino de la desregulación y privatización', in *Reforma y convergencia: Ensayos sobre la transformación de la economía argentina*, ed. Felipe A. M. de la Balze, pp. 223–72. Buenos Aires: ADEBA.

Bouzas, R., and Saúl Keifman (1991). 'El menú de opciones y el programa de capitalización de la deuda externa argentina', *Desarrollo Económico* 116/29 (January–March): 451–76.

Bresser Pereira, Luiz Carlos (1993). *Economic Crisis and State Reform in Brazil: Toward a New Interpretation of Latin America*. Boulder: Lynne Rienner.

—— (1996). *Economic Crisis and State Reform in Brazil: Toward a New Interpretation of Latin America*. Boulder: Lynne Rienner.

—— (1994). 'Brazil', in Wlliamson 1994*a*: 333–54.

—— José María Maravall, and Adam Przeworski (1993). *Economic Reforms in New Democracies: A Social-Democratic Approach*. New York: Cambridge University Press.

Brock, Philip, Michael Connolly, and Claudio González-Vega (eds.) (1989). *Latin American Debt and Adjustment: External Shocks and Macroeconomic Policies*. New York: Praeger.

Bruno, Michael, Guido Di Tella, and Rudiger Dornbusch (eds.) (1988). *Inflation Stabilization: The Experience of Israel, Argentina, Brazil, Bolivia, and Mexico*. Cambridge, Mass.: MIT Press.

Burneo, Kurt (1993). *El desafío de la privatización en el Perú*. Lima: CEDAL.

Cabello, Ricardo, and David Shiguiyama (1998). 'Peru's Privatization Program', in *Privatization and Emerging Equity Markets*, ed. Ira Lieberman and Christopher Kirkness, pp. 32–40. Washington, DC: World Bank–Flemings.

Cameron, Maxwell (1994). *Democracy and Authoritarianism in Peru*. New York: St. Martin's Press.

—— and Philip Mauceri (eds.) (1997). *The Peruvian Labyrinth: Polity, Society, Economy*. University Park, Pa.: Penn State University Press.

Camp, Roderic (1993). *Politics in Mexico*. New York: Oxford University Press.

Canitrot, Adolfo (1993). 'Crisis and Transformation of the Argentine State', in Smith *et al.* 1993: 75–102.

Carbonetto, Daniel, *et al.* (1987). *El Perú heterodoxo: un modelo económico*. Lima: Instituto Nacional de Planificación.

Carrillo, A., and S. García (1983). *Las empresas públicas en México*. Mexico City: Porrúa.

Carrió, Alejandro, and Alberto Garay (1991). *La jurisdición 'per saltum' de la Corte Suprema, su estudio a partir del caso Aerolíneas Argentinas*. Buenos Aires: Abeledo–Perrot.

Castelar Pinheiro, Armando, and A. C. Oliveira (1991). 'Brazilian Privatization: a decade of experience', São Paulo, CEBRAP (Texto de Discussão Interna, 7).

—— and Fabio Giambiagi (1993). 'Brazilian Privatization in the 1990s', mimeo, Rio de Janeiro.

—— and Ben Ross Schneider (1994). 'The Fiscal Impact of Privatization in Latin America', *The Quarterly Review of Economics and Finance* 34, Special Issue: 9–42.

Catterberg, Edgardo (1991). *Argentina Confronts Politics: Political Culture and Public Opinion in the Argentine Transition to Democracy*. Boulder: Lynne Rienner.

CEPAL (1992). *Balance preliminar de la economía de América Latina y el Caribe.* Santiago: CEPAL.

Cerruti, Gabriela (1993). *El Jefe: Vida y obra de Carlos Saúl Menem.* Buenos Aires: Planeta.

—— and Sergio Ciancaglini (1992). *El octavo circulo: Crónica y entretelones de la Argentina menemista.* Buenos Aires: Planeta.

Chisari, Omar, Antonio Estache, and Carlos Romero (1997). 'Winners and Losers from Utility Privatization in Argentina: Lessons from a General Equilibrium Model', *Policy Research Working Paper* 1824 (September), 3–36. Washington DC: World Bank.

CLADE (1988). *Empresas Públicas y politíca de privatizaciones.* Buenos Aires: Fundación Friederich Ebert.

Cook, Paul, and Colin Kirkpatrick (1988). *Privatization in Less Developed Countries.* New York: St. Martin's Press.

COPRI (1993*a*). 'The Turn of Peru', *COPRI Special Supplement*, Lima (May).

—— (1993*b*). *Peru: the Privatization Process.* Lima: COPRI.

Cotler, Julio (1978). *Clases, estado y nación en el Perú.* Lima: Instituto de Estudios Peruanos.

Cowan, Gary (1990). *Privatizing in the Developing World.* New York: Greenwood.

de Abreu, Marcelo, and Rogério L. F. Werneck (1993). 'Privatization and Regulation in Brazil: The 1990–1992 Policies and the Challenges Ahead', *The Quarterly Review of Economics and Finance* 33, Special Issue: 21–44.

de Lima, Venício A. (1998). 'Politíca de Comunicações no Brasil: Novos e Velhos Atores', paper prepared for the XXI International Congress of LASA, Chicago, September 24–6.

de Michele, Roberto (1993). 'Seras Juez', *Sentencia* 9 (May): 44.

de Soto, Hernando (1989). *The Other Path.* New York: Harper.

de Souza, Juarez (1999 forthcoming). 'Privatization in Brazil: Toward and Evolution', in *The Impact of Privatization in Latin America*, ed. Melissa Birch and Jerry Haar. Miami: North–South Center Press at the University of Miami.

Devlin, Robert (1985). *Transnational Banks and the External Finance of Latin America: The Experience of Peru.* Santiago de Chile: United Nations.

—— (1989). *Debt and Crisis in Latin America: The Supply Side of the Story.* Princeton: Princeton University Press.

—— (1993). 'Privatization and Social Welfare', *CEPAL Review* 49 (April): 155–80.

Dietz, Henry (1992). 'Elites in an Unconsolidated Democracy: Peru During the 1980s', in *Elites and Democratic Consolidation in Latin America and Southern Europe*, ed. John Higley and Richard Gunther, pp. 236–56. New York: Cambridge University Press.

Di Tella, Torcuato (1990). *The Transformation of Peronism.* Buenos Aires: Mimeo.

Domíngues, Ricardo (1988). 'Privatizaciones en la Argentina', *Boletín Informativo Techint* (April–May–June): 45–60.

Donahue, John (1989). *The Privatization Decision.* New York: Basic Books.

Dornbusch, Rudiger, and Sebastian Edwards (1989). 'Macroeconomic Populism in Latin America', *NBER Working Paper Series*, no. 2986. Washington DC: National Bureau of Economic Development.

Dupas, Gilberto (1993). 'Competitive Integration and Recovery of Growth: Risks and Prospects', in *Brazil and the Challenge of Economic Reform*, ed. Werner Baer and Joseph Tulchin, pp. 31–7. Washington DC: Woodrow Wilson Center Special Studies.

Durand, Francisco (1987). *Los empresarios y la concertación*. Lima: Fundación Friederich Ebert.

—— (1997). 'The Growth and Limitations of the Peruvian Right', in Cameron and Mauceri 1997: 152–78.

The Economist (1987). 'Brazil: Unstoppable', 25 April: 1–26.

—— (1988). 'Mexican Privatisation. Getting down to Business', 7 May: 65–6.

—— (1993). 'The Greatest Assets Ever Sold', 21 August: 13.

Edwards, Sebastian (1989). *Real Exchange Rates, Devaluation, and Adjustment: Exchange Rate Policy in Developing Countries*. Cambridge, Mass.: MIT Press.

—— (1995). *Crisis and Reform in Latin America: From Despair to Hope*. New York: Oxford University Press.

Estache, Antonio, and David Martimort (1998). 'Institutions and Regulation', paper prepared for the conference, 'Regulation in Post-Privatization Environments: The Latin American Experience', Buenos Aires, 21–2 May.

—— and Martín Rodriguez Pardina (1998). 'Electricity Regulation.' Paper prepared for the conference, *Regulation in Post-Privatization Environments: The Latin American Experience*, Buenos Aires, 21–2 May .

Feigenbaum, Harvey B., and Jeffrey R. Henig (1994). 'The Political Underpinnings of Privatization: A Typology', *World Politics* 46/2 (January): 185–208.

Feinberg, Richard (1992). 'Latin America: Back on the Screen', *International Economic Insights* 3/4 (July–August): 52–6.

FitzGerald, E. V. K. (1979). *The Political Economy of Peru, 1958–78*. Cambridge: Cambridge University Press.

Fleischer, David (1994). 'Political Corruption and Campaign Financing in Brazil', paper prepared for the XVI World Congress of the International Political Science Association, Berlin, Germany, 21–5 August.

—— (1996/7). 'Political Corruption in Brazil: The Delicate Connection with Campaign Finance', *Crime, Law and Social Change* 25/4: 297–321.

Fontana, Andrés (1986). 'Armed Forces and Neoconservative Ideology: State Shrinking in Argentina, 1976–1981', in Glade 1986: 62–74.

Franco, Gustavo, and Winston Fritsch (1992). 'The Political Economy of Trade and Industrial Policy in Brazil', CEPAL, unpublished paper.

Frieden, Jeffrey (1991). *Debt, Development, and Democracy: Modern Political Economy and Latin America, 1965–1985*. Princeton: Princeton University Press.

Fundación de Investigaciones Ecónomicas Latinoamericanas (1987*a*). *El Fracaso del estatismo*. Buenos Aires: Sudamericana-Planeta.

—— (1987*b*). *El Gasto Público en la Argentina 1960–1985*. Buenos Aires: FIEL.

Galal, Ahmed, Leroy Jones, Pankaj Tandon, and Ingo Vogelsang (1994): *Welfare Consequences of Selling Public Enterprises: An Empirical Analysis*. New York: Oxford University Press.

Galiani, Sebastián, and Diego Petrecolla (1999). 'The Argentine Privatiztion Process and Its Aftermaths: Some Preliminary Conclusions', in *The Impact of*

Privatization in Latin America, ed. Jerry Harr, and Melissa Birch. Miami: North–South Center Press at the University of Miami.

Galvão de Almeida, Fernando (1997). 'A privatizaçã na era do Real', *Conjuntura Econômica* (July): 16–20.

Garavito, Rosa Albina (1985). 'Reestructuración de las paraestatales', *El Cotidiano* 2/4 (January–February)

George, Alexander (1980). *Presidential Decisionmaking in Foreign Policy*. Boulder: Westview Press.

Gerchunoff, Pablo, and Alfredo Visintini (1991). 'Privatizaciones en un contexto de inflación e incertitumbre', in *Economia de las empresas publicas*, ed. Alberto Porto, pp. 161–212. Buenos Aires: TESIS.

Gerchunoff, Pablo, and Germán Coloma (1993). 'Privatization in Argentina', in *Privatization in Latin America*, ed. Manuel Sánchez and Rossana Corona, pp. 251–99. Washington DC: Inter-American Development Bank.

Gerchunoff, Pablo, and Guillero Cánovas (1995). 'Privatization en un contexto de emergencia económica', *Desarrollo Económico* 34 (January–March): 483–512.

Gershenson, Antonio (1987). 'Privatización: quien debe decidir?' *La Jornada* 11 (December): 7.

Gibson, Edward (1996). *Class & Conservative Parties: Argentina in* Comparative Perspective. Baltimore: Johns Hopkins University Press.

—— (1990). 'Democracy and the New Electoral Right in Argentina', *Journal of Interamerican Studies and World Affairs* 32/3 (Fall): 177–228.

Giussani, Pablo (1990). *Menem: Su lógica secreta*. Buenos Aires: Sudamericana.

Glade, William (ed.) (1986). *State Shrinking*. Austin: University of Texas Press.

—— (1989). 'Privatization in Rent-Seeking Societies', *World Development* 17: 673–82.

—— (ed.) (1991). *Privatization of Public Enterprises in Latin America*. San Francisco: ICS Press.

Goldstein, Andrea (1997). 'Brazilian Privatization in International Perspective. The Rocky Path from State Capitalism to Regulatory Capitalism', *Fondazione Enrico Mattei Working Paper*, no. 95–7 (November).

Gonzales de Olarte, Efraín (1994). 'Contribuye la privatización al desarrollo del Perú?' *Argumentos-IEP* 23–4/2 (October): 13–16.

—— (ed.) (1996*a*). *The Peruvian Economy and Structural Adjustment: Past, Present, and Future*. Miami: North–South Center Press.

—— (1996*b*). 'Introduction', in Gonzales de Olarte 1996*a*: 1–9.

Gónzalez Fraga, Javier (1991). 'Argentine Privatization in Retrospect', in Glade 1991: 75–98.

Goretti, Matteo, and Delia Ferreira Rubio (1994). 'Gobierno por decreto en Argentina (1989–1993)', mimeo, Buenos Aires: Centro de Estudios para Políticas Públicas Aplicada.

Gorriti, Gustavo (1994). 'Fujimori's Svengali', *CovertAction* 49 (Summer): 4–12, 54–8.

Gosman, Eleonora (1991). 'Aerolíneas Argentinas', in *Privatizaciones: Reestructuración del Estado y la sociedad*, ed. Arnaldo Bocco and Naum Minsburg, pp. 245–58. Buenos Aires: Letra Buena.

Grindle, Merilee S., and John W. Thomas (1991). *Public Choices and Policy Change: The Political Economy of Reform in Developing Countries*. Baltimore: Johns Hopkins University Press.

Hachette, Dominique, and Rolf Lüders (1993). *Privatization in Chile: An Economic Appraisal*. San Francisco: International Center for Economic Growth.

Haggard, Stephan, and Robert Kaufman (eds.) (1992). *The Politics of Adjustment*. Princeton: Princeton University Press.

—— —— (1995) *The Political Economy of Democratic Transitions*. Princeton: Princeton University Press.

Haggard, Stephan, and Steven B. Webb (1992). 'What Do We Know About the Political Economy of Policy Reform?' *World Bank Research Observer* 8/2: 143–68.

—— —— (eds.) (1994). *Voting for Reform: Democracy, Political Liberalization, and Economic Adjustment*. New York: Oxford University Press.

Henke, Steve (ed.) (1986). *Privatization in the Developing World*. Washington DC: The Heritage Foundation.

—— (ed.) (1987). *Prospects for Privatization*. New York: Proceedings of the American Academy of Political Science.

Hemming, Richard, and Ali Mansoor (1988). *Privatization and Public Enterprise*. Washington DC: IMF.

Hill, Alice, and Manuel Abdala (1996). 'Argentina: The Sequencing of Privatization and Regulation', in Levy and Spiller 1996: 202–49.

Holden, Paul and Rajapatirana, Sarath (1995). *Unshackling the Private Sector: A Latin American Story*. Washington, DC: World Bank.

Hunt, Shane (1996). 'The Current Economic Situation in Long-Term Perspective', in Gonzales de Olarte 1996a: 11–57.

Iazzetta, Osvaldo (1996). *Las privatizaciones en Brasil y Argentina: Una aproximación desde la técnica y la política*. Rosario: Ediciones Homo Sapiens.

Iglesias, Enrique (1992). *Reflections on Economic Development: Toward a New Latin American Consensus*. Washington, DC: IDB.

Ikenberry, G. John (1990). 'The International Spread of Privatization Policies: Inducements, Learning, and "Policy Bandwagoning"', in Suleiman and Waterbury 1990a: 88–110.

Indacochea, Alejandro (1993). *Privatizar la privatización y reflexiones sobre el nuevo orden económico mundial*. Lima: ESAN/IDE.

Instituto de Economia do Setor Público (1993). *Proceso de Privatização no Brasil: A Experiencia dos Anos 1990–92*. São Paulo: IESP.

Inter-American Development Bank (1991). *Economic and Social Progress in Latin America*. Baltimore: Johns Hopkins University Press.

International Finance Corporation (1997). *Emerging Stock Markets Factbook 1997*. Washington DC: IFC.

Jochamowitz, Luis (1994). *Ciudadano Fujimori: La construcción de un político*, 2nd edn. Lima: PEISA.

Jones, Leroy, Pankaj Tandon, and Ingo Vogelsang (1990). *Selling Public Enterprises*. Boston, Mass.: MIT Press.

Kahler, Miles (1990). 'Orthodoxy and Its Alternatives: Explaining Approaches to Stabilization and Adjustment', in Nelson 1990a: 33–62.

—— (1992). 'External Influence, Conditionality, and the Politics of Adjustment', in Haggard and Kaufman 1992: 89–136.

Kaufman, Robert R. (1990). 'Stabilization and Adjustment in Argentina, Brazil, and Mexico', in Nelson 1990*a*: 63–111.

Kay, Bruce (1995). ' "Fujipopulism" and The Liberal State in Peru, 1990–1995', *Journal of Interamerican Studies and World Affairs* 21 (Winter): 55–98.

Kay, John, and David Thompson (1988). 'Privatization: A Policy in Search of a Rationale', *Economic Journal* 96.

Keifman, Saúl (1991). 'Privatizaciones y capitalización de la deuda externa: Solución para la Argentina o para los bancos?' In *Privatizaciones: Reestructuración del Estado y la sociedad*, ed. Arnaldo Bocco and Naum Minsburg, pp. 197–217. Buenos Aires: Letra Buena.

Kiewiet, Roderick, and Matthew McCubbins (1991). *The Logic of Delegation*. Chicago: University of Chicago Press.

Kikeri, Sunita, John Nellis, and Mary Shirley (1992). *Privatization: The Lessons of Experience*. Washington, DC: World Bank.

King, Gary (1989). *Unifying Political Methodology: The Likelihood Theory of Statistical Inference*. New York: Cambridge University Press.

—— Robert Keohane, and Sidney Verba (1994). *Designing Social Inquiry: Scientific Inference in Qualitative Research*. Princeton: Princeton University Press.

Kingstone, Peter (1998). 'Political Continuity Versus Social Change: The Sustainability of Neoliberal Reform in Brazil', *Nafta: Law and Business Review of the Americas* 4/2 (Spring): 38–56.

Klaiber, Jeffery (1990). 'Fujimori: Race and Religion in Peru', *America* 163/6 (September): 133–5.

Krieger, Gustavo, Luiz Antônio Novaes, and Tales Faria (1992). *Todos os socios do presidente*. São Paulo: Scritta.

Krueger, Anne (1974). 'The Political Economy of the Rent-Seeking Society', *American Economic Review* (June).

Kuczynski, Pedro Pablo (1977). *Peruvian Economy under Economic Stress: An Account of the Belaunde Administration, 1963–68*. Princeton: Princeton University Press.

—— (1988). *Latin American Debt*. Baltimore: Johns Hopkins University Press/ Twentieth Century Fund.

—— and Felipe Ortiz de Zevallos (1990). *Respuestas para los 90's*. Lima: APOYO.

Lamounier, Bolívar (July 1994). 'Brazil at an Impasse', *Journal of Democracy* 5/3: 73–87.

Landi, Oscar, and Marcelo Cavarozzi (1991). 'Menem: El Fin del Peronismo? (Crisis y Prostración en la Argentina)', *Cuaderno CEDES*, 66.

Lawton, Jorge A. (ed.) (1995). *Privatization and Poverty: Contemporary Challenges in Latin American Political Economy*. Miami: Nort–South Center Press.

Levy, Brian, and Pablo Spiller (eds.) (1996). *Regulations, Institutions, and Commitment*. New York: Cambridge University Press.

Leyden Patrick, and Albert Link (1993). 'Privatization, Bureaucracy, and Risk Aversion', *Public Choice* 76: 199–213.

Lieberman, Ira W., and Christopher D. Kirkness (eds.) (1998). *Privatization and Emerging Equity Markets*. Washington DC: World Bank and Flemings Securities.

Longo, Carlos Alberto (1982). 'Uma Quantificação do Setor Público', in *A Crise do 'Bom Patrão'*, ed. Paulo Rabello de Castro *et al.*, pp. 78–91. Rio De Janeiro: CEDES/APEC.

Llach, Juan (1991). 'La nueva economia institucional y la destatización de las empresas públicas', in *Economía de las empresas públicas*, ed. Alberto Porto, pp. 214–314. Buenos Aires: TESIS.

Luna, M. (1987). 'Hacia un corporativismo liberal? Los empresarios y el corporativismo', *Estudios sociológicos* 5/5.

Machinea, José Luis (1993). 'Stabilisation under Alfonsín', in *Argentina in the Crisis Years (1983–1990)*, ed. Colin M. Lewis and Nissa Torrents, pp. 124–43. London: Institute of Latin American Stduies, University of London.

Maciel, Mario (1989). 'Privatización y Finanzas Publicas: el caso de Chile, 1985–88', *Colección Estudios CIEPLAN* 26 (June): 5–60.

Mainwaring, Scott, and Matthew Shugart (eds.) (1997). *Presidentialism and Democracy in Latin America*. New York: Cambridge University Press.

Majul, Luis (1993). *Los Dueños de la Argentina: La cara oculta de los negocios*. Buenos Aires: Sudamericana.

—— (1994). *Los Dueños de la Argentina II: Los secretos del verdadero poder*. Buenos Aires: Sudamericana.

Marti, Lisa (1994). *Coercive Cooperation*. Princeton: Princeton University Press.

McClintock, Cynthia (1994). 'Presidents, Messiahs, and Constitutional Breakdowns in Peru', in *The Failure of Presidential Democracy*, ed. Juan Linz and Arturo Valenzuela, pp. 286–321. Baltimore: Johns Hopkins University Press.

—— and Abraham Lowenthal (eds.) (1983). *The Peruvian Experiment Reconsidered*. Princeton: Princeton University Press.

McGuire, James W. (1997). *Peronism without Perón: Unions, Parties, and Democracy*. Stanford: Stanford University Press.

Mead, Gary (1990). 'Menem Succeeds Where Others Have Failed Despite a Host of Troubles Along the Way', *Privatization International* (August).

Meller, Patricio (1992). 'A Review of the Chilean Privatization Experience', *The Quarterly Review of Economics and Finance* 33: 95–112.

Mello, M. (1990). 'A Privatização no Brasil: Análise dos seus Fundamentos e Experiências Internacionais', Ph.D. diss. Universidade de São Paulo.

—— (1992). 'A Privatizacão no Brasil: análise dos seus fundamentos e experiéncias internacionais, São Paulo: Universidade de São Paulo.

Mendes, J. C. (1987). 'Uma análise do programa brasileiro de privatizaçao', *Conjuntura econômica* (September).

Menem, Carlos, and Eduardo Duhalde (1989). *La revolución productiva*. Buenos Aires: Lillo.

Menem, Carlos, and Roberto Dromi (1990). *Reforma del estado y transformación nacional*. Buenos Aires: Ciencias de la Administración.

Molano, Walter (1997). *The Logic of Privatization: The Case of Telecommunications in the Southern Cone of Latin America*. Westport: Greenwood.

Montoya, Carlos (1992). 'Dinámica de la privatización', in Portocarrero 1992*a*: 51–62.

Mora y Araujo, Manuel (1991). *Ensayo y Error*. Buenos Aires: Planeta.

—— (1993). 'Las demandas sociales y la legitimidad de la política de ajuste', in *Reforma y convergencia: Ensayos sobre la transformación de la economía argentina*, ed. Felipe A. M. de la Balze, pp. 301–35. Buenos Aires: ADEBA.

Moreno, Oscar (1991). 'El Menemismo: El peronismo de los noventa?' paper prepared for the XV Congress of the International Political Science Association. Buenos Aires, 21–5 July.

Moreno Ocampo, Luis (1993). *En defensa propria: Cómo salir de la corrupción.* Buenos Aires: Planeta.

Most, Benjamin, and Harvey Starr (1984). 'International Relations Theory, Foreign Policy Substitutability, and "Nice" Laws', *World Politics* 36/3: 323–406.

—— (1989). *Inquiry, Logic and International Politics.* Columbia: University of South Carolina Press.

Muñoz, Heraldo (1991). 'Chile: The Limits of Success', in *Exporting Democracy: The United States and Latin America*, ed. Abraham Lownthal pp. 161–74. Baltimore: Johns Hopkins.

Mustapich, Ana María, and Natalia Ferretti (1994). 'El veto presidencial', mimeo. Buenos Aires: Instituto Torcuato Di Tella.

Natale, Alberto (1993). *Privatizaciones en Privado.* Buenos Aires: Planeta.

Nelson, Joan (1984). 'The Political Economy of Stabilization', *World Development* 12, pp. 983–1006 no. 10.

—— (ed.) (1990a). *Economic Crisis and Policy Choice: The Politics of Adjustment in the Third World.* Princeton: Princeton University Press.

—— (1990b). 'Introduction: The Politics of Economic Adjustment in Developing Nations', in Nelson 1990a: 3–32.

—— (1990c). 'Conclusions', in Nelson 1990a: 321–62.

—— (1994). 'Discussion', in Williamson 1994a: 472–9.

Newland, Dan (1993). 'Argentina: The Powers to Be', *US/Latin Trade* (February): 48–53.

O'Donnell, Guillermo (1994). 'Delegative Democracy', *Journal of Democracy* 5/1 (January): 53–69.

Ostiguy, Pierre (1990). *Los capitanes de la industria. Grandes empresarios, política y economía en la Argentina de los años 80.* Buenos Aires: Legasa.

Ott, Attiat (1991). *Privatization and Economic Efficiency.* London: Edward Elgar.

Palermo, Vincente, and Marcos Novaro (1996). *Política y Poder en el gobierno de Menem.* Buenos Aires: Flacso and Grupo Editorial Norma.

Palmer, David Scott (1990). 'Peru's Persistent Problems', *Current History* 89, 543 (January): 5–8, 31–4.

—— (1994) *The Shining Path of Peru.* New York: St. Martin's Press.

Passanezi Filho, Reynaldo (1993). 'Questoes sobre privatização no Brasil', *Notas Técnicas IESP* 4 (May).

—— (1994). 'Impactos fiscais da privatização: aspectos conceituais e análise do caso brasileiro', IESP/FUNDAP 20 (November).

Payne, Leigh A. (1994). *Brazilian Industrialists and Democratic Change.* Baltimore: Johns Hopkins University Press.

Peralta Ramos, Mónica (1992). *The Political Economy of Argentina: Power and Class since 1930.* Boulder: Westview.

Petrazzini, Ben (1995). 'Telephone Privatization in a Hurry', in *Privatizing Monopolies: Lessons from the Telecommunications and Transport Sectors in Latin America*, ed. Ravi Ramamurti, pp. 108–46. Baltimore: Johns Hopkins University Press (1996).

Petrecolla, Alberto, Alberto Porto, Pablo Gerchunoff, and Guillermo Canovas (1993). 'Privatization in Argentina', *The Quarterly Review of Economics and Finance* 33: 67–93.

Piñera, José (1994). 'Chile', in Williamson 1994*a*: 225–31.

Pinzás, Teobaldo (1993). 'La marcha de la privatización', *Argumentos-IEP* (Lima) 7/2 (May): 7–8.

Pirie, Masden (1985). *Dismantling the State: The Theory and Practice of Privatization*. Dallas: National Center for Policy Analysis.

Pirker, Elizabeth (1991). 'Participación de las empresas estatales en la economía argentina', in *Privatizaciones: Reestructuración del Estado y la sociedad*, ed. Arnaldo Bocco and Naum Minsburg, pp. 67–89. Buenos Aires: Letra Buena.

Política Económica (1988). 'Reestructuración del sector paraestatal', 20 December: ii–xvii.

Portocarrero, Gonzalo (1983). 'Ideologías, Funciones del estado y Políticas Económicas: Perú 1900–1980', *Debates en Sociología* 9.

Portocarrero, Javier (ed.) (1992*a*). *Proceso de privatización en el Perú*. Lima: Foro Económico.

—— (1992*b*). 'Síntesis del debate', in Portocarrero 1992*a*: 63–71.

Power, Timothy J. (1994). 'The Pen is Mighter Than the Congress: Presidential Decree Power in Brazil'. Paper prepared for the XVIII International Congress of LASA, Atlanta, 10–12 March.

Prado, Sérgio (1993). 'Processo de privatização no Brasil: a experiência dos anos 1990–92', São Paulo, IESP/FUNDAP (Relatórios de Pesquisa, 11).

Przeworski, Adam (1991). *Democracy and the Market*. Cambridge: Cambridge University Press.

—— (1995). *Sustainable Democracy*. New York: Cambridge University Press.

—— and Henry Teune (1970). *The Logic of Comparative Social Inquiry*. New York: Wiley-Interscience.

Psacharopoulos, George, *et al.* (1992). *Poverty and Income Distribution in Latin America: The Story of the 1980s*. Latin America and the Caribbean Technical Department, Report no. 27. Washington DC: World Bank.

Ramamurti, Ravi (1992). 'The Impact of Privatization on the Latin American debt Problem', *Journal of Interamerican Studies and World Affairs* 34/2 (Summer): 93–126.

—— (1996). 'The New Frontier of Privatization', in *Privatizing Monopolies: Lessons from the Telecommunications and Transport Sectors in Latin America*, pp. 1–45. Baltimore: Johns Hopkins University Press.

—— and Raymond Vernon (eds.) (1991). *Privatization and Control of State-Owned Enterprises*. Washington DC: World Bank.

Rangel, Ignácio (1987). *Economia brasileira contemporanea*. São Paulo: Bienal.

Reichstul, Henri, and Luciano Coutinho (1983). 'Investimento Estatal 1974–1980: Ciclo e Crise', in *Desenvolvimiento Capitalista no Brasil*, ed. Luiz Gonzaga Belluzo and Renata Coutinho. São Paulo: Brasilense.

Roberts, Kenneth, and Moisés Arce (1998). 'Neoliberalism and Lower-Class Voting Behavior in Peru', *Comparative Political Studies* 31/2 (April): 217–46.

Roett, Riordan (1992). *Brazil: Politics in a Patrimonial Society*, 4th edn. New York: Praeger.

—— (1997). 'Brazilian Politics at the Century's End', in *Brazil Under Cardoso*, ed. Susan Kaufman Purcell and Riordan Roett, pp. 19–41. Boulder: Lynne Rienner.

Rojo, Pablo, and Jeffrey Hoberman (1993). 'Deregulation in Argentina: A Policy-Maker's View'. Published in *Quarterly Review of Economics and Statistics*, 34 (1994): 151–77.

Rose-Ackerman, Susan (1992). *Rethinking the Progressive Agenda: The Reform of the American Regulatory State*. New York: Free Press.

Rosenn, Keith (1990). 'Brazil's New Constitution Ten Years Later: An Exercise in Transient Constitutionalism for a Transitional Society', *American Journal of Comparative Law* 38 (Fall): 773–802.

—— (1998). 'Judicial Reform in Brazil', *Nafta: Law and Business Review of the Americas* 4/2 (Spring): 19–56.

Russett, Bruce, and Harvey Starr (1985). *World Politics: The Menu For Choice*, 2nd edn. San Francisco: W. H. Freeman.

Sachs, Jeffrey (1991). 'Accelerating Privatization in Eastern Europe', paper prepared for the World Bank Annual Conference on Development Economics. Washington DC.

—— (1994). 'Life in the Economic Emergency Room', in Wlliamson 1994*a*: 501–24.

Sader, Frank (1995). 'Privatizing Public Enterprises and Foreign Investment in the Developing Countries, 1988–93', Foreign Investment Advisory Service (FIAS) Occasional Paper. Washington, DC: International Finance Corporation and World Bank.

Salcedo, J. M. (1990). *Tsunami presidente*. Lima: Venus.

Saulniers, Alfred (1988). *Public Enterprises in Peru: Public Sector Growth and Reform*. Boulder: Westview Press.

Savas, E. S. (1987). *The Key to Better Government*. New York: Chatham House.

Schamis, Héctor (1991). 'Privatization as Policy and Politics: Comparative Reflections on Latin America and Western Europe', paper prepared for the XVI International Congress of LASA, Washington DC, 4–7 April.

—— (1992). 'Conservative Political Economy in Latin America and Western Europe: The Political Sources of Privatization', in *The Right and Democracy in Latin America*, ed. Douglas Chalmers, Maria do Carmo Campello de Souza, and Atilio Borón, pp. 48–67. New York: Praeger.

Schneider, Ben Ross (1988–9). 'Partly for Sale: Privatization and State Strength in Brazil and Mexico', *Journal of Interamerican Studies and World Affairs* 30 (Winter): 89–115.

—— (1990). 'The Politics of Privatization in Brazil and Mexico: Variations on a Statist Theme', in Suleiman and Waterbury 1990*a*: 319–345.

—— (1992). 'Privatization in the Collor Government: Triumph of Liberalism or Collapse of the Development State?' in *The Right and Democracy in Latin America*, ed. Douglas Chalmers, Maria do Carmo Campello de Souza, and Atilio Borón, pp. 225–38. New York: Praeger.

—— (1997–8). 'Organized Business Politics in Democratic Brazil', *Journal of Interamerican Studies and World Affairs* 39/4 (Winter): 95–127.

—— (forthcoming). 'Elusive Sinergy: Business-Government Relations and Development', *Comparative Politics*.

Schvarzer, Jorge (1977). 'Las empresas industriales más grandes de la Argentina. Una evaluación', *Desarrollo Económico* 17/66 (July–September): 319–38.

—— (1981). 'Expansión económica del estado subsidiario 1976–1981', Buenos Aires: CISEA.

—— (1992). 'La reestructuración de la economía argentina en nuevas condiciones políticas', *Documento CISEA*, Buenos Aires, November.

—— (1993). 'El Proceso de privatizations en la Argentina', *Realidad Económica* (November–December): 42–70.

SELA (1995). 'The Latin American and Caribbean Region's Bet on Privatization', paper prepared for the 21st Regular Meeting of the Latin American Council, San Salvador, El Salvador, 10–13 July 1995.

Selcher, Wayne (1998). 'The Politics of Decentralized Federalism, National Diversification, and Regionalism in Brazil', *Journal of Interamerican and World Affairs* 40/4 (Winter): 25–60.

Sguiglia, Eduardo (1992). *El club de los Poderosos*. Buenos Aires: Planeta.

Sheahan, John (1987). *Patterns of Development in Latin America: Poverty, Repression, and Economic Strategy*. Princeton: Princeton University Press.

Sikkink, Kathryn (1990). *Ideas and Institutions: Developmentalism in Brazil and Argentina*. Ithaca: Cornell University Press.

Siverson, Randolph, and Harvey Starr (1990). 'Opportunity, Willingness, and the Diffusion of War', *American Political Science Review* 84/1: 47–67.

Smith, Amber (1987). 'Mexico Sustains Adjustment Efforts, Realizing Sizable Reductions of Imbalances: Simultaneous Progress made With Trade Liberalization and Privatization', *IMF Survey* 17/13 (June): 210–13.

Smith, William C., and Nizar Messari (1998). 'Democracy and Reform in Cardoso's Brazil: Caught Between Clientelism and Global Markets?' *North–South Agenda Papers* 33 (September).

—— Carlos H. Acuña, and Eduardo A. Gamarra (eds.) (1994). *Democracy, Markets, and Structural Reform in Latin America: Argentina, Bolivia, Brazil, Chile, and Mexico*. New Brunswick: Transaction/North South Center.

Snow, Peter (1979). *Political Forces in Argentina*, rev. edn. New York: Praeger.

Sola, Lourdes (1993). 'The State, Structural Reform, and Democratization in Brazil', in Smith *et al.* 1993: 151–81.

Sotero, Paulo (1996). 'Privatization Program Begins to Roll', *Hemisfile* 7/4 (July/August): 3–4.

Sprout, Harold, and Margaret Sprout (1969). 'Environmental Factors in the Study of International Politics', in *International Politics and Foreign Policy*, rev. edn. ed. James Rosenau, pp. 41–56. New York: The Free Press.

Stallings, Barbara (1990). 'Politics and Economic Crisis: A Comparative Study of Chile, Peru, and Colombia', in Nelson 1990*a*: 113–67.

Starr, Harvey (1978). ' "Opportunity" and "Willingness" as Ordering Concepts in the Study of War', *International Interactions* 4: 363–87.

Stiles, Kendall (1987). 'Argentina's Bargaining with the IMF', *Journal of Interamerican and World Affairs* 29/1 (Fall): 55–85.

Stokes, S. (1996). 'Economic Reform and Public Opinion in Peru, 1990–1995', *Comparative Political Studies* 28/5: 544–65.

Street, James (1987). 'Mexico's Development Crisis', *Current History* 86/518 (March): 101–4.

Suleiman, Ezra, and John Waterbury (eds.) (1990*a*). *The Political Economy of Public Sector Reform and Privatization*. Boulder: Westview.

——— (1990*b*). 'Introduction: Analyzing Privatization in Industrial and Developing Countries', in Suleiman and Waterbury 1990*a*: 1–21.

Suzigan Wilson (1993). 'Industrial Policy and the Challenge of Competitiveness', in *Brazil and the Challenge of Economic Reform*, ed. Werner Baer and Joseph Tulchin, pp. 119–47. (Washington DC: Woodrow Wilson Center Special Studies).

Swiss Bank Warburg (1997). *Privatization in Latin America*. New York: SBW.

Tenenbaum, Bernard (1995). 'The Real World of Power Sector Regulation', *World Bank Viewpoint*, Note no. 50 (June): 1–4.

Terragno, Rodolfo (1992). *Privatizaciones en la Argentina*. Buenos Aires: Fundación Omega Seguros.

Thorp, Rosemary (1977). 'The Post Import-Substitution Era: The Case of Peru', *World Development* 5 (January–February): 125–36.

Torre, Juan Carlos (1993). 'Conflict and Cooperation in Governing the Economic Emergency: The Alfonsín Years', in *Argentina in the Crisis Years (1983–1990)*, ed. Colin M. Lewis and Nissa Torrents, pp. 124–43. London: Institute of Latin American Studies, University of London.

Turner, Frederick, Enrique Zuleta Puceiro, and Carlos R. Miranda (1988). 'El Justicialismo en las provincias', in *Racionalidad del Peronismo*, ed. José Enrique Miguens, and Frederick Turner. Buenos Aires: Planeta.

Urbiztondo, Santiago, Daniel Artana, and Fernando Navajas (1997). *La autonomía de los Entes Reguladores Argentinos*. Buenos Aires: FIEL.

Verbitsky, Horacio (1991). *Robo para la corona*. Buenos Aires: Planeta.

——— (1993). *Hacer la Corte: la construcción de un poder absoluto sin justicia ni control*. Buenos Aires: Planeta.

Vernon, Raymond (ed.) (1988). *The Promise of Privatization*. New York: Council of Foreign Relations.

Vickers, J., and George Yarrow (1988). *Privatization—An Economic Analysis*. Cambridge: MIT Press.

Vispo, Adolfo (1998). 'Los Entes de Regulación. Problemas de diseño y contexto', Unpublished manuscript. Buenos Aires: Flacso.

Waterbury, John (1993). *Exposed to Innumerable Delusions: Public Enterprises and State Power in Egypt, India, Mexico, and Turkey*. New York: Cambridge University Press.

Webb, Richard (1991). 'Prologue', in *Peru's Path to Recovery*, ed. Carlos Peredes and Jeffrey Sachs. Washington, DC: The Brookings Institution.

——— (1994). 'Peru', in Williamson 1994*a*: 355–24.

——— and Graciela Fernández Baca (1991). *Perú en números 1991*. Lima: Cuánto S.A.

Welch, John (1993). 'The New Face of Latin America: Financial Flows, Markets and Institutions in the 1990s', *Journal of Latin American Studies* 25/1 (February): 1–24.

Wellenius, Bjorn (1998). 'Telecommunication Regulation'. Paper prepared for the conference *Regulation in Post-Privatization Environments: The Latin American Experience*, Buenos Aires, May 21–2.

Werlich, David (1991). 'Fujimori and the "Disaster" in Peru', *Current History* 86, 553 (February): 61–4, 81–3.

Werneck, Rogério L. (1991). 'The Uneasy Steps toward Privatization in Brazil', in Glade 1991: 59–74.

—— (1993). 'Government Failure and Wretched Statecraft: Lessons from the Brazilian Vicious Circle', Working Paper no. 301. Pontifical Catholic University of Rio de Janeiro.

Weyland, Kurt (1993). 'The Rise and Fall of President Collor and Its Impact on Brazilian Democracy', *Journal of Interamerican Studies and World Affairs* 35/1 (Spring): 1–37.

—— (1997–8). 'The Brazilian State in the New Democracy', *Journal of Interamerican Studies and World Affairs* 39/4 (Winter): 63–93.

—— (1998). 'Swallowing the Bitter Pill: Sources of Popular Support for Neoliberal Reform in Latin America', *Comparative Political Studies* 31/5 (October): 539–68.

Williamson, John (1990). *The Progress of Policy Reform in Latin America.* Washington, DC: Institute for Financial Economics.

—— (1994a). *The Political Economy of Policy Reform.* Washington: Institute for International Economics.

—— (1994b). 'In Search of a Manual for Technopols', in Williamson 1994a: 11–34.

—— and Stephan Haggard (1994). 'The Political Conditions of Economic Reform', in Williamson 1994a: 11–34.

Wirth, John D. (1970). *The Politics of Brazilian Development, 1930–1954.* Stanford: Stanford University Press.

Wise, Carol (1994). 'The Politics of Peruvian Economic Reform: Overcoming the Legacies of State-Led Development', *Journal of Interamerican Studies and World Affairs* 36/1 (Spring): 75–125.

World Bank (1988). *Peru: Policies to Stop Hyperinflation and Initiate Economic Recovery.* Washington DC: World Bank.

—— (1989). *Brazil: Prospects for Privatization.* Washington DC: World Bank.

—— (1995) *Bureaucrats in Business: The Economics and Politics of Government Ownership.* New York: Oxford University Press.

Wynia, Gary (1992). *Argentina: Illusions & Reality*, 2nd edn. New York: Holmes & Meier.

Yotopoulos, Pan A. (1989). 'The (Rip)Tide of Privatization: Lessons from Chile', *World Development* 17: 683–702.

Zahariadis, Nicholaos (1995). *Markets, States, and Public Policy: Privatization in Britain and France.* Ann Arbor: University of Michigan Press.

Index

350 *Index*

ANTEL 223
Antinori, Marcelo 291 n.
anti-privatization lobby 13, 23, 317–18, 328
  Argentina 91, 94–5, 98–9, 113
  Brazil 194, 197–202, 214, 225, 230 n.,
    297; implementation 187–90
  during 1980s 34, 49, 52, 68
AP (Acción Popular) 56, 62, 233, 259, 261
Apauye 130
APOYO 245, 248–50, 254, 292 n.
APRA (Acción Popular Revolucionaria del
    Peru) 62, 64, 232, 236, 261, 316
Arab Banking Co. 124
Aracruz Celulose 52, 54
Arafértil 163, 170, 177, 205, 211
Arce, Moisés 259
Arcor 136, 138, 149 n.
Argentina 71–149
  and Brazil 221–2
  and Peru 250, 257, 271–2, 277
  privatization: implementation 89–119,
    government capabilities 89–94,
    political responses 94–9; opportunity
    84–9; political economy of 5, 11,
    29–30; during 1980s 32–3, 35–46,
    64, 67–8; theory and practice 295,
    298–315, 318–31; transactions
    (1990–98) 102–7
  technical difficulties 99–108
  see also airlines; debt; electricity;
    inflation; petroleum; postal service;
    privatization; telecommunications;
    transparency; transportation
Argentina de Maritimos 131
Argentine Consumer Protection Law 328
Argentine General Accounting Office 134
Argentine Investment Co. 128
Argentine Private Development Trust Co.
    Limited 88–9
Argon 128, 130
Arinco 269
Armijo, Leslie 3, 8, 14
Arpetro 126
Artana, Daniel 117
Arzac, Alberto González 143 n.
Asia 1–2, 7
  financial crisis (1997) 196–7, 240
  see also Japan; Korea
Asociadas Petroleras 126
Asociados de Electricidad 129
Aspen Marine 131
Astilleros Domeq García 35
Astra 95, 125–7, 130, 135–8, 149 n.
Atahualpa 128

Atila, Carlos 230 n.
Atrium DTVM 178
Aubert Duval 131
auctions, public 106–7, 162–3, 169–72,
    268–73, 303
Augustine, St 331
Aurora 46
austerity policies, see orthodoxy
Austin, James 7
Austral Líneas Aereas 35, 43, 45–6, 112–13
Austral Plan 37–8, 41, 85
Australia 123
Australito 38, 41
authoritarianism, see military regimes
automobiles 138
aviation, see airlines
Aylwin, Patricio 72
Azpiazu, Daniel 83, 99, 136–7, 139–40

Babai, Don 8
Baca, Jorge (Jorge Baca) 255
Baer, Monica 49
Baer, Werner 164
Bagley 138, 148 n.
Bahia 55, 197, 212–13
balance of payments 281, 285, 300
Balbi, Maria Rosa 262
Balbín, Carlos 148 n.
Balbín, Ricardo 35
Balcerowicz, L. 295
Banco Agrario 264
Banco America do Sul 175
Banco Atlantico 124
Banco Bamerindus 175–6
Banco Bilbao Vizcaya 271, 283
Banco Boavista 174
Banco Bradesco 174
Banco Central de Espana 124
Banco Comercial Bancesa 176
Banco Continental 243, 264, 271, 283
Banco de Boston 147 n.
Banco de Galicia 118, 129
Banco de la Nacion 264
Banco de Latin America Nacion Argentina 107
Banco de Vivienda 264
Banco del Comercio 242, 269, 274, 282
Banco do Brasil 176–7, 226 n.
Banco Economico 174–5
Banco Feigin 129
Banco Frances 130
Banco Hipotecario 264
Banco Hispanoamericano 124
Banco Holandes 131
Banco Industria e Comercio 177

Index